URBAN INTERACTIONS

Fig. 1. Hieronymus Bosch, *Ship of Fools* (1490–1500)

First published in 2020 by Gracchi Books, Binghamton, NY,
an imprint of punctum books, Earth, Milky Way.
https://punctumbooks.com

ISBN-13: 978-1-953035-05-9 (print)
ISBN-13: 978-1-953035-06-6 (ePDF)

DOI: 10.21983/P3.300.1.00

LCCN: 2020945542
Library of Congress Cataloging Data is available from the Library of Congress

Copyediting: Adele Kreager
Book design: Vincent W.J. van Gerven Oei
Cover image: Stephen Downes, Carthage

p. punctumbooks
spontaneous acts of scholarly combustion

GRACCHI

"Too many echoes, not enough voices."
— Cornel West

Michael J. Kelly &
Michael Burrows (eds.)

Urban Interactions

Communication and
Competition in
Late Antiquity and
the Early Middle Ages

Contents

Acknowledgments

To those exciting and delightful surprises that awaken your passion, fill your heart, and give you reason to live.

— Michael J. Kelly

This project has been long in the making but I am really pleased with the results. Indeed, the relevance of this book today seems greater now than at its inception. It has been a pleasure to work with all our contributors and their efforts and patience are sincerely appreciated. My warm wishes go out to friends, colleagues and comrades from the School of History and Institute for Medieval Studies at the University of Leeds who are now spread out across the world. I hope to see you all at future IMCs! I must also express deepest gratitude to my fellow editor Michael J. Kelly, whose relentless effort has brought this project to fruition. Finally, thank you to my mother, my father, my sister, my partner and most of all to my grandma; her love and kindness are missed but remain an example to those who knew her.

— Michael Burrows

Iberian Rivalries

Michael J. Kelly

Jamona (today's Ciudadela) vs. Magona (today's Mahon) is one of the most famous urban rivalries of late antiquity. According to the *Epistola Severi* (*Letter of Severus*) — written only a month or two after the events in question (February 418) — in the latter part of the year 416 CE, the Christian theologian and historian Orosius had stopped in the Balearics, specifically in Minorca, on his return to Galicia to bring relics back to bishop Balconius of Braga.[1] He did not make it back, due to the war being waged by the Visigoths as Roman federates led by Wallia (r. 415–418) against the Alans and Vandals in the peninsula.[2] However, what Orosius did bring, straight from Jerusalem, were relics of St. Ste-

---

1 Severus, *Ep.*, 4.1. For all references to and translations of the *Letter of Severus*, see *Severus of Minorca: Letter on the Conversion of the Jews*, ed. and trans. Scott Bradbury (Oxford: Clarendon Press, 1996). On the dating of events, see the introduction.

2 On the Visigothic victories in Hispania in 417–418, see Orosius *Hist.*, 7.43.13 and Hydatius, *Chron.*, 24 (a. 418): "Vandali Silingi in Betica per Valliam regem omnes extincti." For the Orosius, see the translation by Andrew T. Fear, *Orosius: Seven Books of History against the Pagans* (Liverpool: Liverpool University Press, 2010) and the edition of Marie-Pierre Arnaud-Lindet, *Historiarum adversus paganos libri septem* (Paris: Les Belles Lettres, 1990). For the edition and translation of Hydatius's *Chronicles* see Richard W. Burgess, *The "Chronicle" of Hydatius and the "Consularia Constantinopolitana": Two*

phen (5–34), the martyr stoned in front of the eyes of the as yet unconverted Paul.[3]

The rivalry between Christian Jamona and Jewish Magona apparently began with the arrival of the relics and the zeal they unleashed amongst the Christian population. This passion was presumably directed by Severus, the leader of Jamona's small flock. The breakdown of relationships between the communities of the two cities over the course of about a year and a half, from late 416 to February 418, led to a situation in which both "sides," i.e., the Christian and Jewish communities of each respective city, were on the point of war with one another. Although an obvious and longstanding trope, Severus claims that the Jews were even stockpiling weapons in their synagogue in Magona.[4] The Christians, on the other hand, were equally ready to defend their faith. This increasingly heated situation culminated in Severus leading the Christians of Jamona to Magona to "check" the synagogue for weapons. Of course, no weapons are found. Nevertheless, Severus's flock burns the synagogue and Severus subsequently "convinces" the legitimate leader of the island, the Jewish-Roman aristocrat Theodorus of Majorca, to promise to convert himself and his people.

The construction and growth of the urban rivalry between Jamona and Magona ruined the friendly relationships and public cordiality between the people of the two cities. Under Jewish-Roman authority, the people of the two cities lived peacefully, it would seem, even engaging in the mutual prayers of the other. The "miraculous" arrival of the relics of St. Stephen prompted, supposedly, a zeal in the Christian community to quickly turn against their Jewish neighbors and demand St. Stephen, or rath-

---

Contemporary Accounts of the Final Years of the Roman Empire (Oxford: Clarendon Press, 1993), 69–123.

3   New Testament: Acts 6–7.
4   See, for example, Philo of Alexandria, *On Flaccus,* ch. 11. The text here is edited and translated in *Philo, Volume IX* by F. H. Colson (Cambridge: Harvard University Press, 1941), 349–57.

er the bishop Severus, become their patron.[5] As such, the clear imposition from the top of a new power structure leading to the emergence of a violent rivalry and breakdown of peace is actually a reflection of the will of the people, the will of God, and the emergence from historical conflict of everlasting communion under the *patronus communis* Stephen.[6]

The attempt to replace the patron of the two cities with another — to place a Christian city and a Jewish city (only thirty miles apart from each other, on the same, small island) under the patronage of St. Stephen, instead of the "secular" Jewish jurist, manager of the synagogue, and *defensor civitatis,* Theodorus — was a clear political move by Severus to supersede the island's imperial appointment.[7] The actions of Severus were motivated by secular matters (which is not to discount genuine religious enthusiasm, but only to add to the factors), in particular, to make himself the leader of the island. However, any real rivalry between the towns was likely fueled by additional, pre-existing dynamics Severus could have exploited to encourage his smaller community to rise up effectively in revolt.

At around the same modest size of c. 1,000–3000 people, the rivalry between the two cities was nevertheless a dynamic one.[8] The entire island was governed by a doctor of Jewish law and head of the synagogue, Theodorus, yet it also had a significant Christian population that included monks and at least one Christian member of the Roman provincial system, the *vir honoratus* Julius.[9] While this does not seem to have been a substantive issue, in his *Letter* Severus frames the cohabitation as an existential state of being so intense that Jews were said to be, by their very essence as Jews, unable to physically exist in Jamona:

5 Severus, *Ep.,* 4.
6 *Liber de miraculis sancti Stephani,* in *Les miracles de saint Étienne: Recherches sur le recueil pseudo-augustinien (BHL 7860–1),* ed. Jean Meyers et al. (Turnhout: Brepols, 2006), 263–368, at 308, 2.1 ln. 46.
7 Severus, *Ep.,* 6.2, and 20.5.
8 Bradbury, *Severus of Minorca,* 28.
9 Severus, *Ep.,* 10.1, 20.4–5.

upon entering they would be stricken down in supernatural ways (i.e., killed by Christians?).[10] Beyond this rhetoric and any real religious antagonisms, which seem to have developed with the arrival of the relics, and Severus, there were also political rifts related to the authority of the groups on the island. Minorca had an established Christian community, yet it also had a more ancient Jewish population. The latter community seems clearly to have been, according to Severus's *Epistula,* the more powerful one.

The persecution against Magona led by Severus was grounded also in an economic competition between the cities, or rather, the economic dominance of Magona. Jamona's leader Severus was less powerful than Theodorus, and his bishopric was not particularly important. Moreover, Jamona had a less functional harbor and was a poorer city. Magona, in contrast, was the seat of the prefect and its leaders were the appointed Roman officials. This is suggested by an early imperial inscription which hints at Magona as the capital of the island.[11] Magona's Jewish community also seems to have been more educated, or, at least, some of its leading figures were, such as Theodorus, as well as Innocentius: "'Brother Innocentius, you are learned not only in Latin literature, but in Greek literature as well, and you meditate constantly on the law."[12] As such, Severus's position would become more impressive if he could control also Magona, establish his see there, and expand his political influence by turning the city's Jewish inhabitants and leaders into Christians to be shepherded by him.

Speculatively, if there is any truth in the increased demand for Severus to lead the island, we could also detect in this urban rivalry a call for local control of the cities in contrast to being

---

10 Severus, *Ep.,* 3.2.
11 *Corpus Inscriptionum Latinarum, Volume 2: Inscriptiones Hispaniae,* ed. Emil Hübner (Berlin: Georgium Reimer, 1892), 3711: "ter duumviratu in insula functus etiam flaminatu provinciae Hispaniae citerioris."
12 Severus, *Ep.,* 18.15: "Innocenti frater, qui non solum Latinis verum etiam Graecis litteris eruditus es et legem iugiter meditaris."

ruled by a Roman *defensor* elsewhere. This could mirror broader late antique and early medieval patterns of people choosing the local over the international, rejecting a level of material comfort in exchange for local autonomy. Yet, if so, it is a strange sort of "thinking local" juxtaposed with the physical presence of the relics, which carried with them the universality of their meaning and power.[13]

Most importantly, what we learn from this urban rivalry, as constructed almost exclusively by Severus, concerns a dissonance between the rhetorical construction of urban rivalries — with places, things, people, and names used as metaphors to construct certain narratives of morality — and the reality of life in those cities. Most people, from the various constructed categories — Christians, Jews, etc. — lived together in ordinary fashion, living, working, marrying, eating, and even praying together. This dissonance is the critical literary warning we must heed when exploring urban rivalries: even the landscape, the archaeological evidence, which can suggest certain antagonisms, must be approached cautiously.

Words do create life and life does create meaning (illocutionary and perlocutionary). This is evident in the world of late antiquity, in which the Word was the origin of authority and extra-divine substance, e.g., the Word of God to Moses; the emperor in edicts; the bishops; the "Law of Citations" (issued 426) and the opinions of Papinian, Gaius, Ulpian, Paulus, and Modestinus; the oral traditions edited into the Mishnah; the commentary of the Talmud's sages and rabbis, and so on. The living words of Severus effectuated an intensified urban rivalry that led to a transformed existence.[14]

---

13 For discussions of this episode and St. Stephen's relics see: Peter Brown, *The Cult of Saints: Its Rise and Function in Late Antiquity* (Chicago: University of Chicago Press, 1981); Robert Wisniewski, *The Beginnings of the Cult of Relics* (Oxford: Oxford University Press, 2019), 103–5, 105, 124–25.

14 For more on the power of the word in creating consciousness, especially within illiterate communities, see Paulo Freire, *Pedagogy of the Oppressed*, trans. Myra Bergman Ramos (New York: Continuum, 1990).

A useful counterpart to the Jamona–Magona urban rivalry and its miraculous outcome is the intra- and inter-city collaboration and competition on the mainland of Hispania during its final Visigothic century, the seventh. In this instance, the leader of a mainly Christian but certainly diverse community attempted to effect change by creating social, urban antagonisms through a primarily narrativic revision of the *Liber Iudiciorum* (Visigothic Code) of one of his royal predecessor's, Recceswinth (r. 649/653–672). The *Liber Iudiciorum* is a legal code and artifact of Visigothic literature constructed and promulgated by Recceswinth at the Eighth Council of Toledo in 653 in the "Praetorian Church of Sts. Peter and Paul."[15] Early into his reign, the Visigothic King Ervig (r. 680–687) began to revise and re-narrate Recceswinth's *Liber Iudiciorum,* and subsequently request-

---

15 See *Chron.,* 754, 35; XII Toledo 4; and the opening of VIII Toledo: "Anno quinto orthodoxi atque gloriosi et vera clementiae dignitate praespicui Recesuinthi regis, cum nos omnes divinae ordinatio voluntatis euisdem principis serenissimo iussu in basilicam sanctorum apostolorum ad sacrum synodi coegisset aggregari conventum" (*CCH* 5, p. 366). This church would become the site where kings were anointed and blessed before going off to war and was raised by Wamba to the status of being its own see. Thus, just outside the walls of Toledo there was a competing bishop and site of royal, ecclesiastical authority. The progress towards total royal authority in the king seems to have reached new heights, to the extent that the king created a parallel church authority. This may have been the reason for Julian of Toledo apparently leading a coup to overthrow Wamba, and then in XII Toledo 4 abolishing the praetorian church and Wamba's new diocese at Aquis (Chaves), Lusitania. For the primary evidence of this, see XII Toledo 9, and, for discussion, see Roger Collins, *Visigothic Spain: 409–711* (Malden: Blackwell Publishing, 2004), 100. XII Toledo is also the council in which Gundemar's actions over the church were reintroduced into the record. For the *Chronicle of 754,* see José Eduardo López Pereira, ed. and trans., *Crónica mozárabe de 754: edición crítica y traducción* (Zaragoza: Anúbar, 1991); Theodor Mommsen, ed., *Chronica Minora,* Monumenta Germaniae Historica, Auctores Antiquissimi 10, 334–60 (Berlin: Weidmann, 1894); and, Ann Christys, *Christians in Al-Andalus, 711–1000,* 2nd edn. (New York: Routledge, 2010), 28–51, esp. 33–35. References to the Iberian councils are to the authoritative edition edited by Gonzalo Martínez Díez and (from 1982 forward as co-editor) Félix Rodríguez, *La Colección Canónica Hispana,* 6 vols. (Madrid: C.S.I.C., 1966–2002), referred to in these notes as *CCH.*

ed approval of his laws at the Twelfth Council of Toledo (681).[16] Ervig's new version was promulgated on 21 October 681.[17] Ervig reframed the code with both an alternative introduction and a new conclusion, which inserted thirty-four new laws — twenty-eight (eighty-two percent) of which concerned the Jewish community. Ervig's novel book — Book 12.3 — with its dozens of anti-Jewish constitutions provides an alternative ending from the original version by Recceswinth. In Ervig's code, the new happy ending is effectively the elimination of Judaism from the Christian Visigothic kingdom and the conversion of all Jews.[18] However, Ervig's actions seem to have further fueled an existing spirit of urban cooperation, especially between Christians and Jews, in the face of the king's and council's attempts at social disruption and forced homogeneity.[19]

The narrative structure of Ervig's *Liber Iudiciorum* is reminiscent of that of Severus's *Letter*. In both stories, there is a wise and just Christian lawmaker operating in conjunction with the authority of God (this is part also of the original narrative of Recceswinth's *Liber Iudiciorum*)[20] who eagerly converts his

---

16 For the canons of XII Toledo see *La Colección Canónica Hispana* V, ed. Gonzalo Martínez Díez and Félix Rodríguez (Madrid: C.S.I.C., 2002), 135–204. For the *Liber Iudiciorum* (*LI*) see the *Leges Visigothorum antiquiores, MGH Legum,* ed. Karl Zeumer (Hanover and Leipzig: Impensis Bibliopolii Hahniani, 1902), 33–456.

17 *LI*, 2.1.1 (in the 1902 composite edition of Zeumer).

18 For more on Ervig's revision of the *Liber Iudiciorum*, see Michael J. Kelly, "The *Liber Iudiciorum*: A Visigothic Literary Guide to Institutional Authority and Self-Interest," in *The Visigothic Kingdom of Toledo: Concepts and Forms of Power*, ed. Paulo Pachá and Sabine Panzram (Amsterdam: Amsterdam University Press, in press).

19 The laws of Ervig, in the *Liber Iudiciorum* and the councils, represent the main body of evidence for his reign.

20 Although the sovereignty of the Visigothic king as derived from God is not declared as such, and certainly not in the place one would expect — the opening "Constitution" of the Code — there are several places that explain the monarch's role as head of the people and in solemn devotion to God. See, for instance, *LI*, 2.14: "Quod antea ordinari oportuit negotia principum et postea populorum."

whole domain, via various measures. This diversity in forms of conversion — an extreme product of competition — is almost a standard literary trope in Iberian and Visigothic literature from Severus to Ervig, evidenced also clearly in *De origine Gothorum* by Isidore of Seville (bishop of Seville c. 600–636), in which Isidore uses conversion stories to elevate Seville's theopolitical importance above Toledo's.[21] In Severus and Ervig, we see the (literary) struggle against the Jews resolved by numerous means: discussion and persuasive speech, appeals to emotions, confessions and oaths, the inversion of power, gendered politics and, of course, miracles.[22] Finally, through that competition to achieve conversion, another ontological existence has emerged.

In contrast, though, to the neatness of the code, it is evident from other sources that, when confronted with such Visigothic legal-historical efforts to create violence and intra-urban rivalries in the seventh century, communities worked together. For example, a canon of Isidore of Seville's Third Council of Seville in 624 reveals that the reality on the ground in the cities of the kingdom did not necessarily, and certainly not in some places, reflect the narrative of Christian domination and Jewish "salvation" as a universal or genuine social rivalry. On the contrary, the canon describes Christian and Jewish neighbors working together to fight the "system." In the face of the threat of forced baptism, Jews and Christians would secretly swap babies so that the Jewish infants would avoid the baptism while the Christian infants underwent a second meaningless one.[23] This was not

---

21 See Michael J. Kelly, "Writing History, Narrating Fulfillment: The 'Isidore-Moment' and the Struggle for the Past in Visigothic Iberia" (Ph.D. diss., University of Leeds, 2014), ch. 3.

22 For more on the gendered aspects of domination in the story of Severus, see Ross S. Kraemer, "Jewish Women's Resistance to Christianity in the Early Fifth Century: The Account of Severus, Bishop of Minorca," *Journal of Early Christian Studies* 17, no. 4 (2009): 635–65.

23 For the canon of III Seville see the *Excerptum Canonicum* after VIII Toledo in *La Colección Canónica Hispana* V, 482–85. For further discussion of the canon, see Wolfram Drews, "Jews as Pagans? Polemical Definitions of Identity in Visigothic Spain," *Early Medieval Europe* 2, no. 3 (2003): 189–207.

only a reality of the 620s, but must also have been of concern at the time of the construction of the *Liber Iudiciorum* since the canon is preserved after the records of the Eighth Council of Toledo.

The text of Ervig's revision demonstrates, furthermore, that in addition to Christians protecting their neighbors' infants from baptisms unwanted by their parents, Christians were also offering their Jewish neighbors safe places and ways to avoid legal attack, and, at times, they were also, it would seem, either converting to or at least learning about the Jewish faith.[24] Ervig's Book 12 makes it clear too that members of the clergy, from clerks to bishops, were investing their Jewish neighbors with certain authority over matters within the church, while lay people in the cities (or at least Toledo) were hiring local Jewish people as house and estate managers.[25] Priests were also, apparently, having sex with Jewish women.[26] At the level of real interaction, priests seem not have been too fussed about the legal proscriptions.[27] In this, they and their friends and neighbors, were in direct confrontation with the legal-polemical rivalry between them and the "state." The intra-city rivalries of late Visigothic Hispania were thus multifaceted, with overlapping levels of real and *faux* collaboration and conflict, one that could be said to have been a materialist dialectical series leading to a new truth, a new historical moment. In Minorca, a Christian unity had emerged, and so the truth of God had become manifest. In late Visigothic Hispania, perhaps what was revealed was the ontological caesura between neighbors and the "state."

This type of fight is not what scholars typically have in mind when thinking about "urban rivalry" in the period, yet, this both demonstrates a very sincere intra-city and inter-city struggle. In contrast to the story of the rivalry between Jamona and Magona

---

24 *LI*, 12.3.9.
25 *LI*, 12.3.19.
26 *LI*, 12.3.21.
27 *LI*, 12.3.23–24.

in which a regime change was forced from the top and remembered in guise as a miraculous awakening of the people, in the case of late Visigothic Hispania the force failed to create rivalries on the ground level, instead leading to further (or simply highlighting the existence of) collaboration between Christians and Jews in the cities in their mutual struggle against the "state." The ultimately perlocutionary words of Ervig's *Liber Iudiciorum* narrate victory and a happy ending all the same.

The overlapping layers of antagonism in both historical contexts were also those of cooperation, between actual Christians and Jews on the ground, and, as such, serve as an excellent example of some of the components of dialectical and non-dialectical urban rivalry. And yet, as Ian Wood notes in his Introduction to this volume, lacking an abundance of ancient graffiti in the vein of "town 'x' sucks," we need to be careful to distinguish between actual urban rivalries versus personal conflicts between a small circle, of usually elite people, in "rival" cities and other urban landscapes. The case of Magona and Jamona seems to provide a good example of the urban populations actually in competition with one another, not only on a simple combative level, but also in dialectical form of antagonistically working together, resulting in the birth of a new ontological situation. In other words, what is evident is the classic Hegelian (idealist) dialectical concept of the "progress" of history,[28] which I elsewhere demonstrate is the case between certain cities in Visigothic Hispania.[29] On other occasions, as in the late Visigothic kingdom, urban networks compete un-dialectically in a Kantian sense of the aim of one victorious truth (or the separation of spheres, in contrast to Hegel's concern with unity).[30]

28 See Georg Lukács, *The Young Hegel: Studies in the Relations between Dialectics and Economics,* trans. Rodney Livingstone (Cambridge: MIT Press, 1976), ch. 3.4.

29 See especially the case for Seville and other Baetican cities in Kelly, *Writing History, Narrating Fulfillment,* ch. 3.4.

30 Lukács, *The Young Hegel,* ch. 2.4.

This volume intends to demonstrate through a number of case studies several of the intense urban rivalries that shaped the Mediterranean communities of late antiquity. But it also intends to elicit the historical circumstances of the rivalries, the various forms they could take, and the actions of collaboration and competition that co-existed within antagonistic spheres. In the Introduction that follows, Ian Wood elaborates on the relationship between the studies of this volume. In so doing, he shows how their entanglement reveals the presence of local rivalries, their origins, and the centrality of the Church, or, as he argues, churches, to urban relations in late antiquity. Wood demonstrates also how complementing scholarly methods — particularly history and archaeology — affect this information and our understanding of the forms of competition within and between cities, what that may have meant for people, and how we are to interpret urban rivalry in late antiquity — a period of intense urbanism.[31]

---

31 For a glimpse at this urban vibrancy, as evidenced in the Iberian Peninsula, see Joachim Henning et al., "Reccopolis Revealed: The First Geomagnetic Mapping of the Early Medieval Visigothic Royal Town," *Antiquity* 93, no. 369 (2019): 735–51.

Bibliography

Primary

Chronicle of 754. In *Chronica Minora,* edited by Theodor Mommsen. Monumenta Germaniae Historica, Auctores Antiquissimi 10, 334–60. Berlin: Weidmann, 1894.

Hydatius. *Chronicles.* Translated by Richard W. Burgess. In *The "Chronicle" of Hydatius and the "Consularia Constantinopolitana": Two Contemporary Accounts of the Final Years of the Roman Empire,* 69–123. Oxford: Clarendon Press, 1993.

La Colección Canónica Hispana. 6 Volumes. Edited by Gonzalo Martínez Díez and (from 1982 forward as co-editor) Félix Rodríguez. Madrid: C.S.I.C., 1966–2002.

Corpus Inscriptionum Latinarum, Volume 2: Inscriptiones Hispaniae. Edited by Emil Hübner. Berlin: George Reimer, 1892.

Crónica mozárabe de 754: edición crítica y traducción. Edited and translated (Sp.) by José Eduardo López Pereira. Zaragoza: Anúbar, 1991.

Liber de miraculis sancti Stephani. In *Les miracles de saint Étienne: recherches sur le recueil pseudo-augustinien (BHL 7860-1),* edited by Jean Meyers et al., 263–368. Turnhout: Brepols, 2006. DOI: 10.1484/M.HAG-EB.5.106043.

Liber Iudiciorum. In *Leges Visigothorum antiquiores, MGH Legum,* edited by Karl Zeumer, 33–456. Hanover and Leipzig: Impensis Bibliopolii Hahniani, 1902.

Orosius. *Historiarum adversum paganos libri VII.* Edited by Marie-Pierre Arnaud-Lindet. Paris: Les Belles Lettres, 1990.

———. *Orosius: Seven Books of History against the Pagans.* Translated by Andrew T. Fear. Liverpool: Liverpool University Press, 2010.

Philo of Alexandria. *On Flaccus.* In *Philo, Volume IX,* edited and translated by F. H. Colson, 349–57. Cambridge: Harvard University Press, 1941.

Severus of Minorca. *Epistola Severi.* In *Severus of Minorca: Letter on the Conversion of the Jews,* edited and translated by Scott Bradbury, 79–125. Oxford: Clarendon Press, 1996.

Secondary

Brown, Peter. *The Cult of Saints: Its Rise and Function in Late Antiquity.* Chicago: University of Chicago Press, 1981.

Christys, Ann. *Christians in Al-Andalus, 711–1000.* 2nd Edition. New York: Routledge, 2010. DOI: 10.4324/9780203037409

Collins, Roger. *Visigothic Spain: 409–711.* Malden: Blackwell Publishing, 2004. DOI: 10.1002/9780470754610

Drews, Wolfram. "Jews as Pagans?" Polemical definitions of identity in Visigothic Spain." *Early Medieval Europe* 2, no. 3 (2003): 189–207. DOI: 10.1046/j.0963-9462.2002.00108.x

Freire, Paulo. *Pedagogy of the Oppressed.* Translated by Myra Bergman Ramos. New York: Continuum, 1990.

Henning, Joachim, Michael McCormick, Lauro Olmo Enciso, Knut Rassmann, and Eyub Fikrit Eyub. "Reccopolis Revealed: The First Geomagnetic Mapping of the Early Medieval Visigothic Royal Town." *Antiquity* 93, no. 369 (2019): 735–51. DOI: 10.15184/aqy.2019.66

Kelly, Michael J. "The *Liber Iudiciorum*: A Visigothic Literary Guide to Institutional Authority and Self-Interest." In *The Visigothic Kingdom of Toledo: Concepts and Forms of Power,* edited by Paulo Pachá and Sabine Panzram. Amsterdam: Amsterdam University Press, in press.

———. "Writing History, Narrating Fulfillment: The 'Isidore-Moment' and the Struggle for the Past in Visigothic Iberia." Ph.D. diss., University of Leeds, 2014.

Kraemer, Ross S. "Jewish Women's Resistance to Christianity in the Early Fifth Century: The Account of Severus, Bishop of Minorca." *Journal of Early Christian Studies* 17, no. 4 (2009): 635–65. DOI: 10.1353/earl.0.0292

Lukács, Georg. *The Young Hegel: Studies in the Relations between Dialectics and Economics.* Translated by Rodney Livingstone. Cambridge: MIT Press, 1976.

Wisniewski, Robert. *The Beginnings of the Cult of Relics.* Oxford: Oxford University Press, 2019. DOI: 10.1093/oso/9780199675562.001.0001

Introduction

Ian Wood

The history of the city in the late and post-Roman West is not a particularly happy one. Cities declined, and some effectively vanished. For the most part, however, urban life continued — albeit at an impoverished level[1] — in spite of a changing climate, and an ever-present, but escalating, threat of disease.[2] Cities survived into the fifth and sixth centuries and beyond, despite the arrival of barbarians, whose impact varied enormously from place to place. In some cities the incomers did considerable damage (one thinks of the impact of the Huns in the Balkans); some they re-invigorated, choosing them to be the capitals of new states (among them Toledo); and on some they had very little impact. The major force for transformation, indeed, came not from the barbarians, but from religion, and the growth of Christianity as a physical institution. In southern and central Spain, with the coming of Islam, the seat of power changed once

---

1   Simon Esmonde Cleary, *The Roman West, AD 200–500* (Cambridge: Cambridge University Press, 2013), 97–149; Bryan Ward-Perkins, *The Fall of Rome and the End of Civilization* (Oxford: Oxford University Press, 2005); *Urbes Extinctae: Archaeologies of Abandoned Classical Towns*, ed. Neil Christie and Andrea Augenti (Farnham: Ashgate, 2012).
2   Kyle Harper, *The Fate of Rome: Climate, Disease, and the End of an Empire* (Princeton: Princeton University Press, 2017).

again, initially with the emergence of Córdoba as the Umayyad capital: and the Church lost its pre-eminence. Almost everywhere, except generally in Britain[3] and in parts of the Balkans, cities survived, but they were in a constant state of change, as indeed they had always been. And this meant that relations within and between cities changed too.

Archaeology has thrown sharp light onto changes in public space within cities, and thus also on shifts in social interaction and public life implied by such changes in space. In his chapter, Douglas Underwood points to the erection of walls around the cities of the Mediterranean–Aude–Garonne–Atlantic axis in the third century, listing those at Bordeaux and Narbonne, as well as less securely dated fortifications at Toulouse, Bazas, and Carcassonne. In Gaul, the building of walls, usually protecting a reduced area of the city, may well be linked primarily (although not exclusively) to the threats posed by the barbarians, and more generally of the political unrest, of the Third Century Crisis.[4] In Spain, Isabel Sánchez Ramos points rather to the Visigothic walling of cities in Toledo, Valencia, Zaragoza, Seville, Mérida, and Barcelona as marking centers of secular power. This element of public display was not, in fact, confined to Spain, nor indeed to the Visigothic period. Some of the most spectacular walling to survive from Late Roman Gaul also speaks of a desire to impress, and to protect resources, as much as a need for defense against marauding barbarians.

Among other secular public buildings to survive or even to be erected, some were clearly associated with the exercise of power. Pedro Mateos Cruz notes the development of building in fourth-century Mérida to fit its new role as the capital of the Diocesis Hispaniarum, pointing to its connections with Baetica Tarraconensis, and Carthaginiensis, to which one should also

3   Simon T. Loseby, "Power and Towns in Late Roman Britain and Early Anglo-Saxon England," in *Sedes Regiae (ann. 400–800),* ed. Gisela Ripoll, José Maria Gurt, and Alexandra Chavarria Arnau (Barcelona: Reial Acadèmia des Bones Lletres de Barcelona, 2000), 319–70, at 357.
4   Esmonde Cleary, *The Roman West,* AD 200–500, 62–76, 122–36.

add Mauretania Tingitana.[5] The regular presence of an emperor had, of course, an even stronger impact. The evidence for Trier, Milan, Ravenna, Thessaloniki, and, above all, Constantinople is well known. To these examples Dimitris Kyrtatas adds Nicomedia in the days of Diocletian. In the post-Roman period, some of these cities remained central: most obviously Ravenna under the Ostrogoths, and, as Mark Tizzoni remarks, Carthage, where the Vandals essentially took over the pre-existing buildings of government. But some other cities also came to the fore for the first time as centers of royal power.[6] In the case of the Visigoths there is the evidence for building in their two capitals, Toulouse[7] and, later, Toledo, although the archaeological evidence for the situation of the palace in the latter city is still open to question, as Sánchez Ramos argues. Our clearest illustration of royal building in Visigothic Spain, as Javier Martínez Jiménez notes, comes from the *ex novo* foundation of Reccopolis. With the fall of Visigothic Spain, the Muslim incomers established Córdoba as a new city of government, as described by Ann Christys.

Walls and palace buildings (whether for kings or their agents) were types of monument that continued to be of use. Several other types of Roman public monument lost all functional significance and fell into disuse or were put to other uses: most notably theatres, amphitheaters, and circuses, as noted for Spain by Cruz, and for Gaul by Underwood. In Spain, the most striking reuse of an amphitheater is the placing of a church in the middle of that at Tarragona. But other amphitheaters and theatres were put to domestic or military use.[8] The amphitheater at Spoleto was used as a fortress in the Gothic Wars against

---

5   Michael Kulikowski, *Late Roman Spain and Its Cities* (Baltimore: Johns Hopkins University Press, 2011), 71–76.

6   See in general *Sedes Regiae (ann. 400–800)*, ed. Ripoll et al.

7   Jean Guyon, "Toulouse, la première capitale du royaume wisigoth," in *Sedes Regiae (ann. 400–800)*, ed. Ripoll et al., 219–40.

8   Esmonde Cleary, *The Roman West, AD 200–500*, 117–19, 173.

Justinian:[9] at Tours, this became a significant part of the city's very much reduced walled center.[10]

All these developments in the public spaces of cities point to change at the level of social interaction. The complexity of the change is finely illustrated by Michael Mulryan's examination of the "Oriental Quarter" of late Antique Ostia, where the archaeology reveals a remarkable process of invasion of public and (pagan) religious space, and its replacement by low-level private occupation. In Mérida, Cruz points to a similar fragmentation of space, but of big city villas, rather than of minor religious institutions.

The developments in Mérida clearly relate to the larger question of the relations between the city and its aristocracy. Martínez Jiménez points directly to the problem of identifying where the elite is to be found. Cruz notes the fragmentation of big villas in Mérida, suggesting that the aristocracy moved out of the city. Sánchez Ramos cites the discovery of privileged dwellings by the Tagus, outside the walls of Toledo, and points to villas in the countryside surrounding Toledo. If the elite did reside primarily in rural villas, this would, of course, be no more than an extension of what was already common practice in the later Empire. Quite apart from the great late Roman villas that are known from excavation, one can look to the literary evidence. The *Mosella* of Ausonius provides descriptions of villas overlooking the river Moselle. In his *De reditu suo*, Rutilius Namatianus visits or passes the rural villas of numerous of his friends and equals as he travels from Rome to Gaul. Sidonius Apollinaris describes the villa of his father-in-law (the emperor Avitus) at Aydat, as well as the rural residences of other of his

---

9   Neil Christie, *From Constantine to Charlemagne: An Archaeology of Italy AD 300–800* (Aldershot: Ashgate, 2006), 223, 214–27 for general changes to public space in Italy.

10 Henri Galinié, "Tours de Grégoire, Tours des archives du sol," in *Grégoire de Tours et l'espace gaulois,* ed. Nancy Gauthier and Henri Galinié (Tours: Revue archéologique du Centre de la France, 1997), 65–80.

friends and colleagues.[11] This is a reminder that *otium* for the Roman aristocrat had long implied the possibility of moving out to his estate in the country, as a balance to his actions within the city in administration, public service and private business (*negotium*). In all probability aristocrats (other than those holding public office) were less inclined to spend time in the cities of the post-Roman period — but that is no more than hypothesis.

In other words, there is evidence for secular interaction within cities of the post-Roman period. For some cities (including the Carthage of Dracontius and Luxurius,[12] described by Tizzoni), this evidence is very considerable, albeit patchy, and for the most part it is archaeological. A much more vibrant image emerges when one turns to the Church, where the written evidence is at least as strong as that of the archaeology.

Bryan Ward-Perkins has downplayed the evidence for church-building in the post-Roman period, drawing attention to the size difference between the great imperial churches of the fourth and early fifth centuries, and those that were built subsequently.[13] The matter of scale is unquestionably an important consideration, as is that of a declining quality of workmanship. On the other hand, however, there is the sheer number of churches built from the fifth century onwards, and their growing importance as the key feature of a transformed understanding of public space. As Sánchez Ramos remarks, pointing to the evidence for building in Toledo, monumentalization was to be found far more in the churches of Visigothic Spain than in any other type of public structure of the period. Martínez Jiménez contrasts the secular building at Reccopolis with the ecclesiastical monuments of Eio. Still in Spain, Cruz notes the development of Christian edifices in Mérida, and especially of the church of Sta. Eulalia. In the Islamic period, the churches

11 Sidonius Apollinaris, *Carmen* 22; *Epistle* 2.2, 2.9, 5.14, in *Sidoine Apollinaire,* vols. 1 & 2, ed. André Loyen (Paris: Belles Lettres, 1960–1970).

12 Nigel M. Kay, *Epigrams from the "Anthologia Latina"* (London: Duckworth, 2006).

13 Ward-Perkins, *The Fall of Rome and the End of Civilization,* 148–50.

inevitably lost their role in the city, which was at least partially filled by the Friday mosque, or, in Córdoba, the Great Mosque.

Church-building was, of course, not just a Spanish phenomenon. The best-known church buildings are those of Rome, Ravenna, and Constantinople. In some cases, the foundation of a church was clearly straightforward, involving the property of only one donor. But in a confined urban area it could involve a complex process of land acquisition, and an equally complex building history. Brigitte Boissavit-Camus and Christian Sapin have remarked with regard to the funding of churches:

Although in those complexes that are located in places of residence, the donors were undoubtedly private individuals (Geneva, Barcelona [...]), this may not have been the case when a building or a public space was taken over or dismantled (Aix- en-Provence, Rodez): the surroundings of the city walls also lent themselves well to public land use. When construction was accompanied by major changes to the parcel of land and to the roads (Poitiers, Geneva), the approval of the municipal authorities must have been required.[14]

The process of establishing a *domus ecclesiae* may be glimpsed at Poitiers.[15] The creation of an ecclesiastical zone within a city

---

14 Brigitte Boissavit-Camus and Christian Sapin, "De la cathédrale paléochrétienne à la cathédrale romane," *Les Cahiers de Saint-Michel de Cuxa* 54 (2013): 19–38, at 20–21: "Si pour les complexes implantés dans des habitations, les donateurs étaient sans doute des particuliers (Genève, Barcelone [...]), ce ne devait pas être le cas lorsqu'on récupérait ou qu'on démantelait un édifice ou un espace public (Aix-en-Provence, Rodez): les abords de l'enceinte urbaine se prêtaient bien aussi à des opérations foncières publiques. Quand la construction s'accompagne de modifications importantes du parcellaire et de la voirie (Poitiers, Genève), l'accord des autorités municipales a dû être requis."

15 Brigitte Boissavit-Camus, "La *domus ecclesiae* de Poitiers," in *Des "domus ecclesiae" aux palais épiscopaux: Actes du colloque tenu à Autun du 26–28 novembre 2009*, ed. Sylvie Balcon-Berry, François Baratte, Jean-Pierre Caillet, and Dany Sandron (Turnhout: Brepols, 2012), 61–75.

would have required a considerable amount of negotiation in those cases where there was no simple transfer of fiscal land.

Although our literary texts tell us little or nothing about such a process, they do shed considerable light on the Christianization of cities, through the development of cult and especially of the cult of the saints. Brigitte Beaujard's study of the cult of saints in Gaul moves from a discussion of hagiography to an analysis of the relation between "the saint, the Church and the city,"[16] and finally of "the cult of saints in the city: the conquest of time"[17] — that is to say, the effect of the Christian calendar on urban life.

Alongside the evidence of the hagiography, one can set that of the homiletic literature, most especially the sermons of Caesarius of Arles.[18] As Lisa Kaaren Bailey argues in her analysis of the extraordinary Homily 11 of the *Eusebius Gallicanus* collection, the preacher used the martyrs of Lyon to build a common local congregational unity, and did so by making explicit comparison between local saints and the Holy Innocents of Bethlehem. Exactly who wrote or commissioned this strange text is unclear — although I would be more inclined to look to Patiens rather than to his predecessor Eucherius, for the simple reason that the latter was firmly associated with the cult of the nonlocal saint Maurice, and his companions in the Theban legion, whereas we can be sure that Patiens promoted the cult of the local Justus, and indeed that he was buried in the Church of St. Just, which had previously been dedicated to the Maccabees.[19]

16 Brigitte Beaujard, *Le culte des saints en Gaule* (Paris: Cerf, 2000), 333–98.

17 Ibid., 455–510.

18 William E. Klingshirn, *Caesarius of Arles: The Making of a Christian Community in Late Antique Gaul* (Cambridge: Cambridge University Press, 1994). See also Lisa Kaaren Bailey, *Christianity's Quiet Success: The Eusebius Gallicanus Sermon Collection and the Power of the Church in Late Antique Gaul* (South Bend: University of Notre Dame Press, 2010).

19 Jean-François Reynaud, *Lyon aux premiers temps chrétiens* (Paris: Imprimerie nationale, 1986), 54–76.

Patiens has a known form, with regard to the promotion of local saints.

Lyon, guarded, as it is, by cemeterial basilicas containing the relics of local saints (a concrete manifestation of the idea that a city was protected as much by its saints as by its walls), is among the best-studied ecclesiastical topographies of late antiquity and the early Middle Ages. But for an understanding of the urban interactions that might be behind the development of a new Christian topography, one can turn equally profitably to the neighboring city of Vienne, and to the first of bishop Avitus's (c. 450–519) homilies on Rogation. Here Avitus recounts how his predecessor Mamertus negotiated the establishment of three days of liturgical processions. Following a devastating earthquake, the bishop decided that the city needed to make a public demonstration of penitence, so he approached the local senate, which we are told was still functioning, and laid out his plans. Once the senate had agreed, he designed a first day of procession, which was deliberately short, so as to test the willingness of the population to participate in the three-day liturgy.[20] As Sidonius noted, previous attempts to organize equivalent public prayers had been troubled by the fact that potters and gardeners wanted different types of weather.[21]

The archaeological and the written evidence points, therefore, to a history of interaction within the late and post-Roman city, which came to be dominated increasingly by the Church. This tends to be the case even for the capitals of the successor states (although Lombard Pavia might be an exception before

---

20 Avitus, "Homily 6," in *Alcimi Ecdicii Aviti Viennensis episcopi Opera quae supersunt*, ed. Rudolf Peiper, Monumenta Germaniae Historica, Auctores Antiquissimi 6.2 (Berlin: Weidmann, 1883); Danuta Shanzer and Ian Wood, trans., *Avitus of Vienne: Letters and Selected Prose* (Liverpool: Liverpool University Press, 2002), 381–88.

21 Sidonius Apollinaris, *Ep.*, 5.14.

the days of Liutprand [r. 712–744]).[22] We know more of the churches of Ravenna and of Toledo than we do of their palaces.

It is worth noting that the urban establishment of the Church is not simply a substitution of Christian for pagan cult. There had certainly been plenty of temples in Roman cities, but they were differently staffed — pagan priesthoods generally being honorific posts (with the major exception of the Vestal Virgins in Rome), and, for the most part, not requiring substantial resources of property (as opposed to gifts of treasure, which they certainly did receive).[23] The interactions that lay behind the physical establishment of the Church in the cities of the Roman and post-Roman West, and behind the continuing provision of cult, were not a mere replica of what had gone before. It is also worth noting that in terms of endowment and of manpower the Christian Church also differed from Islam, with its mosques and imams.[24] The Islamic conquest of Spain would issue in a different set of urban interactions.

Interaction within cities raises one set of questions: some of these recur in the context of interaction between cities, but here other issues impinge as well. One factor that has to be taken into account when considering intercity relations is that of geography and communication — and although the geography of the Mediterranean World remained relatively stable in the late and post-Roman periods, political change had a profound impact on the safety of travel. The major road network of the Roman Empire is well known from archaeology as well as the written sources — although even a work as official as the *Tabula*

---

22 For Lombard capitals, Gian Pietro Brogiolo, "Capitali e residenze regie nell'Italia longobarda," in *Sedes Regiae (ann. 400–800)*, ed. Ripoll et al., 135–62. http://www.rmoa.unina.it/2268/.

23 Ian Wood, *The Transformation of the Roman West* (Leeds: ARC Humanities Press, 2018), 96–97.

24 Alejandro García Sanjuán, *Till God Inherit the Earth: Islamic Pious Endowments in al-Andalus (9th–15th Centuries)* (Leiden: Brill, 2007), 243–92.

Peutingeriana poses questions of interpretation.[25] Equally well known are the maritime connections across the Mediterranean, which were relatively trouble-free (storms apart) from the moment that Pompey cleared the sea of pirates in 67 BCE until the Vandal crossing to Africa in 429 CE.[26] The establishment of the barbarian kingdoms undoubtedly complicated long-distance communications. And, as Christys shows, the expansion of Islam into the West, and the establishment of an Umayyad capital at Córdoba further complicated matters. Although works of geography do exist, it is often more revealing to look at the narrative accounts of journeys. Geographical descriptions sometimes owe more to literary considerations and to the world-view of the author than to the realities of travel.[27]

The importance of the presence of rulers or provincial governors in a city's interconnectedness is clear from the discussions of Nicomedia, Mérida, Carthage, Toledo, Reccopolis, and Córdoba by Kyrtatas, Cruz, Tizzoni, Martínez Jiménez, and Christys. To political significance, we can also add that of trade, in Mulryan's account of the changing face of Ostia, which is also noted in Underwood's study of the route from the Mediterranean, across south-western Gaul. Above all, there is the pivotal position of the harbor of Carthage, touched on by Tizzoni. Trade relations are better evidenced in the archaeological than in the written record of late antiquity and the early Middle Ages, since the latter tends not to cover mercantile activity — although Gregory of Tours (538–594) does, on occasion, note the importance of merchants,[28] especially those he describes as Syrians, while the

25 Most recently Richard J.A. Talbert, *Rome's World: The Peutinger Map Reconsidered* (Cambridge: Cambridge University Press, 2010). See also the review by Florin Fodorean, *Plekos* 13.2011.9–19 — http://www.plekos.uni-muenchen.de/2011/r-talbert.pdf, 9–19.

26 Peregrine Horden and Nicholas Purcell, *The Corrupting Sea: A Study of Mediterranean History* (Oxford: Blackwell, 2000), 137–43, 153–72.

27 See also Andrew H. Merrills, *History and Geography in Late Antiquity* (Cambridge: Cambridge University Press, 2005).

28 Stéphane Lebecq, "Grégoire de Tours et la vie d'échanges dans la Gaule du VIᵉ siècle," in *Grégoire de Tours et l'espace gaulois*, ed. Gauthier and Galinié,

Vitas Patrum Emeritensium talks of the presence of Greek merchants in the city of Mérida. This information has been queried
by Javier Arce, who has seen in it a Thousand-and-One-Nights
type fable.[29] But the archaeological evidence for the mercantile
importance of some Spanish cities in the post-Roman period is
extremely strong, and the evidence increases year by year. The
significance of Vigo as a trading port has, for instance, only recently been revealed.[30]

In the literary record it is, once again, the Church that is
dominant. Some of the most interesting travel accounts are pilgrim documents — the itineraries of the Bordeaux Pilgrim, Ege-
ria (later fourth century), and, later, Willibald (eighth century).[31]
And, at a more local level, there are the miracle records, which
give a picture of pilgrims traveling to shrines, such as that of
Martin at Tours (336–397), although as Raymond Van Dam
has noted, the vast majority of visitors to the tomb of Martin
came from a relatively limited area.[32] The ecclesiastical record
does, however, cast light on more long-distance communication, even leaving aside pious travel to the Holy Land or to
Rome, and the Church features heavily in diplomatic accounts,
not least because churchmen were employed as diplomats. We
hear of diplomatic journeys by the likes of Germanus of Aux-
erre (378–448), who traveled to Ravenna on behalf of the Ba-
caudae of the Loire, and of Epiphanius of Pavia, who was sent
by Theodoric the Ostrogoth (r. 475–526) to negotiate with the
Gibichung ruler in Lyon, Gundobad (r. 473–516), for the return

169–76.
29 Javier Arce, "The City of Mérida (Emerita) in the *Vitas Patrum Emeriten-
    sium* (VIth century A.D.)," in *East and West: Modes of Communication*, ed.
    Evangelos Chrysos and Ian Wood (Leiden: Brill, 1999), 1–14, at 11–14.
30 Adolfo Fernández, *El comercio tardoantiquo (ss. IV–VII) en el Noroeste pen-
    insular a través del registro cerámico de la Ría di Vigo* (Oxford: Archaeo-
    press, 2014).
31 The itineraries are conveniently edited in *Itineraria et alia geographica*, Cor-
    pus Christianorum Series Latina 175–76 (Turnhout: Brepols, 1965).
32 Raymond Van Dam, *Saints and Their Miracles in Late Antique Gaul* (Princ-
    eton: Princeton University Press, 1993), 117–18.

of prisoners taken from Liguria.[33] In the tenth century we hear of John of Gorze, undertaking a mission to Abd-ar-Rahman III (r. 912–961) in Córdoba at the request of Otto I (r. 936–973).[34]

Clerics made good ambassadors of the kingdoms to which they belonged, because of their literacy. But they also represented their own cities. The connection made between Lyon and Bethlehem in Homily 11 of the *Eusebius Gallicanus* collection discussed by Bailey can hardly be taken as evidence for actual contact between the Gallic and Palestinian city — although Avitus of Vienne did write directly to the Patriarch of Jerusalem only a few decades after the composition of the sermon.[35] But, as Bailey notes, there was a long-standing tradition of urban rivalry in the Roman World. This did not end with the dissolution of the Empire. If anything, the coming of Christianity added further fields of competition. Bailey points to the rivalry between saint cults, and indeed to the way that cults might draw cities together: Lyon and Vienne were united in their association with the Martyrs of 177. One can talk here of *coopétition,* a concept, pointing to simultaneous cooperation and competition, introduced into early medieval studies by Régine Le Jan.[36] Vienne's great rival was Arles, and the fourth, fifth, and sixth centuries saw a long struggle between the two over their relative status.[37]

---

33 Andrew Gillett, *Envoys and Political Communication in the Late Antique West, 411–533* (Cambridge: Cambridge University Press, 2003), 115–38, 148–71.

34 *Hystoria de vita domni Iohannis Gorzie coenobii abbatis. Die Geschichte vom Leben des Johannes, Abt des Klosters Gorze,* ed. Peter Christian Jacobsen, 115–36, Monumenta Germaniae Historica, Scriptores in usum scholarum separatim editi 81 (Wiesbaden: Harrassowitz, 2016).

35 Avitus, *Ep.* 25: Shanzer and Wood, *Avitus of Vienne: Letters and Selected Prose,* 155–56.

36 Régine Le Jan, Geneviève Buhrer-Thierry and Stefano Gasparri, eds., *Coopétition: rivaliser, coopérer dans les sociétés du haut moyen âge (500–1000)* (Turnhout: Brepols, 2017).

37 Nathanaël Nimmegeers, *Évêques entre Bourgogne et Provence. La province ecclésiastique de Vienne au haut Moyen Âge (V^e–XIe siècle)* (Rennes: Presses universitaires de Rennes, 2011), 35–38, 50–51.

Burrows provides a fine example of ecclesiastical rivalry: be-tween Tours and Bourges, although perhaps it is worth pausing to ask whether the rivalry was between the two cities, or be-tween the bishop of Tours, Gregory, and certain of his episco-pal colleagues. There most certainly was rivalry between cities in North-Western Gaul in Gregory's day. He himself recounts a very bloody conflict between the men of Orléans, supported by the citizens of Blois, and those of Châteaudun, backed by the men of Chartres.[38] But there was also rivalry between groups within individual cities, as is clear enough from the histories of bishops Nicetius and Priscus of Lyon,[39] or between Gregory and members of his own clergy, as well as the count, in Tours.[40] A bishop might, therefore, not be representative of the opinions of his diocese. Gregory was an individual, coming from a very particular family:[41] his hostility to the bishop of Bourges might as well be personal as a mark of intercity rivalry.

Whether or not the rivalry between Tours and Bourges was long-standing or was the reflection of personal animus between Gregory and his episcopal colleagues, the conflict was expressed in religious terms. It would, of course, be wrong to reduce the whole of late antique and early medieval history to religious his-tory. Although some aspects of political history cannot be dis-sociated from that of religion, the Church is scarcely a dominant force in the international trade of the period, and although it reacted to the vagaries of climate and disease, it did not cause them. At the same time, the institutional establishment of Chris-tianity in the fourth and fifth centuries, and its social, political

---

38 Gregory of Tours, *Decem libri historiarum,* ed. Bruno Krusch and Wilhelm Levison, Monumenta Germaniae Historica, Scriptores Rerum Merovingi-carum 1.1 (Hanover: Hahn, 1951), 7.2.

39 Ibid., 4.36; Peter Brown, "Eastern and Western Christendom in Late An-tiquity: A Parting of the Ways," in *Society and the Holy in Late Antiquity* (London: Faber and Faber, 1982), 166–95, at 185–86.

40 Gregory, *Decem libri historiarum,* 5.46–49.

41 Ian Wood, "The Individuality of Gregory of Tours," in *The World of Gregory of Tours,* ed. Kathleen Mitchell and Ian Wood (Leiden: Brill, 2002), 29–46.

and economic, as well as spiritual, influence, put it at the heart of the history of urban interaction, from the reign of Theodosius I at least down to the coming of Islam to southern and central Spain. Elsewhere its importance continued almost unchecked. Whether the mosque ever played a similar role to that of the churches of the early Middle Ages (despite the importance of the Great Mosque of Córdoba, or that of Friday mosques elsewhere), is an open question,[42] although the Great Mosque was certainly where the oath of allegiance to a new caliph was taken. However, neither the funding of mosques nor the position of the imam look comparable to the support for the Church and the clergy. And it is not just that the majority of our written material from 400 onwards comes from the pens of churchmen. As we have already noted, in the archaeological record churches constitute the major monumental buildings from the age of Constantine onwards, and it is the Church, or churches, that comes to dominate public space. It is scarcely surprising that it also comes to play a central role, arguably *the* central role, in relations between cities.

---

42 García Sanjuán, *Till God Inherit the Earth*, 238–42 deals with the cemetery as public space.

Bibliography

Primary

Avitus. "Homily 6." In *Alcimi Ecdicii Aviti Viennensis episcopi Opera quae supersunt,* edited by Rudolf Peiper, 108–12. Monumenta Germaniae Historica, Auctores Antiquissimi 6.2. Berlin: Weidmann, 1883.

———. "Homily 6." In *Avitus of Vienne: Letters and Selected Prose,* translated by Danuta Shanzer and Ian Wood, 381–88. Liverpool: Liverpool University Press, 2002.

Gregory of Tours. *Decem libri historiarum.* Edited by Bruno Krusch and Wilhelm Levison. Monumenta Germaniae Historica, Scriptores Rerum Merovingicarum 1.1. Hanover: Hahn, 1951.

Hystoria de vita domni Iohannis Gorzie coenobii abbatis. Die Geschichte vom Leben des Johannes, Abt des Klosters Gorze. Edited by Peter Christian Jacobsen, 115–36. Monumenta Germaniae Historica, Scriptores in usum scholarum separatim editi 81. Wiesbaden: Harrassowitz, 2016.

Itineraria et alia geographica. Edited by Françoise Glorie. Corpus Christianorum Series Latina 175–76. Turnhout: Brepols, 1965.

Sidonius Apollinaris. *Sidoine Apollinaire.* 3 Volumes. Edited by André Loyen. Paris: Belles Lettres, 1960–1970.

Secondary

Arce, Javier. "The City of Mérida (Emerita) in the *Vitas Patrum Emeritensium* (VIth century A.D.)." In *East and West: Modes of Communication,* edited by Evangelos Chrysos and Ian Wood, 1–14. Leiden: Brill, 1999.

Bailey, Lisa Kaaren. *Christianity's Quiet Success: The Eusebius Gallicanus Sermon Collection and the Power of the Church in Late Antique Gaul.* South Bend: University of Notre Dame Press, 2010. DOI: 10.2307/j.ctvpj7d4d.

Beaujard, Brigitte. *Le culte des saints en Gaule.* Paris: Cerf, 2000.

Boissavit-Camus, Brigitte. "La *domus ecclesiae* de Poitiers." In *Des "domus ecclesiae" aux palais épiscopaux: Actes du col-*

loque tenu à Autun du 26–28 novembre 2009, edited by Sylvie Balcon-Berry, François Baratte, Jean-Pierre Caillet, and Dany Sandron, 61–75. Turnhout: Brepols, 2012. DOI: 10.1017/cbo9781139043199 10.1484/m.bat-eb.1.101290.

Boissavit-Camus, Brigitte, and Christian Sapin. "De la cathédrale paléochrétienne à la cathédrale romane." *Les Cahiers de Saint-Michel de Cuxa* 54 (2013): 19–38.

Brogiolo, Gian Pietro. "Capitali e residenze regie nell'Italia longobarda." In *Sedes Regiae (ann. 400–800),* edited by Gisela Ripoll, José Maria Gurt, and Alexandra Chavarria Arnau, 135–62. Barcelona: Reial Acadèmia des Bones Lletres de Barcelona, 2000.

Brown, Peter. *Society and the Holy in Late Antiquity.* London: Faber and Faber, 1982.

Christie, Neil. *From Constantine to Charlemagne: An Archaeology of Italy AD 300–800.* Aldershot: Ashgate, 2006.

Christie, Neil, and Andrea Augenti. *Urbes Extinctae: Archaeologies of Abandoned Classical Towns.* Farnham: Ashgate, 2012.

Chrysos, Evangelos, and Ian Wood, eds. *East and West: Modes of Communication.* Leiden: Brill, 1999.

Esmonde Cleary, Simon. *The Roman West, AD 200–500.* Cambridge: Cambridge University Press, 2013. DOI: 10.1017/cbo9781139043199.

Fernández, Adolfo. *El comercio tardoantiquo (ss. IV–VII) en el Noroeste peninsular a través del registro cerámico de la Ría di Vigo.* Oxford: Archaeopress, 2014. DOI: 10.2307/j.ctvz937ss.

Galinié, Henri. "Tours de Grégoire, Tours des archives du sol." In *Grégoire de Tours et l'espace gaulois,* edited by Nancy Gauthier and Henri Galinié, 65–80. Tours: Revue archéologique du Centre de la France, 1997.

García Sanjuán, Alejandro. *Till God Inherit the Earth: Islamic Pious Endowments in al-Andalus (9th–15th Centuries).* Leiden: Brill, 2007. DOI: 10.1163/ej.9789004153585.i-549.

Gauthier, Nancy, and Henri Galinié, eds. *Grégoire de Tours et l'espace gaulois.* Tours: Revue archéologique du Centre de la France, 1997.

Gillett, Andrew. *Envoys and Political Communication in the Late Antique West, 411–533.* Cambridge: Cambridge University Press, 2003. DOI: 10.1017/cbo9780511496318.

Guyon, Jean. "Toulouse, la première capitale du royaume wisigoth." In *Sedes Regiae (ann. 400–800),* edited by Gisela Ripoll, José Maria Gurt, and Alexandria Chavarria Arnau, 219–40. Barcelona: Reial Acadèmia des Bones Lletres de Barcelona, 2000.

Harper, Kyle. *The Fate of Rome: Climate, Disease, and the End of an Empire.* Princeton: Princeton University Press, 2017. DOI: 10.2307/j.ctv9b2txr.

Horden, Peregrine, and Nicholas Purcell. *The Corrupting Sea: A Study of Mediterranean History.* Oxford: Blackwell, 2000.

Kay, Nigel M. *Epigrams from the Anthologia Latina.* London: Duckworth, 2006.

Klingshirn, William E. *Caesarius of Arles: The Making of a Christian Community in Late Antique Gaul.* Cambridge: Cambridge University Press, 1994. DOI: 10.3828/978-0-85323-368-8.

Kulikowski, Michael. *Late Roman Spain and Its Cities.* Baltimore: Johns Hopkins University Press, 2011.

Le Jan, Régine, Geneviève Buhrer-Thierry, and Stefano Gasparri, eds. *Coopétition: rivaliser, coopérer dans les sociétés du haut moyen âge (500–1000).* Turnhout: Brepols, 2017. DOI: 10.1484/M.HAMA-EB.5.114234.

Lebecq, Stéphane. "Grégoire de Tours et la vie d'échanges dans la Gaule du VIᵉ siècle." In *Grégoire de Tours et l'espace gaulois,* edited by Nancy Gauthier and Henri Galinié, 169–76. Tours: Revue archéologique du Centre de la France, 1997.

Loseby, Simon T. "Power and Towns in Late Roman Britain and Early Anglo-Saxon England." In *Sedes Regiae (ann. 400–800),* edited by Gisela Ripoll, José Maria Gurt, and Alexandria Chavarria Arnau, 319–70. Barcelona: Reial Acadèmia des Bones Lletres de Barcelona, 2000.

Merrills, Andrew H. *History and Geography in Late Antiquity.* Cambridge: Cambridge University Press, 2005. DOI: 10.1017/cbo9780511496370.

Mitchell, Kathleen, and Ian Wood. *The World of Gregory of Tours*. Leiden: Brill, 2002.

Nimmegeers, Nathanaël. *Évêques entre Bourgogne et Provence. La province ecclésiastique de Vienne au haut Moyen Âge (Ve-XIe siècle)*. Rennes: Presses universitaires de Rennes, 2011.

Reynaud, Jean-François. *Lyon aux premiers temps chrétiens*. Paris: Imprimerie nationale, 1986.

Ripoll, Gisela, José Maria Gurt, and Alexandra Chavarria Arnau, eds. *Sedes Regiae (ann. 400–800)*. Barcelona: Reial Acadèmia des Bones Lletres de Barcelona, 2000.

Talbert, Richard J.A. *Rome's World: The Peutinger Map Reconsidered*. Cambridge: Cambridge University Press, 2010. DOI: 10.1017/cbo9780511686863.

Van Dam, Raymond. *Saints and Their Miracles in Late Antique Gaul*. Princeton: Princeton University Press, 1993.

Ward-Perkins, Bryan. *The Fall of Rome and the End of Civilization*. Oxford: Oxford University Press, 2005.

Wood, Ian. "The Individuality of Gregory of Tours," in *The World of Gregory of Tours,* edited by Kathleen Mitchell and Ian N. Wood, 29–46. Leiden: Brill, 2002.

———. *The Transformation of the Roman West*. Leeds: ARC Humanities Press, 2018. DOI: 10.1515/9781942401445.

1

"The Innocence of the Dead Crowned You, the Glory of the Triumphant Crowned Me": The Strange Rivalry between Bethlehem and Lyon in *Eusebius Gallicanus* Sermon 11

Lisa Kaaren Bailey

The anonymous collection of fifth-century Gallic sermons known as the *Eusebius Gallicanus* contains one especially striking entry. Sermon eleven, which honors the martyrs killed in Lyon in the persecution of 177 CE, includes an extensive address to the city of Bethlehem, in the persona of Lyon. This address systematically denigrated the martyrdom value of the children commonly known as the "Holy Innocents," who were killed by Herod in his efforts to destroy the Christ-child. These children become a rhetorical foil by which to elevate the martyrs of Lyon, who were depicted by the preacher as superior, and whose sufferings were described in gruesome detail. Bethlehem here served as a counterpoint, and the subject of a very strange urban rivalry. It was a statement of local and parochial pride, which nonetheless also placed Lyon upon an international stage, in a manner which reflected some of the tensions surrounding the development and promotion of saints' cults in this period.

Eusebius Gallicanus sermon eleven has never before been translated in full into a modern language, so, in order to facilitate discussion below, I have provided a translation here.[1] It is based on Françoise Glorie's edition, *Eusebius "Gallicanus." Collectio homiliarum. Sermones extravagantes.*[2]

1. Even if we were paying our pious debt of prayers to martyrs from foreign lands, we would surely be ensuring our own benefits and advantages: faith would make them ours, and howsoever remote from our country they might be, they would still collect for us the longed-for patronage, because prayers of this kind are dependent on zeal, not place. So, in the household of God, you earn as much intercession as you expend in veneration. Therefore, it is more fitting that religious devotion should unite strangers to us, than that irreligious and neglectful indifference should alienate our own from us.

2. We recognize, dearly beloved, the abundant wealth of divine gifts around our church. The people of a city exult if they are defended by the relics of even one martyr; and behold, we possess an entire populace of martyrs. Our land should rejoice to be the nurse of heavenly soldiers and fertile parent of such virtues. Behold, the profane enemy could by no means profit from such obedience as he profited from the sword; for, just as the feasts of these most sacred days show, as much as sin abounded against virtue, so much grace then abounded in the virtue of the blessed.

1   Many thanks to my colleagues Maxine Lewis and Matthew Trundle who kindly assisted me in putting together the translation of the sermon.

2   Eusebius Gallicanus, *Collectio homiliarum. Sermones extravagantes,* ed. Françoise Glorie, Corpus Christianorum Series Latina 101 (Turnhout: Brepols, 1970), 131–34.

3. We read that "in Bethlehem" thousands of fortunate boys were killed by Herod, while he was looking for Christ; "as the prophet said: 'Rachel was weeping for her children and would not be comforted because they are not.'" [Matt. 2:17–18] Thus, blessed parent and illustrious fatherland of triumphant warriors, you deserve the wealth of such children. Even if [Bethlehem] seemed for a moment in the eyes of the unenlightened to be bereaved, it did not, in fact, need to be consoled at all and it did not weep for its children whom, when lost through enviable sorrow, it had acquired. I can say confidently to you, O Bethlehem, Jewish land, who endured the cruelty of Herod in killing the children, who at one time merited to offer to God the pure-white multitude of peaceful infants, that our Lyon competes worthily with you, O Bethlehem, and contends in speech as if in opposition to you about the divine blessings you have both enjoyed, speaking thus: "O Bethlehem: in the glory of our martyrs, you perhaps surpass in numbers, but I surpass in merit; in yours there was killing, but there was not confession; in mine was the struggle of martyrdom, in yours there was only the opportunity and occasion of happiness; their passing enriched you with a blessing, virtue enriched me; you were able to see the dying of small children in blood, you could not await their struggling; the innocence of the dying crowned you, the glory of the triumphant crowned me; yours reached the reward of the kingdom without consciousness of martyrdom, mine, however, reached it afflicted by torments, confirmed by prayers, cooked in the manner of a sacrifice by savage flames; as much pain as they suffered in their flesh, so much they obtained crowns in the spirit through the blows of torments and slow tortures, and thus they were consecrated before they were killed; you offered those young in years, I those already perfected in virtues; I offered those who were victorious through their torments, who had prevailed when tested in their faith; you offered those who could have the reward of dying, but could not

fear the danger of denying; you offered weak people, lest the sacrilegious one would find Christ, I offered a strong crowd, through whose example of service in the saving of persecutors, Christ even acquired the sacrilegious. Finally, Herod, by means of that blessed slaughter when he sought out only the sacred boy, immolated so many boys. One sex merited your triumph, both merited mine; my fight obtained the prize from the prince of the world even with women; my troop could have had your innocents among its boys, your troop could not have had my Blandina.

4. Divine providence excelled amidst all this: that in such sacrifices of the homeland even a bishop was present. Our blessed father Photinus, in the fullness of old age, bishop of our church, was seized for impious questioning; and, so that we might believe through the merit of his instruction, he was joined to his flock and after the sacrifice of the body to the Lord he offered himself as a new sacrifice given to Christ through the profane tribunals; the infirmity of an old man thus chose a quick death through the injuries and torments of the raging torturers, so that you might see him reserved to a unique martyrdom at that time. Happy is he, standing at the threshold of his life, to whom it was granted that he owed his death more to glory than to nature.

5. Pious minds have been strengthened by the example of such a parent, and the prepared offerings did not so much follow as rush after him. The diverse tricks of the multifarious savagery and the extraordinary torture made the hearts of the saints unconquered within themselves. They conquered by despising the unbearable weight of evil deeds and they showed by enduring that they would not feel: the fires were lit under them but they are known to be strong enough that they consecrate; the beasts were roused, but the beasts can only marvel at their prey and so remain hungry. The flames sanctify the limbs lacerated by

various types of torture, while they do not know that they should consume; the beasts honor them, while they do not know that they should rage. Where are those who say that veneration should not be offered to the sacred bodies of the martyrs? Behold the barbarity of bloodthirsty savagery, which does not accept the meaning of religion, but offers the obedience of veneration, and, ignorant, does not have the power of discernment, but recognizes, to the damnation of the evil ones, what is owed in honors to the saints. And thus, the agent and deed of punishment, in a marvelous way, is a witness of their merits and, while the reverence of piety excels, the silent judgement of impiety is carried out.

6. When therefore, dearly beloved, our church is adorned by such trophies of faith, it demonstrates the benefit to be derived from iniquity, so that iniquity triumphs in new terrible deeds. They give sacred bodies to the flames, depriving them of funeral honors; and after the death of man they battle against humanity itself, and, although the cause of their anger has died, they do not bring an end to the cruelty. However, all unwilling, they were witnesses of their blessedness, they even envied those who had died. As always, malice was married with stupidity! They reduced the bones which should be venerated to ashes, as if their merits could truly be consumed by the flames and their virtues cremated along with their remains. Such confused madness! They acquired heaven for those to whom they denied this earth. Therefore, unheard-of savagery, you made nothing. In vain you believed that you had wiped out their memory, whose glory you had spread. You dispersed the dust of the saints in the waves of the Rhône lest it rise again, but resurrection is not destroyed by water, which through the grace of regeneration is celebrated by the gift of water. You entrusted to the Rhône the relics which should be adored: the strength of the water dissolved the temporal flesh. Therefore, whatever the

birds took from human flesh, the beasts devoured or the waves swallowed up, even if it is not enclosed by a tomb, it is contained within the bosom of the world. The renewal of man does not consist in the way of earth, but in the law of nature and in the virtue of renewal. This is witnessed by a truthful statement: I am the resurrection and the life, who lives in the age of ages.

The collection now known as the *Eusebius Gallicanus* has been something of a puzzle to scholars — even the name is misleading, as it cannot be connected to any "Eusebius of Gaul." Indeed, the sermons are anonymous and although there has been considerable speculation over the authorship of specific texts within it, and of the collection as a whole, the question remains unsettled.[3] However, most scholars agree that the sermons date, in their original form, to the fifth century and reflect the milieu of southern and central Gaul. Jean Leroy, who produced the first extended analysis of the collection, argued that the sermons were written by Faustus, who was bishop of Riez (c. 457–490), and this has been accepted by Brigitte Beaujard, who analyzes sermon eleven as a work of Faustus.[4] As I have argued elsewhere, however, the case for a single author of the collection is not compelling, and sermon eleven tells strongly against it.[5] It reads very much as the work of a local bishop, appealing to his own congregation, and repeatedly claiming the saints as "ours": specific to Lyon, not to a broader Christian community. Sermon eleven may well be the work of Eucherius of Lyon (d. c. 450), as

3   For a full discussion of the authorship issue see Lisa Kaaren Bailey, *Christianity's Quiet Success: The "Eusebius Gallicanus" Sermon Collection and the Power of the Church in Late Antique Gaul* (Notre Dame: University of Notre Dame Press, 2006), 29–38.

4   Jean Leroy, "L'oeuvre oratoire de s. Fauste de Riez: La collection gallicane dite d'Eusèbe d'Émese" (Ph.D. diss., University of Strasbourg, 1954), 1: 212–3; Brigitte Beaujard, "Cités, évêques et martyrs en Gaule à la fin de l'époque romaine," in *Les Fonctions des Saints dans le monde occidental (IIIᵉ–XIIIᵉ siècle)* (Rome: École française de Rome, 1991), 175–91.

5   Bailey, *Christianity's Quiet Success*, 33.

proposed by Jill Harries, or Patiens of Lyon (d. c. 480), as argued by Ralph Mathisen.[6] Both of these bishops were part of the same circle as Faustus of Riez, so it is plausible that he could have received copies of their sermons which were then retained in his church archive. At some subsequent point, probably in the sixth century, a compiler pulled together seventy-six sermons, perhaps drawing from this archive, to form what we know as the *Eusebius Gallicanus* collection. This transmission story is complicated, however, by the existence of a sermon which has been edited as the work of both Augustine of Hippo (d. 430) and of Caesarius of Arles (d. 542), which displays some strong parallels with *Eusebius Gallicanus* sermon eleven, and yet has completely different pastoral goals. Without further work on the possible authorship and dating of this second sermon it is difficult to know how it relates to the *Eusebius Gallicanus* one, but I will offer some thoughts on this below.

Eusebius Gallicanus sermon eleven takes as its subject the martyrdoms of a group of Christians in Lyon and Vienne in 177. The details of their deaths had been recorded for posterity in a letter sent by surviving members of the community back to the churches in Asia and Phrygia. This letter was quoted at length by Eusebius of Caesarea in his *Ecclesiastical History,* and circulated in the West in the rather loose translation by Rufinus of Aquileia (344/345–411).[7] It is possible that independent local stories about these martyrs also circulated — certainly by the late sixth century, Gregory of Tours was providing details about the survival of their relics which contradicted the letter's emphasis on

6 Jill Harries, *Sidonius Apollinaris and the Fall of Rome, A.D. 407–485* (Oxford: Oxford University Press, 1994), 44; Ralph W. Mathisen, *Ecclesiastical Factionalism and Ecclesiastical Controversy in Fifth-Century Gaul* (Washington, DC.: Catholic University of America Press, 1989), 233.

7 Eusebius of Caesarea, *Historia ecclesiastica,* 5.1; Louis Neyrand, "Le récit de la passion de martyrs de Lyon dans la traduction de Rufin," in *Les martyrs de Lyon (177),* ed. Jean Rougé and Robert Turcan (Paris: CNRS, 1978), 289–98; Jean François Reynaud, *Lugdunum christianum: Lyon du IVe au VIIIe s.: topographie, nécropoles et édifices religieux* (Paris: Éditions de la Maison des Sciences de l'Homme, 1998), 24.

the destruction of their bodies.[8] Gregory tells us that by his time Lyon possessed a church dedicated to the martyrs of 177, which held the martyrs' ashes within its altar, a detail which reflects his own sense of the importance of physical remains in establishing a cult for saints and a proper location for worship. The letter quoted by Eusebius of Caesarea, in contrast, states that the bodies were either consumed by dogs or burnt, with the ashes thrown into the Rhône, in order to deny the cherished remains to the Christian community. The *Eusebius Gallicanus* sermon follows this version of events, although the preacher expressed some anxiety about it. He was at pains to stress that the destruction of the martyrs' bodies did not wipe out their memory or their glory, he presented the Rhône almost as though it were a proper reliquary ("adorandas reliquias Rhodano tradis"), and argued that although the remains were not enclosed by a tomb, they are contained within the bosom of the world ("intra mundi gremium continetur"). We may here be seeing a transition stage between a fourth-century rejection of the importance of physical remains to martyr veneration and a late sixth-century desire for such tangible connections to sanctity. Unfortunately, it is impossible to know whether the church described by Gregory was in existence when the *Eusebius Gallicanus* sermon was preached, and no archaeological traces have even established its location within Lyon. The state of the cult of these martyrs in the fifth century is therefore unclear, an important consideration to which I will return.

The story of the martyrs of 177 is reasonably familiar. The approach taken to it by the preacher of *Eusebius Gallicanus* sermon eleven, however, is not. Indeed, there are many features of this sermon which strike the modern reader as strange. The central section of the sermon is a prolonged boast by a personification of Lyon about the superiority of this city's martyrs to

---

8   Gregory of Tours, *Liber in gloria martyrum,* ed. Bruno Krusch, Monumenta Germaniae Historica, Scriptores Rerum Merovingicarum 1.2 (Hanover: Hahn, 1885), 48.

the children killed by Herod in Bethlehem when he sought to destroy the infant Jesus. Rivalry, as scholars have noted, was inherent to Greco-Roman urbanism, and this volume shows how the dynamic continued into late antiquity.[9] Lyon's main rival was Vienne, just down the road and the prime competitor for prestige and episcopal power in the Rhône valley.[10] Vienne, however, shared in claiming the martyrs of 177, so was not an appropriate rival in this instance. Instead, the preacher chose to build his sermon around a comparison with Bethlehem. Bethlehem was an unusual choice. It was not a particular draw for pilgrims, neither did it come close to the veneration which Jerusalem received in late antiquity.[11] Bethlehem was chiefly famous for being the location of Jesus's birth, but even this received only slight reference in the *Eusebius Gallicanus* sermon, which instead focused on the children who were killed there. Even stranger, to modern sensibilities, is the way the preacher repeatedly downplayed the deaths of children in order to build up his own local martyrs as superior. Indeed, although section two of the sermon began by establishing a tone of pathos, the preacher quickly moved on to insist that the "Holy Innocents" lacked merit and virtue because they did not suffer as much as the martyrs of Lyon: they therefore did not struggle, did not attain glory, they were not perfected, they had not passed any test; they were not, in point of fact, proper martyrs at all, when compared with those who died in 177. Even as he made this argument, however, the preacher stressed the youth, innocence, and blood-soaked deaths of these children, evoking pity even as he proudly cited Lyon's superiority. It is difficult to assess the aesthetic response of a fifth-cen-

9   On urban rivalry see also Ray Laurence, Simon Esmonde Cleary, and Gareth Sears, *The City in the Roman West, c. 250 BC–AD 250* (Cambridge: Cambridge University Press, 2011), 123.

10 Jill Harries, "Christianity and the City in Late Antique Gaul," in *The City in Late Antiquity*, ed. John Rich (London and New York: Routledge, 2002), 85.

11 P.W.L. Walker, *Holy City, Holy Places? Christian Attitudes to Jerusalem and the Holy Land in the Fourth Century* (Oxford: Clarendon Press, 1990), 171–98.

tury congregation to this rhetoric, but the fact remains that the preacher's choices require explanation. What was he trying to achieve in this sermon?

Some of the preacher's goals were standard ones. The section extolling the virtues and roles of the martyred bishop Photinus, for example, built up the role of the bishop as a *pater* and *parens* of the church, someone of immense *gravitas* who nonetheless sacrificed himself in order to be with his flock and who thereby strengthened others in his example. This paean to an ideal bishop, probably preached by a bishop, clearly reinforced the importance of this position to the church, to the congregation, and to its sense of how to be properly Christian. Other aspects of the sermon are less expected, however, such as the preacher's pride in the gender inclusivity of Lyon's martyrs. Although the letter in Eusebius of Caesarea had singled out a number of different martyrs, and the names of many of them were recorded also by Gregory of Tours, only two were named in *Eusebius Gallicanus* sermon eleven: the aforementioned Photinus and the martyr Blandina, who was held up for particular attention as a woman. Herod, the preacher noted, had killed only boys. Lyon's martyrs were superior, therefore, because whereas only one sex merited triumph in Bethlehem both did in Lyon. Indeed, although the boys of Bethlehem could have been among the martyrs of Lyon, since the group included both genders, Bethlehem's dead could not have included "Blandinam meam" ("my Blandina"). This focus may reflect a particular interest in Blandina as a cult figure within Lyon. Indeed, the title of the sermon in the surviving manuscript is: *De sancta Blandina Lugdunensi*. The preacher did not, however, include any of the detail recorded in the original letter about Blandina's servile status or the stages of her martyrdom. Perhaps he felt that gender-inclusivity was an important note to strike for his congregation; perhaps he particularly wanted to note a female *exemplum*. Although his motives are not clear, this represents another interesting feature of the text.

Also striking is the preacher's emphasis on the physicality of and tortures experienced by the martyrs. Although this was a major component of the account preserved in Eusebius of Caesarea, it was not the necessary response to martyr cults in the fifth and sixth centuries. Augustine, for example, had much preferred to depict the martyrs as models of steadfastness rather than corporeal suffering. Caesarius's sermons on martyrs depicted them as highly generalized moral *exempla* and contained almost nothing on the actual physical torments suffered by the martyrs themselves. The preacher of *Eusebius Gallicanus* sermon eleven, by contrast, had much to say about torture. The sermon is filled with references to the struggles of the martyrs, the affliction of their torments, the way they were cooked like sacrifices by the flames, the pain they suffered in their flesh, and the tormenting blows to which they were subjected. Photinus was described as crushed "per iniurias et afflictiones" ("through injuries and torments"), and the entire group of martyrs were perfected by the diverse cruelties, with lacerated limbs sanctified by fire and subjected to savage and hungry beasts. This stress upon physicality was followed up by an insistence on the consequent importance of physical relics: "Where are those who say that veneration should not be offered to the sacred bodies of the martyrs?" The preacher goes on to provide an extended, slightly anxious commentary on the fate of the martyrs' physical remains, noting repeatedly that although their bodies had been destroyed, their memory and glory lived on, the resurrection was not denied, and the waters of the Rhône acted almost as a force of regeneration. The preacher clearly felt a strong need to address the lack of proper relics for these local martyrs, which may have been a difficulty for the cult. This perhaps explains why, by the late sixth century, the story was being told quite differently.

Most obviously, however, sermon eleven was an attempt to establish pride in a set of local saints over and against a more "international" group. The preacher established the local and international dynamic from the start of the sermon, although he approached it obliquely, insisting that martyrs from foreign lands could still be "ours" through faith and could provide *patrocinia,* regardless of geographical distance. The second section of the sermon, however, insisted loudly that Lyon should be proud of the martyrs which were particularly its own: "the abundant wealth of divine gifts around our church." The preacher particularly emphasized the number of local martyrs: whereas other cities might be pleased even to have one, "we possess an entire *populos* of martyrs." These martyrs were presented, moreover, as particularly connected to Lyon, as the city was their *nutricia* and *parens fecunda*. The third section of the sermon then provided the comparison with Bethlehem's murdered infants, setting up the pathos of their deaths, before insisting that *Lugdunus nostra* could compete in merit and contend in speech. The speech by Lyon which followed was an extended assertion of local pride, consisting in a detailed breakdown of the tests and sufferings experienced by the martyrs in 177, with Bethlehem's children presented as having escaped lightly by comparison. As I have argued elsewhere, this represents an effort by the preacher to build a common congregational identity which was local, specific, and, therefore, potentially resilient in a world where the international identity of the Roman Empire was crumbling.[12] As Beaujard has pointed out, this was not an eschatological perspective, "mais sur terre, dans le présent."[13] It was a pragmatic response by a local leader to the difficulties of his times. The striking insistence on local rather than international cult is explicable in this context.

Sermon eleven therefore needs to be read alongside the other sermon in the *Eusebius Gallicanus* collection which deals with saints from Lyon: sermon fifty-five on Epipodius and Alexander. This sermon, which may be by the same preacher, makes many of the same rhetorical moves. It compares local to international cults and argues for the primary importance of the former: "Indeed it is a great thing, to offer our prayers in public and general celebrations, but a certain kind of festival should be judged even

---

12 Lisa Kaaren Bailey, "Building Urban Christian Communities: Sermons on Local Saints in the *Eusebius Gallicanus* Collection," *Early Medieval Europe* 12 (2003): 1–24.

13 Brigitte Beaujard, *Le culte des saints en Gaule: les premiers temps. D'Hilaire de Poitiers à la fin du VIᵉ siècle* (Paris: Les Éditions du Cerf, 2000), 133.

more excellent: to rejoice in local virtues."[14] These saints were described by the preacher as natives of Lyon and fellow citizens of its current inhabitants, tying them closely and repeatedly to the soil and landscape of the city. The preacher also insisted that Epipodius and Alexander were the local equals of Rome's apostolic protectors.

> We, however, possess the splendid gift of those blessed ones whole and entire, and what could suffice for the entire world, we hold enclosed exclusively within the bosom of this city and we raise up those twin palms of triumph rivalling the apostolic city, and, having also our own Peter and Paul, we vie with our two supporters against that exalted see.[15]

The message about the importance and value of local cults is identical to that found in sermon eleven. The comparison undertaken in sermon fifty-five, however, was much more smoothly done. Rome was an obvious parallel, with two recognized and successful patron saints, and the preacher offered Epipodius and Alexander as worthy subjects of local attention, without ever downgrading or dismissing the apostles, or their city. In other words, sermon fifty-five engaged in comparison without rivalry and made an effective argument for local pride in the process.

These two sermons, taken together, demonstrate the perceived need for a local identity in Lyon. The goals of the preacher of sermon eleven also need to be read, however, in the context of epideictic rhetoric, a praise speech for a city which had a long

---

14 *Eusebius Gallicanus*, 55.1: "Magnum quidem est: publicis atque communibus dare uota sollemnitatibus; sed excellentior quaedam festiuitas iudicanda est: alumnis exsultare uirtutibus."

15 *Eusebius Gallicanus*, 55.4: "Nos uero beatorum illustre munus totum atque integrum possidemus, et, quod uniuerso mundo possit sufficere, intra gremium ciuitatis huius peculiariter conclusum tenemus; et geminas palmas triumphi aemulas apostolicae urbi attolimus, atque, habentes et nos Petrum Paulumque nostrum, cum sublimi illa sede binos suffragatores certamus."

history and of which Claudian was a late Roman master.[16] The content of the sermon is different from the expected elements in such a speech, but many of the strategies are the same. As Laurent Pernot points out, such speeches engaged in a kind of personification of the city and were particularly marked by the use of apostrophe, hyperbole, and comparison. Indeed, Pernot argues that blame can function in such speeches as a necessary corollary to praise, so that something which is usually praised, and widely recognized as praiseworthy, is blamed in order to exaggerate very deliberately the merits of the speech's subject. If we understand this sermon as a species of epideictic rhetoric, then some of its strangeness makes more sense. The preacher was going over the top in a way which his audience would presumably recognize and understand. Indeed, by taking the most sympathetic universal martyrs — a group of slaughtered children — and using them as his foil, the preacher created a hyperbolic atmosphere and greatly amplified his message. Such speeches, moreover, were fundamentally about communal unity. As Pernot puts it: "Epideictic rhetoric is the social order's rejuvenating bath. It instantiates a moment of communication, in which a community, or a microcommunity, presents itself with a show of its own unity [...]. It delineates images and beliefs common to the group; it defines and justifies accepted values; and sometimes it grants currency to new values."[17] The preacher may have been deliberately using such rhetoric in order to evoke a feeling of consensus and connectedness within his congregation.

Did he succeed? Part of the challenge which this sermon poses comes in interpreting its reception. While Harries asserts that these martyrs were a prominent presence in fifth-century Lyon, our only real evidence for this is the *Eusebius Gallicanus*

---

16 Alan Cameron, *Claudian: Poetry and Propaganda at the Court of Honorius* (Oxford: Clarendon Press, 1970).

17 Laurent Pernot, *Epideictic Rhetoric: Questioning the Stakes of Ancient Praise* (Austin: University of Texas, 2015), 98.

sermon itself. No archaeological or inscriptional remains substantiate the cult of the martyrs of 177, and without Gregory of Tours's mention we would not know that there was a late antique church dedicated to them. Beaujard, indeed, argues that this sermon, as well as the one on Epipodius and Alexander, were attempts to create cults where they had not existed before.[18] Until the church is located and dated this cannot be resolved, but it serves as a reminder not to assume that the preacher spoke for his congregation in the way he claimed to do.

There are many reasons why a bishop of mid-fifth-century Lyon may have wished to establish or bolster a local saint's cult. Lyon had long been a fractured city, with a monumental center on the Fourvière hill, topographically isolated from both the commercial district on the river banks and the Croix-Russe region which centered on the Altar of the Three Gauls and the amphitheater where the martyrs had been paraded.[19] Christian churches were also spread around these disparate areas of the city. The episcopal group emerged in the mid-fourth century along the banks of the Saône and developed into a complex which included churches dedicated to St. John the Baptist, St. Stephen and the Holy Cross, as well as an episcopal residence and various service buildings.[20] On the hill above it, however, in areas which had previously been cemeteries, were two martyrial churches. One, dating to the late fourth or early fifth century, may have originally been dedicated to the Maccabees, but later took the name of St. Justus, after an early bishop of Lyon who was buried there. Not far from it was another fifth-century funerary zone church, now dedicated to St. Irenaeus, whose body it housed, along with those of Epipodius and Alexander, but originally dedicated to St. John. Near one of the entrances to

18 Beaujard, "Cités, évêques et martyrs," 181.
19 Lisa Kaaren Bailey, *The Religious Worlds of the Laity in Late Antique Gaul* (London: Bloomsbury, 2016), 84–87; Reynaud, *Lugdunum christianum,* 18.
20 Nancy Gauthier and Jean-Charles Picard, eds., *Topographie chrétienne des cités de la Gaule des origines au milieu du VIIIe siècle,* vol. 4: *Province ecclesiastique de Lyon (Lugdunensis prima)* (Paris: De Boccard, 1986), 22–26.

the city was a fifth- or early sixth-century church dedicated to St. Lawrence, and our textual sources tell us that the city also housed churches dedicated to St. Mary and to St. Peter, as well as the one for the martyrs of 177.[21] By 600, Lyon had a minimum of fourteen religious buildings scattered throughout the city, and none of these, not even the episcopal group, seems to have acted as a single religious center.[22] Late antique Lyon itself was also a city of diminished proportions. Although both Reynaud and Harries argue that the fifth century was a time of some revival and rebuilding in the city, it still had seen better days, and its inhabitants would have dwelt among monuments which reminded them of a now-lost moment when Lyon had been a center of imperial administration in Gaul.[23] Lyon was a city built around long-distance trade, and that was fading in importance in fifth-century Gaul. After the Frankish conquest in the early sixth century, Lyon played no further significant role in Gallic politics or administration, although its bishop continued to be a prestigious figure, and played an important role in regional church councils.[24]

Lyon was therefore a divided city struggling to find its new place on a markedly less international stage. The preacher's emphasis on unity, and on a coherent local identity, set in stark contrast to a more universal Christianity, makes sense within this context. Lyon was not known as a pilgrimage center — even those outsiders whom we know visited religious sites there

---

21 Gregory of Tours, *Liber in gloria martyrum,* 48; Gregory of Tours, *Liber in gloria confessorum,* ed. Bruno Krusch, Monumenta Germaniae Historica, Scriptores Rerum Merovingicarum 1.2 (Hanover: Hahn, 1885), 21, 22, 63, 64; Gregory of Tours, *Decem libri historiarum,* 3.5; Bernard de Vrégille in *Les diocèse de Lyon,* ed. Jacques Gadille and René Fédou (Paris: Beauchesne, 1983), 25; *Topographie chrétienne, volume 4,* 26–34; May Viellard-Troiekouroff, *Les monuments religieux de la Gaule d'après les ouevres de Grégoire de Tours* (Paris: K.H. Krüger, 1976), 142–50.

22 de Vrégille in *Diocèse de Lyon,* ed. Gadille and Fédou, 32.

23 Reynaud, *Lugdunum christianum,* 199, 263–64.

24 Ibid., 20–21.

were passing through on their way elsewhere.[25] The promotion of local saints was therefore aimed at local residents and took place, as in the sermon, at the expense of broader conceptions of Christian identity. This is a development in accord with the expansion, for example of the cult of St. Justus in Lyon, so that he eventually had four different annual festivals dedicated in his honor.[26] However, as my list of churches should have made clear, international saints continued to be well represented in Lyon. Early church dedications were to John the Baptist, the Maccabees, Mary, Stephen, and Peter. Only gradually did some of these churches come to be associated with local figures, and this may have happened well after the *Eusebius Gallicanus* sermon was preached. The last of the late Roman churches to be built in Lyon was dedicated to St. Lawrence, not to a local saint. This was not a city turning entirely inwards, but one trying to self-locate in a new and confusing world, where even what it meant to be "international" was up for redefinition.[27] The *Eusebius Gallicanus* sermon eleven, therefore, needs to be understood as an *argument* for the prevailing importance of local saints, not as a statement of community consensus on the issue. It may have been an entrance into a local conversation and a statement within a shifting dynamic. This would explain the stark sense of rivalry which permeates the text, and the strange lengths to which the preacher went to make his case. The sermon has a slight air of desperation about it.

It is worth, then, finally, making some comparisons to the alternate course taken in a sermon on the Feast of the Holy Innocents, which displays some very strong parallels to *Eusebius Gallicanus* sermon eleven. This sermon was previously edited

---

25 Bailey, *Religious Worlds*, 91.
26 Reynaud, *Lugdunum christianum*, 24; Beaujard, *Culte des saints*, 472–73.
27 Helmut Reimitz, "The Providential Past: Visions of Frankish Identity in the Early Medieval History of Gregory of Tours' Historiae (Sixth-Ninth Century)," in *Visions of Community in the Post-Roman World: The West, Byzantium and the Islamic World, 300–1100*, ed. Walter Pohl, Clemens Ganter, and Richard Payne (Farnham and Burlington: Ashgate, 2012), 109–11.

as Augustine of Hippo, sermon 220, but has most recently been included as sermon 222 among the works of Caesarius of Arles, as edited by Germain Morin. As the title indicates, it is a sermon for the festival of the children killed by Herod, and section one very closely parallels section two and parts of section three of the *Eusebius Gallicanus* sermon on the martyrs of 177, albeit with no reference to any local martyrs or festivals and with even more emphasis upon the pathos of the children's deaths. Subsequently, however, this sermon takes a completely different path and develops into a general discussion of apparent suffering in this world, and the reassurance that justice will come in the afterlife, ending with some comments on the nature of true riches as opposed to false ones. Whereas the *Eusebius Gallicanus* sermon, therefore, has a focus on this world and the identities and connections which are made within it, the Augustinian/Caesarian sermon focuses entirely on the next world and the importance of directing attention to what will come rather than what is immediately around you. It would be wonderful to know which version came first. Did the Eusebian preacher take an Augustinian sermon on the Holy Innocents and adapt it to suit his own pastoral goals? Did Caesarius take the Eusebian sermon and strip out the local references to build a more generic and "mainstream" sermon on the Holy Innocents? Considerably more work needs to be done on the authorship and dating of the sermons attributed to Caesarius before we can answer these questions. We can at least say, however, that by the sixth century both versions of the sermon were in circulation in Gaul. The Holy Innocents sermon therefore represents an alternate path not taken by the Eusebian preacher and the collection's compiler. They instead chose a this-worldly, pragmatic, local focus which used the martyrs of 177 as a mechanism by which to build a strong Christian community within Lyon. Urban rivalry with Bethlehem was a means to this end.

Bibliography

Primary

Caesarius of Arles. *Sermones.* Edited by Germain Morin. Corpus Christianorum Series Latina 103–104. Turnhout: Brepols, 1953.

Eusebius "Gallicanus." Collectio homilarum. Sermones extravagantes. Edited by Françoise Glorie. Corpus Christianorum Series Latina 101. Turnhout: Brepols, 1970.

Eusebius of Caesarea. *Ecclesiastical History, Vol. 1: Books 1–5.* Translated by Kirsopp Lake. Loeb Classical Library 153. Cambridge: Harvard University Press, 1926. DOI: 10.4159/DLCL. eusebius-ecclesiastical_history.1926.

Gregory of Tours. *Decem libri historiarum.* Edited by Bruno Krusch and Wilhelm Levison. Monumenta Germaniae Historica, Scriptores Rerum Merovingicarum 1.1. Hanover: Hahn, 1951.

———. *Liber in gloria confessorum.* Edited by Bruno Krusch. Monumenta Germaniae Historica, Scriptores Rerum Merovingicarum 1.2. Hanover: Hahn, 1885.

———. *Liber in gloria martyrum.* Edited by Bruno Krusch. Monumenta Germaniae Historica, Scriptores Rerum Merovingicarum 1.2. Hanover: Hahn, 1885.

Secondary

Bailey, Lisa Kaaren. "Building Urban Christian Communities: Sermons on Local Saints in the *Eusebius Gallicanus* Collection." *Early Medieval Europe* 12 (2003): 1–24. DOI: 10.1111/j.0963–9462.2003.00119.x.

———. *Christianity's Quiet Success: The Eusebius Gallicanus Sermon Collection and the Power of the Church in Late Antique Gaul.* Notre Dame: University of Notre Dame Press, 2006.

———. *The Religious Worlds of the Laity in Late Antique Gaul.* London: Bloomsbury, 2016.

Beaujard, Brigitte. "Cités, évêques et martyrs en Gaule à la fin de l'époque romaine." In *Les Fonctions des Saints dans le monde occidental (IIIe–XIIIe siècle)*, edited by Jean-Yves Tilliette, 175–91. Rome: École française de Rome, 1991.

———. *Le culte des saints en Gaule: les premiers temps. D'Hilaire de Poitiers à la fin du VIe siècle*. Paris: Les Éditions du Cerf, 2000.

Cameron, Alan. *Claudian: Poetry and Propaganda at the Court of Honorius*. Oxford: Clarendon Press, 1970.

Gadille, Jacques, and René Fédou, eds. *Les diocèse de Lyon*. Paris: Beauchesne, 1983. DOI: 10.14375/NP.9782701010663.

Gauthier, Nancy, and Jean-Charles Picard. *Topographie chrétienne des cités de la Gaule des origines au milieu du VIIIe siècle, volume 4, Province ecclesiastique de Lyon (Lugdunensis prima)*. Paris: De Boccard, 1986.

Harries, Jill. "Christianity and the City in Late Antique Gaul." In *The City in Late Antiquity*, edited by John Rich, 77–98. London and New York: Routledge, 2002.

———. *Sidonius Apollinaris and the Fall of Rome, A.D. 407–485*. Oxford: Oxford University Press, 1994.

Laurence, Ray, Simon Esmonde Cleary, and Gareth Sears. *The City in the Roman West, c. 250 BC–AD 250*. Cambridge: Cambridge University Press, 2011. DOI: 10.1017/CBO9780511975882.

Leroy, Jean. "L'oeuvre oratoire de s. Fauste de Riez: La collection gallicane dite d'Eusèbe d'Émese." Ph.D. diss., University of Strasbourg, 1954.

Mathisen, Ralph W. *Ecclesiastical Factionalism and Ecclesiastical Controversy in Fifth-Century Gaul*. Washington, DC: Catholic University of America Press, 1989.

Neyrand, Louis. "Le récit de la passion de martyrs de Lyon dans la traduction de Rufin." In *Les martyrs de Lyon (177)*, edited by Jean Rougé and Robert Turcan, 289–98. Paris: CNRS, 1978.

Pernot, Laurent. *Epideictic Rhetoric: Questioning the Stakes of Ancient Praise*. Austin: University of Texas, 2015.

Reimitz, Helmut. "The Providential Past: Visions of Frankish Identity in the Early Medieval History of Gregory of Tours' Historiae (Sixth–Ninth Century)." In *Visions of Community in the Post-Roman World: The West, Byzantium and the Is-*

lamic World, 300–1100, edited by Walter Pohl, Clemens Ganter, and Richaerd Payne, 109–35. Burlington: Ashgate, 2012.

Reynaud, Jean François. *Lugdunum christianum: Lyon du IVe au VIIIe s.: topographie, nécropoles et édifices religieux.* Paris: Éditions de la Maison des Sciences de l'Homme, 1998.

Viellard-Troiekouroff, May. *Les monuments religieux de la Gaule d'après les oeuvres de Grégoire de Tours.* Paris: K.H. Krüger, 1976.

Walker, P.W.L. *Holy City, Holy Places? Christian Attitudes to Jerusalem and the Holy Land in the Fourth Century.* Oxford: Clarendon Press, 1990.

2

Tours vs. Bourges: The Secular and Ecclesiastical Discourse of Inter-City Relationships in the Accounts of Gregory of Tours

Michael Burrows

Introduction: Inter-City Rivalry and Gregory of Tours

Over recent decades, our understanding of the writings of bishop Gregory of Tours (c. 538–594) has developed dramatically. Gregory, author of perhaps the most important and prolific sources that derive from the "barbarian" successor states to the Roman Empire, was once perceived as a credulous and unsophisticated recorder of events. Today however, the complexity of both his historical and hagiographical observations is much better understood.[1] For example, we have come to recognize that Gregory was partisan in his advocacy for certain saint's cults;

---

1   See for example, Walter A. Goffart, *The Narrators of Barbarian History (A.D. 550–800): Jordanes, Gregory of Tours, Bede, and Paul the Deacon* (Princeton: Princeton University Press, 1988); Martin Heinzelmann, *Gregory of Tours: History and Society in the Sixth Century,* trans. Christopher Carroll (Cambridge: Cambridge University Press, 2001); and Kathleen Mitchell and Ian Wood, eds., *The World of Gregory of Tours* (Boston and Leiden: Brill, 2002).

especially those of Julian (d. 311), Martin (d. 397), and Nicetius (d. 566). Furthermore, we can discern particular interest in his own family and their Auvergnat homeland, and likewise hostility toward parties that were hostile to them.

Recognition of these biases substantially adds to our interpretation of the content of Gregory's various works. For example, a superficial reading of the *Decem libri historiarum* (henceforth DLH) suggests a furious dislike for the Neustrian king Chilperic (r. 561–584) and a profound admiration for his brother Guntram, king of Burgundy (r. 561–592), yet a more precise analysis reveals a less binary juxtaposition.[2] Gregory surely liked Guntram more than Chilperic (he describes the former as a "good king," and the latter as contemporary Herod), but his politics were nuanced; he does not seem to have perceived of Chilperic and Guntram as morally polar opposites. Chilperic, for example, seems to have maintained fairly good relations with Gregory at times, while the excoriating review of his reign, which has perhaps skewed our understanding of Gregory's position, may have been written in a context where Guntram — an enemy of Chilperic — was the newly imposed ruler of Tours.[3] If

2 Gregory of Tours, *Decem libri historiarum*, ed. Bruno Krusch and Wilhelm Levison, Monumenta Germaniae Historica, Scriptores Rerum Merovingicarum 1.1 (Hanover: Hahn, 1951). Quotes in English, with page numbers, derive from Gregory of Tours, *The History of the Franks,* trans. Lewis Thorpe (Harmondsworth: Penguin, 1974).

3 Guy Halsall, "Nero and Herod? The Death of Chilperic and Gregory's Writings of History," in *The World of Gregory of Tours,* ed. Mitchell and Wood, 337–50 and Ian Wood "The Secret Histories of Gregory of Tours," *Revue belge de philologie et d'histoire* 71 (1993): 253–70. Alexander C. Murray, "Chronology and the Composition of the Histories of Gregory of Tours," *Journal of Late Antiquity* 1 (2008): 157–96, criticizes these interpretations on the basis that they rely on a synchronicity with events that he rejects. For the purposes of this chapter, however, it is sufficient to note that Murray also stresses the complexity of portrayal in Gregory's narrative. If, as he argues, the DLH was composed entirely after 585, then Gregory nevertheless is more nuanced about Chilperic than has sometimes been allowed, while his depiction of Guntram is also not uncomplicatedly positive.

so, it was surely politically expedient in this context for Gregory to emphasize his antipathy toward the previous regime.

Similarly, though Gregory is clearly effusive in his praise of Guntram at times, the king is not depicted as the exemplar of a perfect monarch. Subtle criticism of his policies and personality occur regularly in the narrative, and Gregory is openly scathing about some of Guntram's more sinful underlings.[4] As a result of reappraisals of Gregory's work, we come to see that kings are not simply bad or good, but subject to change and influence. Moreover, we can determine that his own perspectives and narratives were likewise no less malleable.

With this in mind, I will explore a new approach by which we might better understand aspects of the myriad intertwining themes of Gregory's works; specifically, the matter of inter-city rivalries. Much has been written on the subject of identity in late antiquity/early medieval Europe, yet the majority of it pertains to issues of ethnicity or faith. This is not without good reason, but the issue of the city as an aspect of identity seems largely overlooked. Today, inter-city rivalries are most commonly expressed through sport. Intra-city city rivalries between football clubs, such as the "Old Firm" in Glasgow, AC Milan vs. Inter Milan, or Roma vs. Lazio are often the most notorious in European soccer, but not exclusively so: inter-city contests between the likes of Liverpool and Manchester United, Real Madrid and Barcelona, and Juventus and Fiorentina can be just as hotly contested. For partisan fans, participation in such games has a significant impact on civic identity.[5]

Sport may have played a role in the expression in inter-city rivalries throughout much of history; the minor Italian cities of Gubbio and Sansepolcro have contested a crossbow-shooting

---

4 Michael Burrows, "Gregory of Tours, Political Criticism and Lower-Class Violence," *Mirabilia* 18 (2014): 32–44.

5 Richard Giulianotti and Gary Armstrong, "Avenues of Contestation. Football Hooligans Running and Ruling Urban Spaces," *Social Anthropology* 10 (2002): 211–38 and Anthony King, "Football Fandom and Post-national Identity in the New Europe," *British Journal of Sociology* 51 (2000): 419–42.

competition annually almost every year since 1461, while success in Olympic competition was a great boon for Greek city-
states over their neighbors, and continued to be highly valued
under Roman rule.[6] Yet in fifteenth-century Italy and Classical
Greece the expression of inter-city rivalries was not limited to
sport; they competed politically, economically, and militarily.
Through narratives like that of Xenophon (c. 431–354 BCE), the
Athenian-born partisan of Spartan institutions, they even competed for cultural (and historical) prominence.

Under the hegemony of Rome, inter-city rivalries were necessarily somewhat less preeminent, though they were sometimes
fierce nonetheless. However, after Rome's control faded, it seems
that the former cities of the empire had the opportunity for more
antagonistic relationships once again.[7] François Guizot, the
great historian and statesman of the nineteenth century, put it
like this: "Thus we again discover, at the Fall of the Roman Empire, the same fact that we have detected in the cradle of Rome,
namely, the predominance of the municipal form and spirit. The
Roman world had returned to its first condition; towns had constituted it; it dissolved; and the towns remained."[8] It is plausible,
then, that the pre-hegemonic antagonistic rivalries re-emerged
in the late antique context and that these might be discernible
in the detailed, comprehensive narrative of Gregory of Tours.

Gregory's family hailed from the city of Clermont and had
connections with Langres and Dijon. He and his family also
had longstanding ties to Tours where all but five of his episco-

6 For the sporting rivalry of Gubbio and Sansepolcro, see Diana L. Parsell,
   "Crossbow Rivalry of Two Italian Towns Dates to the Middle Ages," *National Geographic News,* September 6, 2002.
7 For inter-city rivalry under the Roman Empire: Juvenal, 15.33–83; Cicero,
   Pro Cluentio, 23–25; and Tacitus, *Annals,* 14.7. These examples and others
   were compiled by Garrett G. Fagan, "Violence in Roman Social Relations,"
   in *The Oxford Handbook of Social Relations in the Roman World,* ed. Michael Peachin (New York: Oxford University Press, 2014), 488–89.
8 François Guizot, *The History of Civilization,* vol. 1, trans. William Hazlitt
   (New York: The Colonial Press, 1899), 27.

pal predecessors had been his relations.[9] However, for the purposes of identifying inter-city rivalry in Merovingian Gaul, it
is important to stress that Tours, though a metropolitan see,
was not metropolitan of Gregory's native Clermont. Clermont's
ecclesiastical overseer was the bishop of Bourges in the old Roman diocese of Aquitania Prima. Gregory himself was bishop
in a city in which he was often considered a foreigner.[10] He was
metropolitan over suffragan bishops who were routinely dis-
obedient, rivals for power and, at worst, were quite literally at
war with Tours. One of those suffragans even conspired in the
murder of Gregory's brother.[11] At times, Gregory must have felt
rather embattled at Tours, and though his loyalty seems certain
(of course, we base this almost exclusively on his own narrative)
his enduring concern for Clermont and the Auvergne is evident
throughout his works.[12] For this reason, Gregory had personal
interest in the actions and administration of the archdiocese of
Bourges.

For the purposes of investigating a sample of inter-city rivalry in Merovingian Gaul and the works of Gregory, it would
seem then that Bourges presents a good candidate as a rival
for Tours and its bishop. We have already seen that Gregory
would have had personal reasons for interest or perhaps grievance against Bourges. However, there were also concerns which
might have influenced the wider population and ecclesiastical
establishment; the cities were rival metropolitans and their territories were contiguous, but were often divided by the political
boundaries between the rival Frankish kings who dominated
during Gregory's episcopacy.

9   *DLH*, 5.49.
10 In *DLH*, 5.49 a conspirator against Gregory intended to rid Tours of "the
    rabble from Clermont," 321.
11 *DLH*, 5.5.
12 For Gregory's occasional discomfort within his "foreign" diocese and for his
    intimate connection with the Auvergne and the cult of St Julian of Brioude,
    see Brian Brennan, "'Being Martin': Saint and Successor in Sixth-Century
    Tours," *The Journal of Religious History* 21 (1997): 121–35, at 125.

Unfortunately, given our reliance on Gregory for information, it will not be possible to discern with certainty how far his
own biases or rivalry might reflect that of the general population of Tours. We have no other accounts for that city, nor have
we contemporary or equivalent witnesses from Bourges. This
study will therefore focus on Gregory's perspective in particular.

Bourges crops up regularly in his various works. It occurs
with some regularity in the *DLH* and according to the survey
of Pietri — based on Gregory's *miracula* — it supplied more pilgrims than almost any other city to Tours (the exception, Angers, was in any case within the archdiocese of Tours). Indeed,
the Metropolitan district of Bourges supplied more pilgrims to
Tours than even Tours's own Metropolitan district![13] Given this
relative abundance of evidence, it is striking that almost every
reference to Bourges is critical or, at best, non-complimentary.
In order to explain this evidence in the context of inter-city rivalry, it will be broken down into categories that best reflect the
particular issue or grievance. It is hoped that these will elucidate
some of the ways in which city rivalries might have developed
and been given expression in Merovingian Gaul, as well as shed
some light on Gregory's complexity as an author and source.

Bourges as a Rival Cult Center

Interestingly, one of the few seemingly positive comments that
Gregory has for the city of Bourges is that it possessed one of
the first churches in Gaul. This notice, however, recorded in *DLH*
1.31, seems to be loaded with oblique criticism. The preceding
two chapters record the events of the arrival of Christianity in
Gaul. It first became established in Lyons, where bishop Photinus (d. 177) and his successor Irenaeus (d. 202) quickly converted most of the city, which seems to have been very open to
Christianity, despite a series of persecutions and the martyrdom

---

13   Luce Pietri, *La ville de Tours du IVe au VIe siècle. Naissance d'une cite chrétienne* (Rome: École française de Rome, 1983), 550–52 and n. 109.

of numerous early Christians. Among these early martyrs were numbered both Photinus, Irenaeus, and an ancestor of Gregory's named Vettius Epagatus.[14] Sometime later, the other major cities of Gaul received Seven Bishops; the most prominent of which was Saturninus at Toulouse, followed by Gatianus for Tours and others for the cities of Arles, Narbonne, Paris, Clermont, and Limoges.[15] It was only through the actions of one of their disciples, St. Ursinus (unnamed in *DLH* but probably described by Gregory in the *Glory of the Confessors,* henceforth *GC*), that the word of Christianity came to Bourges.[16] However, unlike in the other cities, where converts seem to have been numerous, Gregory claims that Ursinus's reception in Bourges was rather more lukewarm. The few believers attempted to develop the institutions of a bishopric, but could not find a building for a church since the leading men of the town remained committed to paganism. In the end, they had to petition a prominent senator from outside the city, but who owned a property there, for the donation of a church-house. Gregory mentions that this senator, Leocadius, was of the family of Vettius Epagatus (who had been martyred at Lyons); it would seem then that from its origin the see of Bourges was indebted to Gregory's Auvergnat family.[17] These inauspicious beginnings of Christianity at Bourg-

14 *DLH*, 1.29. See also Gregory of Tours, *Glory of the Martyrs,* 48, trans. Raymond Van Dam, Translated Texts for Historians 4 (Liverpool: Liverpool University Press, 2004); the placement is surely intentional: chapter 48 for the forty-eight martyrs. *Glory of the Martyrs* will henceforth be *GM*.

15 *DLH*, 1.30. It is significant that while Tours, Narbonne, and Arles were all provincial capitals and became metropolitan sees, Paris, Toulouse, Clermont, and Limoges were suffragan bishoprics. It is perhaps even more significant that the latter three were all suffragans of Bourges. More on this below.

16 Gregory of Tours, *Glory of the Confessors,* 79, trans. Raymond Van Dam, Translated Texts for Historians 5 (Liverpool: Liverpool University Press, 2004), 59, and see n. 88.

17 *DLH*, 1.31. Indeed, we are even informed in Gregory of Tours, *Life of the Fathers* 6.1, trans. Edward James (Liverpool: Liverpool University Press, 1991), 33 that Leocadius was Gregory's great-grandfather. *Life of the Fathers* will henceforth be *VP*.

es, described directly after the illustrious stories of the Lyons martyrs and the Seven Bishops, place Bourges in a very distant third rank in Gregory's spiritual genealogy of Gaul.

Even after this rocky start, Christianity at Bourges — as told by Gregory — had teething problems. Bishop Ursinus created the foundations of the Church in Bourges, but the people did not know how to venerate their bishops at that time, and so they planted a vineyard over his grave and buried all memory of their first bishop. It was not until the reign of bishop Probianus in the mid-sixth century, several hundred years later, that these origins were uncovered.[18]

Why does Gregory provide such detail regarding the troubled and dubious origins of Christianity in Bourges? It is the contention of this chapter that Gregory, as a native of the Auvergne and bishop of Tours, felt antagonistic toward Bourges, which was metropolitan over Clermont and contiguous to Gregory's own metropolitan see of Tours, and that his references to Bourges constitute a hostile discourse. One probable reason for this antagonistic relationship is the competition for supremacy in prestige of saint's cults and episcopal influence over them. The primary saint of Merovingian Bourges was, as it remains today, St. Stephen, whose relics were brought to Gaul in the aftermath of their discovery in 415.[19] Their arrival seems to have attracted some considerable attention and, during the fifth century, the cult of Stephen — the proto-martyr — may well have been more widespread than that of St. Martin.[20] For Gregory, the advocation of the cult of St. Martin, the former bishop

---

18 *GC*, 79. More on the reluctance of the ecclesiastical hierarchy of Bourges to recognize this below.

19 *GM*, 33, trans. Van Dam, 30, n. 37.

20 Allan Scott McKinley, "The First Two Centuries of Saint Martin at Tours," *Early Medieval Europe* 14 (2006), 173–200, at 181, suggests that during the fifth century, at least, there is little evidence that the cult of Martin was widely revered. For an overview of the spread of worship of Saint Stephen to the West, see François Bovon, "The Dossier on Saint Stephen: The First Martyr," *The Harvard Theological Review* 96 (2003): 302–5.

of Tours, was vital to his own prestige, political and ecclesiastical clout, and status as a Turonian.[21] This alone might have been reason enough for hostility to a powerful neighboring cult, but Gregory was also heavily invested in the cult of St. Julian at Clermont. Both potentially stood to suffer at the hands of a vigorous rival at Bourges.[22]

It is, of course, well known that Gregory was an active champion of the causes of both St. Martin and St. Julian, but he has little to say on the matter of St. Stephen. This relative silence makes it hard to gauge his opinion on the cult at Bourges with certainty, but may in itself be telling. For example, Raymond Van Dam, editor and translator of Gregory's hagiography and *miracula*, has noted that the ignoble placement of Stephen in the thirty-third chapter of his book on martyrs reveals a certain ambivalence or even hostility toward the "first of all martyrs," which perhaps reflects on his feelings toward Bourges.[23]

In addition to the lowly placement of St. Stephen in the *Glory of the Martyrs*, henceforth GM, the rest of the chapter also hints at doubt regarding its credibility. Gregory notes that an oratory to Stephen in Touraine was found, upon renovation, to house none of the relics that tradition claimed to exist. By implication, Gregory may also impugn the relics of Stephen at Bourges. Immediately after tale of traditional but non-existent relics at the oratory near Tours, he goes on to say: "There is a relic of blood of this holy deacon, as is popularly claimed, in the altar

---

21 Brennan, "'Being Martin,'" 126.
22 Indeed, Julian's cult may have already done so. In the fifth century, the wife of bishop Namatius of Clermont had built a suburban church dedicated to Stephen (*DLH*, 2.17), which was clearly in receipt of episcopal patronage still in the sixth century since in 525 Bishop Quintianus was buried there, *VP* 4.5. Raymond Van Dam, *Saints and Their Miracles in Late Antique Gaul* (Princeton: Princeton University Press, 1993), 44, notes that Quintianus was not associated with the cult of Julian and suggests that the cult of Stephen was stronger in Clermont during the early sixth century.
23 GM 33, trans. Van Dam, 30, n. 37.

of a church at Bourges."[24] It is by no means clear, but given the position of Stephen in the *GM,* and his hostility to Bourges, this attestation of credibility to popular belief alone may have been designed to induce a certain cynicism. In stark contrast is the final miracle story attributed to Stephen, in Bordeaux, where a vision of the Saint, still wet with saltwater from his rescue of a floundering ship, appeared to a lamplighter at the church. She was able to mop up the tangible drips that remained after the vision and presented them to her bishop as a new, and definitively credible, relic.[25] This contrast seems to imply that Gregory was not antagonistic to the cult of Stephen generally, but was at least hesitant to endorse it in the neighboring diocese.

It is difficult to prove, with certainty, that Gregory was actively hostile to the cult of Stephen at Bourges, but there is enough veiled criticism in his accounts of both the Christian origins of that city and its sacred patron, to indicate reservations. Gregory was surely not inclined to clumsily lambast the faith of the neighboring diocese, nor openly denounce their most precious relics, but he nevertheless provides enough detail to undermine both. This should not surprise us. Ecclesiastical historians and hagiographers typically tended to construct their narratives so that their favored protagonist triumphed in confrontations with secular, heretical or demonic adversaries. These same narratives were then exploited to build the influence and power of bishops such as Gregory, who relied upon his position as advocate and inheritor of St. Martin to negotiate with kings, counts and fellow churchmen.[26] Given the political significance of the saint's cults, competition between them was surely common. Gregory's descriptions of the dubious Christian origins of Bourges and its cult seem laden with the veiled criticism and faint praise that in-

---

24 *GM* 33, trans. Van Dam, 31: "Pars enim beati sanguinis sacrosancti levitae huius, sicut celebre fertur, in altari Biturigae eclesiae contenetur."
25 *GM* 33.
26 Brennan, "'Being Martin,'" 128, 129–32.

dicate a careful narrative denigration of that see in comparison to its neighbors.

Bourges as a Rival Metropolitan

If Gregory's feelings toward Bourges as a cult center were veiled, he is certainly more candid in his criticism of the episcopal and metropolitan administration of the city. Though he does not seem to have been openly critical about every bishop of Bourges, his descriptions portray three sixth-century bishops of that rival city as variously irreverent, incompetent or foolish in the extreme. These three accounts will be the focus of this section, since in combination they imply a specifically antagonistic discourse. Additionally, attention will also be paid to what might be considered symptoms of metropolitan and episcopal mismanagement, and the consequences of that mismanagement for Bourges's suffragan bishops, the people of Bourges, Aquitania Prima and Gregory's own neighboring diocese.

Firstly, let us consider how Gregory describes the role bishop Probianus (c. 550–560), in the discovery of St. Ursinus the founder of Christianity at Bourges. As we have seen, the remains of this disciple of the earliest Gallic bishops was forgotten by the people of the city who planted vines over his grave. A crippled man named Agustus, from the household of Probianus's predecessor Desideratus, was directed by God to build an oratory to St. Martin in Brives, a village within the Bourges district but close to the boundary with the diocese of Tours. He was healed by the relics of Martin that he placed there and gathered a community of monks. Probianus, perhaps hostile to the intrusion of Martinian monasticism within his see, ordained Agustus abbot for the church of St. Symphronius within the sight of the walls of Bourges, but Agustus refused to leave Brives and appointed a prior to rule in his stead.[27] He then was visited in a dream by St. Ursinus who revealed the location of his remains, but Pro-

27 *GC*, 79.

bianus was disinterested and took no action. It took the visit of an outsider, bishop Germanus of Paris for the final discovery to be made; Ursinus appeared again to both Agustus and Germanus and together they secretly excavated the tomb by night, accompanied by a single cleric to hold a candle for them, and discovered the body of Ursinus still untouched by decay. Only with this revelation was Probianus convinced and the proper reinternment and commemoration of Ursinus begun.[28]

Given our lack of information about Probianus's interests, it is impossible to know the reasons for his hesitance. Van Dam supposes that Agustus might have been an erstwhile partisan of Desideratus and therefore potential rival, but if that was the case Probianus would presumably have found his location at distant Brives preferable.[29] My suspicion is that Probianus's concern was regarding the growth of Martin's cult within his own diocese, just as Gregory seems to have doubted the oratory to Stephen in Touraine which proved to have non-existent relics.[30] The relocation of Agustus to the church of St. Symphronius might have been designed to curtail any enthusiasm for Martin, while the hesitance over Ursinus was, perhaps, a response to Agustus's refusal to move.

In any case, Gregory's opinions about the episcopal behavior of Probianus seem fairly condemnatory. Just as the ancient people of Bourges lacked proper reverence for their Christian founder, so did their modern bishop. Where Gregory's own family had once provided the Church for the city, so now Martin's influence sponsored the rediscovery of Ursinus. Furthermore, just as Bourges had once relied on a disciple from other cities for the word of God, they now relied on the bishop of Paris — a diocese that received one of the original Seven Bishops — to reveal the tomb of that disciple. The message seems clear; despite

---

28 Ibid.
29 *GC*, trans. Van Dam, n. 89.
30 *GM*, 33.

the passage of generations there had been little improvement in *reverentia* in the diocese of Bourges.

Still more hostile is Gregory's depiction of metropolitan management, or lack thereof, at Bourges. Where Probianus seems irreverent, his successor Remigius (c. 570–584), is depicted as incompetent. In *DLH* 6.38, Gregory describes how the succession to the see of Rodez (a suffragan of Bourges), after the death of the incumbent Theodosius, was marred by lobbying and rivalry during which the precious vessels of the church were looted. Eventually Innocentius, Count of Javols (also within Aquitania Prima), was elected through the patronage of Brunhild at the expense of Transobadus, a local priest.[31] Gregory clearly thought this an egregious choice; in the previous chapter, he describes how Innocentius had brought charges of libel against Lupentius, Abbot at Javols, for which he was eventually found not guilty. Not content with the verdict however, Innocentius waylaid Lupentius, killed and beheaded him, and dumped the pieces in a river.[32] After his election at Rodez, Innocentius quickly lived up to his reputation; he harassed his neighbor Ursicinus of Cahors (another Bourges suffragan) and tried to seize certain parishes from him. This scandal dragged on for years until the metropolitan convened a council of the provinces of Clermont and resolved the issue in favor of Ursicinus. The phrasing here seems significant. Gregory names neither Bourges, nor Remigius as metropolitan, but rather describes Aquitania Prima as the provinces of Clermont.[33] The implication of metropolitan mismanagement is clear and Gregory seems to minimize the role of Bourges in the eventual settlement of the affair. Instead Clermont is named in the context of arbitration.[34] Significantly, Remigius is only named in the following chapter, and the only

31 *DLH*, 6.38.
32 *DLH*, 6.37.
33 *DLH*, 6.38: "post aliquot annos coniunctus metropolis cum suis provincialibus apud urbem Arvernum."
34 We will return to the apparent primacy of ranking of Clermont again below.

recognition is that he died.[35] At this juncture it is noted that it was his successor, Sulpicius, who organized the council to resolve the ownership of the disputed parishes. Gregory does not explicitly blame Remigius, but the proximity of these notes makes his incompetence apparent. Remigius ignored or failed in his metropolitan responsibilities both by allowing the chaotic succession by which the criminal Innocentius came to power[36] and by ignoring his misdeeds and persecutions for years thereafter. In Gregory's mind and narrative, it was perhaps not by chance that the greater part of the city of Bourges burned down shortly after Remigius's death.[37]

Far worse than either Probianus or Remigius however, was their predecessor Arcadius (c. 535–549).[38] In c.525,[39] this Arcadius, a senator of Auvergne, plotted to hand over the city of Clermont to Childebert I upon hearing a rumor that the rightful king, Theuderic I, had died in Thuringia. Childebert arrived quickly at Clermont but found the gates locked until the traitorous Arcadius sawed the locks away and opened the city to him.[40] Theuderic then arrived back safely, and Childebert left the city. Soon after Childebert and Clothar I went to war against

---

35 *DLH*, 6.39.

36 Gregory seems to draw specific attention to the bribery and mishandling of the succession to the see of Javols, which Remigius oversaw, by drawing contrast to his own succession which was overseen by Guntram. In his description of the election, Gregory has Guntram deliver a speech which decried the sale of bishoprics as simony. *DLH*, 6.38.

37 *DLH*, 6.39.

38 The bishop Arcadius attested in Gregory's *VP* 9.1 is almost certainly the same who was responsible for the devastation in Clermont described in *DLH* 3.9 and 12. The *DLH* describes him as a senator of Clermont who ended up in Bourges, while the *VP* describes him as a grandson of Sidonius Apollinaris, himself a senator of Clermont, and as Bishop of Bourges. Given Gregory's distaste for him, the absence of a fuller biography is unsurprising. See also, *VP* 66, trans. James, n. 5 and Van Dam, *Saints and Their Miracles in Late Antique Gaul*, 172, n. 11.

39 The dating is uncertain, but we know it corresponds with Quintianus's episcopate. See *VP*, 23, trans. James, n. 9.

40 *DLH*, 3.9.

Burgundy and invited Theuderic to join them. Theuderic was unwilling, but felt it necessary to placate his army which was keen for plunder, so he turned on the Auvergne because of the treacherous surrender of Clermont. What followed was "one of the most cataclysmic events in the history of the area."[41] Theuderic reportedly told his men repeatedly that they had no restrictions in their freedom to plunder and enslave the property and people.[42] This clearly had an enormous impact on Gregory; the event and its implications are described many times throughout his works.[43] Meanwhile Arcadius, the fool who was responsible for the devastation of Clermont and the Auvergne, made good his escape to Bourges.[44]

Only around a decade later do we again hear of Arcadius, this time in the *Life of the Fathers* (henceforth *VP*) and now consecrated bishop of Bourges, where his treachery had apparently been no obstacle to an ecclesiastical career under Clothar's rule. He was sought out by Patroclus, a devout man from the district of Bourges who had been educated under Childebert but returned home upon his father's death, rejected marriage and sought out bishop Arcadius and begged him for admittance into the clergy.[45] This Arcadius granted and Patroclus — who was devoted to fasting, vigils, study and prayer — quickly became deacon. But the archdeacon (the metaphorical *oculus episcopi*) of the church at Bourges became very annoyed when Patroclus's devotion kept him from attending the communal table and so he was sent away. Patroclus came to the village of Néris, on the road between Bourges and Clermont, and built an oratory to St.

---

41 *VP*, 23, trans. James, n. 9.

42 *DLH*, 3.12.

43 For example: *DLH*, 3.11–13, 16; *GM*, 51; *VP*, 4.2, 5.2; and the *Life of Saint Julian*, 13, 14, 23. For the Life of Saint Julian, see Van Dam, *Saints and Their Miracles in Late Antique Gaul*.

44 Bourges, unlike Clermont, was at that time inside the kingdom of Chlodomer (d. 524) and was inherited by Clothar I. Arcadius was therefore safe from Theuderic, unlike some of his family who were captured in Cahors, had their goods seized, and were sent into exile. See *DLH*, 3.12.

45 *VP*, 9.1.

Martin. Arcadius plays only a minor role in this hagiographical account, but it seems that the implication of this story is that the ecclesiastical hierarchy at Bourges rejected the holy Patroclus (or was rejected by him), who then found purpose through devotion to Martin.[46] Given Arcadius's foolish and disastrous history in secular affairs in Aquitania Prima, it is no surprise that Gregory hints at his role in consigning the church of Bourges to the loss of blessed St. Patroclus. This loss might not have been exactly equivalent to the sufferings of the Auvergne that resulted from Arcadius's foolishness, but perhaps Gregory thought it poetic that this time the loss was St. Martin's gain.

These descriptions of metropolitan mismanagement clearly indicate that Gregory held some of his fellow metropolitans at Bourges in contempt. When these examples are taken in conjunction with the evidence of competition between rival saint's cults and the generally hostile tone of Gregory's descriptions of Bourges and its occupants (or at least those who did not seek redemption from St. Martin),[47] it would seem reasonable to assume that he held the metropolitans of Bourges at least partially responsible for troubles in that district. If so, then it seems sensible to cast the net wider and attempt to determine whether accounts of disastrous, evil or irreverent behavior or events in the metropolitan district of Bourges are indicative of the malign influence of the metropolitan rivals of Gregory.

We have already seen hints from the reign of bishop Probianus that the spread of the cult of St. Martin in the territories of Bourges was received with some hostility by the local episcopal hierarchy. It is possible that Patroclus's choice of Martin as his patron was likewise a conscious rejection of Arcadius, his met-

---

46 See Lisa Kaaren Bailey, "Within and Without: Lay People and the Church in Gregory of Tours' Miracle Stories," *Journal of Late Antiquity* 5 (2012): 119–44, at 134–35.

47 Patroclus, for example, was a native of the district of Bourges, but was clearly redeemed — in Gregory's eyes — by devotion to Martin. The same seems to be true of Augustus.

ropolitan.[48] Further events, contemporary with Gregory's episcopate, suggest that the bishops of Bourges may have continued
a policy of hostility to St. Martin. During the reign of Sulpicius
(584–591), whose role in the resolution of the contested parishes
of Cahors Gregory acknowledged, the army of king Guntram
was gathered to attack the usurper Gundovald. Ullo, Count of
Bourges, was a prominent leader in Guntram's army and was
personally involved in the death of Gundovald.[49] Shortly after
the campaign, he dispatched representatives to one of the religious houses devoted to St. Martin in the region to fine them for
not delivering troops for the campaign. These representatives
were met by the *agens* (steward) of the house, who argued that
it was not proper for a religious house to provide soldiers and
refused to pay the fine. The leader of Ullo's representatives entered the courtyard of the house to forcefully seize the payment,
where he apparently collapsed in great pain, pleaded with the
agens and his men for his well-being and was promptly thrown
out the door. The rest of the count's representatives gathered up
their stricken leader and left, and soon after, through fervent
prayer to Martin, the leader was cured of his miraculous ail-
ment.[50]

It is clear from the account of this episode that Gregory was
hostile to the levying of soldiers from religious houses, and especially so since the house was devoted to Martin.[51] Because
Gregory was disapproving of the secular leaders who had de-

48 Because of the relatively early dating of these events in the vita of St. Patroclus, in the c. 530s, it is more difficult to be sure of competition between the
cults of Bourges and Tours than in times more contemporary with Gregory's writing. However, it is likely that Gregory nevertheless conceived and
described these events with the rivalry in mind.

49 *DLH*, 7.38.

50 *DLH*, 7.42.

51 Bailey, "Within and Without," 143, argues that even though the men of this
house were not clergymen, they were still distinct from ordinary saeculares.
Laury Sarti, "The Military, the Clergy and Christian Faith in Sixth-century
Gaul," *Early Medieval Europe* 25 (2017): 162–85, provides some useful discussion of Gregory's attitude toward military interactions and outrages

creed both the levies and the fine, his hostility toward Ullo, Count of Bourges is assured.[52] Whether the criticism in this passage extends to the ecclesiastical administration of Bourges is less clear but it seems likely. Gregory certainly felt that it was the responsibility of a bishop to protect his flock from unjust secular exactions. He himself had defended the citizens of Tours from the imposition of taxes by Childebert II, which he claimed were illegal because of immunities granted by Clothar I out of respect to the city of Martin. Gregory's predecessor Eufronius had defended the city from Charibert's taxation on the same basis. [53] Episcopal responsibility for the people was not limited to the issue of taxation; Gregory also provided a robust defense of refugees who sought sanctuary in his church against the ire of armies and kings, even when he personally despised the fugitives.[54] By contrast, and according to the perspective of Gregory, we might judge the bishop of Bourges to have failed in his moral responsibility to the people of his diocese.

If Gregory thought the bishops of Bourges were responsible for not defending their people against unjust secular demands, then he may have also thought them responsible for failing in their spiritual obligations to the people and church in the district. It is perhaps significant then that Gregory provides many examples of lack of proper reverence within that region. Taken

---

against the clergy, but mistakenly identifies the tax-collecting representatives as beholden to the Count of Tours (175–77).

52 His behavior during the Gundovald campaign is described by Gregory as deceitful *DLH*, 7.38, while the troops under his command were undisciplined and ravaged the common people and churches *DLH*, 7.35.

53 *DLH*, 9.30.

54 *DLH*, 5.14 and 7.21 and 29. In book 5, the refugee was Merovech, Chilperic's estranged son, while in book 7 it was Eberulf, the erstwhile treasurer of Chilperic who was accused of his murder. In both cases Gregory defied royal pressure and the intent of the Count of Tours. He might, therefore, have reasonably expected Sulpicius to have done the same. Nor was the pressure put on Gregory a vain threat; in the first instance Touraine was devastated in punishment for Gregory's moral fortitude, while in the latter a lethal fracas broke out in the church itself.

in isolation, they are not necessarily remarkable, but together, and in conjunction with his other comments on Bourges, these examples seem to be indicative of Gregory's rivalry with, and distaste for his metropolitan neighbor. Peter Brown, in his seminal study on the "Rise and Function" of the cult of saints in late antiquity, juxtaposes *reverentia* with *rusticitas* as antithetical poles in the matter of Christian faith. *Reverentia* was typified by intense spirituality that was precise and refined. The reverent man was "constantly aware, in the play of human action around him, that good and bad fortune was directly related to good or bad relations with [Christ and the saints]."[55] Rustics, by contrast, were boorish, typically rural, and whose lives were ungoverned by the careful ceremonies of Christian etiquette toward the divine. Such people were the rhetorical enemies of the Catholic Church (at least in the absence of neighboring heretics) and represented fundamental enemies of the clergy.[56] It is no surprise then, given what we have seen in this article so far, that the two archetypes of rusticity in Gregory's work both originate from Bourges. In *GC* 80, he recounts a story of how the people of Bourges disrespected the festival of the local hermit Marianus. A man brewed beer during his festival and mocked his more pious neighbors as well as Marianus, so fire burnt all his property and left those of the reverent untouched. Gregory related the message in plain words: "What do you do now, o coarse rusticity? Because you always murmur against God and his friends, you receive catastrophe upon yourself."[57] In a similar case, related in the *Virtues of Bishop Martin of Tours,* henceforth *VM,* a man from Bourges who worked his oxen on a Sunday was struck blind. Gregory describes it as symptomatic of the wider

---

55 Peter Brown, *The Cult of Saints: Its Rise and Function in Latin Christianity* (London: SCM Press, 1981), 119–20.

56 Martin of Braga, a contemporary of Gregory and guardian of relics of Martin of Tours, penned a still extant tract *De correctione rusticorum* on this very topic. Gregory, who held Martin of Braga in high esteem, is likely to have read this work.

57 *GC, 80.*

problem; "Because the ignorance of man does not follow the preaching of bishops, it prepares itself to offend God."[58] This was surely intended primarily as a general comment against rusticity and lack of reverence, but it may in this context, have also been a pointed comment on the efficacy of preaching and general irreverence in Bourges.

Similar examples of criminal activity in Bourges reflect badly on the local church, the reverence of the local people and demonstrate how these issues negatively affected Touraine and its church. A thief stole glass and metal fittings from the church of Yzeures, a village in the south of Tours's district, and took them to Bourges and sold them. He was thereafter afflicted by tumors.[59] In the village of Orbigny, also in Touraine, thieves stole relics of St. Vincentius from the church and sold them to an (unnamed) abbot in Bourges. The abbot received a vision and restored the relics.[60] The theft of church property from Touraine and sale of them in Bourges, and especially the purchase of stolen relics by a cleric, indicate a rusticitas in Bourges and a juxtaposed *reverentia* in Tours.

A far more serious example of *rusticitas* in Bourges can be found in the example of the so-called Pseudo-Christ of Bourges. Sometime around 590 a man from the district was driven insane by a swarm of flies while working in a local forest. He affected the appearance of a wild man and began imitating the behavior of ascetic holy men. From Bourges he travelled south to the district of Arles, presumably via the Auvergne, but returned to Aquitania Prima and the region of Javols where he adopted the persona of Christ and took a female follower as his "Mary". He gathered followers through healing and prophecy and began to

---

58 *VM*, 4.45, in Gregory of Tours, *De virtutibus sancti Martini episcopi*, in *Saints and their Miracles in Late Antique Gaul*, trans. Van Dam. These examples, *GC*, 80 and *VM*, 4.45, are the two that Van Dam uses as examples of divine punishment of stereotypically rustic behavior (at 124), though he does not comment on their common location in the district of Bourges.

59 *GM*, 58.

60 *GM*, 89.

despoil the rich and travelers and distribute the loot among his poor and rustic following.[61] In the troubled context of war, famine and plague, his popularity seems to have snowballed.[62] Even credulous priests joined his cause and his retinue swelled to three thousand, according to Gregory.[63] They seem to have plundered their way from Javols to Le Velay and then to Le Puy, both within the metropolitan district of Bourges, where they seem to have laid siege to the city. Eventually Aurelius, the bishop of Le Puy, who seems to have organized the defense, had to dispatch disguised hitmen to assassinate the Pseudo-Christ.[64]

It is hard to imagine a more spectacular example of *rusticitas*. This irreverent cavalcade committed theft, violence and murder, practiced demoniacal magic and prophecy, impersonated Christ and the Virgin Mary, corrupted clergymen, mocked a bishop with their nakedness and laid siege to an episcopal city. The severity of these outrages and the support that the Pseudo-Christ accumulated must reflect badly on the metropolitan of the district, since he was responsible for the *reverentia* of the people of the district. It is perhaps indicative of Gregory's disapproval that, although the worst of the disturbance took place in the south of Aquitania Prima, he specifically names Bourges as the origin of the perpetrator and perhaps, therefore, lays blame specifically at their door. It may be of significance that the death of Sulpicius, metropolitan of Bourges, is recorded in the follow-

61 *DLH,* 10.25: "Interea coepit quosdam spoliare ac praedare, quos in itinere repperisset; spolia tamen non habentibus largiebatur."
62 Gregory describes the explicit context of famine and plague in the chapter, but adds further detail in *DLH,* 9.22 (for plague) and 7.45 (for famine). Details of the recent and local war are described elsewhere at length. The most significant detail is in 8.30, which describes how Guntram's men devastated the Frankish lands on their way southward to Septimania, were defeated, and devastated them again on their way out again.
63 *DLH,* 10.25: "Seducta est autem per eum multitudo inmensa populi, et non solum rusticiores, verum etiam sacerdotes eclesiastici. Sequebantur autem eum amplius tria milia populi."
64 The whole affair is described in *DLH,* 10.25.

ing chapter of the *DLH*.[65] As we have seen in Gregory's account of the crimes of Innocentius of Javols, Gregory only named the metropolitan at fault (in that case Remigius), in the following chapter which recorded only his death. The naming and death of Sulpicius follows the same structure, perhaps indicating a narrative method of Gregory's for delivering a subtle critique of episcopal rivals. In any case, the failure of the clergy of Bourges seems apparent by contrast to other regions. Several other examples of popular/populist messianic, prophetic or magical figures can be found in the *DLH*.[66] In each of these it is surely significant that the bishop directly confronts the rustic charlatan before his popularity gets out of control. Later, in the chapter discussing the Pseudo-Christ, Gregory suggests that he personally dissuaded several potential rustic rabble-rousers, while elsewhere he describes ousting two such imposters from Tours; one named Desideratus, reputedly from Bordeaux, and another, unnamed but of Spanish origin, whom he expelled and was also later imprisoned by bishop Ragnemod of Paris.[67] The bishops of Bourges seem not to have met the standards set by Gregory himself, or his more worthy fellow bishops such as Ragnemod.

It has hopefully been established, during the course of this section, that Gregory displays consistent hostility toward the metropolitan administration of Bourges and that this seems to have been caused, or at least fueled, by examples of failure to adequately protect the people and suffragan bishops of the district and failure to adequately resist the evils of *rusticitas*. Finally, however, we must assess whether Gregory's distaste for his rival metropolitans at Bourges derived from these failures alone, or something more fundamental. As we have seen, Gregory's account of the Christian origins of Bourges was disparaging, especially in contrast to some of its suffragans, including Clermont, as well as with Tours, the metropolitan of neighbor-

---

65 *DLH*, 10.26.
66 At the close of *DLH*, 10.25 Gregory suggests such characters were common.
67 Both are described in *DLH*, 9.6.

ing Lugdunensis Tertia. Indeed, the fact that Bourges was only evangelized by disciples from its suffragans at Toulouse, Clermont and Limoges may have even, from Gregory's perspective, called its metropolitan status into question. The metropolitan sees of Merovingian Gaul were based closely on the provincial, originally secular, diocese structure of the Roman imperial administration in Gaul. In almost every case the provincial capital became the metropolitan diocese and Bourges was no exception. However, Gregory may have felt that Bourges's less than sparkling Christian heritage counted against the inheritance of this status, especially in comparison to the illustrious Toulouse and his home city of Clermont. Toulouse, of course, was unsettled by its recent history on the borders of the Catholic Frankish and Arian Visigothic realms, but Clermont was among the first Gallic cities to be converted, as told by Gregory, by the Seven Bishops.[68] Bourges, by contrast, relied on lesser disciples of the Seven as well as patronage from Gregory's ancestors, themselves probably from Clermont.[69] Nor indeed was this the only time Bourges relied upon its suffragans. In a high-profile case in 470 Sidonius Apollinaris, bishop of Clermont and still relatively junior, was able to quell political, clerical and theological controversy by overseeing the election of a new bishop in Bourges, with the assistance of Perpetuus, metropolitan of Tours and Gregory's predecessor.[70] Gregory does not mention this intercession, perhaps because he was uncomfortable with the topic

68 See above.

69 Thorpe, "Introduction" in *The History of the Franks,* 11, describes Leocad as "Senator of Bourges," but the narrative seems to imply that his origins were external and that he, like much of the senatorial aristocracy, owned properties across various regions. Given that the embattled early Christians of Bourges reached out to him he was presumably local and already Christian, so it seems reasonable that he came from Clermont. Moreover, as Gregory explains in the *VP,* 6.1, Leocadius was father of Leocadia, Gregory's grandmother and wife of a senator of Clermont.

70 Johannes A. van Waarden, "Episcopal Self-Presentation: Sidonius Apollinaris and the Episcopal Election in Bourges," in *Episcopal Elections in Late Antiquity,* ed. Johan Leemans et al. (Berlin: De Gruyter, 2011), 555–61.

of suffragan involvement in the metropolitan succession, but it seems probable that he was aware of Clermont's historic significance.[71] It was perhaps for this reason that he described the council that finally resolved Innocentius of Javols's false claims to certain parishes of Cahors as "a council of the provinces of Clermont," rather than of Bourges.[72] Given these hints, and his consistent hostility to Bourges, it is plausible that Gregory actually doubted the very metropolitan legitimacy of that diocese. If Gregory believed that ecclesiastical leadership of Aquitania Prima was misplaced and that his home city of Clermont was a more appropriate seat for the metropolitan, then such a fundamental grievance would surely have had had a profound effect on his perception of Bourges and its bishops.

Unfortunately, we cannot be entirely certain that Gregory believed Clermont more deserving of primacy than Bourges, but throughout the course of this section we have established that Gregory was certainly and generally critical of his metropolitan counterparts to the east. Given the consistency, diversity and sometime vehemence of his criticism, and considering it in conjunction with the rivalry between saint's cults at Tours and Bourges, it indicates that — at the very least — Gregory of Tours felt hostility or rivalry toward his neighbors.

Political Rivalry between Tours and Bourges

So far, we have seen substantial evidence which indicates that the bishop of Tours as champion of St. Martin and metropolitan of Lugdunensis Tertia, felt a rivalry toward the advocates of St. Stephen and Aquitania Prima in Bourges. It is difficult to de-

---

71 After all, both Sidonius and Gregory were citizens of Clermont. Indeed, Gregory wrote a book, now lost, on the Masses composed by Sidonius, and Sidonius was a correspondent of Gregory's predecessor Perpetuus of Tours and, perhaps also his successor Volusianus. See *DLH*, 2.22 and Edward James, *VP*, n. 20.

72 *DLH*, 6.38: "coniunctus metropolis cum suis provincialibus apud urbem Arvernum resedens iudicium emanaret."

termine how far this rivalry stretched because we are reliant on Gregory's insight, but given the importance of his writings for our understanding of sixth-century Gaul, evidence of his personal hostility is of great importance in its own right. However, it is probable that Gregory felt particular antagonism toward Bourges because of his personal affiliation to Clermont, but it is plausible that the feeling was shared by other bishops either side of the divide. As we have seen, the ecclesiastical hierarchy at Bourges seems to have been hostile to the expansion of the cult of Martin in its territories and, since numerous bishops of Tours were related to Gregory, it seems reasonable to suppose that they shared some of his biases.[73]

Episcopal rivalries also seem to have spilled over into secular affairs. This is not surprising, since local communities were closely tied to their pastoral ecclesiastical structures, and therefore the biases of one presumably influenced the other, whether through policy, gossip or the pulpit.[74] Moreover, ecclesiastic and lay authorities necessarily interacted, even when relationships were fractious, so it must be expected that secular powers sometimes acted in either support or defiance of ecclesiastical prejudices, depending on their vested interests.[75]

In the following section, we will consider some political interactions between Tours and Bourges as described by Gregory. The specific relationship between these cities has rarely featured in analyses of Merovingian politics, but given the evidence of ecclesiastical rivalry, these episodes can be seen in a new light. Furthermore, the addition of these secular grievances between the cities and their territories adds another strand to the argument: the widespread and fundamental impact of volatile rela-

---

73 *DLH,* 5.49.
74 It was also not unprecedented for personal or familial grievances to be taken up by the wider community. See Cicero, *Pro Cluentio,* 23–25, where the citizens of Lamina take up the cause of the Aurii against the evil Oppianicus.
75 For example, the counts of Bourges seem to have been hostile to the house of Saint Martin in the district. See above and *DLH,* 7.42.

tions between Tours and Bourges perhaps indicates that perceptions of rivalry and hostility extended well beyond the personal vignettes of their bishops.

The geographic locations of Tours and Bourges within the sixth-century Merovingian kingdoms was surely conducive to the development of political rivalry. The two were provincial capitals and cities of historic and contemporary significance. They were located fairly closely together; less than 160 kilometers (100 miles) apart, and the river Cher, and its tributary the Yèvre on which Bourges stands, probably presented more of a highway than a barrier.[76] Bourges and Tours were also contiguous metropolitan sees; this was not unique — Mainz and Trier, and Vienne and Lyons were contiguous as well — but they stood peculiarly divided by their political affiliation. Bourges had been within the old Roman "Seven Provinces" region, while Tours had belonged to "outer" Gaul.[77] Bourges was securely within the Burgundian realm from Guntram's accession in 561 onward, while Tours sat just opposite on a fractious political boundary and belonged, variously, to three kingdoms and four kings during Gregory's reign.

This boundary was exploited by one of Gregory's most prominent personal adversaries, Count Leudast of Tours. Gregory is forthright in his criticism of Leudast in the *DLH,* describing him, variously, as a low-born, fawning, strutting, dishonest, murderous despoiler of church property. It is worth taking a moment to expand upon his convoluted career. Though the son of a slave, he had been made count because he was a favorite of king Charibert's wife, but on Charibert's death, when Tours passed to Sigib-

---

76 We do not know a great deal about rivers as transportation in the time of Gregory, but, on several occasions, he records the use of boats for transport (for example *DLH,* 6.25, 7.46, 10.31). In any case, given the number of pilgrims and others that moved between these contiguous territories, it seems clear that movement was reasonably easy; see Pietri, *La ville de Tours,* 550–57 on the travel of pilgrims to Tours in late antique Gaul.

77 See Alexander C. Murray, ed., *From Roman to Merovingian Gaul: A Reader* (Peterborough: Broadview Press, 2000), 662–69.

ert, Leudast had sided with Chilperic. He was therefore ousted by Sigibert, but when Chilperic's son Theudebert captured the city (several years later), Gregory — who guiltily admits that he was new to the diocese and under severe pressure — reappointed Leudast. During this time Leudast acted respectfully toward the church and townsfolk, because he feared for his position, but he was nevertheless deposed when Sigibert retook the city. He then seems to have spent two years in exile in Brittany, only to take up his position for a third time when Sigibert died and Tours passed to Chilperic. Now comparatively secure, yet still fearful of plots, he paraded the church house in full armor and happily plundered the people to expand his treasury. Chilperic heard of his crimes and instituted a free vote, which resulted in yet another deposition from comital status, but Leudast did not give up; he gained an audience with Chilperic, and accused Gregory of conspiring to hand over Tours to Sigibert's son Childebert II and of claiming that Fredegund had had an affair with bishop Bertram of Bordeaux.[78] Chilperic had Leudast beaten and imprisoned, but Leudast related that his accusations could be corroborated by friends of his in Tours. His cronies, a priest and a subdeacon, both called Riculf, conspired in the plot and the case gathered a degree of momentum. Eventually, Chilperic called a council at Berny-Rivière, near Soissons, to investigate the affair. As Gregory tells it, the case prompted outcry among the people, who thought it illegitimate that a bishop could be implicated by accusations of an inferior. Chilperic and the bishops seem to have agreed, and had the case thrown out. Leudast fled to sanctuary at the Church of St. Peter in Paris but, having learned that he was denied the right to sanctuary, made his way to Tours where he gathered his valuables and fled to Bourges. The priest Riculf who, during Gregory's trial, claimed to have rid Tours of the influence of Clermont, fled to another of Gregory's enemies, his suffragan Felix of Nantes. Meanwhile, Leudast quarreled with the local judge and people in Bourges, and raised

78 *DLH*, 5.49.

some men — including some old cronies from Touraine — and attacked them. He then led these men back across the border to Tours, but Duke Berulf sent troops against him, so Leudast fled to the church of St. Hilary in Poitiers. Fredegund ordered him expelled, and he fled again to Bourges, where he begged allies to conceal him.[79] There he hid for some three years, perhaps continuing to exploit the frontier, until a renewal of hostilities between Chilperic and Guntram provided him with an opportunity for another crack at Tours. While Chilperic was camped with his forces at Melun, outside Bourges, he crossed back to Touraine and demanded re-admittance to the city and communion. Gregory fobbed him off, and he went to seek audience with Chilperic, where the army pleaded in his favor. He accompanied the king to Paris, but could not win Fredegund over, and suffered a prolonged and gruesome end — and a well-deserved one according to Gregory.[80]

From this survey of the activities of Leudast, it should be clear that enterprising individuals could exploit boundaries to gain advantages or refuge during fractious periods of Merovingian politics. Interestingly, this tale provides several details of cross-border refuge; Leudast exploited the Touraine–Bourges boundary, but also took refuge in Brittany, Paris, and Poitiers, while Gregory himself was encouraged to flee to his hometown of Clermont — in the district of Bourges and the kingdom of Guntram — by the new Count of Tours, Eunomius, and Duke Berulf, when the case against him was mounting. Even the priest Riculf crossed the border between the dioceses of Tours and Nantes to shelter with Felix, who was hostile to Gregory. Factionalism, conflict, and rivalry clearly existed within the church, courts, and aristocracy. The Riculfs, and probably also Felix, were hostile to the influence of Clermont in the diocese

79 Ibid.
80 *DLH,* 6.32. A full narrative of his career can also be found in Allen E. Jones, *Social Mobility in Late Antique Gaul* (Cambridge: Cambridge University Press, 2009), 107–14.

of Tours; Riculf the priest claimed to have "purged the city of Tours of the rabble from Clermont."[81] Just as Gregory held prejudices against Bourges as a rival metropolitan and cult center, so Riculf's faction seems to have been prejudiced against Clermont as the origin of their rivals. Similarly, we can assume that the various parties who had been injured by the frontier violence of Leudast and his retinue may have held the neighboring authorities responsible for tolerating or supporting his rapacious behavior.

If Gregory's account is anything to go by, Leudast made many enemies who might have felt aggrieved by the count's exploitation of the Touraine–Bourges frontier. But there were far more significant factors than his vagabondage to create or deepen the rift between the peoples of those cities. The hostility between the royal brothers Chilperic and Guntram that seems to have facilitated the cross-border raids of Leudast only intensified, and when Leudast sought audience with Chipleric at Melun, he found him encamped at the site of one of the major battles of the Merovingian era. Chilperic blamed Guntram for the death of Sigibert and allied with the latter's son, Childebert II against Guntram. In 584, Chilperic sent Duke Berulf with soldiers from Tours, Poitiers, Angers, and Nantes to attack Bourges from the west, along with a second army from Aquitane, led by Desideratus, which approached from the south. According to Gregory, the district of Bourges raised fifteen thousand men to fight Chilperic's generals, but they were nevertheless driven back into the city, with heavy losses on both sides:

> The slaughter was immense, more than seven thousand being killed from the two armies. With what remained of their force [Desideratus] pushed on to Bourges itself, ravaging and destroying everything. The devastation was greater than anything described in ancient times: not a house remained

81 *DLH*, 5.49: "cuius ingenium Turonicam urbem ab Arvernis populis emundavit."

standing, not a vineyard, not an orchard; everything was raised to the ground and utterly ruined.[82]

But the Neustrians could not languish in their victory; Guntram arrived with his main force and slaughtered the greater part of Chilperic's army. Many men from Tours must have died in these engagements, but the losses of the district were redoubled by the devastation of Touraine by Desideratus and Berulf who, on their retreat, stole, burned, and murdered "just as if they were in an enemy country."[83]

Between them, both Tours and Bourges may have had more cause than most cities to grieve the quarreling of the sons of Clothar. Losses of men and property must have been extreme; not only does Gregory emphasize the destruction in context, but also vividly recalled the resultant anguish at the trial of bishop Egidius, six years and four books after the war.[84] Civil war was an egregious matter for sixth-century Gaul; it dominates several aspects of Gregory's narrative and inciting *bellum civile* was the primary accusation leveled at Egidius. When we consider the political violence involved in Leudast's cross border ravaging and the conflict between Chilperic and Guntram in the context of the inter-city rivalry we have already seen in the earlier sections, it seems probable that ill feeling between Tours and Bourges extended beyond just Gregory and his metropolitan neighbor.

If such hostility already existed in 584, it was surely catalyzed in the following years. Chilperic died later that year and

---

82 *DLH*, 6.31: "factaque est ibi stragis magna, ita ut de utroque exercitu amplius quam septim milia caecidissent. Duces quoque cum reliqua parte populi ad civitatem pervenerunt, cuncta deripientes vel devastantes; talisque depopulatio inibi acta est, qualis nec antiquitus est audita fuisse, ut nec domus remaneret nec vinea nec arbores, sed cuncta succiderent, incenderent, debellarent," *The History of the Franks,* trans. Thorpe, 360.

83 *DLH*, 6.31: "sicut solet contra inimicos fieri," *The History of the Franks,* trans. Thorpe, 361.

84 *DLH*, 10.19.

discord soon arose between Guntram and Childebert II over what should happen to his territories and widow Fredegund, who Childebert accused of murder. Guntram sent his envoys to demand loyalty from the cities that Sigibert had taken following the death of Charibert: these included Tours and Poitiers, but both cities preferred the rule of Childebert II instead. The soldiers of Bourges were sent to enforce the loyalty of Tours; they lost no time in revenging their losses sustained in the wars of Chilperic only months previously and burned buildings and churches until Tours capitulated. Willachar, Count of Orléans — another city of Guntram's — was installed as Count of Tours concurrently. Meanwhile Poitiers had accepted the envoys of Childebert, so the men of Bourges and their erstwhile enemies from Tours were sent to attack Poitiers.[85] Much like Tours, the city conceded to Guntram after a certain degree of burning and looting by the invaders, but by late in the year of 585 the Poitevins had broken their oath. Guntram raised a great army from Orléans and Bourges, his principal cities in the region, and sent them to plunder and massacre the area. These soldiers then also ravaged Touraine on their return, even burning churches, to the particular outrage of Gregory since the Tourangeaux had faithfully kept their oath.[86]

Poitiers eventually recognized Guntram, who was by now more concerned with the usurper Gundovald than Childebert. The troops of Bourges and Orléans, which seem to have been of major importance in his army, were sent off to challenge Gundovald along with some men of Tours. Unsurprisingly, given

---

85 *DLH*, 7.12 and 13. This almost immediate integration of previously hostile forces of Tours into Guntram's army is also paralleled by the levy of Châteaudun, who had made war upon Orléans immediately after Chilperic's death but were quickly incorporated under Burgundian rule and operating in co-operation with Willachar, Count of Orléans and Tours. See *DLH*, 7.2 and 7.29. Gregory certainly remained hostile to the forces of Orléans (see 7.21), so we might expect that the Dunois also experienced inter-city rivalry in this case.

86 *DLH*, 7.24.

recent relations between these cities, the Tourangeaux quickly deserted, while the rebellious Poitevins harassed Guntram's men as they passed through the district.[87] Gregory records that during the campaign Guntram's army committed many atrocities and suffered divine retribution for it.[88] Furthermore, Ullo, Count of Bourges, was among the leaders of this army and personally behaved deceitfully in the build up to the killing of Gundovald.[89] As we have already seen, he subsequently tried to fine the house of St. Martin for not providing troops for the campaign.[90] Gregory is openly hostile in his description of these actions, and places the men of Bourges at the scene of every crime. If the actions of the Torangeaux and Poitevins are anything to go by, they felt little affection toward their new allies.[91] This does not necessarily constitute a rivalry in the manner that Gregory seems to have felt, but the intensity of conflict and uneasy alliance between Bourges and Tours in the mid-580s apparently created a wider perception of hostility.

There is, however, one episode that might constitute evidence of a long-standing rivalry between secular citizens of Tours and Bourges. The so-called feud of Sichar and Chramnesind is a notorious instance of spiraling violence that has elicited a great deal of scholarly attention. During the Christmas festivities in 585, in the village of Manthelan, some thirty kilometers (eighteen miles) south of Tours, a priest was killed by the followers of Austregisil. Violence then broke out between these men and Sichar, son of John, who had been a friend of the priest. Some of

---

87 *DLH*, 7.28.

88 *DLH*, 7.35.

89 *DLH*, 7.38.

90 *DLH*, 7.42.

91 In addition to lackluster participation of Tours and open hostility of Poitevins in the Gundovald campaign, Gregory also informs us of a couple of instances of violent attacks by Tourangeaux on the occupying forces of Guntram; see *DLH*, 7.21 and 7.29. It is my opinion that Gregory uses these examples, and the prolonged emphasis on the bad behavior of Burgundian soldiers, as a method of political critique: see Burrows, "Gregory of Tours, Political Criticism and Lower-Class Violence."

Sichar's properties were burned and looted and Austregisil was condemned for homicide and theft. Meanwhile Sichar, discontented with legal arbitration, went to seize back his goods from where they had been left with Auno and, in doing so, butchered Auno and several members of his family. Gregory tried to call a halt to the dispute by offering compensation to Auno's surviving son, Chramnesind, but he instead went and burned down further properties of Sichar. They were then brought to arbitration, and because of Chramnesind's violence, the compensation owed to him by Sichar was halved.[92] Two or three years later Sichar and Chramnesind were fully reconciled and shared a meal at Chramnesind's house. There, Sichar got drunk and boasted that Chramnesind had benefitted from the murder of his kin and that the compensation had made him wealthy. Chramnesind responded by hacking Sichar's skull open, stripping his corpse, and hanging it from a fence post. He then rushed to the king to plead for clemency, but was rebuffed by Brunhild who had considered Sichar her favorite. It is at this point that we are informed that Chramnesind, and his family, came from Bourges.[93]

This tale has been variously interpreted as evidence for the particular violence of Merovingian society, for Frankish traditions of blood feud and as an example of the darkness of the "Dark Ages."[94] Many of the more dramatic reactions to this episode are now out of fashion, but the tale still attracts attention. It is my proposal that it can be reinterpreted in light of the rivalry

92 *DLH,* 7.47.
93 *DLH,* 9.19.
94 For Samuel Dill, *Roman Society in Gaul in the Merovingian Age* (London: Macmillan, 1926), 304–6, this example of post-Roman violence was particularly egregious, depressing, and noticeably "medieval" in character. For Erich Auerbach, in his seminal work of literary criticism, *Mimesis,* the discord was exemplary of the shrunken world-view of the post-Roman historian: Erich Auerbach and Edward W. Said, *Mimesis: The Representation of Reality in Western Literature* (Princeton: Princeton University Press, 2013), 77–95. For a review of the episode and its historiography, see Ian Wood, "The Bloodfeud of the Franks: A Historiographical Legend," *Early Medieval Europe* 14 (2006): 489–504.

between Tours and Bourges. The discord arose within months of the violent occupation of Touraine by the forces of Guntram, among whom soldiers from Orléans and Bourges featured prominently as we have seen. Several instances of violence between the Tourangeaux and these occupiers are acknowledged by Gregory.[95] At the very least, we can interpret the Sichar-Chramnesind conflict within the pattern of hostility between Tours and Bourges, both in the context of the wars with Guntram and more generally. However, it is reasonable to push the argument further in order to flesh out the story. As we have seen, Guntram imposed at least some new secular authorities in the region with the replacement of Eunomius, the previous Count of Tours, with Willachar of Orléans.[96] Given that Chramnesind and Auno derived from Bourges, it seems plausible that they were among the followers of Guntram who were rewarded with property in Touraine at the same time. Sichar's origins are less certain, but we know he lived and held property in Tours and also in Poitiers and that he had the favor of Brunhild.[97] Both cities had belonged to Sigibert and attempted to side with Childebert II (against Guntram) after Chilperic died, and Brunhild was Sigibert's wife and Childebert II's mother. Since Sichar was only around twenty years old at the time of his death, it seems likely that both the property and favor were inherited from his family, probably his

---

95 *DLH*, 7.13, 21, 29.

96 *DLH*, 7.13.

97 He might also be identified with the Sichar who, along with Willachar, led troops from Tours and Bourges against Poitiers in c. 584. Martindale argues that this Sichar was either a *dux* in command of the expedition, or Count of Bourges and commanding their contingent. The latter seems unlikely since Ullo was Count of Bourges and leading those troops against Gundovald in 585. If this Sichar was Count of Bourges, then it is very unlikely that he can be the same Sichar, son of John, who fought with Chramnesind, since his comital status would surely have warranted some mention. It is also unlikely that the Sichar, son of John, would have been a *dux* in c. 584 since he was around twenty years old in 587. We can therefore follow Martindale in assuming that they were not related; John R. Martindale, *Prosopography of the Later Roman Empire*, vol. 3 (London: Cambridge University Press, 1981), 1145.

father, a certain John. Though these associations do not prove that Sichar's family were Sigibert/Childebert loyalists, it seems plausible and would certainly explain his hostility toward Auno and Chramnesind. If we believe these assertions, then the conflict was not simply a feud following the death of a priest, but the product of friction between factions in the aristocracy of Touraine; one side new incomers imposed from the enemies in Bourges, the other local and loyalists of the family of Sigibert. Personal revenge clearly had a role, but I would argue political rivalry and factionalism were major factors.

This interpretation may also help us to understand the timeline of events; in 585 Gregory and the Count of Tours, almost certainly Willachar, mediated between the parties and though Chramnesind's actions halved his compensation, they still considered Sichar the guilty party. The tension between the parties then faded, presumably much as the conflict between the cities of Tours and Bourges faded into the past. However, whereas in 585 Chramnesind could perhaps count on the support of Willachar and Guntram, in 587 his position had altered, since the treaty of Andelot gave Childebert II control of Tours.[98] We know that Sichar had the favor of Brunhild and if he was indeed a Sigibert/Childebert loyalist, then the treaty certainly boosted his standing and perhaps initiated the incautious boasting that caused his death. Chramnesind, by contrast, was weakened by this development and it is no surprise that he fled back to Bourges and the territory of Guntram when he heard of Brunhild's anger.[99]

---

98 *DLH*, 9.11. By exploiting similar circumstances, the treasurer of Chilperic's son Clovis also fled across the political frontier to Bourges to shelter from Fredegund's anger under the aegis of Guntram; *DLH* 5.39.

99 Willachar, Guntram's appointment, was also removed from his position as Count of Tours, perhaps as early as 587 but certainly by 590. He is named as count by Gregory in 590 while serving Guntram against the Bretons, where he was accused of complicity with the Breton leader Waroch and was dismissed, but he may have only been Count of Orléans at this time (*DLH*, 10.9). Sometime between 587 and 590, Gregory's friend Galienus became Count of Tours. If Willachar was replaced prior to 587, this could be inter-

I would argue that the identification of Auno's family as part of the imposition of a loyal aristocracy by Guntram in 584 and the family of Sichar as local rivals and supporters of Sigibert/Childebert add considerably to our understanding of the conflict that arose between them. However, even if this detail were to be rejected, we still have clear evidence of hostility from occupants of Touraine toward a family from Bourges immediately after the cities had been at war, and simmering on for a few years thereafter. We know that Gregory was hostile to leadership in Bourges, both ecclesiastical and secular, and was highly critical of their actions. We have also seen that the frontier between the territories lent opportunity to violent raiders like Leudast and his cronies and that the open warfare between Tours and Bourges was particularly brutal. All this seems to have caused the Tourangeaux to be hostile to occupying forces in the mid-580s and perhaps toward Bourges in particular. The citizens of Bourges perhaps felt similar distaste. Given that Gregory is our source for these episodes, it is difficult to speculate about how widely grievances and rivalries were felt among the general population in these territories. It is also difficult to prove that these constituted or contributed to a long-standing rivalry rather than just hostility in the context of war between the cities. However, Gregory's own biases themselves provide a clue to this; his outrage over the devastation of the Auvergne at the hands of Theuderic and the mismanagement that lead to it are probably personal to him and his kin, but the existence of such lingering resentment and hostility is telling. Given the conflict between Bourges and Tours in the later sixth century, it seems likely that similar perspectives were held by aggrieved parties on both sides of the conflict.[100] Bourges was sacked, Tours occupied by hostile forces and both territories were devastated. Rogues

---

preted as more evidence of hostility to the aristocracy imposed by Guntram, but it is not possible to be sure.

100 At the very least, we know that the wounds were still sore six years later at the trial of bishop Egidius, who was blamed for the sack and waste of the city of Bourges; DLH, 10.19.

and vagabonds exploited the instability of the border to wreak havoc on both sides. In such a context it would be surprising if rivalry did not exist, and the behavior of the characters in the Sichar and Chramnesind affair would seem to confirm this residual, mutual dislike.

Conclusion: Gregory's Rivalry or Tours's Rivalry?

It is clear that cities had great significance in Merovingian Gaul, and a deal of political autonomy. They raised their own militias and could negotiate their own tax statuses. The kings who ruled over them sometimes tried to centralize affairs, but these efforts were met with resistance, and misrule could invite rebellion or overtures to a rival. Unfortunately, however, we have very little evidence to assess the institutions of these cities, save the words of Gregory himself.

Because of Gregory's singular importance, any new insight about his biases is of great value. We know that, broadly speaking, that Gregory liked Sigibert and Guntram, and liked Chilperic rather less.[101] Similarly, it has long been recognized that he favored Tours, Clermont, St. Martin, and St. Julian, but in this case evidence of opposing negative biases has never been considered systematically. In this article, I propose that we can discern a sustained hostility towards the city of Bourges throughout the works of Gregory. If, rhetorically at least, Chilperic was the "Herod" counterpart to "good king" Guntram, then perhaps we can say Bourges was the "Gomorrah" counterpart to hallowed Tours and Clermont.

I have argued that there seem to be three main reasons for Gregory's hostility; firstly, the competition of St. Stephen's cult at Bourges with his favored St. Martin at Tours and St. Julian at Clermont; secondly, the perceived mismanagement of the suffragans in the district of Bourges by the metropolitan (whose very status Gregory seems to have resented); thirdly, the po-

---

101 On this issue, see the Introduction above and n. 3.

litical rivalry of these provincial capitals whose proximity and recent bloody interactions fueled aversion. These seem ample enough reasons to fuel Gregory's personal hostility. In the case of Bourges, his discourse is consistently and structurally antagonistic. This certainly has implications for how we read references to Bourges, but if we accept that he held biases based on inter-city rivalry, then perhaps we ought to consider yet another layer of complexity in our analyses of his works; references to cities — just like allusions to kings, emperors, peoples, states or the Bible — should be considered in light of the cache of knowledge and experiences which accompanied them. Gregory liked some cities, and disliked others. These preferences shaped his narrative and were shaped in turn by his upbringing, environment and experiences, and we must be mindful of these as best we can when we study Gregory's works.

The implications of these biases for Gregorian studies are significant enough, but are even more important if these antagonisms can be seen to have been held by populations at large. As with so much in Merovingian history, it is difficult to be certain how closely the people of Tours shared the disposition of their bishop. Certain grievances must have been personal; we cannot expect those citizens who considered Gregory "an outsider" to share his soft spot for Clermont.[102] Likewise, they may not have had the same professional and personal concerns over the metropolitan responsibilities and status of Bourges that Gregory harbored. However, the citizens of Tours certainly seem to have been defensive of their Church[103] and some may have shared a competitive attitude toward a neighboring cult center, though this remains speculative. However, the evidence of political strife between Tours and Bourges in Gregory's works seems to indicate a more popular sense of rivalry. The boundary between them was regularly exploited by crooks and refugees from fractious Merovingian politics, often to the detriment of

102 *DLH*, 5.49.
103 Even violently defensive of it! *DLH*, 7.29.

the inhabitants.[104] Moreover, both cities and their districts were cruelly ravaged in warfare, which we know to have had a lasting effect on the populations.[105] These tit-for-tat depredations almost certainly colored popular opinion. In the case of Tours, occupying forces from Guntram's domain were perceived with resentment and sometimes resisted with violence by the people of Touraine.[106] If my analysis is correct, it is exactly these kinds of inter-city rivalries that were to blame for the famous conflict between Sichar and the family of Chramnesind.[107] If, through the study of the rivalry of Tours and Bourges, we can discern a genuine popular hostility, then the implications of this insight are no less significant than the identification of a new set of commonly-held biases in Gregory's *opera*. In the absence of popular representation or revolt, it is all too easy for the historian to forget that ordinary people had opinions and agency, but evidence of a common perception of rivalry and the violent outcomes that resulted from it may help to remind us.

104 See above and *GM*, 58, 89.
105 See above and *DLH*, 3.12.
106 *DLH*, 7.13, 21, 29.
107 See above.

Bibliography

Primary

Gregory of Tours. *Decem libri historiarum.* Edited by Bruno Krusch and Wilhelm Levison. Monumenta Germaniae Historica, Scriptores Rerum Merovingicarum 1.1. Hanover: Hahn, 1951.

———. *De virtutibus sancti Martini episcopi.* In *Saints and Their Miracles in Late Antique Gaul,* translated by Raymond Van Dam, 199–303. Princeton: Princeton University Press, 1993.

———. *Glory of the Confessors.* Translated by Raymond Van Dam. Translated Texts for Historians 5. Liverpool: Liverpool University Press, 2004.

———. *Glory of the Martyrs.* Translated by Raymond Van Dam. Translated Texts for Historians 4. Liverpool: Liverpool University Press, 2004.

———. *Life of the Fathers.* Translated by Edward James. Liverpool: Liverpool University Press, 1991.

———. *Miracula et opera minora.* Edited by Bruno Krusch. Monumenta Germaniae Historica, Scriptores Rerum Merovingicarum, 1.2. Hanover: Hahn, 1885.

———. *The History of the Franks.* Translated by Lewis Thorpe. Harmondsworth: Penguin, 1974.

Secondary

Auerbach, Erich, and Edward W. Said. *Mimesis: The Representation of Reality in Western Literature.* Princeton: Princeton University Press, 2013. DOI: 10.2307/j.ctt3fgz26.

Bailey, Lisa Kaaren. "Within and Without: Lay People and the Church in Gregory of Tours' Miracle Stories." *Journal of Late Antiquity* 5 (2012): 119–44. DOI: 10.1353/jla.2012.0006.

Bovon, François. "The Dossier on Saint Stephen: The First Martyr." *The Harvard Theological Review* 96 (2003): 279–315. DOI: 10.1017/S0017816003000452.

Brennan, Brian. "'Being Martin': Saint and Successor in Sixth-Century Tours." *The Journal of Religious History* 21 (1997): 121–35. DOI: 10.1111/j.1467–9809.1997.tb00481.x.

Brown, Peter. *The Cult of Saints: Its Rise and Function in Latin Christianity.* London: SCM Press, 1981. DOI: 10.7208/chicago/9780226076386.001.0001.

Dill, Samuel. *Roman Society in Gaul in the Merovingian Age.* London: Macmillan, 1926.

Fagan, Garrett G. "Violence in Roman Social Relations." In *The Oxford Handbook of Social Relations in the Roman World,* edited by Michael Peachin, 467–95. New York: Oxford University Press, 2014.

Giulianotti, Richard, and Gary Armstrong. "Avenues of Contestation. Football Hooligans Running and Ruling Urban Spaces." *Social Anthropology* 10 (2002): 211–38. DOI: 10.1017/S0964028202000149.

Goffart, Walter A. *The Narrators of Barbarian History (A.D. 550–800): Jordanes, Gregory of Tours, Bede, and Paul the Deacon.* Princeton: Princeton University Press, 1988.

Guizot, François. *The History of Civilization.* Volume 1. Translated by W. Hazlitt. New York: The Colonial Press, 1899.

Halsall, Guy. "Nero and Herod? The Death of Chilperic and Gregory's Writings of History." In *The World of Gregory of Tours,* edited by Kathleen Mitchell and Ian N. Wood, 337–50. Leiden: Brill, 2002.

Heinzelmann, Martin. *Gregory of Tours: History and Society in the Sixth Century.* Translated by Christopher Carroll. Cambridge: Cambridge University Press, 2001.

Jones, Allen E. *Social Mobility in Late Antique Gaul.* Cambridge: Cambridge University Press, 2009. DOI: 10.1017/CBO9780511596735.

King, Anthony, "Football Fandom and Post-national Identity in the New Europe." *British Journal of Sociology* 51 (2000): 419–42. DOI: 10.1080/00071310050131602.

Martindale, John R. *Prosopography of the Later Roman Empire.* Volume 3. London: Cambridge University Press, 1981.

McKinley, Allan Scott. "The First Two Centuries of Saint Martin at Tours." *Early Medieval Europe* 14 (2006): 173–200. DOI: 10.1111/j.1468-0254.2006.00179.x.

Mitchell, Kathleen, and Ian Wood, eds. *The World of Gregory of Tours.* Boston and Leiden: Brill, 2002.

Murray, Alexander C. "Chronology and the Composition of the Histories of Gregory of Tours." *Journal of Late Antiquity* 1 (2008): 157–196. DOI: 10.1353/jla.0.0004.

———, ed. *From Roman to Merovingian Gaul: A Reader.* Peterborough: Broadview Press, 2000.

Parsell, Diana L. "Crossbow Rivalry of Two Italian Towns Dates to the Middle Ages." *National Geographic News,* September 6, 2002.

Pietri, Luce. *La ville de Tours du IVe au VIe siècle. Naissance d'une cite chrétienne.* Rome: École française de Rome, 1983.

Sarti, Laury, "The Military, the Clergy and Christian Faith in Sixth-century Gaul." *Early Medieval Europe* 25 (2017): 162–85. DOI: 10.1111/emed.12199.

Thorpe, Lewis. "Introduction". In *Gregory of Tours: The History of the Franks,* translated by Lewis Thorpe, 7–22. Harmondsworth: Penguin, 1974.

Wood, Ian. "The Bloodfeud of the Franks: A Historiographical Legend." *Early Medieval Europe* 14 (2006): 489–504. DOI: 10.1111/j.1468–0254.2006.00192.x.

———. "The Secret Histories of Gregory of Tours." *Revue belge de philologie et d'histoire* 71 (1993): 253–70. DOI: 10.3406/rbph.1993.3879.

Van Dam, Raymond. *Saints and Their Miracles in Late Antique Gaul.* Princeton: Princeton University Press, 1993.

Van Waarden, Johannes A. "Episcopal Self-Presentation: Sidonius Apollinaris and the Episcopal Election in Bourges." In *Episcopal Elections in Late Antiquity,* edited by Johan Leemans et al., 555–61. Berlin: De Gruyter, 2011. DOI: 10.1515/9783110268607.555.

3

Did All Roads Lead to Córdoba under the Umayyads?

Ann Christys

The history of al-Andalus under the Umayyads (AH 138–c.422 / 756–c.1031 CE)[1] is that of the ruling family and of their capital. Apart from Córdoba, only Seville, Mérida, Toledo, and Zaragoza attracted the attention of the chroniclers, as the Umayyads struggled against rebels based in these cities; there were no new foundations until the ninth century.[2] The scene moves from Córdoba only when emirs, caliphs, and their generals leave the capital to campaign against rebels, or against the "Galicians" and the "Franks" to the north. Geographers writing in Arabic from the tenth century onwards recorded some of the roads that these expeditions might have followed, in the form of itineraries that depict Córdoba as the hub of a network of roads that led to all parts of al-Andalus and beyond.

Yet it is not easy to move from itineraries to connectivity, to populate these roads, and the peninsula's navigable rivers, with everyday traffic. This is not because the theme of connectivity

---

1   All dates are henceforth CE unless otherwise noted.
2   Eduardo Manzano, *Conquistadores, Emires y Califas Los Omeyas y la formación de al-Andalus* (Barcelona: Crítica, 2006), 248.

was unknown in medieval Arabic scholarship. An eastern geographer, al-Yaʿqūbī, writing c. 899 about Baghdad commented:

The two great rivers, the Tigris and the Euphrates, run along either side of Baghdad, and merchandise and provisions come to it by water and by land, [...] such that every piece of merchandise carried to it from the eastern and western parts of the land of Islam and that which is outside the land of Islam reaches it. For [merchandise] is carried to [Baghdad] from India, China, Tibet, [the land of the Turks], al-Daylam, [the land of] the Khazars, Ethiopia and the rest of the countries [...] as if all good things on earth are conveyed there.[3]

There is, as far as I know, no similar statement about Córdoba. Details emerge from narrative and other sources of Córdoba's importance as an administrative center, with a monopoly over the control of religion and education. The city attracted scholars from elsewhere in al-Andalus.[4] Chronicles and other written sources, as well as sporadic archaeological finds, attest to the external trade of al-Andalus with North Africa and Egypt and even as far as Khorasan,[5] mainly from the second half of the tenth century onwards. It is assumed that much of this trade served the capital; "Córdoba must have been a large city [...].

---

3   يجري في حافتيه النهران الاعظمان دجلة وافزات فيأتيها التجارات والمير برّاً وبحرا بأيسر السعى حتى تكامل
    بها كلّ متجر يحمل من المشرق والمغرب من اوض الاسلام وغبر ارض الاسلام فانّه يحمل اليها من الهند والسند
    ... والصين والتُبّت والترك والدَيلم والخَزر "والحبشة وسائر البلدان [...] حتى كانّه سيقت اليها خيرات الارض
    Al-Yaʿqūbī, *Kitāb al-buldān*, in *Bibliotheca Geographorum Arabicorum*, vol. 7, ed. Michael J. de Goeje (Boston and Leiden: Brill, 1892), 234; trans. Zayde Antrim, *Routes and Realms. The Power of place in the Early Islamic World* (New York: Oxford University Press, 2012), 39.

4   Manuela Marín, "La transmisión del saber en al-Andalus (hasta 300/912)," *Al-Qanṭara* 8, no. 1 (1987): 87–97.

5   Ibn Ḥawqal, *Kitāb ṣūrat al-arḍ*, 2 vols, ed. Johannes H. Kramers (Boston and Leiden: Brill, 1938–1939), 105–6, 110, 114; translated by Johannes H. Kramers and Gaston Wiet in *Configuration de la terre: Kitab surat al-ard*, 2 vols. (Beirut: Commission internationale pour la traduction des chefs d'oeuvre, 1964), 95, 109, 113.

The demands of such a large concentration of population must have drawn to it agricultural communities not only from the hinterlands, but also from more distant areas."[6] As Córdoba's population is a great unknown[7] and in "the absence of any archaeological or historical study of the structure and organisation of Andalusi trade,"[8] it is difficult to substantiate such statements. The Arabic sources for al-Andalus rarely refer to Córdoba's strategic position as a Central Market Town with a major role in internal and external trade, or to the capital's hinterland, served by local routes that would have connected it with nearby villages supplying the capital with food, building materials, and utility goods. There are surprisingly few references to the difficulties of travel, to seasonal hazards or to the risks of encountering bandits. These references will be reviewed in this chapter, although the main focus will be on the value of the Arabic geographies as evidence for travel in al-Andalus in the tenth century and for the importance of the other cities of al-Andalus in relation to the Umayyad capital.

The study of geography did not have a high profile in medieval Islam. Much of what we would call geographical information is scattered through works of a more encyclopedic nature. Biographical details about Muslim scholars in other fields — historians, poets, and experts on law and theology — were assembled in dictionaries which often gave the scholar's origin, dates of birth and death, education, a list of his works, and a number of more-or-less plausible anecdotes. In contrast, the medieval Arabic scholars who are now remembered for their writings on

6 Florin Curta, "Markets in Tenth-Century al-Andalus and Volga Bulghāria: Contrasting Views of Trade in Muslim Europe," *Al-Masāq* 25, no. 3 (2013): 305–30.

7 The figures quoted are often implausible: Antonio Almagro ("Planimetría de las ciudades hispanomusulmanes," *Al-Qanṭara* 8 (1987): 421–48) estimated that Córdoba's walled *madīna*, with an area of 185 ha., might have held some 65,000 inhabitants, to which should be added an unknown number of people living in the more sparsely-populated suburbs.

8 Curta, "Markets in Tenth-Century al-Andalus and Volga Bulghāria," 329.

geography are known mainly from manuscripts that carry their name either at the beginning or in a colophon, which may also give the date when the text was copied. Geography in the Islamic world, sometimes called *jugrāfiya,* is thought of as being part of the inheritance from the Greek world, translated into Arabic from the ninth century onwards.[9] Its origins, which may be legendary, are with the caliph al-Ma'mūn (813–833), who gave his name to a geography (or possibly a map) which does not survive, although a later author claimed to have seen it.[10] Yet the Persian inheritance was equally important. Geographers who claimed to be citing Ptolemy of Alexandria (c. 150) used Greek vocabulary — such as the term *iqlim,* or climate — even in works based on the Persian geographical tradition, which had its own way of dividing the world.

One of the earliest surviving Arabic geographies is the *Book of Routes and Realms* compiled by a Persian administrator, Ibn Khurradādhbih (c. 820–912), who served at the Abbasid court in Baghdad and Samarra, holding a title that translates as "head post master." The *Book of Routes and Realms*[11] is sometimes supposed to have been of practical value for those traveling the empire on the caliph's service, but it was probably more concerned with displaying the extent of the caliph's power.[12] Ibn Khurradādhbih is not known to have surveyed the routes he

---

9 Dimitri Gutas, *Greek Thought, Arabic Culture: The Graeco-Arabic Translation Movement in Baghdad and Early 'Abbasid Society (2nd/4th–8th/10th Centuries)* (London and New York: Routledge 1998); André Miquel, *La géographie humaine du monde musulman jusqu'au milieu du IIᵉ siècle. Géographie et géographie humaine dans la literature arabe des origins à 1050,* vol. 1 (Paris: Mouton, 1967), 12.

10 Al-Mas'ūdī, *Al-Tanbih wa-l-Ishraf,* ed. Michael J. de Goeje (Boston and Leiden: Brill, 1894), 183–85.

11 Ibn Khurradādhbih, *Al-Masālik wa-l-mamālik,* ed. Michael J. de Goeje (Boston and Leiden: Brill, 1889), Charles Barbier de Meynard, "Le livre des routes et des provinces, par Ibn Khoradhbeh, publié, traduit et annoté par M. Barbier de Meynard," *Journal Asiatique* 6, no. 5 (1865): 5–127, 227–96, 446–532.

12 Antrim, *Routes and Realms,* 102–6.

mentioned and he also included stories of real and imaginary travelers, among them Sallām the interpreter who set off to look for the wall that Alexander the Great had built to keep out Gog and Magog.[13] Viewed from Baghdad, al-Andalus, which together with North Africa was known as the Maghreb, appeared remote and of little interest. Some Arabic geographies omit al-Andalus altogether and most have little information about Islam's most westerly outpost. Ibn Khurradādhbih's brief comment on the peninsula was not well-informed:

On the other side of the sea is the land of al-Andalus. Córdoba is five days journey from the sea. From Granada on the coast of [the province of] Córdoba as far as Narbonne, the furthest extent of al-Andalus, where lies Franja, [the land of the Franks] is a distance of one thousand miles. Toledo, where the king resided, is twenty days' journey from Córdoba. In al-Andalus there are forty cities including Mérida, Zaragoza, Narbonne, Girona and al-Bayḍā. [Al-Andalus] borders on Franja and the lands of polytheists that border it. The length and breadth of al-Andalus is a month's march [in each direction]. It is fertile and abundant in fruit. On its northern borders with the Rūm (Christians, especially Byzantines) and Franja are the mountains of al-Andalus, covered in snow. From the furthest point in this direction is a mountain where a fire [emitting] rocks and earth burns and never becomes clear. The king of al-Andalus when it was conquered was called Lodarik, of the people of Isfahān and from Isfahān the people of Córdoba were called the Ispān.[14]

13 Emeri van Donzel and Andrea Schmidt with Claudia Ott, *Gog and Magog in Early Eastern Christian and Islamic Sources: Sallam's Quest for Alexander's Wall* (Boston and Leiden: Brill, 2010).

14 ما وراء البحر بلاد الاندلس وهي قرطبة وبينها وبين الساحل مسيرة خمس ليال ومن ساحل قرطبة غرناطة الى أربونة وهي آخر الاندلس مما يلي فرنجة الف ميل، وطليطلة وبها كان ينزل الملك ومن طليطلة الى قرطبة عشرون ليلة، وللاندلس اربعون مدينة فمنها ماردة وسرقسطة وأربونة وجرندة والبيضا، وتجاور الاندلس فرنجة وما ولاها من يلاد الشرك، والاندلس مسيرة اكثر من شهر في شهر، وهي خصبة كثيرة الخير كثيرة الفواكه. ومما يلي الشمال والروم وفرنجة من جبال الاندلس تثلج وفي آخر ذلك الوجه جبل فيه نار تتقد في حجارة وتراب

Some geographers did travel, and they emphasized what they had learned from this. Yet the relationship between book-learning and observation was not straightforward. A prominent ninth-century scholar, al-Jāhiz, described Kūfa in Iraq from his own observation, yet he wrote about another city, Basra, which is where he actually lived, by copying outworn clichés.[15] Authors' claims to eye-witness status do not always make their descriptions more reliable; hence the inconclusive debates over such episodes as Ibn Fadlan's descriptions of a Viking burial on the Volga.[16] Ibn Khurradādhbih's combination of plausible — although often inaccurate — data, folk etymology creating spurious links between people and places with similar-sounding names, and tales of the downright fantastical is typical of geography in Arabic.

A second *Book of Routes and Realms* composed in the middle of the tenth century has a little more information about the peninsula. It is attributed to al-Istakhrī (d. 957), who came from the town of Istakhr, built in the Sasanian period from the ruins of nearby Persepolis. Al-Istakhrī traveled, but not to the Maghreb, and it has been assumed that he copied his information on this part of the Islamic world from an earlier work or works. Al-Istakhrī emphasized the liminal position of al-Andalus, bordered on two sides by the lands of unbelief and on the other two sides by the Mediterranean and the Encircling Ocean, beyond which there was nothing. Yet he praised the cities of al-Andalus, above all Córdoba, and listed fourteen itineraries, of which ten start or finish in the capital:[17]

لم تصفأ قط. وكان ملك الاندلس حين فُتحت يقال له لوذريق من اهل اصبهان واصبهان سمى اهل قرطبة الاسبان. Ibn Khurradādhbih, *Kitāb al-masālik*, ed. de Goeje, 89–90; all translations, unless credited, are by the author.

15 In Houari Touati, *Islam et voyage au Moyen Âge: Histoire et anthropologie d'une pratique lettrée* (Paris: Éditions du Seuil, 2000); trans. Lydia G. Cochrane, *Islam and Travel in the Middle Ages* (Chicago: University of Chicago Press, 2010), 105–18; Miquel, *La géographie humaine,* 1:38–45.

16 Miquel, *La géographie humaine,* 1:136–38.

17 Évariste Lévi-Provençal, *Histoire de l'Espagne musulmane,* vol. 3, 2nd edn. (Paris: Maisonneuve and Larose, 1950, repr. 1999), 317–25.

Al-Andalus is wide, with many cities [and] very fertile [...] the greatest city is Córdoba [...] none of the cities approaches Córdoba in size and the number of its stone buildings, which are buildings from the Jāhilīya (the period before Islam). There are no new cities except Pechina and Santarem [...] where they weave hair [of camels and goats] into clothes and dye them to make costly items exclusively for the Umayyads.[18]

[...] The region of Elvira (near Granada) is known for its silk of the very best quality. In al-Andalus there are many gold mines and there are silver mines in Elvira and Murcia and at a place called Kurtash near Córdoba.[19] [...] From the Maghreb come black slaves from the land of al-Sūdān (the blacks) and white slaves from al-Andalus, valuable female slaves — even those who use no art on their appearance sell for 1,000 dinars or more —, Maghrebi felts, riding mules, coral, ambergris, gold, honey, oil (coarse hide used for polishing), silk, and sable.[20]

A reference to the Banū Ḥafṣūn, rebels against the Umayyads between 880 and 928, and to the current ruler as ʿAbd al-Raḥmān III (r. 912–961) narrows the time that al-Istakhrī was writing to the second or third decade of the tenth century. This gives added credence to the itineraries that al-Istakhrī included, which are recorded in different ways. Sometimes al-Istakhrī merely stated the time needed for the journey — from Córdoba to Zaragoza,

---

18 الاندلس بلدان عريضة كثيرة المدن خصبة واسعة. ومدينتها الظمى تسمع قرطبة [...] وليس فيها ما يقارب قرطبة في العظم الكبر واكثر ابنيتها من حجرة وهى ابنية جاهليّة. لا تعرف فيها مدينة محدثة الا بجّانة [...] وشنترين [...] يقع منها وبر [...] وهو عزيز وتنسج منه ثياب فتتلون [...] ويحجر عليها ملوك بني اميّة.
Al-Istakhrī, *Kitāb al-masālik wa al-mamālik: Viae regnorum description dictionis Moslemicae*, ed. Michael J. de Goeje, Bibliotheca Geographorum Arabicorum 1 (Boston and Leiden: Brill, 1873; repr. London: Brill, 1927), 41–42.

19 وبكورة إلبيرة حرير كثير يفضل ويقدم على غيره. وبلادلندلس معادن كثيرة من الذهب وبها معادن فضّة بناحية إلبيرة وموسية وبقرب قرطبة بموضع يقال له كرتش. Ibid., 47.

20 يقع من المغرب الخدم السود من بلاد السودان والخدم البيض من الاندلس والجواري المثمنة تاخذ الجارية الخادم عن غير صناعة على وجوههما الف دينار واكثر وتقع منها البود المغربيّة وانيغال للسرج والمرجان والعنبر والذهب والعسل والزيت والسفن والحرير والسمور. Ibid., 45.

for instance, takes fifteen days — but other itineraries include the intermediate stations and the distances between them. He ended his description of the peninsula with the statement: "and these are all the distances of al-Andalus."[21]

The most extensive description of al-Andalus in the Umayyad period was compiled by a Persian geographer from the generation after al-Istakhrī. Born in Nishapur, Ibn Ḥawqal traveled widely in the Islamic world over more than thirty years and made his last trip, to Sicily, in 977. The purpose of his travels is obscure; it has been suggested that he was an agent or propagandist for the Fatimid rulers of Egypt, but he could also have been a merchant. His *Description of the Earth* was compiled towards the end of his life in c. 988. According to the introduction, the work was an account of "everything there is to know about each region: the various sources of riches, taxation, tithes, property taxes, itineraries, its imports, and commerce."[22] The work was illustrated with maps which defined "the location of every town in relation to its neighbour and its position in relation to north and south, east, and west."[23]

Ibn Ḥawqal began with a eulogy of its climate and fruitfulness that is reminiscent of Isidore's *Laus Spaniae*:

Al-Andalus is one of the most magnificent of all peninsulas. [...] I entered Spain at the beginning of the year 337 (11 July 948–30 June 949) when the ruler was ʿAbd al-Raḥmān III [...]. Most of the land is cultivated and well populated. Everywhere there are running waters, woods, and fruit trees, as well as sweet water. Abundance and contentment dominate all aspects of life, the enjoyment of goods and the means of acquiring wealth are common to rich and poor alike thanks to light taxation, the excellent state of the land and the riches

---

21 فهذه جوامع المسافات بالادلس. Ibid., 47.

22 ما يُحتاج الى معرفته من جوامع ما يشتمل عليه ذلك الإقليم من وجوه الأموال والجبايات والأعشار واخاراجات الطرقات وما قيه من المجالب والتجارات. والمسافات في Ibn Ḥawqal, *Kitāb ṣūrat al-arḍ*, 3.

23 وموقع كلّ مدينةٍ من مدينةٍ تجاورها وموضعها من شمالها وجنوبها وكونها بالمرتبة من شرقها وغربها. Ibid., 5.

of the ruler [...] the abundance of his treasures and possessions [...] and the customs revenue on the copious merchandise that comes in and goes out aboard ships.[24]

Ibn Ḥawqal's comment on Córdoba is often cited:

There is nothing to equal it in the whole of North Africa or
even in Upper Mesopotamia, Syria or Egypt, for the number
of its inhabitants, its extent, the vast area taken up by markets, its cleanliness, the architecture of the mosques or the
great number of baths and caravanserais. Several travellers
from this city who have visited Baghdad, say that it is the
size of one of the two sides of that city [...]. Córdoba is not
perhaps equal to half the size of Baghdad, but is not far off
being so. It is a city with a stone wall, with handsome districts
and vast squares.[25]

Ibn Ḥawqal included two itineraries that are not in al-Istakhrī.
Both of them link Córdoba with Toledo, but in one case by a
very roundabout route, as we shall see.

There are problems in accepting Ibn Ḥawqal's description of
al-Andalus as an eye-witness account, especially when read in
conjunction with his description of Sicily, which is much longer
and, unlike the account of al-Andalus, full of the sort of information that would strike a visitor. Ibn Ḥawqal characterized
Sicily as an island well-situated in relation to al-Andalus, North
Africa, and Byzantium, with mountains, castles, and fortifica-

24 فاما الاندلس فهي من نفائس جزائر البحر[...] ودخلتها في أوّل سنة سبع وثلثين وثلثمائة والقيّم بها أبو
المطرّف عبد الرحمن [...] وأكثرها عامر مأهول ويغلب عليه المياه الجارية والشجر والثمر والانهار العذبة
والرخص والسعة في جميع الأحوال الى نيل النعيم والتملّك الفاشي في الخاصّة والعامّة فينال ذلك أهل مهنهم
وأرباب صنائعهم لقلّة مؤنهم وصلاح بلادهم ويسار ملكهم [...] ووفور خزانته وأمواله [...] وما يقبض من
الأموال الوافرة على المراكب الواردة اليهم والصادرة عنهم. Ibid., 108.

25 وأعظم مدينة بالاندلس قرطبة وليس بجميع المغرب لها شبيه ولا بالجزيرة والسأم ومصر ما يدانيها في كثرة
أهل وسعة رُقعة وفُسحة أسواق ونظافة محالّ وعمارة مساجد وكثرة حمّامات وفنادق ويزعم قوم من سافرتها
الواصلين الى مدينة السلام أنّها كأحد جانبي بغداد [...] وقرطبة وإن لم تكُ كأحد جانبي بغداد فهي قريبة من
ذلك ولاحقة به وهي مدينة ذات سور من حجارة ومحالّ حسنة ورحاب فسيحة. Ibid., 111–12.

tions and mostly under cultivation.[26] The sole city worthy of note is Palermo, which Ibn Ḥawqal described in a long section.[27] In Palermo, according to Ibn Ḥawqal, there is a main mosque large enough for seven thousand worshippers, and there are more than three hundred other mosques. This compares with five hundred mosques in Córdoba — or so he has been told; he cannot verify this figure, whereas in Sicily he has visited most of them. Ibn Ḥawqal claimed to have seen as many as ten mosques built side-by-side, because every family who could afford to do so built their own. He also went into detail about such local matters as the sources of water and the properties of Sicily's onions, citing people he had met in Palermo as his informants — including, for one meeting, the date and time of day and the fact that it was raining. In addition, Ibn Ḥawqal said that he had summarized both the merits and the faults of Sicily and its inhabitants in a "Book on Sicily."[28] His cursory treatment of al-Andalus, on the other hand seems to be based on information copied from his Iranian predecessors. Ibn Ḥawqal said that he took with him a copy of Ibn Khurradādhbih's *Routes and Realms.*[29] His own account "does not coincide with information given by Ibn Khurradādhbih,"[30] although he cited the earlier work on the time taken to cross the peninsula. Some of the many similarities with al-Istakhrī's work are discussed below.

Although Ibn Ḥawqal and al-Istakhrī's geographies have different titles, they are very similar in construction and in many places almost identical in wording. In an appendix to his four-volume study of medieval Arabic geography to 1050, André Miquel laid out the opening paragraphs of the two geographers' works as they appear in the modern editions to demonstrate their close relationship.[31] Elements of Ibn Ḥawqal's account of

26 Ibid., 118; trans. Kramers and Wiet, 117.
27 Ibn Ḥawqal, *Kitāb ṣūrat al-arḍ*, 118–28; trans. Kramers and Wiet, 117–27.
28 Ibn Ḥawqal, *Kitāb ṣūrat al-arḍ*, 129; trans. Kramers and Wiet, 128.
29 Ibn Ḥawqal, *Kitāb ṣūrat al-arḍ*, 329; trans. Kramers and Wiet, 322.
30 لا يوافق رسم ابن خرداذبه. Ibn Ḥawqal, *Kitāb ṣūrat al-arḍ*, 5.
31 Miquel, *La géographie humaine*, 1: 299ff and Appendix 1.

al-Andalus already present in al-Istakhrī's text include a comment on the size of Córdoba. As al-Istakhrī had not seen Córdoba, it seems that his information about al-Andalus came either from a written source or from a traveler, although he does not mention either of these. Ibn Ḥawqal's text in turn served as one of the main sources for al-Idrīsī's geography, composed for Roger II of Sicily in the 1160s, favored over al-Idrīsī's first-hand knowledge of al-Andalus. By the time al-Idrīsī, was writing, Córdoba's days of glories under the Umayyads were long gone, and the city was no longer the center of power. Of the Umayyad palace of Madīnāt al-Zahrā' outside Córdoba he remarked "today this city is in ruins and on the point of disappearing;"[32] Yet al-Idrīsī incorporated events from the tenth-century history of the city into his geography as though they were current[33] and he made no attempt to revise routes that may no longer have been in use.[34]

It seems that much of these geographers' data for al-Andalus came from their libraries, whether or not they themselves had traveled. In the introduction to the *Description of the Earth* Ibn Ḥawqal stated his debt to al-Istakhrī, saying that he bumped into al-Istakhrī on the Indus and promised to do further work on the older man's text. Many of the surviving manuscripts of Ibn Ḥawqal and al-Istakhrī's geographies have maps. Indeed, Ibn Ḥawqal characterized his geography as a guide to his maps, which he drew under the eyes of his mentor. He noted that al-Istakhrī had "drawn a map of the Indus region, but he had made some mistakes, and he had also drawn Iran, which he had done extremely well. For my part, I had drawn the map of Azerbaijan which occurs on the following page and of which he approved, as well as that of Iraq which he considered excellent. My map

---

32 وهي الآن خراب في حال الذهاب. Al-Idrīsī, *Nuzhat al-mushtāq fī ikhtirāq al-atāq, Description de l'Afrique et de l'Espagne*, ed. Rheinhart Dozy and Michael J. de Goeje (Amsterdam: Oriental Press, 1969), 212.

33 Al-Idrīsī, ed. Dozy and De Goeje, 208–12; trans., 256–65.

34 Al-Idrīsī, *La première géographie de l'occident*, trans. P.A. Jaubert (1840), rev. H. Bresc and Annliese Nef (Paris: Flammarion, 1999), 15–20, 32.

of Egypt, however, he condemned as wholly bad and that of the Maghreb as for the most part inaccurate." Ibn Ḥawqal added: "Here is the map of the Maghreb [...] within the limits of my capacities, either through personal observation or with the aid of eye-witness testimony."[35] Thus we are led to believe that the maps in the surviving manuscripts are versions of what the two men actually drew, perhaps continuing an existing tradition.

Yet the reality of the relationship between the works attributed to al-Istakhri and Ibn Ḥawqal is more complicated than one would imagine from reading modern editions and studies of them. As is often the case, the editors who worked so hard to bring medieval Arabic texts to light in the nineteenth and twentieth centuries also confused our understanding of them. They placed undue emphasis on the titles of the manuscripts, trying to make "routes and realms" into one category and "description of the earth" into another. These texts were popular, possibly because of the maps that accompanied them (in some manuscripts spaces have been left for the maps to be added later). [36] Editors were faced with compilations of different lengths with different titles, written in Arabic or Persian from the eleventh to nineteenth centuries; at least thirty-eight manuscripts have al-Istakhri's name in the title or colophon, while eleven name Ibn Ḥawqal, and more are being discovered. In the 1870s, Michael De Goeje made an edition of "al-Istakhrī" and another of "Ibn Ḥawqal" based on manuscripts copied in the twelfth to the sixteenth centuries. In the 1930s, Johannes Kramers made a new edition of "Ibn Ḥawqal" from a manuscript with this author's name that De Goeje did not see: a *Description of the Earth* dated 1086. Kramers noted that this has "many so far unknown additions to Ibn Ḥawqal's text, especially in the description of the western part of the Islamic world"[37] and in particular a much

---

35 ما أذت الاستطاعة اليه ووقفتُ بالمشاهد والخبر الصحيح بالمفاوهة عليه. فهذه صورة المغرب [...] Ibn Ḥawqal, *Kitāb ṣūrat al-arḍ*, 66.

36 Karen C. Pinto, *Medieval Islamic Maps: An Exploration* (Chicago and London: University of Chicago Press, 2016).

37 Ibn Ḥawqal, *Kitāb ṣūrat al-arḍ*, v–vi.

longer section on Sicily.[38] Kramers included, with due acknowl-
edgement, material from De Goeje's edition; "some material
has also been added from other sources where a more complete
version of Ibn Ḥawqal seems to be quoted. It has also been
deemed necessary sometimes to go back to the Iṣṭakhrī text, a
procedure which De Goeje too had frequently been obliged to
adopt."[39] Some of the opening section, however, including the
apparently verbatim citation from Ibn Ḥawqal on his meeting with al-Istakhrī, is not in the earliest manuscript. Thus, the
contents of the various manuscripts used for the editions are
difficult to explain as the result of diachronic copying. To give
some examples: eight of the ten itineraries from Córdoba that
De Goeje included in his edition of al-Istakhri are also in a Persian compilation with the title *Book of Routes and Realms*,[40] that
'fell into the hands' of Sir William Ouseley towards the end of
the eighteenth century, although the details are not identical.
This manuscript does not have the name of the author. However
Ouseley attributed the work to Ibn Ḥawqal, noting that two passages in the Persian text are almost identical to passages copied
by the Ayyubid historian, Abū al-Fidā' (d. 1331), which begin
"Ibn Ḥawqal said."[41] Until much more work has been done on
the manuscripts of the Arabic geographers, it will be impossible
to draw meaningful conclusions about their authorship. It appears that what went into De Goeje's editions was based on his
opinion about which section of a given manuscript belonged to
which author. Modern scholars made further distinctions based
on the appearance of the maps, if any, so that a manuscript with
one author's name can be classified under the maps attributed to

38 Ibid., 118–31.
39 Ibid., vi; for example, two paragraphs of the introduction to "Ibn Ḥawqal"
    do not appear in the 1086 manuscript: ibid. 3; trans. Kramers and Wiet, 2–3.
40 William Ouseley, ed. and trans., *The Oriental Geography of Ibn Ḥawqal,
    an Arabian traveller of the tenth century* (London: Oriental Press, 1800), vi,
    available from https://archive.org/details/orientalgeograpooagoog/page/
    n13/mode/2up.
41 Ibid., 254, 264.

another.[42] Thus, the editions of the two geographers' works are far from definitive, leaving unexplained discrepancies. It may be argued that neither "al-Istakhrī" nor "Ibn Ḥawqal" represent a single author, and that all the surviving manuscripts contain material that was added after the fall of the Umayyads. Thus, Ibn Ḥawqal's description of al-Andalus may represent nostalgia for the lost Córdoba of the Umayyads rather than an eye-witness account. Summing up the early medieval Arabic geographers, Miquel concluded that each made his own synthesis from the written material available to him, to which he might or might not add his own observations.[43] This was also true of the copyists and/or compilers of later manuscripts of these texts. Rather than come to an overarching conclusion about "Islamic geography" we must try to work out what and how each compiler selected from his sources at a given moment. Without new critical editions of the works of al-Istakhrī and Ibn Ḥawqal — an enormous task — "al-Istakhrī" is used in this chapter to mean De Goeje's version of the work of an author who did not travel to al-Andalus and "Ibn Ḥawqal" means Kramers's version with its possible origin with a traveler to Córdoba in the tenth century.

Al-Istakhrī did not describe the itineraries in as much detail as Ibn Ḥawqal and what he says is inconsistent. He noted that it took three days to go from Córdoba to Seville, perhaps following the route where the railway now runs, a distance of 135 kilometers (84 miles), or 45 kilometers (28 miles) per day. From Córdoba to Guadalajara, 360 kilometers (224 miles) as the crow flies, took eight days according to al-Istakhrī, again about 45 kilometers a day. But for the journey from Córdoba to Zamora on the river Duero, al-Istakhrī gave an improbable twenty-two days. An account in an eleventh-century source of a campaign mounted against Zamora from Córdoba gives details

---

42 Gerald R. Tibbetts, "The Balkhī School of Geographers," in *The History of Cartography,* vol. 2, book 1, ed. J.B. Hartley and David Woodward, Cartography in the Traditional Islamic and South Asian Societies (Chicago: Chicago University Press, 1992), 108–36.

43 Miquel, *La géographie humaine,* 1: 151.

of the route, but unfortunately the place names are obscure, and it is not clear which way they went.[44] Córdoba to Zamora by modern roads is 582 kilometers (362 miles), or about thirteen days journey at 45 kilometers per day. As with the description of Spain by the postmaster Ibn Khurradādhbih, this information is too unreliable to be used by travelers.

The two geographers listed three different routes from Córdoba to Toledo, which I will analyze in some detail to illustrate the potential and the difficulties of this material. The routes to Toledo that appear in Ibn Ḥawqal's *Description* do not appear to have come from al-Istakhrī, who simply said that the journey from Córdoba to Toledo took six days without giving its intermediate points.[45] The first of Ibn Ḥawqal's itineraries, to Medinaceli via Toledo is as follows:

Córdoba — Caracuel four days — Calatrava one day — Malagon one stage — Yebenes one stage — Toledo one stage — Magan 1 stage — Gharra 1 stage — Guadalajara — Sha'ra al-Qawarir one stage — Medinaceli 1 stage.[46]

It is not clear what was meant by a stage, but if this is equivalent to a day's journey, the journey takes two days longer than al-Istakhrī suggested. Ibn Ḥawqal also gave as an itinerary the following route to Toledo via a huge loop up to the coast, which makes little sense as a single journey:

---

44 Ibn Ḥayyān, *Al-Muktabis. Tome troisième. Chronique du règne du calife Umaiyade ʿAbd Allah à Cordoue,* ed. Melchor M. Antuña (Paris: Libraire Orientaliste Paul Geuthner, 1937), 134.

45 Al-Istakhrī, *Kitāb al-masālik,* 46.

46 إربعة أيّام [...] ومن كركويه الى قعلة رباح [...] ومن قعلة رباح الى ماقون [...] ومن قرطبة الى كركويه المدينة مرحلة ومنها الى انبش [...] مرحلة ومن انبش الى طليطلة مرحلة [...] ومن طليطلة الى مغام [...] مرحلة ومن مغام الى الغُرّاء [...] مرحلة، ومنها الى وادى الحجارة [...] ومنها الى شعراء القوارير مرحلة [...] مرحلة [....]. ومنها الى مدينة السلام مرحلة. Ibn Ḥawqal, *Kitāb ṣūrat al-arḍ,* 116; for a discussion of the toponyms, see Félix Hernández, "El camino de Córdoba a Toledo en la época musulmana," *Al-Andalus* 24 (1959): 1–62.

Córdoba — Murad one day — Gharghira one stage — Seville
two days — Niebla two days — Gibraleon two days — Lepe
three days — Ocsonaba four days — Silves six days — Alcacer do Sal five days — Almada, the mouth of the river three
days — Lisbon one day — Cintra two days — Santarem two
days — Aviz four days — Juromenha two days — Elvas one
day — Badajoz (where one crosses the river) one day — Qa-
ntarat al-Sif four days — Mérida one day — Medellín two
days — Trujillo two days — Caceres two days — Miknasa
two days — Makhadat al-Balat one day — Talavera — three
days — Toledo three days.[47]

Ibn Ḥawqal's treatment of the cities of al-Andalus outside the
capital is brief, but he inserted comments on some of the stations on the itineraries, noting for instance that Seville was a
prosperous city, situated on the same river as Córdoba, with
many orchards and vineyards, and was particularly known for
its figs, whilst the towns of Alcacer do Sal and Calatrava (both
from Arabic terms meaning "fortress") were protected by walls.
At Toledo, a great stone bridge spanned the river Tagus. There
is a lot of information of this sort in Arabic geographies. Modern studies of the medieval Islamic world have picked data from
them with the aim of saying what various places were like at the
time of writing, but without appreciating the problems inherent
in the transmission of this information.

The most direct route from Córdoba to Toledo, 230 kilometers (143 miles) as the crow flies over the mountains of the Sierra

47 فمن قرطبة الى مراد مرحلة ومن مراد الى غرغيرة مرحلة ومن غرغيرة الى اشبيليه يومان [...] ومن اشبيليه
الى لبله بومان [...] ومنها الى جبل العُيون يومان [...] ومن جبل العيون الى لب ثلثة ايّام [...] ومن لب الى
اخشنبه [...] أربعة أيّام ومن اخشنبه الى مدينة شلب ستة ايّام ومن شلب الى قصر بنى ورداسن خمسة ايّام
[...] ومنها الى المعدن وهو فم النهر ثلثة ايّام [...] ومن فم النهر الى لشبونه يوم ومن لشبونه الى شنترة يومان
ومن شتارة الى شنترين يومان ومن شنترين الى بيزه أربعة ايّام ومن بيزة الى جلمانية يومان ومن جلمانية الى
البش يوم ومن البش الى بطليوس يعبر النهر يوم ومن بطليوس الى قنطرة السيف الى ماردة يوم ومن ماردة الى
مدلَين يومان ومن مدلَين الى ترجيله يومان ومن ترجيله الى قصراش يومان ومن قصراش الى مكناسه يومان ومن
مكناسه الى مخاضة البلاط يوم ومن مخاضة الى طليبره خمسة ايّام ومن طليبره الى طليذلة ثلثة ايّام. Ibn
Ḥawqal, *Kitāb ṣūrat al-arḍ*, 115–16; Ibn Ḥawqal says that one can travel from
Córdoba to Badajoz by the main road in six stages, but not name them.

Morena, is not necessarily the easiest; the traveler has also to cross the rivers Guadiana and Tagus. In a series of articles Félix Hernández studied the itineraries of al-Andalus in the tenth century in an attempt to explain the routes with reference to Spain's geography and changing political realities.[48] Hernández began with a careful study of topography which took into account the effect of the seasons on river and mountain crossings and the existence of transport infrastructure.[49] He brought in a wide range of sources, supplementing Arabic geographies with references in the chronicles to the routes that emirs, caliphs and their armies took on summer campaigns. To give one example, an account, perhaps dating to the tenth century, of the crucial battle between the governor of al-Andalus Yusuf al-Fihri and the first Umayyad to rule the peninsula ʿAbd al-Raḥmān I in 756 shows them traveling along opposite banks of Guadalquivir.[50] The tradition that Ṭāriq ibn Ziyād and Mūsā ibn Nusayr took separate routes through their conquest of the peninsula, meeting at Almarad/Almaraz on the Tagus, seem to have arisen in the tenth century.[51] This is the way people were likely to have gone at the time of writing, even if the stories themselves may not be true. Nor it is clear that the route taken by an army on horseback was the same as that followed by merchants, embassies and other travelers in more peaceful times. Even the sup-

48 Félix Hernández, "Estudios de Geografía Histórica Española VII: Gāfiq, Gahet, Gahete = Belalcázar," *Al-Andalus* 9 (1944): 71–109; Hernandez, "El camino de Córdoba a Toledo"; Félix Hernández, "Los caminos de Córdoba hacia noroeste en época musulmana," *Al-Andalus* 32 (1967): 37–123, 277–355.

49 For the impact of seasonal travel on society see, e.g., Ariel López, "Life on Schedule: Monks and the Agricultural Cycle in Late Antique Europe," in *Motions of Late Antiquity: Essays on Religion, Politics and Society in Honour of Peter Brown,* ed. Jamie Kreiner and Helmut Reimitz, Cultural Encounters in Late Antiquity and the Middle Ages 20 (Turnhout: Brepols, 2016), 187–208.

50 *Ajbar Machmía (Colección de tradiciones),* ed. and trans. E. Lafuente y Alcántara (Madrid: Real Academia de la Historia, 1867), 85–86; trans. 83.

51 Luis Molina, "Un relato de la conquista de al-Andalus," *Al-Qanṭara* 19 (1998): 39–65; Nicola Clarke, *The Muslim Conquest of Iberia: Medieval Arabic Narratives* (Abingdon and New York: Routledge, 2012), 38.

position that travelers used the Roman roads cannot be proven; since they were going on horseback or donkey, paved roads were less necessary. Hernández also cast his net wider and looked at routes mentioned in Latin and Romance chronicles from the later Middle Ages and in the *Repartimientos* (distribution) of land and other properties taken in the Christian re-conquest. Hernández discovered, for example, that the Christians who took Córdoba in 1236, had first to make a detour of 100 kilometers (62 miles) to the west to cross the Tagus, which was in flood. Hernández also used a description of the peninsula which Fernando, the son of Christopher Columbus, left unfinished in 1523, as well as modern maps and local informants, who showed him the site of a ford that is not mentioned in any of the written sources. These gleanings helped him to decode obscure place names and to suggest reasons why a traveler might sometimes be obliged to make a wide detour to reach his destination.

Hernández's sources mention a direct route from Córdoba to Toledo, crossing the mountains of the Sierra Morena. It was used at least twice when campaigning against the north, in 1003 and 1005, by 'Abd al-Malik and Sanchuelo, the sons of the last powerful ruler of al-Andalus in the early Islamic period, al-Manṣūr. Of the earlier campaign the chronicler says that it took fourteen days to reach Toledo, but this may have included delays to assemble the troops or to deal with opposition.[52] Parts of the same route were used by Muslim armies attacking Toledo in the thirteenth century.[53] Ibn Ḥawqal's shorter route crossed to the east of the Sierra Morena, which meant a detour, but would have been easier because it is not so steep.[54] Ibn Ḥawqal did not mention a direct route to Mérida from Córdoba that almost certainly existed in his time, as we shall see; the actual route is now obscure although Hernández reconstructed it from "old roads"

---

52   Ibn Idhārī, *Kitāb Bayān al-Maghrib*, vol. 3, ed. Évariste Lévi-Provençal (Paris: P. Guethner, 1930), 5.

53   Hernández, "El camino."

54   Ibid.

mentioned in a variety of sources. From Mérida Ibn Ḥawqal's long route goes on to Toledo via Trujillo. From Trujillo it should have been possible to cross the Tagus at Talavera de la Reina and enter Toledo following the right bank of the river. Ibn Ḥawqal's route, however, veered slightly to the west and north to another crossing point, at Makhadāt al-Balāṭ, near present-day Almaraz. A bridge was built here in the sixteenth century, but a century earlier one crossed by boat.

Hernández concluded that political considerations can account for Ibn Ḥawqal's proposed detour. His source, Ibn Idhārī, writing in Morocco c. 1300, gave a second account of the campaigns of ʿAbd al-Malik and Sanchuelo. The chronicler explained that the expeditions were not able to leave Córdoba by its northern gates because of the proximity of rebels.[55] Perhaps they made a detour to the west. However, this does not explain why, more than a century later, al-Idrīsī still gave as the route to Toledo an itinerary which began by going west, perhaps to Mérida, continued along the banks of the Guadiana as far as Calatrava and then turned towards Toledo.[56] Hernández calculated that a traveler following this route had to go 160 kilometers (99 miles) to the northwest of Córdoba to reach a point 34 kilometers (21 miles) west of the city and then turn some 150 kilometers (93 miles) towards the northeast.[57] It is possible that the convoluted routes in the geographies are partly explicable by strategic issues that applied only for a short period, but they continued to be copied and mixed with information from other sources.

As we have seen, Ibn Ḥawqal characterized his text as a guide to the maps. These survive as a sequence that is common to most of the manuscripts of al-Istakhrī and Ibn Ḥawqal: a world map and twenty regional maps that follow the order of the text.[58] The world maps are schematic, showing the world as circular

---

55 Ibn ʿIdhārī, *Kitāb Bayān al-Maghrib*, 3: 11.
56 Al-Idrīsī, *Description*, trans. Dozy and de Goeje, 263–65.
57 Hernández, "El camino."
58 Pinto, *Medieval Islamic Maps*, 55.

in the midst of an Encircling Ocean beyond which, most geographers believed, lay only cold and darkness; they complement the *mappae mundi* of the Latin cartographic tradition, of which the earliest peninsular example is in an eighth-century manuscript from Albi.[59] From the Peutinger Table, dating perhaps to the beginning of the fourth century, which placed Rome in the center of the world, to the Hereford *mappa mundi,* where the focus is Jerusalem, world maps represented to the viewer what was important. The Peutinger Table also gave the routes that led to Rome, not, it has been argued, as a guide for travelers, but to show that all roads led to the capital.[60] No similar graphic representation of itineraries survives in the earliest Islamic maps, which were in any case not centered on capitals such as Baghdad and Córdoba but on the holy cities of Mecca and Medina. In this world view, al-Andalus does not appear as important. In the 1086 world map, the whole of the land of the Christians, the country of the Rūm, from Constantinople to the western tip of Europe, is squeezed into one corner. Al-Andalus is a yet smaller corner of this corner and although Constantinople is located, Córdoba is not. If the map was truly a graphic statement of what Ibn Ḥawqal thought was important, both Córdoba and al-Andalus are of minor significance.

Although it would be rash to suggest that tenth-century travelers took the long and winding road to Toledo that Ibn Ḥawqal recorded, we may be in a position to account for it at least in part by reference to the Roman roads listed in the third-century *Itinerarium provinciarum Anto[ni]ni Augusti.*[61] In the Roman

---

59 *Mappa mundi e codice Albigensi 29 accedunt indeculum quod maria vel venti sunt et (Pauli Orosii) Discriptio terrarum ex eodem codice, in Itineraria et alia geographica,* ed. François Glorie, Corpus Christianorum Series Latina 175 (Turnhout: Brepols, 1965), 473–87.

60 Richard Talbert, *Rome's World: The Peutinger Map Reconsidered* (Cambridge: Cambridge University Press, 2010), 162–63.

61 One copy may have been in the possession of Eulogius of Córdoba: Gonzalo Menéndez Pidal, *Los Caminos en la Historia de España* (Madrid: Cultura Hispánica, 1992), 34, 56.

road network Córdoba was one of number of nodal points. *The Barrington Atlas of the Greek and Roman World,* using material and written evidence, retraces five roads leading from Córdoba.[62] The most important was the Via Augusta, which ran from Cádiz, the Pillars of Hercules, via Barcelona and Girona to join the Via Domitia to Rome.[63] One of Córdoba's other main roads, the Via Emerita, which crossed a tributary of the Guadalquivir by the Roman bridge, still extant, led to Mérida, capital of late Roman Spain and another nodal point. Like Córdoba, Mérida has a Roman bridge and other monuments of the pre-Islamic and Islamic periods, but it has a much less prominent place in Arabic historiography and geography. From Mérida, the main road north led to Zaragoza, passing through Toledo. One might well travel from Córdoba to Toledo via Mérida, particularly if Mérida's bridge was one of the best places to cross the Guadiana. Chroniclers noted that the Roman bridges at Córdoba and Mérida were repaired in the Islamic period, but others may have fallen into disuse. References to Roman roads in the Arabic sources are rare, but a fourteenth-century text, the *Chronicle of the Moor Rasis*[64] notes that whoever sets off from Carmona (near Seville) to travel to Narbonne will never have to leave "the paved road [...] built by Hercules," a clear reference to the Via Augusta.[65] This is one of a number of references to a paved road, *balāṭ* in Arabic, the origin of the place name Albalata which is common in Spain today.

The Via Emerita was one of two Roman routes leaving Córdoba that could have been used to travel to Toledo. The other, which left Córdoba on the Via Augusta, is the one followed by

---

62 Richard Talbert, ed., *Barrington Atlas of the Greek and Roman World* (Princeton: Princeton University Press, 2000), 24–27.

63 John Richardson, *The Romans in Spain* (Malden: Blackwell, 1996 and 1998), 160–62.

64 See below.

65 *Crónica del Moro Rasis,* ed. Diego Catalan y María Soledad de Andres (Madrid: Editorial Gredos, 1975), 98; for the challenges posed by this text, see below.

the modern road and must have existed in the Islamic period, although the Arabic geographers did not mention it. The direct route to Toledo over the mountains does not seem to have Roman antecedents, which may explain Hernández's failure to find either material or written evidence for it that is later than the thirteenth century, not even so much as a sheep drovers' road. The road from Toledo via Mérida was one of the peninsula's most important routes throughout the Middle Ages.[66] But it did not lead to Córdoba — rather, it led to Seville. It is listed in the itineraries of Alfonso VI of Castile in the eleventh century and later maps label it the "royal road to Seville."

It is plausible that Roman roads were still the main arteries of peninsular travel in the Umayyad period. Nor is it surprising that, in the tenth century and later, geographers writing in Arabic remembered some of the detail of these roads, albeit sometimes confused. We have no idea, however, whether they were copying from earlier written sources — and if so which — or in Ibn Ḥawqal's case at least, speaking from experience. This however was not the only way of writing about the peninsula. Geographers from the end of the eleventh century onwards were to give more detail about connectivity between the towns and cities of al-Andalus. The picture that emerges from their work is not dominated by Córdoba but by Seville.

An alternative way of writing about al-Andalus seems to have begun with a historian whom Ibn Ḥawqal could have met in Córdoba. Aḥmad al-Rāzī was prominent at the court of ʿAbd al-Raḥmān III and died in 955. He was remembered as the author of chronicles and at least one geography. Unfortunately, his works do not survive in anything like their original state. Many Muslim compilers of the eleventh century and later cited al-Rāzī extensively for the history of the peninsula up to his day. Interpretation of the geography, in contrast, depends on a strange text that purports to be a description of al-Andalus with an account of the conquest that was translated from Arabic into Portuguese

---

66 Hernández, "Estudios de Geografía."

and then into Castilian. The *Chronicle of the Moor Rasis,* as it is known, is almost impossible to use. The historical section has clearly been rewritten from a Romance chronicle and it bears no resemblance to citations of al-Rāzī by Muslim historians. Parts of the geographical section, however, could have originated with al-Rāzī, such as the statement that "Córdoba is the mother of cities and was always the seat of the greatest princes and the house of kings. And people go there from all parts."[67]

There are many similarities between the *Chronicle of the Moor Rasis* and a number of Arabic geographies compiled in the eleventh to the fourteenth centuries.[68] The starting point of these works was the description of the peninsula in Orosius's *Seven Books of History against the Pagans* that begins "Spain is triangular." A much-interpolated version of Orosius exists that seems to have been translated into Arabic at the end of the ninth century.[69] Most of the Arabic geographers used only Orosius's geographical introduction,[70] which also circulated in Spain in Latin independently from the rest of the text. The dominance of the Orosian model meant that as late as the fifteenth century, when the Muslims were confined to the area around Granada, geographers continued to give the term "al-Andalus" to the whole of the peninsula, saying as Orosius had, that Hispania, now al-Andalus, ended at Narbonne. More importantly for the present discussion, these geographers followed the opening description of Spain with a gazetteer of the peninsula: brief accounts of the cities and towns with episodes from their history and the routes

---

67 "Cordoua [...] es madre de las çibdades, e fue sienpre morada de los mayores prínçipes e casas de los rreyes. E de todas las partes vienen en ella." *Crónica del Moro Rasis,* 19.

68 Emmanuelle Tixier du Mesnil, *Géographes d'al-Andalus. De l'inventaire d'un territoire à la construction d'une mémoire* (Paris: Publications de la Sorbonne, 2014).

69 *Kitāb Hurūshiyūsh (Traddución Árabe de las Historiae Adversus Paganos de Orosio),* ed. Mayte Penelas (Madrid: Centro Superior de Investigaciones Científicas, 2001).

70 Luis Molina, "Orosio y los Geógrafos Hispanomusulmanes," *Al-Qanṭara* 5 (1984): 62–92.

between them. To give one example: after his description of Valencia, al-'Udhrī, writing in Almería at the end of the eleventh century, noted "the roads from Valencia to the places which are controlled by her."[71] Al-'Udhrī and his near-contemporary, al-Bakrī describe the places that remained under Muslim control at the time they were composed. Córdoba, said al-Bakrī was no longer, destroyed in the civil strife which according to al-Bakrī lasted from 400 AH (1009–10) until his own times (al-Bakrī was writing c.1167): "her traces became empty and [the loss of] her people was lamented."[72] This chain of geographers did not allow Córdoba to monopolize their descriptions of the peninsula, although they continued to acknowledge the city's importance and gave long descriptions of the Great Mosque. Their focus on Córdoba was an inherited tradition, established at the Umayyad court by al-Rāzī, the *Moor Rasis,* which did not reflect the reality of the writers' own times.

There was another obvious way to travel that medieval Muslim writers in general hardly mentioned — by water. We may assume that it was often quicker to travel by boat along the coast than overland, but the sources rarely say so. The earliest such reference seems to be from the eleventh century, a journey by sea from Almería to Valencia.[73] The Arabic geographers' neglect of river transport is difficult to explain, since Strabo commented as much on river travel as on roads, and noted that the Guadalquivir was navigable as far as Córdoba, although from Se-

---

71   Al-'Udhrī, *Nuṣūṣ 'an al-Andalus min kitāb tarsī' al-akhbār wa tanwī al-athār,* in *Fragmentos geográfico-históricos de al-Masālik ilā Gamī al-Mamālik,* ed. 'Abd al-Azīz al-Ahwānī (Madrid: Instituto de Estudios Islámicos, 1965), 19.

72   Al-Bakri, *The Geography of al-Andalus and Europe from the Book "Al-masalik wa-l-mamalik,"* ed. 'Abd al-Raḥmān El-Hajji (Beirut: Dar al-Ishad, 1968), 106.

73   Ibn Ḥazm, *El Collar de la Paloma,* trans. Emilio García, 2nd edn. (Madrid: Sociedad de Estudios y Publicaciones, 1967), 261; Olivia Remie Constable, *Trade and Traders in Muslim Spain: The Commercial Realignment of the Iberian Peninsula, 900–1500* (Cambridge: Cambridge University Press, 1996), 16.

ville it was necessary to transfer to smaller vessels.[74] The river probably flooded about once every five years[75] and sources for the Umayyad period mention floods and also droughts in summer, which made navigation difficult. Perhaps this is one of the reasons why Vikings did not reach Córdoba in their expedition against al-Andalus of September-November 844, although they occupied Lisbon and Seville and ranged across a wide area of open country in the southwest.[76] Arabic sources rarely refer to boats on the Guadalquivir, giving little indication that river traffic to the capital was significant.[77] The Guadalquivir was still navigable to Córdoba after the Christian re-conquest, although the increasing number of mills along the river hindered the passage of boats. Recent archaeology has pointed to the continuing importance in the Islamic period of a fortification added to the southwest corner of Córdoba's walls in the Visigothic period, which defended the river approaches.[78] This area was further strengthened in the Islamic period to protect against floods and to provide a pavement between the Alcázar, which adjoined the inside of the south wall of the city, and the river. Downstream of the bridge the pavement took a completely new course in the Islamic period, providing protection for the esplanade between the Alcázar and the bridge. It is likely that these developments

74 Richardson, *Romans in Spain,* 162.
75 Karen Carr, *Vandals to Visigoths. Rural Settlement Patterns in Early Medieval Spain* (Ann Arbor: University of Michigan Press, 2002), 15.
76 Ann Christys, *Vikings in the South: Voyages to Iberia and the Mediterranean* (London and New York: Bloomsbury, 2015), 29–45.
77 Ibn Ḥayyan, *Al-Muqtabas min anbā' ahl al-andalus, ed. Maḥmūd 'Alī Makki* (Beirut: Dār al-kitāb al-'arabī, 1973), 19; Al-Mas'udi, *Al-Tanbih wa-l-Ishraf,* ed. de Goeje, 68; Constable, *Trade and Traders,* 22.
78 Juan F. Murillo, Alberto León Muñoz, Elena Castro, María Teresa Casal, Raimundo Ortiz, and Antonio J. González, "La transición de la civitas clásica cristianizada a la madina islámica a través de las transformaciones operadas en las áreas suburbiales," in *El anfiteatro romana de Córdoba y su entorno urbano. Analysis arqueológico (ss.I–XIII d.C.),* ed. Desiderio Vazquerizo and Juan F. Murillo, Monografías de arqueología cordobesa 19.2 (Córdoba: Universidad de Córdoba y Gerencia Municipal de Urbanismo del Ayuntamiento, 2010), 503–46.

also served a commercial port, although no evidence for port activity has so far been found. There is no doubt, however, that Seville's superiority as a port was one factor in its pre-eminence over Córdoba in the Roman period, which it regained after the fall of the Umayyads and maintained until the river started to silt up in the seventeenth century.

Information about everyday travel in the Umayyad period is hard to find. When people travel in the Arabic sources, unless they are on campaign, they are going to Córdoba. Arabic chroniclers mentioned embassies from Christian rulers,[79] but they focused on their arrival in Córdoba and gave little or no detail of the route taken or the hazards and inconveniences of the journey. Scholars claimed that they had traveled in search of learning, although this may be a *topos*. According to a tenth-century biographical dictionary, the father of Ibn Ḥabīb (d. 853) sent him to Jerusalem and the Hijāz with a thousand dinars and the instruction "Take these and use them in the search for knowledge and it is not to be spent on anything else unless you need to purchase a chaste female slave" but he received no advice on the perils of travel.[80] One of Ibn Ḥabīb's pupils left his home in Toledo to study in Córdoba, but his sole worry was that he arrived without a letter of introduction to Ibn Ḥabīb.[81] The biographies of teachers born outside Córdoba in the period to 961 shows that many scholars in the provinces with large follow-

---

79 E.g., Ibn Hayyān, *Muqtabas*, ed. Makkī, 27; Ibn Hayyān, *Annales palatinos del calife de Córdoba al-Hakam II, por 'Isa ibn Ahmad al-Razi (360–364 H. = 971–975 J.C.),* trans. Emilio García Gómez (Madrid: Sociedad de Estudios y Publicaciones, 1967), 75, 90, 185, 187, 201, 227; 'Abd al-Raḥmān El-Hajjī, *Andalusian Diplomatic Relations with Western Europe During the Umayyad Period (AH138–366/AD755–976): An Historical Study* (Beirut: Dār al-Irshād, 1970).

80 خذ هذه واستعن بها في طلب العلم ولا تنفق منها شيئا إلا في سبيل العلم إلا إن احتجت إلى ابتياع جارية تتعفف بها, Muḥammad b. Ḥārīth al-Jushanī, *Ajbār al-fuqahā' wa-l-muḥaddithīn (Historia de los alfaquíes y tradicionalistas de al-Andalus),* ed. María Luisa Avila and Luis Molina, Fuentes Arábico-Hispanas 3 (Madrid: Centro Superior de Investigaciones Científicas, 1992), 245.

81 Ibid., 246.

ings had not studied in Córdoba, or were marginally influenced by the capital.[82] Muslims may have been actively discouraged from traveling. The Maliki school of Islamic law, dominant in al-Andalus from the ninth century, allowed the ruler to prohibit the pilgrimage; although the earliest surviving legal ruling to this effect dates from the twelfth century, Ibn Khaldūn believed that it had already applied under the Umayyads.[83]

Nor are the Latin sources for al-Andalus more helpful. There are few references to journeys and, like the Arabic chroniclers, the Latin authors rarely mention the mechanics of the journey. In his letter to bishop Wilesindus of Pamplona of 851, Eulogius, the hagiographer of the martyrs of Córdoba, noted that he set off to find his brothers in Gaul, a dangerous road because of thieves and now completely blocked to him because of the rebellion of William of Septimania, so he turned aside to visit the monasteries around Pamplona, returning to Córdoba via Zaragoza, Sigüenza, Alcalá, and Toledo. The difficulties of travel between Córdoba and Christian Pamplona means that he has delayed sending Wilesindus the relics he promised him until he could entrust them to the heir to Pamplona, returning to that city.[84] This is an exceptional reference to what may have been commonplace difficulties. There are people on the move in hagiographies, such as the account of the embassy of John of Gorze to Córdoba in the tenth century.[85] John of Gorze traveled with a

---

82 Maribel Fierro and Manuela Marín, "La islamización de las ciudades andalusíes a través de sus ulemas (s.II/VIII — comienzos s.IV/X)," in *Genèse de la ville islamique en al-andalus et au Maghreb occidental*, ed. Patrice Cressier and Mercedes García Arenal (Madrid: Casa de Velázquez, 1998), 65–98.

83 Ibn Khaldūn, *The Muqaddimah: An Introduction to History*, vol. 2, trans. Franz Rosenthal, 2nd edn. (London: Routledge, 1967), 99–100; Jocelyn Hendrickson, "Prohibiting the Pilgrimage: Politics and Fiction in Mālikī Fatwās," *Islamic Law and Society* 23 (2016): 161–238.

84 Eulogius, *Epistula tertia ad Wiliesindum*, in *Corpus Scriptorum Muzarabicorum*, vol. 1, ed. Juan Gil (Madrid: Instituto Antonio de Nebrija, 1973), 497.

85 John, Abbot of Saint-Arnoul, *Vita Johannis Gorzensis, in Annales, chronica et historiae aevi Carolini et Saxonici*, ed. Georg Pertz, Monumenta Germaniae Historica, Scriptores IV (Hanover: Hahn, 1841): 335–77.

deacon and a merchant from Verdun via Langres, Beaune, Dijon, Lyons to the Rhône; the boat capsized and he lost his luggage, but he arrived in Barcelona. From there, he traveled via Tortosa and Zaragoza, reaching the capital in 954. The return mission of bishop Recemund of Elvira, near Granada, in 955, took ten weeks to reach Otto's court in Frankfurt, but John of Gorze's biographer does not say what route they took. The passions of two Christians who traveled to Córdoba in the 920s and met their martyrdom in the capital both cite the same warning that "the road of life is straight and narrow but the road that leads to perdition is wide';"[86] this was more important to the hagiographers than the physical roads that the martyrs traveled.

Merchants appear occasionally in the sources, perhaps trading mainly in slaves, although there are references to Córdoban leather in sources from Francia;[87] Christian merchants from Northern Spain and elsewhere in Europe were required to have a safe conduct (*aman*) which gave them temporary *dhimmi* status, in order to trade in Andalusi markets. Without it they themselves could be enslaved.[88] Yet, as Curta pointed out, our evidence for trade in the early medieval period is exiguous.[89] There has been much debate about whether al-Andalus was a "tributary" or a "feudal" economy, even though much remains unknown about fundamentals such as markets, the products

---

86 "Unde itaque Dominus dicit uiam esse artam ad uitam, latam uero et spatiosam que ducit ad perditionem." Cf. Matthew 7:13–14; *La Pasión de San Pelayo*, ed. Celso Rodríguez Fernández (Santiago de Compostela: Universidad de Santiago de Compostela and Universidad de Vigo, 1991), 44; "Intrate per angustam portam, quia ampla et spatiosa est uia, que ducit ad perdictionem," *Passio Argentea*, in *Pasionario Hispánico*, intro., ed., and trans. Pilar Riesco Chueca, 4, 254; cf. Matthew 7:13–14.

87 E.g., charter of donation to Corbie dated 716 including "10 Córdoban skins": Theo Kölzer, ed., *Die Urkunden der Merovinger*, Monumenta Germaniae Historica Diplomata regum Francorum e stirpe Merovingica (Hanover: Hahnsche Buchhandlung, 2001), 215–16.

88 John Wansborough, "The Safe-conduct in Muslim Chancery Practice," *Bulletin of the School of Oriental and African Studies* 34, no. 1 (1971): 20–35.

89 Curta, "Markets."

traded or coinage. Recent archaeology is pointing to the importance of local factors in the connectivity of the peninsula[90] and further excavation will help to shed light on these questions.[91] Much of this information comes from ceramic finds, which are mainly of locally-produced pots, often of poor quality, until glazed ware became more widely-distributed in the second half of the tenth century.[92] Markets have been excavated in rescue digs of Córdoba's suburbs[93] and the delineation of *munyas* (villas with market gardens and orchards) around the *madīna,* from the written sources and from archaeology, show that much of Córdoba's consumption may have been very local. Market treatises survive from the tenth century onwards. They deal mainly with the types of frauds perpetrated by poor people trading in small quantities of local products. Only rarely is there a reference to a specific market.[94]

Thus, it is difficult at the present time to see how or why people traveled within al-Andalus. In the future a single big pottery find could change our current perception that the peninsula was very regional and provide a basis for a more nuanced reading of the itineraries of the Arabic geographers. Roman

90 José C. Carvajal and Miguel Jiménez, "Studies of the Early Medieval Pottery of al-Andalus," *Early Medieval Europe* 19, no. 4 (2011): 411–35.

91 José C. Carvajal, "Review Article: The Archaeology of al-Andalus: Past, Present and Future," *Medieval Archaeology* 58 (2014): 318–39.

92 Claire Déléry, "Using cuerda seca Ceramics as a Historical Source to Evaluate Trade and Cultural Relations Between Christian Ruled Lands and al-Andalus, from the Tenth to Thirteenth Centuries," *Al-Masaq* 21, no. 1 (2009): 31–58; Chris Wickham, *Framing the Middle Ages. Europe and the Mediterranean 400–800* (Oxford: Oxford University Press, 2005), 742–45; James L. Boone, *Lost Civilization: The Contested Islamic Past in Spain and Portugal* (London: Duckworth, 2009), 138; Jairus Banaji, *Exploring the Economy of Late Antiquity: Selected Essays* (Cambridge: Cambridge University Press, 2016), 19–34, 211.

93 Murillo et al., "La transición."

94 Pedro Chalmeta, "EI 'Kitab fi adab al-hisba' (Libro del buen gobierno del zoco) de al-Saqati," *Al-Andalus* 32 (1967): 125–62, 359–97; 33 (1968): 143–95, 367–434 at 385–86 has an anecdote about the markets of Córdoba and Almería that may date to the Umayyad period.

roads may still have been the main arteries of peninsula travel in the Umayyad period since some of the same routes are still in use today. It is more surprising that, in the tenth century or later, geographers writing in Arabic recorded the detail of these roads, although sometimes in a garbled fashion. This information may have been copied from written sources rather than from travels through the peninsula. Where the eastern Islamic world learned the geography of Spain, however, remains a mystery. Geographers writing about the peninsula from the end of the eleventh century onwards were to give more detail about connectivity between the towns and cities of al-Andalus. Some of them were describing the world of their own day and the picture that emerges from their work differs from that of al-Istakhrī and Ibn Ḥawqal. It is dominated not by Córdoba but by Seville. This may not simply be a reflection of political change after the fall of the Umayyads but also of the reality of travel, in particular, that Seville was easier to get to both by road and by river. When al-Istakhrī and Ibn Ḥawqal listed all the roads that led to and from Córdoba they may have obscured the truth about interconnectivity between other centers in the peninsula. It was, for instance, almost certainly true that Seville and Mérida were important regional centers, but the geographers and chroniclers make them look very much subordinate to the capital. Córdoba was at the center of al-Andalus, but only for a relatively brief period under the Umayyads. Only for those looking back to a Golden Age did Córdoba look bigger and more important than it was, so that all roads appeared to lead there, even if it meant going a long way round.

Bibliography

Primary

Ajbar Machmua (Colección de tradiciones). Edited and translated by E. Lafuente y Alcántara. Madrid: Real Academia de la Historia, 1867.

Al-Bakri. *The Geography of al-Andalus and Europe from the Book "Al-masalik wa-l-mamalik."* Edited by Abd al-Raḥmān El-Hajji. Beirut: Dar al-Ishad, 1968.

Al-Idrīsī. *Nuzhat al-mushtāq fī ikhtirāq al-atā. Description de l'Afrique et de l'Espagne.* Edited by Rheinhart Dozy and Michael J. de Goeje. Amsterdam: Oriental Press, 1969.

———. *La première géographie de l'occident.* Translated by P. A. Jaubert (1840) and reviewed by H. Bresc and Annliese Nef. Paris: Flammarion, 1999.

Al-Istakhrī. *Kitāb al-masālik wa al-mamālik: Viae regnorum description dictionis Moslemicae.* Edited by Michael J. de Goeje. Bibliotheca Geographorum Arabicorum 1. Boston and Leiden: Brill, 1873; repr. London: Brill, 1927.

Al-Masʿūdī. *Al-Tanbih wa-l-Ishraf.* Edited by Michael J. de Goeje. Boston and Leiden: Brill, 1894, repr. 2013.

Al-ʿUdhrī. *Nuṣūṣ ʿan al-Andalus min kitāb tarsīʾ al-akhbār wa tanwīʾ al-athār.* In *Fragmentos geográfico-históricos de al-Masālik ilā Gamī al-Mamālik,* edited by ʿAbd al-Azīz al-Ahwānī. Madrid: Instituto de Estudios Islámicos, 1965.

Al-Yaʿqūbī. *Kitāb al-buldān.* In *Bibliotheca Geographorum Arabicorum,* volume 7, edited by Michael J. de Goeje. Boston and Leiden: Brill, 1892.

Crónica del Moro Rasis. Edited by Diego Catalan y María Soledad de Andres. Madrid: Editorial Gredos, 1975.

Eulogius. *Epistula tertia ad Wiliesindum.* In *Corpus Scriptorum Muzarabicorum,* volume 1, edited by Juan Gil. Madrid: Instituto Antonio de Nebrija, 1973.

Ibn Ḥawqal. *Kitāb ṣūrat al-arḍ.* 2 Volumes. Edited by Johannes H. Kramers. Boston and Leiden: Brill, 1938–1939.

———. *Configuration de la terre: Kitab surat al-ard.* 2 Volumes. Translated by Johannes H. Kramers and Gaston Wiet. Beirut: Commission internationale pour la traduction des chefs d'oeuvre, 1964.

Ibn Ḥayyān. *Al-Muktabis. Tome troisième. Chronique du règne du calife Umaiyade 'Abd Allah à Cordoue.* Edited by Melchor M. Antuña. Paris: Librarie Orientaliste Paul Geuthner, 1937.

———. *Al-Muqtabas min anbā' ahl al-andalus.* Edited by Maḥmūd 'Alī Makki. Beirut; Dār al-kitāb al-'arabī, 1973.

———. *Annales palatinos del calife de Córdoba al-Hakam II, por 'Isa ibn Ahmad al-Razi (360–364 H. = 971–975 J.C).* Translated by Emilio García Gómez. Madrid: Sociedad de Estudios y Publicaciones, 1967.

Ibn Ḥazm. *El Collar de la Paloma.* Translated by Emilio García. 2nd edition. Madrid: Sociedad de Estudios y Publicaciones, 1967.

Ibn Idhārī. *Kitāb Bayān al-Maghrib.* Volume 3. Edited by Évariste Lévi-Provençal. Paris: P. Guethner, 1930.

Ibn Khaldūn. *The Muqaddimah: An Introduction to History.* Volume 2. Translated by Franz Rosenthal. 2nd Edition. London: Routledge, 1967.

Ibn Khurradādhbih. *Kitāb al-Masālik wa-l-mamālik.* Edited by Michael J. de Goeje. Boston and Leiden: Brill, 1889, repr. 2013.

John, Abbot of Saint-Arnoul. *Vita Johannis Gorzensis.* In *Annales, chronica et historiae aevi Carolini et Saxonici,* edited by Georg Pertz. Monumenta Germaniae Historica, Scriptores 4. Hanover: Hahn, 1841.

Kitāb Hurūshiyūsh (Traddución Árabe de las Historiae Adversus Paganos de Orosio). Edited by Mayte Penelas. Madrid: Centro Superior de Investigaciones Científicas, 2001.

La Pasión de San Pelayo. Edited by Celso Rodríguez Fernández. Santiago de Compostela: Universidad de Santiago de Compostela and Universidad de Vigo, 1991.

Mappa mundi e codice Albigensi 29 accedunt indeculum quod maria vel venti sunt et (Pauli Orosii) Discriptio terrarum ex eodem codice. In *Itineraria et alia geographica,* edited by Françoise Glorie. Corpus Christianorum Series Latina 175. Turnhout: Brepols, 1965.

Muḥammad b. Ḥārīth al-Jushanī. *Ajbār al-fuqahā' wa-l-muḥaddithīn (Historia de los alfaquíes y tradicionalistas de al-Andalus).* Edited by María Luisa Avila and Luis Molina. Fuentes Arábico-Hispanas 3. Madrid: Centro Superior de Investigaciones Científicas, 1992.

Orosius. *Historiarum adversum paganos libri VII.* Edited by Marie-Pierre Arnaud-Lindet. Paris: Les Belles Lettres, 1990.

———. *Orosius: Seven Books of History against the Pagans.* Translated by Andrew T. Fear. Liverpool: Liverpool University Press, 2010.

Passio Argentea. In *Pasionario Hispánico. Introducción, edición crítica y traducción.* Edited by Pilar Riesco Chueca, Seville: Universidad de Sevilla Secretariado de Publicactiones, 1995.

Secondary

Almagro, Antonio. "Planimetría de las ciudades hispanomusulmanes." *Al-Qanṭara* 8 (1987): 421–48.

Antrim, Zayde. *Routes and Realms: The Power of Place in the Early Islamic World.* New York: Oxford University Press, 2012. DOI: 10.1093/acprof:oso/9780199913879.001.0001

Banaji, Jairus. *Exploring the Economy of Late Antiquity: Selected Essays.* Cambridge: Cambridge University Press, 2016. DOI: 10.1017/CBO9781316182314.

Barbier de Meynard, Charles. "Le livre des routes et des provinces, par Ibn Khoradhbeh, publié, traduit et annoté par M. Barbier de Meynard." *Journal Asiatique* 6, no. 5 (1865): 5–127, 227–96, 446–532.

Boone, James L. *Lost Civilization: The Contested Islamic Past in Spain and Portugal.* London: Duckworth, 2009.

Carr, Karen. *Vandals to Visigoths: Rural Settlement Patterns in Early Medieval Spain.* Ann Arbor: University of Michigan Press, 2002. DOI: 10.3998/mpub.15681.

Carvajal, José C. "Review Article: The Archaeology of al-Andalus: Past, Present and Future." *Medieval Archaeology* 58 (2014): 318–39. DOI: 10.1179/0076609714Z.00000000041.

Carvajal, José C., and Miguel Jiménez. "Studies of the Early Medieval Pottery of al-Andalus." *Early Medieval Europe* 19, no. 4 (2011): 411–35. DOI: 10.1111/j.1468–0254.2011.00330.x.

Chalmeta, Pedro. "El 'Kitab fi adab al-hisba' (Libro del buen gobierno del zoco) de al-Saqati." *Al-Andalus* 32 (1967): 359–97 and *Al-Andalus* 33 (1968): 143–95, 367–434.

Christys, Ann. *Vikings in the South: Voyages to Iberia and the Mediterranean.* London and New York: Bloomsbury, 2015. DOI: 10.5040/9781474213790.

Clarke, Nicola. *The Muslim Conquest of Iberia. Medieval Arabic Narratives.* Abingdon and New York: Routledge, 2012. DOI: 10.4324/9780203180891.

Cochrane, Lydia G., trans. *Islam and Travel in the Middle Ages.* Chicago: University of Chicago Press, 2010.

Constable, Olivia Remie. *Trade and Traders in Muslim Spain: The Commercial Realignment of the Iberian Peninsula, 900–1500.* Cambridge: Cambridge University Press, 1996.

Curta, Florin. "Markets in Tenth-Century al-Andalus and Volga Bulghāria: Contrasting Views of Trade in Muslim Europe." *Al-Masāq* 25, no. 3 (2013): 305–30. DOI: 10.1080/09503110.2013.844503.

Déléry, Claire. "Using cuerda seca Ceramics as a Historical Source to Evaluate Trade and Cultural Relations between Christian Ruled Lands and al-Andalus, from the Tenth to Thirteenth Centuries." *Al-Masaq* 21, no. 1 (2009): 31–58. DOI: 10.1080/09503110802704411.

Donzel, Emeri van, and Andrea Schmidt with Claudia Ott, *Gog and Magog in Early Eastern Christian and Islamic Sources: Sallam's Quest for Alexander's Wall.* Boston and Leiden: Brill, 2010. DOI: 10.1163/ej.9789004174160.i-280.

El-Hajjī, 'Abd al-Raḥmān. *Andalusian Diplomatic Relations with Western Europe during the Umayyad period (AH138–366/ AD755–976): An Historical Study.* Beirut: Dār al-Irshād, 1970.

Fierro, Maribel, and Manuela Marín. "La islamización de las ciudades andalusíes a través de sus ulemas (s.II/VIII — comienzos s.IV/X)." In *Genèse de la ville islamique en al-andalus et au Maghreb occidental,* edited by Patrice Cressier and

Mercedes García Arenal, 65–98. Madrid: Casa de Velázquez, 1998.

Gutas, Dimitri. *Greek Thought, Arabic Culture: The Graeco-Arabic Translation Movement in Baghdad and Early 'Abbasid Society (2nd/4th–8th/10th Centuries).* London and New York: Routledge 1998.

Hendrickson, Jocelyn. "Prohibiting the Pilgrimage: Politics and Fiction in Mālikī Fatwās." *Islamic Law and Society* 23 (2016): 161–238. DOI: 10.1163/15685195–00233p01.

Hernández, Félix. "El camino de Córdoba a Toledo en la época musulmana." *Al-Andalus* 24 (1959): 1–62.

———. "Estudios de Geografía Histórica Española VII: Gāfiq, Gahet, Gahete = Belalcázar." *Al-Andalus* 9 (1944): 71–109.

———. "Los caminos de Córdoba hacia noroeste en época musulmana." *Al-Andalus* 32 (1967): 37–123, 277–355.

Kölzer, Theo, ed. *Die Urkunden der Merovinger. Monumenta Germaniae Historica Diplomata regum Francorum e stirpe Merovingica.* Hanover: Hahnsche Buchhandlung, 2001.

Lévi-Provençal, Évariste. *Histoire de l'Espagne musulmane.* Volume 3. 2nd edition. Paris: Maisonneuve and Larose, 1950, repr. 1999.

López, Ariel. "Life on Schedule: Monks and the Agricultural Cycle in Late Antique Europe." In *Motions of Late Antiquity. Essays on Religion, Politics and Society in Honour of Peter Brown,* edited by Jamie Kreiner and Helmut Reimitz. Cultural Encounters in Late Antiquity and the Middle Ages 20, 187–208. Turnhout: Brepols, 2016. DOI: 10.1484/M.CELA-MA-EB.5.108245.

Manzano, Eduardo. *Conquistadores, Emires y Califas Los Omeyas y la formación de al-Andalus.* Barcelona: Crítica, 2006.

Marín, Manuela. "La transmisión del saber en al-Andalus (hasta 300/912)." *Al-Qanṭara* 8, no. 1 (1987): 87–97.

Menéndez Pidal, Gonzalo. *Los Caminos en la Historia de España.* Madrid: Cultura Hispánica, 1992.

Mesnil, Emmanuelle Tixier du. *Géographes d'al-Andalus. De l'inventaire d'un territoire à la construction d'une mémoire.* Paris: Publications de la Sorbonne, 2014.

Miquel, André. *La géographie humaine du monde musulman jusqu'au milieu du II*e *siècle. Géographie et géographie humaine dans la literature arabe des origins à 1050.* Volume 1. Paris: Mouton, 1967.

Molina, Luis. "Orosio y los Geógrafos Hispanomusulmanes." *Al-Qanṭara* 5 (1984): 62–92.

Molina, Luis. "Un relato de la conquista de al-Andalus." *Al-Qanṭara* 19 (1998): 39–65. DOI: 10.3989/alqantara.1998.v19.i1.485.

Murillo, Juan F., Alberto León Muñoz, Elena Castro, María Teresa Casal, Raimundo Ortiz, and Antonio J. González. "La transición de la civitas clásica cristianizada a la madina islámica a través de las transformaciones operadas en las áreas suburbiales." In *El anfiteatro romana de Córdoba y su entorno urbano: Analysis arqueológico (ss.I–XIII d.C.),* edited by Desiderio Vazquerizo and Juan F. Murillo, 503–46. Monografías de arqueología cordobesa 19.2. Córdoba: Universidad de Córdoba y Gerencia Municipal de Urbanismo del Ayuntamiento, 2010.

Ouseley, William, ed. and trans. *The Oriental Geography of Ibn Ḥawqal.* London: Oriental Press, 1800.

Pinto, Karen C. *Medieval Islamic Maps. An Exploration.* Chicago and London: University of Chicago Press, 2016. DOI: 10.7208/chicago/9780226127019.001.0001.

Richardson, John. *The Romans in Spain.* Malden: Blackwell, 1996/1998.

Talbert, Richard J.A., ed. *Barrington Atlas of the Greek and Roman World.* Princeton: Princeton University Press, 2000.

———. *Rome's World: The Peutinger Map Reconsidered.* Cambridge: Cambridge University Press, 2010.

Tibbetts, Gerald R. "The Balkhī School of Geographers." In *The History of Cartography,* Volume 2, Book 1, edited by J. B. Hartley and David Woodward, 108–36. Cartography in the Traditional Islamic and South Asian Societies. Chicago: Chicago University Press, 1992.

Touati, Houari. *Islam et Voyage au Moyen Âge: Histoire et anthropologie d'une pratique lettrée.* Paris: Éditions du Seuil, 2000.

Wansborough, John. "The Safe-Conduct in Muslim Chancery Practice." *Bulletin of the School of Oriental and African Studies* 34, no. 1 (1971): 20–35. DOI: 10.1017/S0041977X00141552.

Wickham, Chris. *Framing the Middle Ages: Europe and the Mediterranean 400–800.* Oxford: Oxford University Press, 2005. DOI: 10.1093/acprof:oso/9780199264490.001.0001.

4

Religious Conflict in Roman Nicomedia

Dimitris J. Kyrtatas

Late in 311 CE, citizens of Nicomedia, holding images of their gods in their hands, presented themselves to Emperor Maximinus (r. 308–313), who was residing in their city. They were requesting the expulsion of their fellow Christians.[1] This was but one of the many similar incidents of the period throughout Roman Asia. For almost ten years, the whole empire was experiencing a severe religious crisis. Similar tensions were present already from the third century, as old cults were being reshaped while new ones were becoming popular. The surviving literary sources have preserved valuable details regarding the ordeals of the Christians, but the adherents of other religious practices were also facing problems. At the turn of the third century, conversions to Judaism were banned,[2] while a few decades later, Mithraism, having reached the peak of its spread, started declin-

---

1 Eusebius, *Ecclesiastical History, Volume II: Books 6–10,* trans. J.E.L. Oulton, Loeb Classical Library 265 (Cambridge: Harvard University Press), 9.9a.4.
2 *Historia Augusta,* "Septimius Severus," vol. 1, trans. David Magie, Loeb Classical Library 139 (Cambridge: Harvard University Press, 1921), 17.1. The measure was probably temporary. See Luis H. Feldman, *Jew and Gentile in the Ancient World* (Princeton: Princeton University Press, 1993), 386–87.

ing, as the army was retreating in the northern frontiers.[3] By the early fourth century, the Manichaeans were being ruthlessly persecuted.[4]

Our main informers regarding the persecution of Christians under the tetrarchy are Eusebius (d. 341), the church historian, who was living in Palestinian Caesarea and had visited Tyre during the persecutions, and Lactantius (c. 250–325), who had served as an official professor of rhetoric under Diocletian in Nicomedia. They both attributed the religious turmoil to the whims of emperors and other powerful state officials, whom they accused of superstition and wickedness. This idea has reasonably influenced modern scholarship to a significant degree, for the increasing religiosity of several third- and fourth-century emperors has been confirmed by many independent witnesses. Consequently, the initiative of some Nicomedians against their fellow Christians was regarded by Eusebius and Lactantius, and is still seen by some modern scholars, as instigated or even fabricated by Maximinus himself.[5]

Emperors and other state officials were indeed very powerful and could easily intervene in the lives of their subjects, especially in matters of public interest. Furthermore, they often took their religious duties and responsibilities extremely seriously and cared to demonstrate their piety and devotion to both the traditional deities and the cults of their own choice.[6] But even

3   The most fervent supporters of Mithraism were soldiers. See Franz Cumont, *The Mysteries of Mithra* (New York: Dover Publications, 1956), 199.
4   The edict against the Manichaeans was probably published in 302.
5   Eusebius, *Ecclesiastical History, Volume II*, 9.2; 9.4.1; Lactantius, *Of the Manner in Which the Persecutors Died*, in *The Ante-Nicene Fathers: Translations of the Writings of the Fathers down to AD 325*, vol. 7, ed. A. Cox Cleveland, Alexander Roberts, and James Donaldson (New York: Christian Literature Publishing, 1885; rpt. 1982), 36. Cf. W.H.C. Frend, *Martyrdom and Persecution in the Early Church* (Oxford: Basil Blackwell, 1965), 514.
6   Third-century coins give a good idea of the numerous deities venerated in Nicomedia. See Hale Güney, "Excavation Coins and Stray Finds, Ancient: Unpublished Coins of Nicomedia," *The Numismatic Chronicle* 176 Offprint (London: The Royal Numismatic Society, 2016), 415.

the accounts provided by our Christian informers often suggest that attributing the religious tensions exclusively or even mainly to the whims of emperors does not fully account for the train of events.

Maximinus, as Eusebius clearly demonstrates, did not need fake delegations to express his anti-Christian sentiments. Whenever he wished to persecute Christians, he did so without pretext. More significantly, in the Nicomedian incident he did not even comply with the request of the delegation. It is thus almost inconceivable to insist that the emperor had machinated an episode if only to turn the demand down.

Eusebius was obliged to interpret the emperor's reservations as resulting from the "compulsion of necessity," not his own desire.[7] By doing so, however, he had to admit that the Roman rulers were not as powerful as he would, otherwise, have us believe. In fact, he presents Maximinus as inconsistent in his religious policy, changing his orders almost constantly, according to circumstances, his relations to other members of the tetrarchy, and his war against the Christian Armenians.[8]

Maximinus, according to Eusebius, was gratified with the request of the Nicomedian embassy. In his reply, he made no secret of his own preferences and his dislike of Christian practices. But having perceived that the Christians of the city were numerous and that the request to expel them was not unanimous, he decided that it was best to reject it.[9] Since the population of Nicomedia at large was obviously divided in its religious sentiments, by stressing the lack of unanimity, he was clearly thinking of the city council.[10] This means that some of the council

---

7   Eusebius, *Ecclesiastical History, Volume II,* 9.9a.10: "ὑπὸ τῆς ἀνάγκης ἐκβεβιασμένος."

8   Ibid., 9.8.2.

9   Ibid., 9.9a.5.

10 Thus A.H.M. Jones, *Constantine and the Conversion of Europe* (New York: The Macmillan Co., 1949), 68; and *The Later Roman Empire,* vol. 1 (Oxford: Basil Blackwell, 1964), 73) who wrongly argues that the petition was accepted; Frend, *Martyrdom and Persecution in the Early Church,* 514.

members were either Christians (and had obviously abstained from the embassy) or pagans who did not agree with the idea of their expulsion. Christian influence was strong and had penetrated the upper sections of society.[11]

By banishing wealthy Christians, Maximinus understood that he would be depriving the city of their public services, which were badly needed at the time.[12] And this was something he definitely wished to avoid, if at all possible.[13] Wealthy citizens were chosen as members of the city councils, while they kept financing, on their own initiative, public spectacles.[14] The emperor, therefore, concluded that it was preferable to leave things as they stood and allow the citizens of Nicomedia to follow the worship of their choice.[15] On the other hand, he had no reservations about banishing Christians from other cities that had sent delegations with similar requests.[16]

Relating the same events, Lactantius also claimed that Maximinus, while residing in Nicomedia, secretly procured himself addresses from various cities (which he does not name) with anti-Christian requests. But according to his account, the emperor was asked to forbid the building of Christian churches within the city walls and to prevent the Christians from worshiping God, not to banish Christians altogether.[17] The difference is interesting, but not particularly important. Without churches to

---

11 See also below.
12 A.H.M. Jones, "The Cities of the Roman Empire," in *The Roman Economy: Studies in Ancient Economic and Administrative History,* ed. P.A. Brunt (Oxford: Basil Blackwell, 1974), 14.
13 Eusebius, *Ecclesiastical History, Volume II,* 9.9a.2.
14 Cf. what Dio Chrysostom had to say about the wealthy citizens of Nicomedia: Dio Chrysostom, *Discourses 37–60,* vol. 4, trans. H. Lamar Crosby, Loeb Classical Library 376 (Cambridge: Harvard University Press, 1946) 38.2, 41.
15 Eusebius, *Ecclesiastical History, Volume II,* 9.9a.8.
16 Ibid., 9.4.1–2.
17 Lactantius, *Of the Manner in Which the Persecutors Died,* 36.

perform their religious ceremonies, Christians could remain steadfast only by abandoning their cities.[18]

Despite their personal interpretations, the hard facts underlying the expositions of Eusebius and Lactantius suggest that Maximinus was mainly responding to the anti-Christian sentiments of his pagan subjects. The emperor certainly had his own religious preferences, but he was prudent enough to adapt his policy according to the prevailing conditions and the interests of his dominion, as he felt best.[19]

Only very few (and rather insignificant) details have survived regarding the spread of Christianity in Nicomedia. Since Bithynia is mentioned in one of the *New Testament* epistles, it is reasonable to assume that the message of Jesus reached its major city at an early stage.[20] But apart from a late and apocryphal tradition relating that the apostle Andrew had passed through it on his way to Achaia, we have to reach the late second century for the first reliable information.[21]

The existence of Christians in Nicomedia is testified for the first time around 170. Dionysius, bishop of Corinth, wrote to them, combating the Marcionites.[22] His letter was apparently not addressed to the local bishop, as was the custom, either because there was none, or because the bishop was supporting the wrong

---

18 The epigraphic evidence seems to be contradictory. A petition from Arycanda in Lycia does not explicitly request the expulsion of Christians, while from Colbasa in Pisidia it does. See *A New Eusebius: Documents Illustrative of the History of the Church to A.D. 337*, ed. James Stevenson (London: SPCK, 1968), 297; Stephen Mitchell, "Maximinus and the Christians in A.D. 312: A New Latin Inscription," *The Journal of Roman Studies* 78 (1988): 105–24, at 108.

19 See Ramsay MacMullen, "Religious Toleration Around the Year 313," *Journal of Early Christian Studies* 22, no. 4 (2014): 499–517.

20 1 Pet. 1:1. The epistle was probably written in the late first century.

21 The tradition regarding Andrew is given by Gregory of Tours. See *The Apocryphal New Testament: A Collection of Apocryphal Christian Literature in an English Translation*, ed. J.K. Elliott (Oxford: Clarendon Press, 1993), 274.

22 Eusebius, *Ecclesiastical History, Volume I: Books 1–5*, trans. Kirsopp Lake, Loeb Classical Library 153 (Cambridge: Harvard University Press, 1926), 4.23.4.

side. But he obviously regarded the Nicomedian Christians as significant, otherwise he would not have taken the trouble to correspond with a divided community so far away from his own. On the other hand, the existence of Marcionites in Nicomedia can be easily explained. Marcion himself was a native of neighboring Pontus, the son of the bishop of Sinope, according to tradition. Before his death around 160, he had established a flourishing and independent Christian Church, throughout the empire.[23]

Christian Nicomedia is lost again from our sight for more than a century. The reasonable assumption is that, despite the efforts of Dionysius, it did not join the developing Catholic movement and continued its own separate course (Marcionite or other) that has not left clear traces in the extant literature. Significantly, no local bishop or prominent Christian of Nicomedia is known by name before the persecution of the early fourth century.

Nicomedia was a significant Hellenistic city and became even more prominent in Roman times.[24] Writing in the early first century CE, Strabo records that it was founded by Nicomedes, who transferred there the inhabitants of neighboring Astacus that had been razed to the ground by Lysimachus. Interestingly, however, although he could surmise that its founder was Nicomedes, he had no idea which one of the four Bithynian kings so-named it had been.[25] For no monument celebrating the event was preserved in his days, as, for example, the tomb of Prusias in the center of Prusa.[26]

23 Adolf von Harnack, *Marcion: The Gospel of an Alien God* (Durham and North Carolina: The Labyrinth Press), 1990.
24 See A.H.M. Jones, *Cities of the Eastern Roman Provinces* (Oxford and New York: Oxford University Press, 1937), 148–74.
25 Strabo, *Geography, Volume V: Books 10–12*, trans. Horace Leonard Jones, Loeb Classical Library 211 (Cambridge: Harvard University Press, 1928), 12.4.2.
26 Dio Chrysostom, *Discourses*, 4: 47.17.

Nicomedia was actually founded in 264 BCE by Nicomedes I, who made it his capital with the intention of Hellenizing his kingdom (Nicomedes himself was given a Greek name by his father Zipoetes, the first ruler of Bithynia to have assumed a royal title).[27] The city may well have been inhabited by the population of neighboring Astacus, but Bithynian villagers would have to be added for the establishment of a prosperous community.

In the late second century BCE, many Bithynian villagers were severely pressured and even enslaved by tax-collectors. Since the kingdom had declared itself a Roman ally, the senate intervened on their behalf, ordering their liberation.[28] On the other hand, during the First Mithridatic War (89–85 BCE), although Bithynia was still affiliated with Rome, its territories were raided by the Roman army, while Nicomedia was sacked and plundered.[29] In 74 BCE, Nicomedia, along with the entire kingdom of Bithynia, was bequeathed to Rome by Nicomedes IV.[30] But a Roman military intervention under Pompeii was also necessary in 64 BCE[31] for the annexation of the area and its reorganization with Pontus into one province.[32]

27 Arrian, *Bithynika*, fragment 63. Arrian's *Bithynika*, which gave details regarding the mythology of the region and its history down to the last Nicomedes has not survived. But extracts are preserved in Photius's Myriobiblos. See *The Library of Photius*, trans. John Henry Freese (London and New York: Society for Promoting Christian Knowledge, 1920).

28 Diodorus Siculus, *The Library of History, Volume XII: Fragments of Books 33–40*, trans. Francis R. Walton, Loeb Classical Library 423 (Cambridge: Harvard University Press, 1967), 36.3. This took place during the reign of Nicomedes III.

29 Ibid., 38/39.8.

30 Appian, *Roman History, Volume II, Book 7, The Mithridatic Wars*, ed. and trans. Brian McGing, Loeb Classical Library 3 (Cambridge: Harvard University Press, 1912–1913), 2.10.

31 Appian, *Roman History, Volume III: The Civil Wars, Books 1–3.26*, trans. Horace White, Loeb Classical Library 4 (Cambridge: Harvard University Press, 1913), 5.14.139.

32 Appian, *Mithridatic Wars*, 17.

Following its annexation, much changed in the province.[33] Most of its fertile land seems to have been redistributed and its population rearranged. Roman military forces were often present in the area, while they normally had to pass through Nicomedia on their way to the eastern frontiers. A patrolling fleet was also stationed in the gulf. Maintaining the army had always been a strain to the local population, but also a contribution to its markets.[34] In the first century CE, the originally mixed population of Nicomedia (if that was the case), could be addressed as being "well-born" and "very Greek."[35] But as several inscriptions make clear, this was not a very precise description. Thracians were also living in the city, while most of the estate owners were probably Roman citizens.[36]

Nicomedia was certainly the largest city in the area, while its harbor served as the main anchorage for any army that had to move from the West to the East or to sail from the Aegean to the Black Sea. It was surrounded by gardens, fertile soil and forests, providing wood and timber of special use for shipbuilding.[37] It had mines and was privileged with local mints, providing coins

33 See Jesper Majbom Madsen, *Eager to Be Roman: Greek Response to Roman Rule in Pontus and Bithynia* (London and New York: Bloomsbury, 2009).

34 On the numismatic evidence see Hale Güney, "The Roman Monetary Economy in Bithynia During the Second Half of the First Century B.C.: The Case of Nicomedia," *Revue Belge de Philologie et Histoire* 93 (2015): 31–53.

35 Dio Chrysostom, *Discourses*, 4: 47.13: "εὐγενεῖς [...] καὶ σφόδρα ῞Ελληνας."

36 See Thomas Corsten, "The Rôle and Status of the Indigenous Population in Bithynia," in *Rome and the Black Sea Region: Domination, Romanisation, Resistance,* ed. Tønnes Bekker-Nielsen (Aarhus: Aarhus University Press, 2006), 85–92.

37 Important information is provided by Libanius in his *A Monody on Nicomedia Destroyed by an Earthquake*. For a translation of this text, see *Select Works of the Emperor Julian,* vol. 2, trans. John Duncombe (London: J. Nichols 1784; rpt. Sydney: Wentworth Press, 2016). Epigraphic evidence suggests that there was also a professional association of ship-owners. See Hale Güney, "The Economic Activities of Roman Nicomedia and Connectivity between the Propontic and the Pontic World," in *Interconnectivity in the Mediterranean and Pontic World during the Hellenistic and Roman Periods,* ed. Victor Cojocaru, Altay Coşkun, and Mădălina Dan (Cluj-Napoca: Mega Publishing House, 2014), 607–10.

that were circulating as far as the Balkans.[38] Of great significance was its marble trade, which reached various parts of the empire, including Rome.[39] Besides marble and timber, it exported farm produce in significant quantities. Its inhabitants were farmers, merchants, public servants, artisans, stonemasons, miners, shopkeepers, bakers, mariners and fishermen, some with nets, some with hooks.[40]

One of Nicomedia's main concerns was its rivalry with neighboring towns. Since it was privileged with the main harbor of the area, it collected significant revenues. Consequently, it constantly received petitions for urgent matters and could grant particular favors to individuals or even entire communities, if its council so wished. According to Dio Chrysostom, however, writing around 81 CE, Nicomedia was in enmity and competition with Nicaea, the second largest city of Bithynia. The two cities were not fighting for land or sea, neither for revenues. Such matters had been arranged, allowing both to benefit from the interchange of their products. Nicomedia and Nicaea had common ancestors, gods, customs, festivals as well as personal ties of blood and friendship. The sole reason for contending was primacy, a mere name that seemed serious enough to create constant and major problems.[41] After the Battle of Cyzicus, fought and won in 193 by Septimius Severus against his rival Pescennius Niger, the Nicomedians welcomed his army. This stance gave them a great advantage over the Nicaeans, who chose to

---

38 Pliny the Younger, *Letters, Volume II: Books 8–10. Panegyricus,* trans. Betty Radice, Loeb Classical Library 59 (Cambridge: Harvard University Press, 1969), 10.31. See Güney, "The Economic Activities of Roman Nicomedia," 612–19.

39 See Güney, "The Economic Activities of Roman Nicomedia," 610–12; Bryan Ward-Perkins, "The Marble Trade and its Organization: Evidence from Nicomedia," *Memoirs of the American Academy in Rome* 36 (1980): 325–38.

40 Pliny, *Letters,* 10.31, 74; Libanius, *Monody,* 9.

41 Dio Chrysostom, *Dicourses,* 4: 38. See Anthony R.R. Sheppard, "Dio Chrysostom: The Bithynian Years," *L'Antiquité Classique* 53 (1984): 163–66.

support the wrong side, and secured for the Nicomedians the symbolic primacy they so passionately desired.[42]

When Pliny became governor of Bithynia and Pontus in 111, large amounts of money had been already spent on two distinct projects for the construction of an aqueduct, both of which had failed. With Trajan's approval, a third one was planned of which several details are given. A new forum was also on its way, adjacent to an older one. Pliny felt that if this new forum was to be made functional, the ancient temple of the Great Mother (i.e., Cybele) had to be rebuilt or moved. Of much greater ambition was the governor's plan to dig a canal that would connect lake Sophon with a river, thereby making the transport of marble, farm produce, and wood and timber for building much easier and cheaper. The idea was given to him by a similar project begun under one of the Bithynian kings.[43] While Pliny was still governor a widespread fire destroyed many private houses as well as two public buildings, the Elder Citizens' Club and the Temple of Isis. He, therefore, asked the emperor's permission to organize a small fire brigade of 150 members. But Trajan was apprehensive because in former years such societies had been responsible for political disturbances. Pliny was only allowed to provide the necessary equipment that would make fire-fighting in the future easier.[44]

Bithynia was not often threatened by external aggression. But when in 256 or soon thereafter it was invaded by Goths (also called Scythians in our sources) many of its cities were destroyed, while Nicomedia was cruelly plundered.[45] According to

---

42 Herodian, *History of the Empire, Volume I: Books 1–4,* trans. C.R. Whittaker, Loeb Classical Library 454 (Cambridge: Harvard University Press, 1969), 3.2.9. See Tønnes Bekker-Nielsen, *Urban Life and Local Politics in Roman Bithynia: The Small World of Dion Chrysostomos* (Aarhus: Aarhus University Press, 2008), 148–50.

43 Pliny, *Letters,* 10.37–38, 41, 49, 61. A functioning aqueduct is mentioned by Libanius in his *Monody* 18. See Madsen, *Eager to Be Roman,* 11–58.

44 Pliny, *Letters,* 10.33–34.

45 *Historia Augusta,* "The Two Gallieni," vol. 3, trans. David Magie, Loeb Classical Library 263 (Cambridge, University Press, 1932), 4.8.

a late account, the invaders marched from Chalcedon against the great city that was celebrated for its affluence. Hearing of their approach, the citizens escaped, carrying along with them all the riches they could. Still, the barbarians were astonished at the vast quantity of valuables they found. At long last, having set fire to Nicomedia and Nicaea, the Goths loaded their spoil in wagons and ships, and began thinking of returning to their homes.[46]

Nicomedia was built on a hill with strong walls (sections of which still survive) and gates. Since it could not be easily stormed, its enemies had to rely mostly on surrenders or betrayals.[47] Not much is known regarding its buildings during the Hellenistic period. Temples of Zeus and Asclepius, Cybele and Isis are clearly mentioned in the sources.[48] But the existence of an early temple of Demeter and her daughter may also be taken for granted, since Arrian, who was born in Nicomedia and had been a priest of their cult, affirms that the city was dedicated to them.[49]

According to Cassius Dio, Augustus (r. 27 BCE–14 CE) permitted the non-Roman inhabitants of Nicomedia, those who were called Hellenes, to consecrate precincts to himself, in a manner that he would have never dared in Rome or Italy.[50] The

---

46 Zosimus, *New History* (London: Green and Chaplin, 1814), 1.35.

47 The walls are mentioned by Appian, *Mithridatic Wars,* 1 and Libanius, in his *Monody,* who also describes the hill. On the fortification of the city see Clive Foss, *Survey of Medieval Castles of Anatolia II: Nicomedia* (Ankara: The British Institute of Archaeology at Ankara, 1996), 29–43.

48 Appian, *Mithridatic Wars,* 1.8; Diodorus Siculus, *Library of History,* 32.21; Pausanias, *Description of Greece, Volume II: Books 3–5,* trans. W.H.S. Jones, Loeb Classical Library 188 (Cambridge, Harvard University Press, 1926), 3.3.8; Pliny, *Letters,* 10.33, 49.

49 Arrian's *Bithynika,* fragment 1, in *The Library of Photius,* trans. John Henry Freese (London and New York: Society for Promoting Christian Knowledge, 1920).

50 Cassius Dio, *Roman History,* vol. 6, trans. Earnest Cary and Herbert Baldwin Foster, Loeb Classical Library 175–76 (Cambridge: Harvard University Press, 1914–1927), 51.20.7. See, however, Jesper Majbom Madsen, "Who Introduced the Imperial Cult in Asia and Bithynia? The Koinon's Role in the

Nicomedians actually obtained from the senate the privilege of celebrating games and of erecting a second imperial temple, dedicated to Commodus (r. 177–192).[51] A third imperial temple is also attested.[52] During the second or early third century, the so-called Antonine baths were built. It was said that they were of a very great size.[53] A circus, a theatre and a palace are also mentioned.[54]

Statues of the emperors could be seen in several sites of Nicomedia.[55] Several emperors are recorded as visiting Nicomedia. Among them was most likely Hadrian (r. 117–138) in 123 (and perhaps some years earlier as well). Since the city had been recently damaged by an earthquake (in 120), the emperor provided generous funds for its rebuilding.[56] More precise information is given regarding Caracalla (r. 198–217), who spent there the winter of 214–215. His entourage included Cassius Dio, who related his conduct with disgust. The emperor, according to the historian, "engaged in gratifying his curiosity in various ways." He drove chariots, slayed wild beasts, fought as a gladiator. While in Nicomedia, Caracalla celebrated the Saturnalia with his friends, conversing with them on cultural and religious matters.[57]

Early Worship of Augustus," in *Kaiserkult in den Provinzen des Römischen Reiches*, ed. Anne Kolb and Marco Vitale (Berlin and Boston: De Gruyter, 2016), 21–35.

51 Cassius Dio, *Roman History*, 73.12.2.

52 See Bekker-Nielsen, *Urban Life and Local Politics in Roman Bithynia*, 153.

53 Procopius, *On Buildings*, trans. H.B. Dewing and Glanville Downey, Loeb Classical Library 343 (Cambridge: Harvard University Press, 1940), 5.3.7. See also below.

54 Cassius Dio, *Roman History*, vol. 9, 78.17; Pliny, *Letters*, 10.31. Of the late fourth century palace, Libanius stated in his *Monody* 10 that it was "glittering" (ἐπαστράπτον) over the bay.

55 Pliny, *Letters*, 10.74 mentions statues of Trajan.

56 See Anthony R. Birley, *Hadrian: The Restless Emperor* (Abingdon: Routledge, 1997), 157.

57 Cassius Dio, *Roman History*, 9: 78.17.4; 79.8.4, trans. Cary and Foster (1929): ἐφιλοπραγμόνει.

Elagabalus (r. 218–222) also spent the winter of 218–219 in the city. It was in Nicomedia that he began his imperial career by practicing ecstatic rites and going

through the ridiculous motions of the priestly office belonging to his local god (Elagabal) in which he was trained. He wore the most expensive types of clothes, woven of purple and gold, and adorned himself with necklaces and bangles. On his head he wore a crown in the shape of tiara glittering with gold and precious stones. The effect was something between the sacred garb of the Phoenicians and the luxurious apparel of the Medes.[58]

Yet the emperor did not wear the appropriate triumphal dress on the Day of the Vows, as was expected by someone, like himself, holding the consulship (unfortunately, we are not told what impression these practices gave to the Nicomedians, but they were certainly very unattractive to most of the traditional Roman aristocracy).[59] Other emperors also wintered in Nicomedia whenever they led their campaigns against the Persians. Diocletian was actually proclaimed emperor by the army very near the city with "heaven-sent unanimity" in 284, having been predisposed himself for the post by the prophecy of a Druidess.[60] He chose Nicomedia as his imperial residence, contributing greatly to its promotion. Important information is given by Lactantius, who was an eye

---

58 Herodian, *History of the Empire, Volume II: Books 5–8*, trans. C.R. Whittaker, Loeb Classical Library 455 (Cambridge: Harvard University Press, 1970), 5.5.3–4: "τήν τε ἱερωσύνην τοῦ ἐπιχωρίου θεοῦ, ᾗ ἐντέθραπτο, περιεργότερον ἐξωρχεῖτο, σχήμασί τε ἐσθῆτος πολυτελεστάτοις χρώμενος, διαχρύσοις τε πόρφυρας ὑφάσμασι περιδεραίοις τε καὶ ψελίοις κοσμούμενος, ἐς εἶδος δὲ τιάρας στεφάνην ἐπικείμενος χρυσῷ καὶ λίθοις ποικίλην τιμίοις. ἤν τε αὐτῷ τὸ σχῆμα μεταξὺ Φοινίσσης ἱερᾶς στολῆς καὶ χλιδῆς Μηδικῆς." Cf. Historia Augusta, "Antoninus Elagabalus," vol. 1, 5.1.
59 Cassius Dio, *Roman History*, 9: 80.8.3.
60 *Historia Augusta*, "Carus," vol. 3, 13–14: "omnes divino consensus."

witness (though an extremely hostile one). The emperor, he asserts, had

> a certain endless passion for building, and on that account,
> endless exactions from the provinces for furnishing wages to
> laborers and artificers, and supplying carriages and whatever
> else was requisite to the works which he projected. Here pub-
> lic halls, there a circus, here a mint, and there a workhouse
> for making implements of war; in one place a habitation for
> his empress, and in another for his daughter. Presently, great
> part of the city was quitted, and all men removed with their
> wives and children, as from a town taken by enemies; and
> when those buildings were completed, to the destruction of
> whole provinces, he said, "They are not right, let them be
> done on another plan." Then they were to be pulled down,
> or altered, to undergo perhaps a future demolition. By such
> folly was he continually endeavoring to equal Nicomedia
> with the city Rome in magnificence.[61]

Rebuilding a city on new plans had always been a straining and,
in many ways, distressing project, for practical but also symbolic
reasons. The Nicomedian council had been at least once praised
for having voluntarily passed a resolution to transfer, for such a
purpose, the city tombs.[62] Upon another occasion, while serving as governor of Bithynia and Pontus, Pliny obtained Trajan's
permission to demolish the ancient temple of Cybele and move

---

61 Lactantius, *Of the Manner in Which the Persecutors Died, 7*: "Huc accedebat
    infinita quaedam cupiditas aedificandi, non minor provinciarum exactio
    in exhibendis operariis et artificibus et plaustris, omnia quaecumque sint
    fabricandis operibus necessaria. Hic basilicae, hic circus, hic moneta, hic
    armorum fabrica, hic uxori domus, hic filiae. Repente magna pars civitatis
    exciditur. Migrabant omnes cum coniugibus ac liberis quasi urbe ab hosti-
    bus capta. Et cum perfecta haec fuerant cum interitu provinciarum, 'non
    recte facta sunt,' aiebat, 'alio modo fiant.' Rursus dirui ac mutari necesse erat
    iterum fortasse casura. Ita semper dementabat Nicomediam studens urbi
    Romae coaequare."

62 Dio Chrysostom, *Discourses, 4*: 47.16.

it to a new site without the loss of its sanctity.[63] It is, therefore, hardly surprising that a large-scale renovation would have also caused many serious complains.

One of the most striking features of late third-century urban development in Nicomedia is the location and size of the Christian church. While Diocletian's project had been more or less executed it was standing prominently on rising ground, within view of the newly renovated palace.[64] It had appropriate utensils and furniture and, as was normal, a repository for the Holy Scripture. Interestingly, the authorities were under the impression that an image of the Divinity would be also stored somewhere within its premises. The church was clearly located within a lively area of the city, for it was surrounded by large buildings.[65] Members of Diocletian's and Galerius's families, as well as Christians serving in the court or the imperial administration would have frequently attended its services.[66]

No information has been preserved regarding the origins of the Nicomedian church building that stood so close to the imperial palace. But an important clue given by Eusebius may serve as a basis for a reasonable hypothesis. For he asserts that while the Christians had been enjoying a long period of peace (lasting for about forty years) before the persecution of his own time, the existing places of prayer were no longer satisfactory. New churches of spacious dimensions were, therefore, being erected from the foundations throughout all the cities.[67] Indeed, in making this suggestion, Eusebius gives the impression that

---

63 Pliny, *Letters,* 10.49.

64 Regarding Diocletian's palace see Socrates, *Ecclesiastical History,* 1.6.

65 Lactantius, *Of the Manner in Which the Persecutors Died,* 12.

66 Ibid., 11, 15; Eusebius, *Ecclesiastical History, Volume II,* 8.1.3.

67 Eusebius, *Ecclesiastical History, Volume II,* 8.1.5. The existence of large church buildings in Pontus is implied from an even earlier period in Gregory Thaumaturgus's *Canonical Epistle.* But the canon 11 may be a later addition.

he had Nicomedia in mind.[68] In this case, its church would have been constructed sometime between 260 and 303.[69]

Diocletian transformed the city in a most impressive way. Before the end of 304, he was able to dedicate, in public, his new circus, having returned to Nicomedia for this purpose after a long circuit along the banks of the Danube.[70] About two generations later, and while some further work was also done by his successors (who were otherwise mostly interested in the development of Constantinople), Nicomedia could be praised by Libanius in a most generous manner:

In beauty also it yielded to these [the cities that were even larger], and was equaled, not excelled, by some others. For stretching forth its promontories with its arms it embraced the sea. It then ascended the hill by four colonnades extending the whole length. Its public buildings were splendid, its private contiguous, rising from the lowest parts to the citadel, like the branches of a cypress, one house above another, watered by rivulets and surrounded by gardens. Its council-chambers, its schools of oratory, the multitude of its temples, the magnificence of its baths, and the commodiousness of its harbor I have seen, but cannot describe.

And besides, Libanius mentions statues, perfect in beauty in every part of the city, winding walks, porticos, fountains, aqueducts, courts of judicature and libraries. As for the baths, he

---

68 Eusebius, *Ecclesiastical History, Volume II,* 8.1.1–4, mentions the imperial palaces and the rulers who allowed the members of their households, wives, children and servants, to openly practice the rituals, clearly implying Diocletian. He also adds two important imperial servants by name, Dorotheus and Gorgonius, who were Christians, both of whom were serving Diocletian in Nicomedia.

69 The Christians of Antioch also possessed an important church building during the same period, requesting the emperor's intervention regarding its lawful ownership. See Eusebius, *Ecclesiastical History, Volume II,* 7.30.19.

70 Lactantius, *Of the Manner in Which the Persecutors Died,* 17.

singles out those named after Antoninus (r. 138–161), that were equal in value to the whole city.[71]

Having reigned successfully for more than nineteen years, Diocletian started persecuting the Christians, successively issuing four edicts on the matter, each one more severe than the previous.[72] Regarding the reasons for this radical change in imperial religious policy, Eusebius and Lactantius, who was living at the time in Nicomedia, provide intriguing pieces of information. Interestingly, neither of them had anything to say about the similar treatment of the Manichaeans, with which the policy of religious persecutions was inaugurated – probably because they both felt that it was well in order.[73]

Diocletian, although religious and scrupulous in his duties, had remained tolerant with Christianity. His wife and daughter were either converts or sympathizers, while his court and army included many Christians who professed their religion openly.[74] His first negative encounter with some Christians occurred, as we are told, in 299, while he was joined in Syria by his Caesar Galerius, who had just returned from a victorious encounter with the Persians.[75] Lactantius relates the following story:

Diocletian, as being of a timorous disposition, was a searcher into futurity, and during his abode in the East he began to slay

---

71 Libanius, *Monody*, 17. This description was given immediately after the disastrous earthquake of 358. See Edward Watts, "The Historical Context: The Rhetoric of Suffering in Libanius' Monodies, Letters and Autobiography," in *Libanius: A Critical Introduction*, ed. Lieve van Hoof (Cambridge: Cambridge University Press), 2014, 39–58; Peter Van Nuffelen, "Earthquakes in A.D. 363–368 and the Date of Libanius, *Oratio* 18," *The Classical Quarterly New Series* 56, no. 2 (2006): 657–61.

72 See G.E.M. de Ste. Croix, "Aspects of the 'Great Persecution,'" in *Christian Persecution, Martyrdom, and Orthodoxy*, ed. Michael Whitby and Joseph Street (Oxford and New York: Oxford University Press 2006), 35–78.

73 Cf. Eusebius, *Ecclesiastical History, Volume II*, 7.31.

74 Lactantius, *Of the Manner in Which the Persecutors Died*, 11, 15; Eusebius, *Ecclesiastical History, Volume II*, 8.1.3.

75 See Timothy D. Barnes, *Constantine and Eusebius* (Cambridge: Harvard University Press, 1981), 18.

victims, that from their livers he might obtain a prognostic of events; and while he sacrificed, some attendants of his, who were Christians, stood by, and they put the immortal sign on their foreheads. At this the demons were chased away, and the holy rites interrupted. The soothsayers trembled, unable to investigate the wonted marks on the entrails of the victims. They frequently repeated the sacrifices, as if the former had been unpropitious; but the victims, slain from time to time, afforded no tokens for divination. At length Tages, the chief of the soothsayers, either from guess or from his own observation, said, "There are profane persons here, who obstruct the rites." Then Diocletian, in furious passion, ordered not only all who were assisting at the holy ceremonies, but also all who resided within the palace, to sacrifice, and, in case of their refusal, to be scourged. And further, by letters to the commanding officers, he enjoined that all soldiers should be forced to the like impiety, under pain of being dismissed the service.[76]

The emperor was probably satisfied with the arrangement and did not wish to take any further action.

Galerius's household, as we are told again by Lactantius, also included many Christians. While his mother, who was a votary of the gods of the mountains, made sacrifices almost every

---

76 Lactantius, *Of the Manner in Which the Persecutors Died,* 10: "Cum ageret in partibus Orientis, ut erat pro timore scrutator rerum futurarum, immolabat pecudes et in iecoribus earum ventura quaerebat. Tum quidem ministrorum scientes dominum cum adsisterent immolanti, imposuerunt frontibus suis inmortale signum; quo facto fugatis daemonibus sacra turbata sunt. Trepidabant aruspices nec solitas in extis notas videbant et, quasi non litassent, saepius immolabant. Verum identidem mactatae hostiae nihil ostendebant, donec magister ille aruspicum Tagis seu suspicione seu visu ait idcirco non respondere sacra, quod rebus divinis profani homines interessent. Tunc ira furens sacrificare non eos tantum qui sacris ministrabant, sed universos qui erant in palatio iussit et in eos, si detrectassent, verberibus animadverti, datisque ad praepositos litteris, etiam milites cogi ad nefanda sacrificia praecepit, ut qui non paruissent, militia solverentur."

day, feasting with her servants on the meat offered to idols, the Christian members of her family would not partake of the entertainments, fasting and praying.[77] On this account, by "woman-like" complaints, she instigated her son, who was no less superstitious. And Galerius, in his turn, kept pressing Diocletian for the whole winter.

Diocletian, who could not easily make up his mind in a matter that would raise disturbances throughout the empire, asked his friends, a few civil magistrates and a few military commanders, for counsel. Although he was encouraged also by them to persecute Christians, he felt that the consent of the gods was also required and so dispatched, accordingly, a soothsayer to inquire of Apollo at Miletus. At long last, he agreed that persecution was necessary, demanding, however, moderation in the treatment of Christians and commanding the business to be carried through without bloodshed.[78]

Eusebius approached the topic in an altogether different manner. He introduces the Diocletianic persecution with a brief but powerful presentation of the great progress that had been already achieved. Many Christians, he argues, were honored by the emperors and entrusted even with the government of provinces (although none such governor is known). They had even filled the imperial palaces, winning over wives, children and servants of emperors. Consequently, great multitudes were gathering in every city, holding regularly and openly their services in churches of spacious dimensions. But then, as a result of their great freedom, Christians started railing against one another, warring upon themselves, as occasion offered, "with weapons and spears formed of words." Church rulers attacked church rulers and laity formed factions against laity, "while unspeakable hypocrisy and pretense pursued their evil course to

---

77 We can only imagine the tension between servants feasting almost continually and servants fasting and abstaining from meat because the only available food had been sacrificed to pagan gods.

78 Lactantius, *Of the Manner in Which the Persecutors Died,* 11.

the furthest end." Behaving in such a way, they provoked the persecution themselves as a divine judgement.[79]

This lamentation has been normally read either as a theological declaration or a rhetorical exaggeration and has never been seriously examined by modern scholars as historical fact. After all, Eusebius adds that he thought it best to pass over the dissensions and the unnatural conduct between Christians and deal instead only with the persecution that followed.[80] And yet, he gives some clues regarding the dimensions of the problem that should not be totally neglected.

Diocletian and Galerius, while both living in Nicomedia, began persecuting Christians in February 303. Their first act was directed against the church building of the city. According to their orders, the prefect, along with chief commanders, tribunes and officers of the treasury, when the day dawned and while it was yet hardly light, forced open the church gates and searched everywhere for an image of the Divinity (*simulacrum dei*). Soon after, they committed to the flames the books of the Holy Scriptures that were kept inside, while abandoning to pillage the utensils and furniture. Galerius was of the opinion to set the whole building on fire, but Diocletian dreaded that once kindled, so great a fire could spread over some part of the city, for the church was surrounded by many large buildings. So, they gave orders to the Pretorian Guards to come in battle array, with axes and other iron instruments, and level the lofty edifice to the ground.[81]

On the next day, the emperors published their first edict against Christians. All churches were to be destroyed, all copies of the Scripture surrendered and burned and all public meet-

79 Eusebius, *Ecclesiastical History, Volume II*, 8.1.1–7: "δόρασιν τοῖς διὰ λόγων ἀρχόντων τε ἄρχουσι προσρηγνύντων καὶ λαῶν ἐπὶ λαοὺς καταστασιαζόντων τῆς τε ὑποκρίσεως ἀφάτου καὶ τῆς εἰρωνείας ἐπὶ πλεῖστον ὅσον κακίας προϊούσης."

80 Ibid., 8.1.2.

81 Lactantius, *Of the Manner in Which the Persecutors Died*, 12; cf. *The Divine Institutes*, 5.2.1; Eusebius, *Ecclesiastical History*, 8.1.9; 8.2.1; 8.2.4.

ings banned. Those who held high positions would lose all civic rights, while those who were employed in the imperial service, would be deprived of their liberty.[82] As soon as the edict was published in Nicomedia, a certain person, "moved by zeal towards God and carried away by his burning faith, seized and tore it to pieces, when posted up in an open and public place, as an unholy and profane thing." And this was done while Diocletian and Galerius were present in the city. The incident, Eusebius explains, besides leading to the execution of the daring Christian, produced outstanding martyrs in the city among the imperial servants, of which he actually names three: Dorotheus, Gorgonius, and Peter.[83]

Interestingly, although both Eusebius and Lactantius mention the first Nicomedian martyrdom, neither of them felt it proper to provide the martyr's name, although, as was said, he was "by no means obscure, but most highly honored as the world counts pre-eminence."[84] Their reluctance can be easily explained, since voluntary martyrdom was condemned by most church leaders of the period, while this particular instance had led to further condemnations that were hardly necessary.[85]

Soon after, a fire broke out in the palace, attributed, by rumors, to the Christians. Eusebius could not explain its cause and Lactantius claimed that it was ordered by Galerius as a provocation. Years later, Emperor Constantine (r. 306–337), who had been also an eye witness, thought that it came as divine justice against Diocletian. Inflamed with anger, Diocletian command-

---

82 Lactantius, *Of the Manner in Which the Persecutors Died,* 13; Eusebius, *Ecclesiastical History, Volume II,* 8.2.4.

83 Eusebius, *Ecclesiastical History, Volume II,* 8.5–6.5; "ζήλῳ τῷ κατὰ θεὸν ὑποκινηθεὶς διαπύρῳ τε ἐφορμήσας τῇ πίστει, ἐν προφανεῖ καὶ δημοσίῳ κειμένην ὡς ἀνοσίαν καὶ ἀσεβεστάτην ἀνελὼν σπαράττει." Cf. Lactantius, *Of the Manner in Which the Persecutors Died,* 13.

84 Eusebius, *Ecclesiastical History, Volume II,* 8.5: "οὐκ ἀσήμων τις, ἀλλὰ καὶ ἄγαν κατὰ τὰς ἐν τῷ βίῳ νενομισμένας ὑπεροχὰς ἐνδοξοτάτων."

85 See G.E.M. de Ste. Croix, "Voluntary Martyrdom in the Early Church," in *Christian Persecution, Martyrdom, and Orthodoxy,* ed. Whitby and Street, 153–200.

ed that all his domestics should be tortured to force a confession of the plot, but to no avail. Two weeks later, a second fire was detected, although this time it was easily extinguished. The destruction of the newly constructed palace led to a further and much more severe persecution.[86]

During those events, the bishop of Nicomedia Anthimus was beheaded. He is the first and only local bishop known by name until the end of the persecution. But strangely, Lactantius, who must have been present at the execution, did not regard the incident as worthy of mention, while Eusebius, our sole informer, had no details to add. He mentions neither the cause, nor the circumstances of the martyrdom. And contrary to his common practice, he does not praise the bishop as virtuous, learned or venerable. He simply records the fact of the beheading, without any comment.[87]

Eusebius adds that many Christians lost their lives in Nicomedia, others by the sword, others by fire, others by drowning. According to the information he was able to collect, "men and women leaped upon the pyre with a divine and unspeakable eagerness."[88] The accounts provided by Eusebius and Lactantius make it clear that neither of them was in cordial relations with at least the leading members of the Nicomedian Christian community. And if such was the case, we may only imagine the feelings of the local, pagan population, not to mention the authorities, who saw the imperial edict torn up in public and the

---

86 Eusebius, *Ecclesiastical History, Volume II*, 8.6.6; Lactantius, *Of the Manner in Which the Persecutors Died*, 14; Constantine, *Oration to the Assembly of the Saints*, 25.2.

87 Eusebius, *Ecclesiastical History, Volume II*, 8.6.6, 8.13.1. Cf. his comments on the martyrdoms of bishop Silvanus of Emesa, who was "exceedingly advanced in age" and had "exercised his ministry for forty years," of bishop Peter of Alexandria, who was "a truly divine example of a bishop on account of his virtuous life and his earnest study of the holy Scriptures" and of presbyter Lucian, who was brought to Nicomedia, "a most excellent man in every respect." Eusebius, *Ecclesiastical History, Volume II*, 9.6.1–3.

88 Ibid., 8.6.6: "προθυμίᾳ θείᾳ τινὶ καὶ ἀρρήτῳ ἄνδρας ἅμα γυναιξὶν ἐπὶ τὴν πυρὰν καθαλέσθαι."

palace twice in flames. For more than ten years, there is no further mention of a bishop in the city, although much is known about bishops in most other important sees.

Maximinus was proclaimed Caesar in 305.[89] The ceremony took place three miles outside Nicomedia, at a site where a pillar with a statue of Jupiter was placed. In the presence of Galerius, Diocletian took off his purple robe and put it on him, while descending from the tribunal and passing through the city in a chariot. Constantine, who had been educated in Nicomedia and had spent many years in the court, was also present. But since he had been passed over in the succession, he found a pretext to leave the city only to return victorious in 324.[90]

At the beginning of his career, Maximinus was not very active in persecuting the Christians.[91] But a year later, in 306, he (probably in agreement with Galerius) issued a new edict against them that was vigorously enforced in parts at least of his domain.[92] Eusebius had much to say about martyrdoms in Palestine, but neither he nor Lactantius record anything in particular regarding Nicomedia.[93]

In 309, Maximinus, having been proclaimed "son of Augustus" by Galerius, turned his mind to religious matters once more, ordering the restoration of the old pagan temples that had been neglected for a long time and the erection of new ones in every city.[94] Two years later, in 311, a new edict was unexpect-

---

89 See Christopher S. Mackay, "Lactantius and the Succession to Diocletian," *Classical Philology* 94 (1999): 198–209.

90 Photius, *The Library*, 1.62; Lactantius, *Of the Manner in Which the Persecutors Died*, 19.

91 Eusebius, *Ecclesiastical History, Volume II*, 9.9a.2. See G.S.R. Thomas, "Maximin Daia's Policy and the Edicts of Toleration," *L'Antiquité Classique* 37, no. 1 (1968): 172–85; Mitchell, "Maximinus and the Christians in A.D. 312."

92 See Ste. Croix, "Aspects of the 'Great Persecution'," 61–62.

93 Cf. Eusebius, *Martyrs of Palestine*, 4.8.

94 Eusebius, *Ecclesiastical History, Volume II*, 8.14.9; *Martyrs of Palestine*, 9.2; Lactantius, *Of the Manner in Which the Persecutors Died*, 32, 36. See R.M. Grant, "The Religion of Maximin Daia," in *Christianity, Judaism and other Greco-Roman cults*, ed. Jacob Neusner (Leiden: Brill, 1975), 143–66; Oliver

edly issued in Nicomedia under the names of Galerius, Licinius and Constantine ordering the termination of the persecutions. The edict was almost certainly promulgated under the name of Maximinus as well, but neither Eusebius nor Lactantius felt it was fit to report it. In any case, Maximinus was obliged to comply.[95] To do so, he commanded his subordinates to put the relevant orders of toleration into writing.[96] When Galerius died only a few days later, Nicomedia fell under his control. It was at this point that he received embassies from the city to expel the Christians.[97]

Although he did not agree to act against the Christians of Nicomedia, Maximinus soon resumed his policy of reviving paganism. In 312, having returned to Nicomedia from Syria and Egypt, he appointed in every province superintendent priests that should appear in white. Of those priests, it was said that they prevented the Christians from erecting churches or worshiping their God, either publicly or in private.[98] Several bishops were executed, while a renowned presbyter of Antioch called Lucian was brought to Nicomedia and led to martyrdom in Maximinus's presence.[99] According to Eusebius, Maximinus was convinced that due to his piety neither famine, nor pestilence, nor even war had taken place in his time.[100]

Nicholson, "The 'Pagan Churches' of Maximinus Daia and Julian the Apostate," *The Journal of Ecclesiastical History* 45, no. 1 (1994): 1–10.

95 Lactantius, *Of the Manner in Which the Persecutors Died,* 34; Eusebius, *Ecclesiastical History,* 8.17. See John R. Knipfing, "The Edict of Galerius (311 A.D.) Re-considered," *Revue Belge de Philologie et d' Histoire* 1, no. 4 (1922): 693–705 and "Religious Tolerance During the Early Part of the Reign of Constantine the Great (306–313)," *The Catholic Historical Review* 4, no. 4 (1925): 483–503; Paul Keresztes, "From the Great Persecution to the Peace of Galerius," *Vigiliae Christianae* 37 (1983): 379–99.

96 Eusebius, *Ecclesiastical History, Volume II,* 9.1.1–7.

97 Ibid., 9.9a.4. See above.

98 See note 94 above.

99 Eusebius, *Ecclesiastical History, Volume II,* 8.13.2–7; 9.6.1–3. The report seems to be rather chronologically confused.

100 Ibid., 9.8.3.

While Maximinus was persecuting the Christians once more, Constantine and Licinius met in Milan and agreed, among other things, upon a common policy of religious toleration.[101] Maximinus, vowing that he was determined to annihilate all Christians, was soon defeated by Licinius.[102] In 313, Licinius entered Nicomedia putting an end to the persecution of Christians by promulgating an order that has been known ever since as the "edict of Milan."[103] Finding himself in a desperate situation, Maximinus issued his own edict of toleration (for purely personal reasons, as may be presumed) and died soon after.

A few years later, Licinius was at war with Constantine. Having lost the Balkans in 317 he moved to Nicomedia. It was probably at that time that Eusebius (not the historian) was translated as bishop from Berytus to the see of Nicomedia and seems to have exercised more general power, being influential at the court. When Constantine became sole emperor, Eusebius may have negotiated over the defeated Licinius's surrender. Constantine resided in Diocletian's palace in Nicomedia, and Eusebius became even more prominent.[104]

Nicomedia was pivotal in the history of Christianity and, more generally, the religious history of the period. By the early fourth century, large sections of its population, including members of the upper classes, the imperial administration, and the imperial families had joined the new religion. Being a significant minority, they made their presence clearly felt by frequenting their church, which stood upon rising ground in a populous area and in full view of the palace.

The Nicomedian Christians, or at least many among them, seem to have been particularly zealous in their beliefs and man-

101 Lactantius, *On the Manner in Which the Persecutors Died,* 44. Cf. Eusebius, *Ecclesiastical History, Volume II,* 9.9.12.

102 Lactantius, *Of the Manner in Which the Persecutors Died,* 46.

103 Ibid., 48; Eusebius, *Ecclesiastical History, Volume II,* 10.5.2–14.

104 Socrates, *Ecclesiastical History, Volume I,* 1.6.5. See Raymond Van Dam, *The Roman Revolution of Constantine* (Cambridge: Cambridge University Press, 2007), 273–74.

ners. They were probably seen by other contemporary Christians as fanatic and prone to the prohibited voluntary martyrdom. Eusebius and Lactantius had precious little to record regarding their history and activities (including their martyrdoms), presumably because they disapproved of their stance and regarded them as having provoked, to a certain degree, the persecution of their own time. Their pagan neighbors, on the other hand, may have regarded them as responsible for calamities, such as earthquakes, invasions by foreign tribes that had befallen the city or conflagrations. Some among them felt that the Christians were offending the traditional gods and that it was, therefore, undesirable to go along living with them.

The idea that disasters of various kinds could be due to divine wrath because of human misconduct was very common among both pagans and Christians. According to Dio Chrysostom, for example, "Gods punish justly for grievous sins with pestilence or earthquakes."[105] Eusebius, on the other hand, claimed that Maximinus's impiety had finally caused his defeat in his war against the Armenians, as well as famine and pestilence in his domain, while the persecution came upon Christians as "divine judgement with a sparing hand," because they had sinned against each other.[106] Who was guilty and who had suffered for tolerating the sinners depended upon each group's religious point of view.

Diocletian, urged by Galerius, made up his mind to persecute the Christians while living in Nicomedia. Although he wished at first to avoid bloodshed, he soon gave his consent for a very violent repression of Christianity in the city and all over the empire. After several years, having been convinced that the persecution had done no good to the empire or personally to himself, it was in Nicomedia that Galerius published his edict

---

105 Dio Chrysostom, *Discourses*, 4: 38.20: "ἐπειδὰν μὲν οὖν λοιμὸς ἢ σεισμὸς γένηται, τοῖς θεοῖς ἐγκαλοῦμεν, ὡς κακῶν παρέχουσιν τοῖς ἀνθρώποις αἰτίας."

106 Eusebius, *Ecclesiastical History, Volume II*, 8.1.7; 9.8: "θεία κρίσις, οἵα φίλον αὐτῇ."

of toleration. And it was in Nicomedia again that Maximinus made new attempts to repress Christianity. Finally, the permanent termination of the persecution was announced by the victorious Licinius in Nicomedia.

Under the reign of two emperors that were friendly to Christianity in East and West, Licinius and Constantine, Nicomedia received its first bishop whose records have survived. Eusebius (not the historian), a fervent supporter of Arius and his doctrines, became one of the most energetic and influential leaders of a faith that was emerging victorious after grievous ordeals. As the church of the city had been demolished at the beginning of the Diocletianic persecution, the Christians were allowed to build a new one in its place, of great magnificence and of boundless height. Its construction has been ascribed to Constantine, but work would have begun in the days of Licinius, sometime between 313 and 324.[107]

By choosing to convene the first ecumenical council in Nicaea and not Nicomedia, as would have been normally expected, and by supporting the anti-Arian side, Constantine revived, at a symbolic but very profound level, the old antagonism between the two cities. The whole empire was divided between the Nicaean and the anti-Nicaean doctrine (with Eusebius of Nicomedia as its main advocate). But then again, by being baptized in Nicomedia by Eusebius himself, who had regained his favor, Constantine reversed the balance. The bishop of Nicomedia was to leave a lasting legacy, not least for ordaining Ulfila and contributing to the conversion of the Goths to Arianism.[108]

---

107 Ibid., 8.1.5; 10.2.1. Interestingly, according to Eusebius the churches that were rebuilt before the persecution of his own time had wider foundations than the previous, while those that were rebuilt after the end of the persecution were much higher. In this context, he does not mention the church of Nicomedia explicitly. But see Eusebius, *Life of Constantine*, 3.50.

108 Ulfila was of Cappadocian Greek origin, but his family had been enslaved during the Gothic invasions. He was probably born in captivity. See E.A. Thompson, *The Visigoths in the Time of Ulfila* (Oxford: Clarendon Press, 1966); Peter J. Heather and John Matthews, *The Goths in the Fourth Century* (Liverpool: Liverpool University Press, 1991), 124–44.

Religious conflict in the early fourth century, and probably earlier, was primarily between paganism and Christianity. At the same time, however, it was also between different versions of Christianity and different varieties of paganism. Although the topic was deliberately avoided by our main informers, along with its history, Christian Nicomedia was influenced by Marcionism, zealots prone to voluntary martyrdom, and Arianism. Paganism, on the other hand, was experimenting with radically new ways of ritual and organization, as the religious policy of Maximinus makes clear. The expulsion of Christians from Nicomedia and other cities was considered by many as necessary for the revival of a profound piety.

Nicomedia had been severely damaged by raiders and earthquakes on several occasions, but had always managed to recover through its vitality and imperial aid. It was only surpassed in population by Rome, Alexandria, Antioch and, gradually, Constantinople. Because of its buildings and public edifices, it was seen by many as of supreme beauty. After the earthquake of 358, however, it never again obtained its former glory. Most of the houses were carried down the slopes of the hills falling one upon another, while the great part of the temples and private houses that might have been saved were consumed by a fire that kept burning for five days. Even the great church built by Constantine was destroyed, while Cecropius, the bishop of the city, was killed along with his fellow bishop of Bosporus who happened to be present. Of the inhabitants, most among those who survived fled. What was left of the city's former glory was destroyed five years later by a new earthquake, and so was a good part of Nicaea.[109] But the Roman Empire was already largely Christian and was proceeding along altogether new religious paths.

---

109 Libanius, *Monody*; Ammianus Marcellinus, *History. Volume I: Books 14–19,* trans. J.C. Rolfe, Loeb Classical Library 300 (Cambridge: Harvard University Press, 1950), 17.7.1; Ammianus Marcellinus, *Volume II: Books 20–26,* trans. J.C. Rolfe, Loeb Classical Library 315 (Cambridge: Harvard University Press, 1940), 22.13.5; Sozomen, *Ecclesiastical History, in Nicene and Post-Nicene Fa-*

Bibliography

Primary

Appian. *Roman History, Volume II. Book 7, The Mithridatic Wars.* Edited and translated by Brian McGing. Loeb Classical Library 3. Cambridge: Harvard University Press, 1912–1913. DOI: 10.4159/DLCL.appian-roman_history_book_xii_mithridatic_wars.1912.

————. *Roman History, Volume III: The Civil Wars,* Books 1–3.26. Translated by Horace White. Loeb Classical Library 4. Cambridge: Harvard University Press, 1913.

Ammianus Marcellinus. *History. Volume I: Books 14–19.* Translated by J.C. Rolfe. Loeb Classical Library 300. Cambridge: Harvard University Press, 1950.

————. History. *Volume II: Books 20–26.* Translated by J.C. Rolfe. Loeb Classical Library 315. Cambridge: Harvard University Press, 1940.

Arrian. *Bithynika,* fragment. *The Library of Photius.* Translated by John Henry Freese. London and New York: Society for Promoting Christian Knowledge, 1920.

Cassius Dio. *Roman History.* 9 Volumes. Translated by Earnest Cary and Herbert Baldwin Foster. Loeb Classical Library 175–76. Cambridge: Harvard University Press, 1914–1927.

Dio Chrysostom. *Discourses 37–60.* Volume 4. Translated by H. Lamar Crosby. Loeb Classical Library 376. Cambridge: Harvard University Press, 1946.

Diodorus Siculus. *The Library of History, Volume XII: Fragments of Books 33–40.* Translated by Francis R. Walton. Loeb Classical Library 423. Cambridge: Harvard University Press, 1933. DOI: 10.4159/DLCL.diodorus_siculus-library_history.1933.

Eusebius. *Ecclesiastical History, Volume I: Books 1–5.* Translated by Kirsopp Lake. Loeb Classical Library 153. Cambridge:

thers, vol. 2, trans. Chester D. Hartranft, ed. Philip Schaff and Henry Wace (Buffalo: Christian Literature Publishing, 1890), 4.16.

Harvard University Press, 1926. DOI: 10.4159/DLCL.eusebius-ecclesiastical_history.1926.

———. *Ecclesiastical History, Volume II: Books 6–10*. Translated by J.E.L. Oulton. Loeb Classical Library 265. Cambridge: Harvard University Press, 1932.

Herodian. *History of the Empire, Volume I: Books 1–4*. Translated by C.R. Whittaker. Loeb Classical Library 454. Cambridge: Harvard University Press, 1969. DOI: 10.4159/DLCL.herodian-history_empire.1969.

———. *History of the Empire, Volume II: Books 5–8*. Translated by C.R. Whittaker. Loeb Classical Library 455. Cambridge: Harvard University Press, 1970.

Historia Augusta. 3 Volumes. Translated by David Magie. Loeb Classical Library 139–40, 263. Cambridge: Harvard University Press, 1921–1932.

Lactantius. *Divine Institutes.* Translated by Anthony Bowen and Peter Garnsey. Translated Texts for Historians 40. Liverpool: Liverpool University Press, 2003.

———. *Of the Manner in Which the Persecutors Died.* In *The Ante-Nicene Fathers: Translations of the Writings of the Fathers down to AD 325, Volume 7,* edited by A. Cox Cleveland, Alexander Roberts, and James Donaldson. New York: Christian Literature Publishing, 1885, rpt. 1982.

Libanius. *A Monody on Nicomedia Destroyed by an Earthquake.* In *Select Works of the Emperor Julian, Volume 2,* translated by John Duncombe. London: J. Nichols 1784; rpt. Sydney: Wentworth Press, 2016.

Pausanias. *Description of Greece, Volume II: Books 3–5.* Translated by W.H.S. Jones. Loeb Classical Library 188. Cambridge: Harvard University Press, 1926.

Photius. *The Library of Photius.* Translated by John Henry Freese. London and New York: Society for Promoting Christian Knowledge, 1920.

Pliny the Younger. *Letters, Volume II: Books 8–10. Panegyricus.* Translated by Betty Radice. Loeb Classical Library 59. Cambridge: Harvard University Press, 1969. DOI: 10.4159/DLCL.pliny_younger-panegyricus.1969.

Procopius. *On Buildings.* Translated by H.B. Dewing and Glanville Downey. Loeb Classical Library 343. Cambridge: Harvard University Press, 1940. DOI: 10.4159/DLCL.procopius-buildings.1940.

Strabo. *Geography, Volume V: Books 10–12.* Translated by Horace Leonard Jones. Loeb Classical Library 211. Cambridge: Harvard University Press, 1928.

Sozomen. *Ecclesiastical History.* In *Nicene and Post-Nicene Fathers, Volume 2,* translated by Chester D. Hartranft, edited by Philip Schaff and Henry Wace. Buffalo: Christian Literature Publishing, 1890.

Zosimus. *New History.* London: Green and Chaplin, 1814.

Secondary

Barnes, Timothy D. *Constantine and Eusebius.* Cambridge: Harvard University Press, 1981.

Bekker-Nielsen, Tønnes. *Urban Life and Local Politics in Roman Bithynia: The Small World of Dion Chrysostomos.* Aarhus: Aarhus University Press, 2008. DOI: 10.2307/j.ctv62hgkr.

Birley, Anthony R. *Hadrian: The Restless Emperor.* Abingdon: Routledge, 1997.

Corsten, Thomas. "The Rôle and Status of the Indigenous Population in Bithynia." In *Rome and the Black Sea Region: Domination, Romanisation, Resistance,* edited by Tønnes Bekker-Nielsen, 85–92. Aarhus: Aarhus University Press, 2006. DOI: 10.2307/j.ctv62hh2z.8.

Cumont, Franz. *The Mysteries of Mithra.* New York: Dover Publications, 1956.

Elliott, J.K., ed. *The Apocryphal New Testament: A Collection of Apocryphal Christian Literature in an English Translation.* Oxford: Clarendon Press, 1993. DOI: 10.1093/0198261829.001.0001.

Feldman, Luis H. *Jew and Gentile in the Ancient World.* Princeton: Princeton University Press, 1993.

Foss, Clive. *Survey of Medieval Castles of Anatolia II: Nicomedia.* Ankara: The British Institute of Archaeology at Ankara, 1996.

Frend, W.H.C. *Martyrdom and Persecution in the Early Church.* Oxford: Basil Blackwell, 1965.

Grant, R. M. "The religion of Maximin Daia." In *Christianity, Judaism and other Greco-Roman Cults,* edited by Jacob Neusner, 143–66. Leiden: Brill, 1975.

Güney, Hale. "Excavation Coins and Stray Finds, Ancient: Unpublished Coins of Nicomedia," *The Numismatic Chronicle* 176 Offprint. London: The Royal Numismatic Society, 2016.

———. "The Economic Activities of Roman Nicomedia and Connectivity between the Propontic and the Pontic World." In *Interconnectivity in the Mediterranean and Pontic World during the Hellenistic and Roman Periods,* edited by Victor Cojocaru, Altay Coşkun, and Mădălina Dan, 605–24. Cluj-Napoca: Mega Publishing House, 2014.

———. "The Roman Monetary Economy in Bithynia During the Second Half of the First Century B.C.: The Case of Nicomedia." *Revue Belge de Philologie et Histoire* 93 (2015): 31–53. DOI: 10.3406/rbph.2015.8646.

Harnack, Adolf von. *Marcion: The Gospel of an Alien God.* Durham: The Labyrinth Press.

Heather, Peter J., and John Matthews. *The Goths in the Fourth Century.* Liverpool: Liverpool University Press, 1991. DOI: 10.3828/978-0-85323-426-5.

Jones, A.H.M. *Cities of the Eastern Roman Provinces.* Oxford and New York: Oxford University Press, 1937.

———. *Constantine and the Conversion of Europe.* New York: The Macmillan Co., 1949.

———. "The Cities of the Roman Empire." In *The Roman Economy: Studies in Ancient Economic and Administrative History,* edited by P.A. Brunt, 1–34. Oxford: Basil Blackwell, 1974.

———. *The Later Roman Empire, 284–602.* Oxford: Basil Blackwell, 1964.

Keresztes, Paul. "From the Great Persecution to the Peace of Galerius." *Vigiliae Christianae* 37 (1983): 379–99. DOI: 10.1163/157007283X00241.

Knipfing, John R. "The Edict of Galerius (311 A.D.) Re-considered." *Revue Belge de Philologie et d' Histoire* 1, no. 4 (1922): 693–705. DOI: 10.3406/rbph.1922.6200.

Knipfing, John R. "Religious Tolerance During the Early Part of the Reign of Constantine the Great (306–313)." *The Catholic Historical Review* 4, no. 4 (1925): 483–503.

Mackay, Christopher S. "Lactantius and the Succession to Diocletian." *Classical Philology* 94 (1999): 198–209. DOI: 10.1086/449431.

MacMullen, Ramsay. "Religious Toleration Around the Year 313." *Journal of Early Christian Studies* 22, no. 4 (2014): 499–517. DOI: 10.1353/earl.2014.0050.

Madsen, Jesper Majbom. *Eager to Be Roman: Greek Response to Roman Rule in Pontus and Bithynia.* London: Bloomsbury, 2009.

———. "Who Introduced the Imperial Cult in Asia and Bithynia? The Koinon's Role in the Early Worship of Augustus." In *Kaiserkult in den Provinzen des Römischen Reiches,* edited by Anne Kolb and Marco Vitale, 21–36. Berlin and Boston: De Gruyter, 2016.

Mitchell, Stephen. "Maximinus and the Christians in A.D. 312: A New Latin Inscription." *The Journal of Roman Studies* 78 (1988): 105– 24. DOI: 10.2307/301453.

Nicholson, Oliver. "The 'Pagan Churches' of Maximinus Daia and Julian the Apostate." *The Journal of Ecclesiastical History* 45, no. 1 (1994): 1–10. DOI: 10.1017/S0022046900016407.

Nuffelen, Peter Van. "Earthquakes in A.D. 363–368 and the Date of Libanius, *Oratio* 18." *The Classical Quarterly New Series* 56, no. 2 (2006): 657–61. DOI: 10.1017/S0009838806000784.

Sheppard, Anthony R.R. "Dio Chrysostom: The Bithynian Years." *L'Antiquité Classique* 53 (1984): 157–73. DOI: 10.3406/antiq.1984.2118.

Ste. Croix, G.E.M. de. "Aspects of the 'Great Persecution.'" In *Christian Persecution, Martyrdom, and Orthodoxy,* edited by Michael Whitby and Joseph Street, 35–78. Oxford: Oxford University Press, 2006. DOI: 10.1093/acprof:oso/9780199278121.003.0001.

————. "Voluntary Martyrdom in the Early Church." In *Christian Persecution, Martyrdom, and Orthodoxy,* edited by Michael Whitby and Joseph Street, 153–200. Oxford: Oxford University Press, 2006. DOI: 10.1093/acprof:oso/9780199278121.003.0004.

Stevenson, James, ed. *A New Eusebius: Documents Illustrative of the History of the Church to A.D. 337.* London: SPCK, 1968.

Thomas, G.S.R. "Maximin Daia's Policy and the Edicts of Toleration." *L'Antiquité Classique* 37, no.1 (1968): 172–85. DOI: 10.3406/antiq.1968.1502.

Thompson, E.A. *The Visigoths in the Time of Ulfila.* Oxford: Clarendon Press, 1966.

Van Dam, Raymond. *The Roman Revolution of Constantine.* Cambridge: Cambridge University Press, 2007. DOI: 10.1017/CBO9780511819476.

Ward-Perkins, Bryan. "The Marble Trade and Its Organization: Evidence from Nicomedia." *Memoirs of the American Academy in Rome* 36 (1980): 325–38. DOI: 10.2307/4238714.

Watts, Edward. "The Historical Context: The Rhetoric of Suffering in Libanius' Monodies, Letters and Autobiography." In *Libanius: A Critical Introduction,* edited by Lieve van Hoof, 39–58. Cambridge: Cambridge University Press 2014. DOI: 10.1017/CBO9781139012089.005.

5

Reccopolitani and Other Town Dwellers in the Southern Meseta during the Visigothic Period of State Formation

Javier Martínez Jiménez[1]

The *ex novo* royal urban foundation of Reccopolis, in a largely de-urbanized territory, near the Visigothic capital of Toledo in the late sixth century CE has had a significant impact on how we understand town life in the post-Roman period. This brief analysis of Reccopolis and what we know about its inhabitants (compared and contrasted with what we know of other regional nuclei such as Toledo, El Tolmo, Complutum, or even Mérida) will give an overview of what it may have been like to dwell in an urban site in the core of the Visigothic kingdom during the

1   I would like to thank Michael J. Kelly for inviting me to contribute to this volume and the members of the ERC "The Impact of the Ancient City Project" for their useful comments. This chapter was written while holding a position as a PDRA in the ERC-funded project "The Impact of the Ancient City," directed by Prof. Andrew Wallace-Hadrill. This project has received funding from the European Research Council (ERC) under the European Union's Horizon 2020 research and innovation program (grant agreement no. 693418).

Fig. 1. Map of the southern Meseta, indicating the sites mentioned in the text. Created by the author.

period of state formation, between the late sixth and early seventh centuries.

This paper is in no way a detailed or thorough account on all the archaeological evidence regarding daily urban life. Rather, it presents a series of broad-brush ideas and interpretations based on secondary work (with only a minor proportion resulting from my own field work). First, a synthetic view of five particular cities of the southern Meseta is presented; then, three main issues are approached through the monumental and archaeological remains of these cities. These issues are: first, how these sites were visually and monumentally (both in existing towns and in new foundations); second, a few ideas on what can be inferred regarding daily life (both at the level of the domestic family and the urban community); and third, what can be said about city dwellers and city identities. These are issues which can be framed within the general topic of "urban interactions" in as much as they involve the interactions within the city: the relationships within the urban community, the townscape in which it is inscribed, and, to an extent, the interaction between different urban communities.

The Evolution of Townscapes Before the Visigothic Kingdom

The southern Meseta (fig. 1) is a territory in the Iberian Peninsula located between the Central ranges to the north, the Sierra Morena to the south, the Portuguese lowlands to the west, and the mountainous ranges that separate the flatlands from the Mediterranean coast in the east. It includes the upper and middle valleys of two of the main rivers of the peninsula (the Tagus and the Guadiana), which form fertile, if unnavigable, corridors in what are otherwise dry and nearly barren flat uplands. In the Iron Age, it was largely divided into north–south territories of various "Celt-Iberian" groups.[2] However, in the Roman period, it was split between the three early Imperial provinces, each of which had a share of this territory, without any clear geographical dividing line. The largest part fell in the Tarraconensis province, and inside the *conventus iuridicus* (a poorly understood provincial subdivision)[3] of Cartagena (Carthago Nova). This link to the Mediterranean town was preserved into late antiquity, when it became a separate province: Carthaginensis.

This territory was articulated along three main roads: a road running E–W between Mérida and Valencia; one running NE–sw linking Zaragoza with Mérida; and one running NW–SE from the northern Meseta towards Cartagena. This territory was dotted with a small number of minor, secondary towns in

2   The term "Celt-Iberian" is highly controversial. In this instance it is only being used because it was the Roman name given to these groups of Vaccei, Vettones, Carpetani, and others, and not as any sort of ethnic label. Cf. Francisco Burillo Mozota, *Los celtíberos. Etnias y estados* (Barcelona: Crítica, 1998).

3   Cf. Pablo Ozcariz Gil, *Los conventus de la Hispania Citerior* (Madrid: Dykinson, 2006).

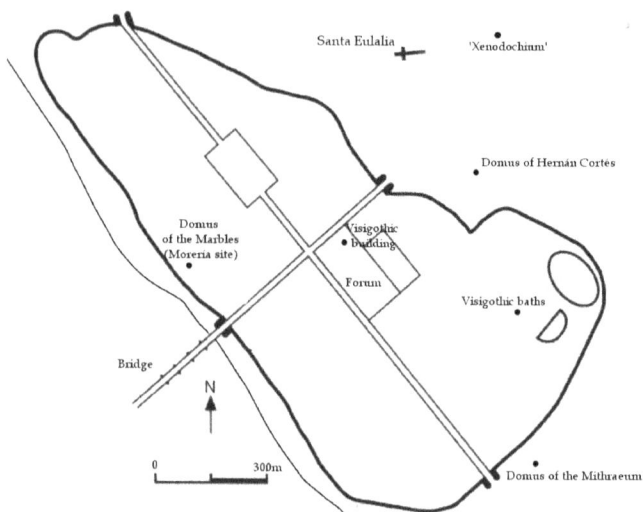

Fig. 2. Plan of Mérida in the Visigothic period. Created by the author.

the Roman period,[4] which, by late antiquity, and especially after the transformations of the fourth century,[5] were reduced to
a handful of real urban settlements in which town life can be
identified. Mérida (the old Roman capital), Toledo (the new Visigothic capital), and Complutum are the best known, together
with the new Visigothic foundations of Eio and, our particular case study, Reccopolis. Other sites such as Valeria, Ercavica,
or Segobriga are far less known and have not provided us with
enough material to discuss their urbanism in the post-Roman
period (and in fact, it is very doubtful that they continued to

4 Pieter Houten, *Civitates Hispaniae: Urbanisation on the Iberian Peninsula
during the High Empire* (PhD diss., Leiden University, 2018).
5 Ángel Fuentes Domínguez, "La antigüedad tardía en Castilla-La Mancha,"
in *Castilla-La Mancha en época romana y antigüedad tardía*, ed. Ángel
Fuentes Domínguez (Ciudad Real: Universidad de Castilla-La Mancha,
2006), 176–213.

function in any urban way at all),[6] even if they existed as Visigothic bishoprics.

From these examples (and in fact, from the whole peninsula), Mérida was certainly the most important city (fig. 2).[7] The former capital of the *dioecesis Hispaniarum* (which included the Iberian Peninsula and northern Morocco) had a large walled enclosure, reinforced in the fifth century to counter the barbarian threat: its capital role and wealth made it the prime target of the raids of Sueves and Visigoths. The spectacle monuments (theater, amphitheater, circus), which had been renewed during the course of the fourth century with imperial patronage, became the main quarry sites during the fifth and sixth centuries (especially for the construction of the reinforced walled enclosure) and were probably out of use.[8] The water supply system seems to have been preserved into the late Roman period, but, by the sixth century, it was largely abandoned—despite some failed attempts to put one of the aqueducts back in use.[9] The fora and other main administrative buildings were similarly quarried and dismantled, although by the temple of the impe-

6   See Adela Cepas Palanca, *Crisis y continuidad en la Hispania del siglo III*, Anejos de Archivo Español de Arqueología 17 (Madrid: CSIC, 1997). On Segóbriga, see Juan Manuel Abascal Palazón, Martín Almagro Gorbea, and Rosario Cebrián Fernández, "Segóbriga visigoda," in *Recópolis y la ciudad en la época visigoda*, ed. Lauro Olmo Enciso, Zona Arqueológica 9 (Alcalá de Henares: Museo Arqueológico Regional, 2008), 221–41.

7   Other than the chapter in this volume by Pedro Mateos Cruz, see Miguel Alba Calzado, and Pedro Mateos Cruz, "El paisaje urbano de Emerita en época visigoda," in *Recópolis y la ciudad en la época visigoda*, ed. Olmo Enciso, 261–73.

8   Large clearing excavations early in the twentieth century prevent us from discussing any late antique occupation of these buildings, as it happened in the theater of Cartagena, the amphitheater of Tarragona, or the circus of Arles. The circus of Mérida may have been still in use during the fifth and into the sixth century: Juan Antonio Jiménez Sánchez, "Los últimos ludi circenses realizados en Hispania en época visigoda," *Faventia* 28, no. 1 (2006): 99–113.

9   Elena Sánchez López and Javier Martínez Jiménez, *Los acueductos de Hispania. Construcción y abandono* (Madrid: Fundación Juanelo Turriano, 2016), 244–57.

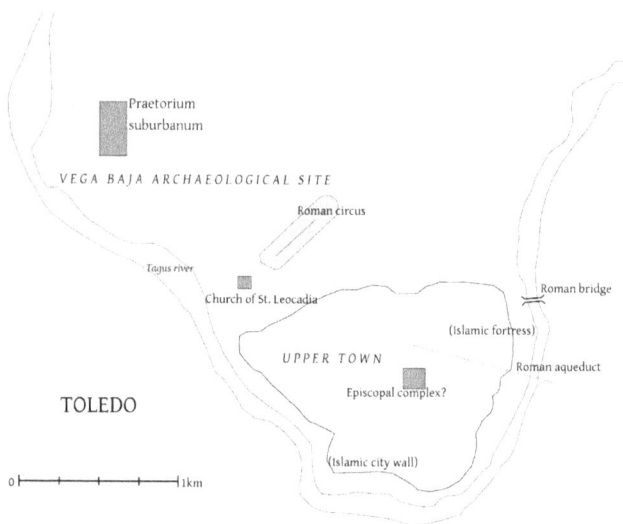

Fig. 3. Plan of late antique Toledo. Created by the author.

rial cult a public(?) building was set up, perhaps linked to the new Visigothic administration of the city.[10] It was, however, the bishops who were responsible for most of the new constructions of the post-Roman period, including the episcopal complex, the suburban basilica of Saint Eulalia with the "xenodochium," and the repairs of the bridge.

Toledo (fig. 3) had been a secondary town in the Roman administrative system all throughout the Classical period, and it only gained importance during the Visigothic period of state formation when it became the royal capital. The reasons why are not clear, but certainly its central location in the Peninsula (which fitted the new Visigothic policies) and the lack of a strong local aristocracy (as in Mérida, Córdoba, or Zaragoza)

10 Pedro Mateos Cruz and Isaac Sastre de Diego, "Elementos arquitectónicos tardoantiguos y altomedievales en el Templo de Diana (Mérida, España)," *Mérida. Excavaciones arqueológicas* 7 (2004): 397–415.

which could contest the royal authority were key. Toledo is, archaeologically, unevenly known: the upper town is still densely inhabited, and there is hardly anything known about its Roman or Visigothic past, other than the street grid and that the cathedral complex was located up there. The walls, allegedly repaired by king Wamba (r. 672–680) were commemorated in an inscription. The lower town (the "Vega Baja"), however, has been subject of much archaeological activity in the recent years. Originally the location of the martyrial basilica of Saint Leocadia,[11] the circus, and some scattered villa occupation, in the late sixth century the whole area was developed, with a new street grid and the monumental remains of what has been identified with the *praetorium suburbanum* (the suburban royal palace) mentioned in the sources.[12]

Lastly, it is worth mentioning the old Roman town of Complutum (fig. 4), which offers a point of contrast with these two other flourishing cities of late antiquity.[13] Complutum had been, like Toledo, a secondary nucleus in the central Meseta, but, from the fourth century onwards, it became an important Christian site thanks to the martyring of two young boys, Saints Justus and Pastor, whose shrine became an important focal point of

11 Josep Maria Gurt Esparraguera and Pilar Diarte Blasco, "La basílica de santa Leocadia y el final de uso del circo romano de Toledo: Una nueva interpretación," *Zephyrus* 69 (2012): 149–63.

12 Lauro Olmo Enciso, "La Vega Baja en época visigoda: una investigación arqueológica en construcción," in *La Vega Baja de Toledo*, ed. Alfonso García and Diego Perís (Toledo: Toletum Visigodo, 2009), 69–94. Cf. Francisco Moreno Martín, "Circulación de modelos y circularidad de argumentación para el conocimiento de la topografía cristiana entre la Antigüedad Tardía y la Alta Edad Media," in *Entre civitas y madina. El mundo de las ciudades en la Península Ibérica y en el norte de África (siglos IV–IX)*, ed. Sabine Panzram and Laurent Callegarin, Collection de la Casa de Velázquez 167 (Madrid: Casa de Velázquez, 2018), 153–72.

13 The late antique phases of Complutum are extensively described in Sebastián Rascón Marqués and Ana Lucía Sánchez Montes, "Complutum tardoantiguo," in *La investigación arqueológica de la época visigoda en la Comunidad de Madrid*, ed. Jorge Morín de Pablos, Zona Arqueológica 8 (Alcalá de Henares: Museo Arqueológico Regional, 2006), 267–91.

Fig. 4. Plan of the sites mentioned for Complutum in the Visigothic period. Created by the author.

cult activity—comparable to Saint Eulalia. The old walled enclosure, with its forum and administrative center (developed and modified in the fourth century) was largely un-urban by the sixth century. By the period of Visigothic state formation the settlement had spread across three main clusters which completely disregarded the old walls, creating a four-mile dispersed habitat along the main Roman road. The three settlements were around the old villa of El Val, clustered around the *Campus Laudabilis* (the martyrial shrine of the Holy Boys), and around the forum area.

The New Foundations

The construction of a new city was a monumental and expensive accomplishment, and a clear statement of state power (and is still nowadays, if we look for instance at the foundations of Canberra in the 1910s, Brasilia in the 1950s, Putrajaya in the 1990s or Naypyidaw in the 2000s). During late antiquity and the early Middle Ages, city building was an activity which was mostly confined to the Eastern Empire and Sassanid Persia (and later taken up by the Umayyads),[14] but in Visigothic Spain we find two unique examples: Reccopolis and Eio. These two sites are exceptional enough in many aspects not to be taken as characteristic, but they nonetheless reflect the trends and ideals of what a city was conceived to have been.

Reccopolis
In the case of Reccopolis, all the information we have about the foundation derives from John of Biclar's (c. 540–621) account (later abridged by Isidore of Seville [c. 560–636]), who mentions this:[15]

> With the tyrants completely destroyed, and the invaders of Spain defeated, King Liuvigild settled his peace with his own people. He founded a city (*civitatem*) named after his son in Celtiberia, which he named Reccopolis, which he endowed with wonderful works within the walls and in the suburbs, and he established privileges for the people of the new city (*urbis*).

We do not know how long the city took to build, or if the date given by John of Biclar of 578 commemorates the beginning of the works or the official inauguration, but the date of 578 coincides with Liuvigild's *decennalia,* the tenth-year commemoration of his reign (in John of Biclar's computation). Founding a city on such a marked occasion was certainly a great celebration,

---

14 Cf. *New Cities in Late Antiquity: Documents and Archaeology,* ed. Efthymios Rizos, Bibliothèque de l'Antiquité Tardive 35 (Turnhout: Brepols, 2017).

15 *Chronica,* 578.4: "Liuvigildus rex extinctis undique tyrannis, et pervasoribus Hispaniae superatis sortitus requiem propriam cum plebe resedit civitatem in Celtiberia ex nomine filii condidit, quae Rec[c]opolis nuncupatur: quam miro opere et in moenibus et suburbanis adornans privilegia populo novae Urbis instituit."

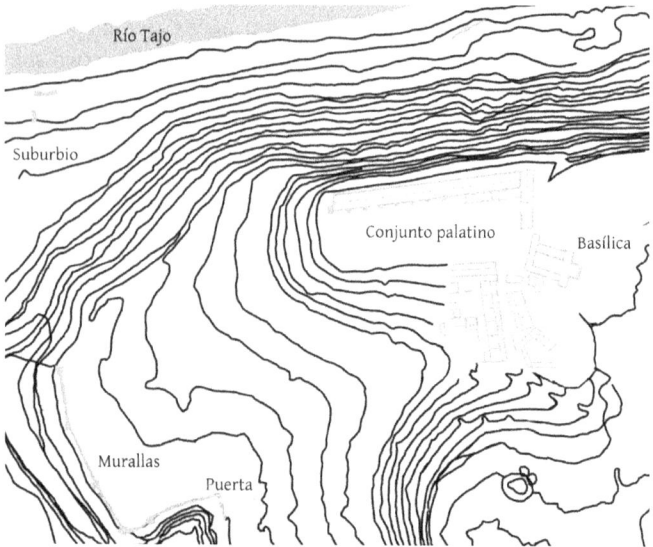

Fig. 5. Plan of the excavations at Reccopolis. Author's original adaptation of an image in Lauro Olmo Enciso, "La ciudad en el centro peninsular durante el proceso de consolidación del estado visigodo de Toledo," *Zona arqueológica* 8, no. 2 (2006): 251–66, at 255.

and by linking it to Reccared it set the foundations for a dynastic succession.[16]

Regarding the site chosen for the foundation of Reccopolis, it is located on a hilltop adjacent to the River Tagus, sixty-eight miles upstream from Toledo, the royal capital. It is twenty-seven miles E of Complutum and fourteen miles SW of Ercavica, the two main Roman towns in that area. Even if it is not located on a main Roman road, it was linked with secondary roads. The site had not been previously settled, although the residual presence of fourth-century material may point towards the existence of a

---

16 This pre-dates Hermenegild's rebellion. All translations are the author's unless otherwise stated.

villa in the surrounding area, from which building material was quarried.

If we look at the urbanism of the new city (fig. 5), from John of Biclar we learn that Liuvigild provided it with "splendid buildings" (*miro opere*), which are not specified. From the archaeology we can guess that these perhaps relate to the basilica and "palatine" complex, located at the upper town.[17] This area includes an open plaza with an apsed basilica on one end and three long, two-story, aisled buildings on three of the sides. This whole complex was accessed through a monumental gate. These buildings are made of mortared rubble and paved with *opus signinum.* An aqueduct is also known to have supplied the city,[18] which may be one of the "splendid buildings," following aqueduct praise in other Gothic royal contexts (in particular, in Ostrogothic Italy).[19] No other public or monumental buildings are known from the excavations, as most of the site lies in private land and is yet unexcavated,[20] but if Reccopolis follows other patterns of late antique and post-Roman urbanism, it is

17 All the archaeological descriptions of Reccopolis in this chapter are taken from the extensive list of publications by Lauro Olmo Enciso, from the University of Alcalá de Henares, to whom I am grateful for the opportunities to work with and dig on the site. The key references would be Lauro Olmo Enciso, "Recópolis: una ciudad en época de transformaciones," in *Recópolis y la ciudad en la época visigoda,* ed. Olmo Enciso, 40–63; Lauro Olmo Enciso, "The Royal Foundation of Recópolis and the Urban Renewal in Iberia During the Second Half of the Sixth Century," in *Post-Roman Towns and Trade in Europe and Byzantium,* ed. Joachim Henning (Berlin: DeGruyter, 2007), 181–99; and Lauro Olmo Enciso, Manuel Castro Priego, Amaya Gómez de la Torre-Verdejo, and Álvaro Sanz Paratcha, "Recópolis y su justificación científica: la secuencia estratigráfica," in *Recópolis y la ciudad en la época visigoda,* ed. Olmo Enciso, 64–75.

18 Javier Martínez Jiménez, "A Preliminary Study of the Aqueduct of Reccopolis," *Oxford Journal of Archaeology* 34, no. 4 (2015): 301–20.

19 *Variae,* 7.6.2: "In formis autem Romanis utrumque praecipuum est, ut fabrica sit mirabilis et aquarum salubritas singularis" ("Moreover, it is particular to the aqueducts of Rome both [their] wonderful construction and the unique wholesomeness of their waters").

20 Recent geophysical surveys have revealed many other structures, but it is imposible to tell their purpose or function without excavation: Joachim

doubtful that others will be found. Amphitheaters and theaters were already out of use, as were civil basilicas, but baths were still popular, as the newly built ones of Mérida or Barcelona (although not of the same monumental scale of classical public baths in Spain).[21] In terms of public amenities, post-Roman town dwellers did not get much else.

Still following John of Biclar's text, Liuvigild also erected walls and built suburbs (which were, as it happens, also privileged with *miro opere*). The location of the walled enclosure is roughly known, with two gates and various towers identified around the hilltop site.[22] The suburbs are less well known, although various walls are still visible on the western side of the hilltop, including some by the river bank, which may relate to a river harbor. We could venture that a suburban church existed (the only type of "splendid building" found in other suburbs in Visigothic Spain), but there are no remains to substantiate this. Unless, of course, we count the aqueduct as a suburban building as well.

As for the privileges, it is impossible to know which these were (other than the fact itself of being granted a plot in a new city), but one can guess that these included urban and rural plots of land to settle and to work. Market rights or workshops could have been one of these privileges for which we could have some indirect archaeological evidence. The N–S street that leads down from the palace complex towards the main E–W road (that linked the two known gates) is flanked by a series of workshops, where glass and gold were worked, and these buildings belong,

Henning et al. "Reccopolis Revealed: First Geomagnetic Mapping of the Early Medieval Visigothic Royal Town," *Antiquity* 93, no. 369 (2019), 735–51.

21 Virginia García-Entero, *Los balnea domésticos — ámbito rural y urbano — en la Hispania romana.* Anejos de Archivo Español de Arqueología 37 (Madrid: CSIC, 2005), 213 (for Barcelona), 527–29 (for Mérida). Note that the date of the bath at Mérida remains unpublished, even if it was excavated recently. I thank Miguel Alba Calzado for pointing this out.

22 Amaya Gómez de la Torre-Verdejo, "La muralla de Recópolis," in *Recópolis y la ciudad en la época visigoda,* ed. Olmo Enciso, 77–86.

stratigraphically, to the same phase as the monuments of the upper town.[23] If the workshops and the monumental center belong to the same phase, it is logical to deduce that they were built with the same constructive effort, which would further suggest that a way to finance the running of the city might have been by renting out these market areas. This would contrast to the development of the dwelling areas, which belong to a second constructive phase, perhaps up to the initiative of the occupants (which would explain the architectural differences between the houses west and east of the workshop street). There are few other privileges that could be granted to town dwellers, although remission of land taxes was a very popular measure in late and post-Roman legislation; if this measure was granted to cities who had just recovered from war,[24] it could certainly apply to the inhabitants of a new city before its fields yield their first crops.

From more technical perspectives, and as is evident from the archaeological remains, it is clear that the resources (manpower, financial, and material) necessary to build the city were immense. Doubtless, the largely abandoned Roman town of Ercavica, despite it still being an active bishopric, served as a large quarry — perhaps taking advantage of the fluvial road link between the two sites. All roofs in Reccopolis are tiled, and even if it seems that they were all newly fired *imbrices,* the large variety of types could also suggest that they were being reused. Marble (not just for decorations, but to be burnt into lime) was probably brought from Ercavica as well, and in large quantities, considering the amount of mortar used at Reccopolis. The burning of the lime and the making of the mortar required large amounts of water, so perhaps the aqueduct was one of the first

---

23 Olmo Enciso et al., "Recópolis y su justificación"; Manuel Castro Priego and Amaya Gómez de la Torre-Verdejo, "La actividad artesanal en Recópolis: la producción de vidrio," in *Recópolis y la ciudad en la época visigoda,* ed. Olmo Enciso, 117–28.

24 As, for instance, Marseilles or Arles in the Ostrogothic period (*Variae,* 3.34, 40, and 41).

Northern necropolis

Walls and gateway

Rock mill

Visigothic episcopal complex

Islamic houses

Visigothic wall

Visigothic acropolis

EIO - EL TOLMO DE MINATEDA

50 m

Fig. 6. Plan of the excavations at El Tolmo de Minateda (Eio). Image printed by permission of Sonia Gutiérrez.

structures set up during the construction. Clay and sandstone for ashlars, rubble, and pisé walls could (and can) still be obtained locally around Reccopolis. The presence of a quarry next to the remains of the aqueduct would suggest that this was done on an ad hoc basis, wherever a rocky outcrop was easily accessible, rather than from a large, centralized quarry (a mode of extraction which had disappeared largely by the fifth century).[25]

---

25 Cf. Anna Gutiérrez García, *Roman Quarries in the Northeast of Hispania (Modern Catalonia)* (Tarragona: ICAC, 2009), esp. 255–60.

Regarding the finances, it is clear that the available funds were obtained mostly through confiscations and war booty from Liuvigild's campaigns in the previous years against the Byzantines and various groups of rebels, as described by John of Biclar, but his monetary reform would have also benefitted this project.[26] As for the manpower, I have suggested elsewhere[27] that the technical and trained personnel (architects and engineers) required for this project were probably foreign (sent from Byzantium?), but vernacular builders were certainly local. Whether the latter were free or slave, or prisoners of war, is open to discussion, but Liuvigild evidently could muster enough workforce.

Eio

The site of El Tolmo de Minateda (fig. 6), a small rocky outcrop in the mostly plain area that links the southern Meseta with the Mediterranean coast (and the territories controlled by the Byzantines since the mid-sixth century) has been identified with the site of Eio.[28] This site lacks a source referring to its foundation (as Reccopolis has with John of Biclar), but its existence is inferred from the acts of Visigothic ecclesiastical councils,

---

26 On Visigothic coinage, see Ruth Pliego Vázquez, *La moneda visigoda I. Historia monetaria del Reino visigodo de Toledo (c. 569–711)* (Seville: Universidad de Sevilla, 2009).

27 Martínez Jiménez, "Aqueduct of Reccopolis."

28 As with Reccopolis, most of the archaeological information presented here from the excavations at El Tolmo has been extensively published by Sonia Gutiérrez Lloret, from the University of Alicante. The most relevant publications are: Lorenzo Abad Casal, Sonia Gutiérrez Lloret, Blanca Gamo Parras, and Pablo Cánovas Guillén, "Una ciudad en el camino: pasado y futuro de El Tolmo de Minateda (Hellín, Albacete)," in *Recópolis y la ciudad en la época visigoda*, ed. Olmo Enciso, 323–36; Sonia Gutiérrez Lloret, Lorenzo Abad Casal, and Blanca Gamo Parras, "'Eio', 'Iyyuh' y el Tolmo de Minateda (Hellín, Albacete): De sede episcopal a 'madīna' islámica," in *VI Reunió d'Arqueologia Cristiana Hispànica*, ed. Josep Maria Gurt and Albert Ribera (Barcelona: IEC, 2005), 345–70; and Sonia Gutiérrez Lloret and Julia Sarabia Bautista, "The Episcopal Complex of Eio-El Tolmo de Minateda (Hellín, Albacete, Spain): Architecture and Spatial Organization, 7th to 8th Centuries AD," *Hortus Artium Medievalium* 19 (2013): 267–300.

where the bishop of Eio or Elo (referred to as *Ecclesia Elotana*) is listed. The creation of this bishopric was done to counter the power (and claim the territory) of the bishop of Ilici, who was most probably inside the Byzantine province,[29] and it can be dated to the 590s (a date supported by the archaeology). In this case, as the foundation is not commented on in the sources, all the information derives from the excavations.

From a technical point of view, the construction of Eio is very similar to that of Reccopolis. In terms of resources, Reccared was as successful as his father in his military campaigns, so he had similar access to manpower and cash; additionally, El Tolmo is located on an early Roman urban site (Ilunum), which had been abandoned since the second century, and thus some building materials were reused from this earlier site. In fact, the fortified gate reuses parts of a large imperial dedicatory inscription. Two characteristic elements of the construction of El Tolmo are that mortar is less prominent than in Reccopolis (explaining perhaps the presence of *opus africanum*) and that the outline of the buildings was chiseled on the bedrock, and then the buildings were erected following those master lines.

Architecturally, the most important monuments at El Tolmo/ Eio are the fortified gate, the episcopal basilica and palace complex, and the fortified acropolis. These elements mirror those of Reccopolis (fortifications, and civil and Church authorities), although in Eio the weight of the ecclesiastical over the civil power reverses the situation of Reccopolis. The episcopal complex at Eio includes a basilica with an apse where the sanctuary is separated with chancel screens, a baptistery, an *ad sanctos* necropolis, an episcopal hall, and residences, together with a series of rain-water cisterns.[30] The acropolis consists of a corner of the

---

29 Javier Martínez Jiménez and José María Moreno Narganes, "*Nunc autem a Gothis subversa*: The Province of Alicante and the Spanish Mediterranean Towns Between the Byzantine and Visigothic periods," *Early Medieval Europe* 23, no. 3 (2015): 263–89.

30 For the cisterns, Javier Martínez Jiménez, "Water Supply in the Visigothic Urban Foundations of Eio (El Tolmo de Minateda) and Reccopolis," in *New*

hill, separated from the rest of the site by a wall, and whereas a couple of dwellings have been identified, only the main fortified gate is preserved as a monument on site.

It is conceivable that the settlers for this new site were also granted some privileges (they were moving to the frontier zone with the Byzantines, after all), although it is more difficult to conjecture at what these were than with Reccopolis. The urban nature of the site could be contested on grounds of its size (some seven hectares [17.3 acres]), but the presence of a bishop (evident through the basilica with baptistery) underlines its urban status — even if only from a legal and administrative perspective. It certainly did not inherit much in terms of Roman monumentality from its second-century predecessor: most of the hill was levelled to the bedrock in order to build the new Visigothic settlement.

Daily Life and Domestic Environments

If compared to Roman imperial foundations (both earlier, Western foundations such as Mérida, Carthage, or Trier, and coeval, Eastern foundations such as Justiniana Prima), the monumental displays of Reccopolis and Eio seem perhaps limited. The lack of colonnaded streets, marble sculptures, amenities such as theaters or baths, or large and lavish basilicas is not just an unfair comparison regarding the substantially different access to resources, but also not really valid, as it does not reflect the underlying social and political circumstances. And this discrepancy between Roman and post-Roman townscapes is not only visible in the monumentality of the cities, but also in their domestic architecture and the objects of daily use, such as pottery. But still, during the post-Roman period there seems to have been an overall similar feel to domestic and daily living in the towns of the central Meseta, both old Roman sites and new Visigothic foundations.

Cities in Late Antiquity, ed. Rizos, 240–41.

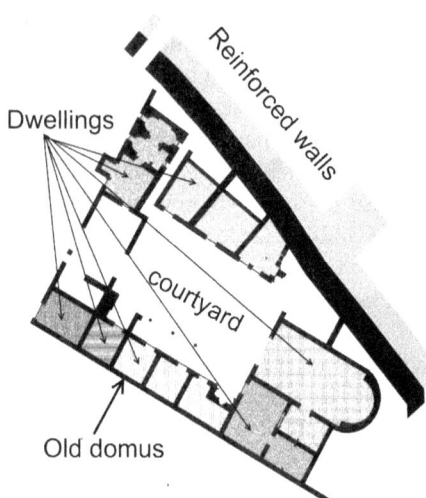

Fig. 7. Plan of the late antique phase domus of the Marbles, excavated at the site of Morería in Mérida. Out of a single-family house of the late Roman period, six different family dwellings are made in the fifth and sixth centuries. Author's original adaption of an image in Miguel Alba Calzado, "La vivienda en Emerita durante la antigüedad tardía: propuesta de un modelo para Hispania," in *VI Reunió d'Arqueologia Cristiana Hispànica,* ed. Josep Maria Gurt and Albert Ribera (Barcelona: IEC, 2005), 121–50, at 145.

Regarding domestic architecture and houses (the home for the basic unit of social interaction: the family), there is a clear transformation when compared to the Roman world. And in this aspect, the dwelling areas of Reccopolis, Eio, Complutum (late phases of the *domus* of Hippolytus and of the Cupids), Mérida (Morería site) and Toledo (Vega Baja houses) show very similar characteristics. By the sixth century, urban housing was not linked to atrium-style *domus*[31] or even to peristyle or

31 The atrium-style domus, despite being the prototype of Classical Roman housing, existed only during a limited chronology, and was not distributed

oecus houses; Visigothic urban housing was (as far as archaeology indicates) based around small single-family dwellings (on
the premise of one hearth per family unit) with multipurpose
rooms (usually no more than two or three linked to the principal room where the hearth is), structured around a courtyard.[32]
In Reccopolis these houses tend to be larger, no doubt because
they were built on empty plots for the early settlers, whereas in
Mérida (in particular, the dwellings of the Visigothic phase of
the *domus* of the Marbles; fig. 7) they have to fit within the re-
used rooms of an earlier Roman house.[33] In this last case, the old
peristyle is turned into a communal courtyard. Trampled earth,
usually mixed with lime, is the most common flooring technique (perhaps used together with esparto rugs), and the walls
were built with pisé on mortared rubble foundations (when not
re-using Roman existing walls), and whitewashed.

These houses included rubbish pits and communal water
points (cisterns, wells) to counter the lack of aqueduct supplies
(in Reccopolis there may have been a public cistern).[34] Although
in Mérida the Roman sewers might have been partially in use,
cesspits were also common, but in Reccopolis the idea of vaulted
underground sewers is wholly abandoned in favor of open air
drains, running in the center of concave streets.[35] Animal pens,

ubiquitously.

32 For a more theoretical and methodological approach to understanding domestic structures see Sonia Gutiérrez Lloret, "Gramática de la casa. Perspectivas de análisis arqueológico de los espacios domésticos medievales
en la Península Ibérica (siglos VII–XIII)," *Arqueología de la Arquitectura* 9
(2012): 139–64.

33 For Reccopolis, see Olmo Enciso et al., "la secuencia estratigráfica." For
Mérida, Miguel Alba Calzado, "La vivienda en Emerita durante la antigüedad tardía: propuesta de un modelo para Hispania," in *VI Reunió
d'Arqueologia Cristiana Hispànica,* ed. Gurt and Ribera, 121–50.

34 Martínez Jiménez, "Aqueduct of Reccopolis."

35 Jesús Acero Pérez and Josep Anton Remolà Vallverdú, *La gestión de los residuos urbanos en Hispania. Xavier Dupré Raventós (1956–2006) in memoriam.* Anejos de Archivo Español de Arqueología 60 (Mérida: CSIC, 2011).
Cf. with the Islamic period: Francisco Vidal Castro, "Agua y urbanismo:
evacuación de aguas en fatwà-s de al-Andalus y el Norte de África," in

small gardens, and other non-residential uses of intra-mural plots have traditionally been seen as indicators of ruralization of the urban landscapes, although for our case studies these appear only in Complutum and the more peripheral areas of Mérida — these have not been identified in the new foundations.

Non-elite domestic pottery assemblages were modified to fit in these contexts where hearths are on the floor instead of built kitchens, and beaten earth flooring is the most common flooring technique. In this way, characteristic Visigothic coarse wares with thicker walls, clays with mineral inclusions, and convex bases were better adapted to this situation.[36] The widespread presence of individual bowls and closed shapes in cooking pots would suggest that eating habits had changed: serving individual portions in the bowls rather than sharing dishes on the table with plates and trays.[37]

This simplification of the domestic structure (if compared to Roman urban housing) is only apparent, because none of these houses are elite residences; and in this aspect, lower and middle classes are much more visible in these urban contexts than they

---

L'urbanisme dans l'occident musulmana u Moyen Âge. Aspects juridiques, ed. Patrice Cressier, Maribel Fierro, and Jean-Pierre van Staëuel (Madrid: Casa Velázquez, 2000), 101–23.

36 Despite the loss of such techniques as the fast potter's wheel or slips. Cf. Miguel Alba Calzado Miguel and Santiago Feijoo Martínez, "Pautas evolutivas de la cerámica común de Mérida en épocas visigoda y emiral," in *Cerámicas tardorromanas y altomedievales en la Península Ibérica,* ed. Luis Caballero, Pedro Mateos Cruz, and Manuel Retuerce, Anejos de Archivo Español de Arqueología 28 (Mérida: CSIC, 2003), 483–504.

37 A thorough study of zooarchaeological, carpological, and archaeobotany remains from urban contexts would give further indications on the nature of urban diets and help to characterize what the urban diet was in the late sixth century; something which exists for rural and urban Islamic contexts: Idoia Grau Sologestoa, *The Zooarchaeology of Medieval Álava in its Iberian Context,* British Archaeological Reports International Series 2769 (Oxford: Archaeopress, 2015); Marcos García García, "Some Remarks on the Provisioning of Animal Products to Urban Centres in Medieval Islamic Iberia: The Cases of Madinat Ilbirah (Granada) and Cercadilla (Córdoba)," *Quaternary International* 460 (2016): 86–96.

are in early Roman towns. This raises the question of where the members of the elite actually lived, episcopal complexes with residences for the clergy and Visigothic palaces apart. Perhaps the houses identified at the Vega Baja in Toledo could be interpreted as residences of the palatine administrative elites, but there is little published about them. Otherwise, late Roman suburban villas in Mérida (like the *domus* of Hernán Cortés or the *domus* of the Mithraeum) and Complutum do not continue in use into this period. I would venture that this is a problem of archaeological visibility, and I would expect these elite dwellings close to the new foci of power: episcopal complexes and Visigothic palaces (the environs of which have not been fully excavated for any of the case studies put forward here).

From the nature of these domestic units, organized around communal areas and courtyards, it is possible to guess that beyond the nuclear family, the next level of social interaction took place at a neighborhood level. It is also a possibility that these communities included (but were not limited just to) extended families, a pattern that could perhaps reflect the organization of kin groups in funerary contexts of this period. This hypothesis would link this Visigothic/late antique pattern of social life of a *vicus,* or neighbor community with later developments in the Islamic period, when this is clearly attested.[38] This would further link back to Classical Roman practices, where belonging to a *vicus* was a layer of identity for town dwellers.[39]

Beyond the immediate surroundings, and the interaction within the neighbor community, the wider body of town dwellers had, in the Visigothic period, various places in which to interact with fellow citizens. After the late Roman shift from a curial administration based on magistracies to a local government based on a centrally-appointed count, the forum had

---

38 Julio Navarro Palazón and Pedro Jiménez Castillo, "Algunas reflexiones sobre el urbanismo islámico," *Artigrama* 22 (2007): 259–98.

39 Alan Kaiser, *Roman Urban Street Networks* (London: Routledge, 2011), esp. 38.

ceased to fulfill a political and administrative role (e.g., for vot-
ing, assembling citizens or delivering speeches).[40] However, this
does not imply that open areas were not needed in post-Roman
cities. It is true that fora were encroached upon and that their
temples, basilicas and decorations were (orderly) dismantled,[41]
but they were still reference landmarks of the city. Even at Reccopolis there was the need for a large open area, even if inside
the palatine complex — would the inhabitants have identified it
as a forum? I would venture so, even if they just used the word
forum simply meaning open urban space, and despite it not being recognizable architecturally as a "Classical" Roman forum.[42]
    In the absence of curiae and of classically functioning fora,
city dwellers would have gone directly to civil and ecclesiastical
palaces (which we know from the archaeology) for their administrative or judicial needs, and our case studies provide various
examples of such places. The episcopal complex at Eio has a hall.
At Reccopolis it is difficult to envisage how the palace worked
(especially considering its layout),[43] but while the lower ground
could have served as a storage for revenue and tax (collected in
kind), the upper floor could have held the administrative and
audience rooms. The *praetorium* of Toledo would have had a
similar (if not grander) function. In Mérida, other than the obscure Visigothic building of the forum there is the sixth-century

---

40 Wolfgang Liebeschuetz, "The End of the Ancient City," in *The City in Late
    Antiquity,* ed. John Rich (Ashgate: London, 1992), 1–50.
41 Fuentes Domínguez, "La antigüedad tardía," 205–6; Mateos and Sastre,
    "Elementos arquitectónicos tardoantiguos y altomedievales en el Templo
    de Diana (Mérida, España);" Rascón and Sánchez, "Complutum tardoanti-
    guo."
42 Or perhaps due to its relationship to the palace, if law was administered
    there, following cautiously Isidore's definition of a forum (*Etym.,* 15.2.27).
43 And despite the doubts of some scholars, it cannot be denied that the site is
    Reccopolis and that the upper town is a site of political representation and
    centralized administration. Cf. Javier Arce, "Recópolis, la ciudad fantasma,"
    in *Doctrina a magistro discipulis tradita. Estudios en homenaje al profesor
    Dr. Luis García Iglesias,* ed. Adolfo Domínguez and Gloria Mora Rodríguez
    (Madrid: Universidad Autónoma de Madrid, 2010), 373–94.

building north of the city, currently identified with the *xenodo-chium* of Masona, a building whose function is not really clear, has a large apsed hall and was decorated with carved marbles, perhaps was used also for holding audiences.[44]

Fora served also as market places in the Roman period. In fact, encroachment could be seen as the permanent occupation of temporary market stalls, so perhaps the presence of a commercial street at Reccopolis can be seen as an indicator that commercial streets were the "market hubs" in late antique towns (as it has been proposed for the East).[45] Archaeology has yet to shed light on this issue for the case-studies put forward here, because not even in El Tolmo have such structures been found. The eminent local nature of commodities such as glass[46] and table wares[47] (as opposed to the abundance of imported wares in the Roman period) may, however, suggest that, as is the case in Reccopolis, production and sales occurred in the same space. This opens two possibilities, which are not necessarily exclusive: production remained largely in the suburbs (so suburbs would be active commercial hubs) or production had partially relocated into the walled enclosures.

Another area where citizen interaction was likely to take place was in religious contexts. It is in this period when church-

---

44 Pedro Mateos Cruz, "La identificación del xenodochium fundado por Masona en Mérida," in *IV Reunió d'Arqueologia Cristiana Hispànica,* ed. Josep Maria Gurt Esparraguera and Nuria Tena (Barcelona: Institut d'Estudis Catalans, 1995), 309–16. I have difficulties seeing this building functioning as a hospital.

45 Classically exposed in John Crawford, *The Byzantine Shops at Sardis* (Cambridge: Harvard University Press, 1990).

46 Ángel Fuentes Domínguez, "Vidrio de la Antigüedad tardía (ss.V–X). Cuestiones de fabricación y comercialización. Problemas de identificación," in *Vidrio islámico en Al-Andalus,* ed. Enrique Rontomé Notario (Madrid: Fundación Centro Nacional del Vidrio, 2007), 13–36.

47 Alfonso Vigil-Escalera and Juan Antonio Quirós Castillo, eds., *La cerámica de la Alta Edad Media en el cuadrante noroeste de la Península Ibérica (siglos V–X)* (Bilbao: Universidad del País Vasco, 2016); Caballero, Mateos Cruz, and Retuerce, eds., *Cerámicas tardorromanas y altomedievales en la Península Ibérica.*

es begin to be built inside the city walls (Mérida, Toledo), something paralleled by the presence of religious buildings in the centers of the new urban foundations (Reccopolis, Eio). Churches and basilicas in this period had clearly segregated areas for ordained and lay members of the congregation, but they still formed gathering areas for the community — especially on holy days. Masona is known to have carried out processions and making a point out of it during Easter.[48] Religious processions, well-known in Gallic examples,[49] may have also existed in Spanish sites at this date.[50] The presence of both cathedrals and martyrs' shrines in Complutum, Mérida, and Toledo, opens the possibility for such processions linking cathedrals with shrines. In Toledo, king Wamba (slightly after our period) paraded into the city with booty and prisoners (including the usurper Paul) in a style which harks back to Roman triumphs.[51] The idea may not have been completely foreign, as similar processions existed in the Roman period.

Lastly, it is worth going back to the lack of Roman amenities described earlier. It is true that by the late sixth century none of the Roman *spectacula* were in use, and they were not set up in the new urban foundations, but the point is that in a Christian urban community where magistrates making payments *ex officio* did not exist, such forms of entertainment did not have a place. They had become completely outdated, even if horse-racing may have continued into the early sixth century.[52] Regarding baths, whereas there is general evidence for continuity of bath-

---

48 Cf. *VPE*, 5.2.12.

49 Simon Esmonde Cleary, *The Roman West, AD 200–500: An Archaeological Study* (Cambridge: Cambridge University Press, 2013), 180.

50 One such procession is described for Zaragoza by Gregory of Tours (*DLH*, 3.29), although not in usual circumstances.

51 *HWR*, 30. Cf. Hendrik Dey, *The Afterlife of the Roman City: Architecture and Ceremony in Late Antiquity and the Early Middle Ages* (Cambridge: Cambridge University Press, 2014), 156–57.

52 Jiménez Sánchez, "Los últimos ludi circenses realizados en Hispania en época visigoda."

ing, there are few examples of the southern Meseta.[53] A combination of the ambiguous position of the Church on public bathing and the high costs of maintaining and running large baths (together with the end of aqueduct supplies) meant that these baths were smaller — even with individual tubs,[54] something that can be seen in the Visigothic baths of Mérida mentioned above. The royal complexes of Toledo and Reccopolis might have had baths, but this is just speculation. The ones known for Complutum were private and certainly out of use by this time. Overall, in terms of public entertainment in these cities there was little on offer that can be seen archaeologically. What other means of post-Roman entertainment city dwellers had is open to interpretation.

Urban Identities?

If we put together the archaeological information at our disposal, together with the small windows into daily life obtained from the scarce texts (and with a great deal of comparison with other, better studied and more informative areas), it may be possible to have a glimpse of the identities of urban dwellers of our proposed case studies. It should be clearly stated here that by "identity" I am describing a complex series of superimposed and intersecting layers taken by an individual and by communities. Identities are not just social, ethnic or linguistic constructs, but the amalgamation of various characteristics that define an individual within his community and against "the other."[55]

---

53 Cf. Javier Martínez Jiménez, *Aqueducts and Urbanism in post-Roman Hispania,* Gorgias Studies in Classical and Late Antiquity 26 (Piscataway: Gorgias Press, 2019).

54 Bryan Ward-Perkins, *From Classical Antiquity to the Middle Ages: Urban Public Building in Northern and Central Italy AD 300–850* (Oxford: Oxford University Press, 1984), 152.

55 Walter Pohl, "Introduction: Strategies of Distinction," in *Strategies of Distinction: The Construction of Ethnic Communities, 300-800,* ed. Walter Pohl and Helmut Reimitz (Leiden: Brill, 1998), 1–15.

One clear element of identity that can be pinpointed is that these urban communities were eminently Christian, and there are no archaeological traces of active pagan activity. This may not be surprising or innovative, but it needs saying, even if it is simply because it may be the only element of identity that we can identify with absolute certainty. Besides the biased texts of the *Lives of the Father of Mérida* (a Christian text about bishops and their deeds), these urban dwellers were building churches, commemorating martyrs' tombs, and burying themselves in Christian fashion and on Christian locations (except for Reccopolis, where the necropolis of Visigothic date is yet to be identified). Even the funerary epigraphy, so abundant in Mérida, is ubiquitous in Christian self-defining epithets such as *servus Dei* or *famulus Dei*.[56] Town dwellers were Christian.

However, one may also point out that at Reccopolis the basilica would have been technically Arian (although liturgically or architectonically there is nothing that distinguishes it from a Catholic/Trinitarian one) as it was founded by Liuvigild, who was a champion of Arianism. Some (if not all?) of the original settlers of Reccopolis might also have been Arians themselves. Liuvigild was trying to achieve unity in his reign, including through the conversion of Catholics into Arianism, Reccopolis might have been a good excuse to have a wholly Arian community.[57] The re-consecration from Arian to Catholic of the cathedral of Saint Mary in Toledo by Reccared after his conversion, as commemorated in an inscription,[58] and the reference to

---

56 José Luis Ramírez Sádaba, "La primera epigrafía cristiana de Mérida," in *Los orígenes del cristianismo en Lusitania*, ed. Antonio González and Agustín Velázquez, Cuadernos Emeritenses 34 (Mérida: MNAR, 2008), 101–22.

57 This is all a suggestion, impossible to prove as a working hypothesis.

58 *IHC*, 155 = *ICERV*, 302: "In nomine d(o)m(i)n(i) consecra|ta ecclesia S(an) ct(a)e Mari(a)e| in cat(h)olico die pridie| idus aprilis anno feli|citer primo regni d(omi)ni| nostri gloriossisimi Fl(avii)| Reccaredi regis (a)era| DCXXV" ("In the name of the Lord, the church of Saint Mary was consecrated on a Catholic holiday the day before the ides of April in the first joyful year of the reign of our lord most glorious king Flavius Reccared. [Given] in the era of 625 [12 April 587 — perhaps Good Friday]").

Arian bishops and communities in *Lives of the Fathers of Mérida* and the acts of church councils also place these religious communities in other main cities of the kingdom. The number and proportion of Arians and Trinitarians is impossible to assess, but these two opposing communities certainly existed. Arianism was also a political marker, as an identity element for the Visigothic ruling elite, and conversions into Arianism would have been ways of climbing up in society.[59]

A small mention should be made of the Jews, whose presence in the Visigothic kingdom is evident through the constant legislation against them. They are also present in the material record (including a *menorah* carved in a hermit's cave near Ercavica), but also in inscriptions, such as the funerary epitaph of rabbi Jacob, from late Visigothic Mérida. Judaism would have been an "other" urban identity, as opposed to Christians.[60]

Town dwellers were also Latin-speaking — another obvious observation. However, there were some exceptional examples of Greek-speaking (or Greek-literate) individuals, especially bishops and other minor members of the clergy and occasional traders, recorded both in the sources and evident in the epigraphy.[61] Regarding Gothic speakers, there is no evidence for or against them, but I think it is doubtful Gothic was much spoken. The Visigoths had been deeply rooted in the Roman system from the end of the fourth century, and by the fifth and sixth they were a very heterogeneous group, with many non-Gothic individuals. Gothic seems to have been used purposefully in the court of Toulouse, but this was incidental and obviously used as a way

59 Manuel Koch, "Arianism and Ethnic Identity in Sixth-century Visigothic Spain," in *Arianism: Roman Heresy and Barbarian Creed,* ed. Guido Berndt and Roland Steinacher (London: Ashgate, 2014), 257–70.

60 Raúl González Salinero, "Fuentes arqueológicas y documentales para el estudio de los judíos en la Hispania Romana y Visigoda," in *¿Una Sefarad inventada?,* ed. Javier Castaño (Córdoba: El Almendro, 2014), 133–60.

61 Edgar Miguel Cruz, Monteiro Fernandes, and Miguel Filipe Grandão Valerio, "Comunidades helenógrafas en la Lusitania visigoda (s. VI)," *Pyrenae* 44, no. 2 (2013): 69–108.

to annoy Roman diplomats. The Arian church seems to have been deeply Latin-based as well, especially if they could conduct theological debates in Latin (in Spain, Gaul, and Africa). The use of personal Gothic names, lastly, is in no way an indicator, as they are simply markers of belonging (or intention to belong to) the Visigothic elite. The limited degree of preservation of Gothic words in Spanish (mostly limited to military terms) would also reinforce this statement.

Regarding ethnicity, ethnic "Romans" (descendants of people who lived in the Peninsula before the fifth century) and ethnic "Goths" (descendants of the Visigoths who settled in Gaul after 418 CE)[62] existed. It is difficult, however, to assess what their sixth-century descendants decided to identify themselves as. In fact, during this period of conflict, the term "Roman" usually depicted the "true Romans," the eastern troops of the "Byzantine" province (although "Goth" and, to a lesser extent, "Roman" still survived to a certain degree as political categories, both eventually simply meaning "citizens of the kingdom").[63] It is more likely that at a local and regional level (as it is the case of Gaul as described by Gregory of Tours)[64] people identified themselves through their extended *familia* rather than their gens (especially if it was a noble, or senatorial family) and through their city and associated local citizenship.[65] The fact that there was active competition amongst the main cities at religious and political levels (which city had the most powerful saint, or which city should be

---

62 The Visigoths were themselves a very heterogeneous group of Gothic and non-Gothic origins; cf. Peter Heather, "Goths and Huns," in *Cambridge Ancient History, Volume XIII: The Late Empire, AD 337–425*, ed. Averil Cameron and Peter Garnsey (Cambridge: Cambridge University Press, 1998), 487–515.

63 Erica Buchberger, *From Romans to Goths and Franks: Ethnic Identities in Sixth- and Seventh-Century Spain and Gaul* (Ph.D. diss, University of Oxford, 2012), esp. 80–82. I would like to thank Erica for her comments and for letting me have a look at her thesis.

64 Ibid., 114–17.

65 Javier Martínez Jiménez, "Urban Identity and Citizenship in the West between the Fifth and Seventh Centuries," *al-Masaq* 32, no. 1 (2020): 81–108.

the seat of the Visigothic kingdom)[66] could potentially underline this sense of citizenship or city identity.

The issue of "ethnic identity" is usually complicated when the archaeological record comes into play, especially when scholars (even today) repeatedly go back to old *etic* interpretative models through which to identify "ethnic" Visigoths through their grave goods.[67] This problem is, besides, based only on the assumption that the "ethnic Visigothic" community needed to identify and separate itself as such, which is not only a modern idea, but also purely hypothetical. These grave goods (usually weapons and *cloisonné* jewelry and other metal objects) are perhaps better understood as *emic* markers of rank and status.[68] In this way, the grave goods are interpreted not only by themselves, but in their specific (individual grave's skeletal remains) and general (within surrounding burials) contexts. The redefinition of the elites after the collapse of the Roman imperial system and during the process of Visigothic state formation required of an arena in which to display and confirm the new social structure.[69] These "Germanic" grave goods are linked to members of the new elite in service of the new monarchy, and this elite status is what separates these burials from the largely unfurnished burials of the non-elites. Therefore, weapons and jewelry displayed in

66 Cf. Sabine Panzram, "Mérida contra Toledo, Eulalia contra Leocadia. Listados 'falsificados' de obispos como medio de autorepresentación municipal," in *Espacios urbanos en el occidente mediterráneo (S. VI–VIII),* ed. Alfonso García (Toledo: Toletum Visigodo, 2010), 123–30.

67 Pots don't equal people: The modern equivalent would be to talk about ethnic "Americans" in Europe through the "iPod culture horizon." Cf. Carlos Tejerizo García, "Ethnicity in Early Middle Age Cemeteries. The Case of the 'Visigothic' Burials," *Arqueología y Territorio Medieval* 18 (2011): 29–43, who explains this in depth.

68 Cf. Heinrich Härke, "The Nature of Burial Data," in *Burials and Society: The Chronological and Social Analysis of Archaeology and Burial Data,* ed. Claus Jensen and Karen Nielsen (Aarhus: Aarhus University Press, 1997), 19–29.

69 Guy Halsall, *Early Medieval Cemeteries: An Introduction to Burial Archaeology in the Post-Roman West* (Skelmorlie: Cruithne Press, 1995), and Guy Halsall, "Ethnicity and Early Medieval Cemeteries," *Arqueología y Territorio Medieval* 18 (2011): 15–28.

burials served to reaffirm the position of the deceased's relatives amongst their community as members of the new aristocracy of the kingdom by the conspicuous destruction of wealth (and not necessarily ethnic markers).

That is the theory; the problem arrives when trying to apply this to urban contexts, because most of the necropoleis where these grave goods are found appear in rural contexts. Urban necropoleis tend to be more sober in their funerary display, perhaps because there were other ways of communicating these meanings of rank and status, and perhaps because urban communities were not as small or closed as rural ones. They follow similar patterns of concentration around "central" tombs or sacred spots, with a decreasing presence of metal objects (personal items, vases, etc.) from the sixth into the seventh century, so that by the end of our period the only grave goods appear to be pottery.[70] As mentioned, there are no burials known for Reccopolis. Near Toledo we find the necropolis of El Carpio de Tajo, with its famous "Visigothic" grave goods, but its location over twenty miles away from Toledo makes it hard to see it as an urban necropolis. If it were an urban necropolis (or linked to inhabitants of Toledo), then the reasons for its distant location are not obvious, and equally intriguing. Mérida, Toledo and Complutum have urban and peri-urban necropoleis, but only the necropolis of Daganzo, near Alcalá de Henares, has any significant finds that could be characterized as "Germanic" (in this case, weapons which simply indicate warrior status).[71]

---

70 Cf. Manuel Contreras Martínez and Antonio Fernández Ugalde, "El espacio funerario en el poblado de época visigoda de Gózquez de Arriba (San Martín de la Vega, Madrid)," in *La investigación arqueológica de la época visigoda en la Comunidad de Madrid*, ed. Jorge Morín de Pablos, Zona Arqueológica 8 (Alcalá de Henares: Museo Arqueológico Regional, 2006), 517–34.

71 Rascón and Sánchez, "Complutum tardoantiguo," 289.

Conclusions

When Michael Kulikowski wrote in 2006 "what those sixth- and seventh-century cities looked like, what it felt like to live in them, is at present completely beyond our power to reconstruct,"[72] he certainly highlighted a gap in our knowledge, a gap that perhaps it is nowadays easier to cast light on. In this very generic approach to the archaeology of Reccopolis and other sites from the southern Meseta, I have addressed an overall view of what cities looked like, what cities dwellers might have expected in them, what information we can reconstruct about their daily life, and, more boldly, how they might have portrayed and defined themselves.

In a daring go at a Homeric inversion, let us summarize the main ideas. The big and old question of ethnogenesis and ethnic identity is difficult to see in urban contexts. This is not only because of the lack of characteristic "Germanic" goods in urban sites, but mainly because these items should not be seen as ethnic markers: they are dialectic ways of consolidating rank and status within the community. It is more likely that city dwellers identified themselves through other means, such as family and lineage or, more simply, as members of their *civitas* and of the kingdom ("Roman" having gone out of fashion long before our period). In this sense, faith and language could have also identified various sub-groups within the body of citizens, which could be antagonized and seen as "the other."

At a more pedestrian level, urban interactions in the late sixth and seventh century took place in the context of Christian monumentality, with some elements that looked back to the Roman past. Most of the public monuments had been set up in a very particular socio-economic system where euergetism and magistracies paying *ex officio* funded a whole set of new

---

72 Michael Kulikowski, "The Late Roman City in Spain," in *Die Stadt in der Spätantike — Niedergang oder Wandel?*, ed. Jens-Uwe Krause and Christian Witschel (Stuttgart: Franz Steiner Verlag, 2006), 143.

buildings for administration and entertainment. After this very particular mode of funding building and entertainment was displaced by the new, late Roman administration, and partially discredited by the new Christian morals, these buildings ceased to fulfill a function and were slowly dismantled. Reccopolis is very illustrative in this sense, because the constructions identified on the site would reflect the ideal or expected urban amenities in a city of the late sixth century. These include an open area, a commercial street, religious and civil administrative centers and a water supply, but no theater, or circus, or a civil basilica. We have a similar view for Eio — El Tolmo de Minateda. The state and the urban elites had new architectural priorities.

Social gatherings and meeting points in these post-Roman towns would have followed Roman patterns, in as much as fora (in their late Roman modified, partially encroached and/or dismantled version) and market areas. In a few cases, baths also existed, but perhaps Christian buildings, especially in holidays also fulfilled this social function — they were, after all, the spiritual centers of the communities. On occasion, and especially in the royal capital, solemn royal celebrations would have provided entertainment. The layout of Reccopolis could suggest that similar events could have been imagined for it (and even taken place). For more mundane administrative and legal situations, "palaces" offered a centralized point of reference.

In terms of housing, and as far as we can tell from excavations, town dwellers lived in close communities, with more shared spaces than in previous periods as houses themselves became simpler in their design. We know little about the housing of the elites in this period (beyond those from the Vega Baja in Toledo), but this may be a problem of archaeological invisibility. Whether in new housing, in new foundations or in dwellings created out of earlier Roman shells, domestic architecture remains quite similar, with very noticeable changes from earlier or classical phases at all levels. These domestic changes in architecture and design also parallel changes in the domestic wares, which had to increasingly rely on local productions, as imported commodities were no longer available.

Overall, the inhabitants of Reccopolis had a daily life very similar to other town dwellers of the main cities of the Visigothic kingdom. The common traits shared by those high-status cities with strong economies (state-driven or not) are linked to the continuity of some elements of late Roman town life. In this sense, late Roman and post-Roman cities should be seen as a far more coherently defined as "late antique," in clear contraposition to "Classical" (or rather, "early imperial") examples. The southern Meseta, due to its direct connections with the Visigothic monarchy, could be compared to those important towns in Baetica or the Mediterranean coast, but those towns in the north or the west, where connections with the wider Mediterranean world seem more limited (and where Roman urbanism does not seem to have been as intense or effective),[73] tell a very different story.

---

73 Javier Martínez Jiménez and Carlos Tejerizo García, "Central Places in the Post-Roman Mediterranean: Regional Models for the Iberian Peninsula," *Journal of Mediterranean Archaeology* 28, no. 1 (2015): 81–104.

Bibliography

Primary

Chronica = John of Biclar. *Chronica a. DLXVII–DXC.* Edited by Theodor Mommsen. Monumenta Germaniae Historica, Auctores Antiquissimi 11. Berlin: Weidmann, 1894.

DLH = Gregory of Tours. *Decem libri historiarum.* Edited by Bruno Krusch and Wilhelm Levison. Monumenta Germaniae Historica, Scriptores Rerum Merovingicarum 1.1. Hanover: Hahn, 1951.

HWR = Julian of Toledo. *Historia Wambae Regis.* Edited by Jocelyn N. Hillgarth and and Wilhem Levison. Corpus Christianorum Series Latina 115. Turnhout: Brepols, 1976.

ICERV = *Inscripciones cristianas de la España romana y visigoda.* Edited by J. Vives. 2nd Edition. Barcelona: Consejo Superior de Investigaciones Científicas 1969.

IHC = *Inscripciones Hispaniae Christianae.* Edited by E. Hübner. Berlin: G. Reimeri, 1871–1900.

Isidore of Seville. *Etymologies. Isidori Hispalensis Episcopi Etymologiarum sive Originum Libri XX.* Edited by W. M. Lindsay, Oxford, 1911. Translation: *The Etymologies of Isidore of Seville.* Translated by Stephen A. Barney, W.J. Lewish, J.A. Beach, and Oliver Berghof. Cambridge: Cambridge University Press, 2006.

Variae = Cassiodorus Senator. *Epistulae Theodoricanae Variae.* Edited by Theodor Mommsen. Monumenta Germaniae Historica, Auctores Antiquissimi 12. Berlin: Weidmann, 1894.

VPE = [Paul the Deacon]. *De vita Patrum Emeritensium.* Edited by Jacques-Paul Migne. Patrologia Latina 80 (Paris: Garnier, 1863).

Secondary

Abad Casal, Lorenzo, Sonia Gutiérrez Lloret, Blanca Gamo Parras, and Pablo Cánovas Guillén. "Una ciudad en el camino: pasado y futuro de El Tolmo de Minateda (Hellín, Albacete)." In *Recópolis y la ciudad en la época visigoda,* edited by Lauro

Olmo Enciso, 323–36. Zona Arqueológica 9. Alcalá de Henares: Museo Arqueológico Regional, 2008.

Abascal Palazón, Juan Manuel, Martín Almagro Gorbea, and Rosario Cebrián Fernández. "Segóbriga visigoda." In *Recópolis y la ciudad en la época visigoda,* edited by Lauro Olmo Enciso, 221–41. Zona Arqueológica 9. Alcalá de Henares: Museo Arqueológico Regional, 2008.

Acero Pérez, Jesús, and Josep Anton Remolà Vallverdú. *La gestión de los residuos urbanos en Hispania. Xavier Dupré Raventós (1956–2006) in memoriam.* Anejos de Archivo Español de Arqueología 60. Mérida: CSIC, 2011.

Alba Calzado, Miguel. "La vivienda en Emerita durante la antigüedad tardía: propuesta de un modelo para Hispania." In *VI Reunió d'Arqueologia Cristiana Hispànica,* edited by Josep Maria Gurt and Albert Ribera, 121–50. Barcelona: IEC, 2005.

Alba Calzado, Miguel, and Pedro Mateos Cruz. "El paisaje urbano de Emerita en época visigoda." In *Recópolis y la ciudad en la época visigoda,* edited by Lauro Olmo Enciso, 261–73. Zona Arqueológica 9. Alcalá de Henares: Museo Arqueológico Regional, 2008.

Alba Calzado, Miguel, and Santiago Feijoo Martínez. "Pautas evolutivas de la cerámica común de Mérida en épocas visigoda y emiral." In *Cerámicas tardorromanas y altomedievales en la Península Ibérica,* edited by Luis Caballero, Pedro Mateos, and Manuel Retuerce, 483–504. Anejos de Archivo Español de Arqueología 28. Mérida: CSIC, 2003.

Arce, Javier. "Recópolis, la ciudad fantasma." In *Doctrina a magistro discipulis tradita. Estudios en homenaje al profesor Dr. Luis García Iglesias,* edited by Adolfo Domínguez and Gloria Mora Rodríguez, 373–94. Madrid: Universidad Autónoma de Madrid, 2010.

Buchberger, Erica. *From Romans to Goths and Franks: Ethnic Identities in Sixth- and Seventh-Century Spain and Gaul.* Ph.D. diss., University of Oxford, 2012. https://ora.ox.ac.uk/objects/uuid:1c70a75a-9556-4642-93ea-220b877155c6.

Burillo Mozota, Francisco. *Los celtíberos. Etnias y estados.* Barcelona: Crítica, 1998.

Caballero Zoreda, Luis, Pedro Mateos Cruz, and Manuel Retuerce, eds. *Cerámicas tardorromanas y altomedievales en la Península Ibérica.* Anejos de Archivo Español de Arqueología 28. Mérida: CSIC, 2003.

Castro Priego, Manuel, and Amaya Gómez de la Torre-Verdejo. "La actividad artesanal en Recópolis: la producción de vidrio." In *Recópolis y la ciudad en la época visigoda,* edited by Lauro Olmo Enciso, 117–28. Zona Arqueológica 9. Alcalá de Henares: Museo Arqueológico Regional, 2008.

Cepas Palanca, Adela. *Crisis y continuidad en la Hispania del siglo III.* Anejos de Archivo Español de Arqueología 17. Madrid: CSIC, 1997.

Contreras Martínez, Manuel, and Antonio Fernández Ugalde. "El espacio funerario en el poblado de época visigoda de Gózquez de Arriba (San Martín de la Vega, Madrid)." In *La investigación arqueológica de la época visigoda en la Comunidad de Madrid,* edited by Jorge Morín de Pablos, 517–34. Zona Arqueológica 8. Alcalá de Henares: Museo Arqueológico Regional, 2006.

Crawford, John. *The Byzantine Shops at Sardis.* Cambridge: Harvard University Press, 1990.

Dey, Hendrik. *The Afterlife of the Roman City: Architecture and Ceremony in Late Antiquity and the Early Middle Ages.* Cambridge: Cambridge University Press, 2014. DOI: 10.1017/ CBO9781107706538.

Esmonde Cleary, Simon. *The Roman West, AD 200–500: An Archaeological Study.* Cambridge: Cambridge University Press, 2013. DOI: 10.1017/CBO9781139043199.

Fernandes, Edgar Miguel Cruz Monteiro, and Miguel Filipe Grandão Valerio. "Comunidades helenógrafas en la Lusitania visigoda (s. VI)." *Pyrenae* 44, no. 2 (2013): 69–108.

Fuentes Domínguez, Ángel. "La antigüedad tardía en Castilla-La Mancha." In *Castilla-La Mancha en época romana y antigüedad tardía,* edited by Ángel Fuentes Domínguez, 176–213. Ciudad Real: Universidad de Castilla-La Mancha, 2006.

———. "Vidrio de la Antigüedad tardía (ss.V–X). Cuestiones de fabricación y comercialización. Problemas de identificación." In *Vidrio islámico en Al-Andalus,* edited by Enrique Rontomé Notario, 13–36. Madrid: Fundación Centro Nacional del Vidrio, 2007.

García García, Marcos. "Some Remarks on the Provisioning of Animal Products to Urban Centres in Medieval Islamic Iberia: The Cases of Madinat Ilbirah (Granada) and Cercadilla (Cordoba)." *Quaternary International* 460 (2016): 86–96. DOI: 10.1016/j.quaint.2016.06.021.

García-Entero, Virginia. *Los balnea domésticos — ámbito rural y urbano — en la Hispania romana.* Anejos de Archivo Español de Arqueología 37. Madrid: CSIC, 2005.

Gómez de la Torre-Verdejo, Amaya. "La muralla de Recópolis." In *Recópolis y la ciudad en la época visigoda,* edited by Lauro Olmo Enciso, 77–86. Zona Arqueológica 9. Alcalá de Henares: Museo Arqueológico Regional, 2008.

González Salinero, Raúl. "Fuentes arqueológicas y documentales para el estudio de los judíos en la Hispania Romana y Visigoda." In *¿Una Sefarad inventada?,* edited by Javier Castaño, 133–60. Córdoba: El Almendro, 2014.

Grau Sologestoa, Idoia. *The Zooarchaeology of Medieval Álava in its Iberian Context.* British Archaeological Reports International Series 2769. Oxford: Archaeopress, 2015.

Gurt Esparraguera, Josep Maria, and Pilar Diarte Blasco. "La basílica de santa Leocadia y el final de uso del circo romano de Toledo: Una nueva interpretación." *Zephyrus* 69 (2012): 149–63.

Gutiérrez García, Anna. *Roman Quarries in the Northeast of Hispania (Modern Catalonia).* Tarragona: ICAC, 2009.

Gutiérrez Lloret, Sonia. "Gramática de la casa. Perspectivas de análisis arqueológico de los espacios domésticos medievales en la Península Ibérica (siglos VII–XIII)." *Arqueología de la Arquitectura* 9 (2012): 139–64. DOI: 10.3989/arqarqt.2012.11602.

Gutiérrez Lloret, Sonia, Lorenzo Abad Casal, and Blanca Gamo Parras. "'Eio', 'Iyyuh' y el Tolmo de Minateda (Hellín, Albacete): de sede episcopal a 'madîna' islámica." In *VI Reunió d'Arqueologia Cristiana Hispànica,* edited by Josep Maria Gurt and Albert Ribera, 345–70. Barcelona: IEC, 2005.

Gutiérrez Lloret, Sonia, and Julia Sarabia Bautista. "The Episcopal Complex of Eio-El Tolmo de Minateda (Hellín, Albacete, Spain). Architecture and Spatial Organization. 7th to 8th Centuries AD." *Hortus Artium Medeivalium* 19 (2013): 267–300. DOI: 10.1484/J.HAM.1.103584.

Härke, Heinrich. "The Nature of Burial Data." In *Burials and Society: The Chronological and Social Analysis of Archaeology and Burial Data,* edited by Claus Jensen and Karen Nielsen, 19–29. Aarhus: Aarhus University Press, 1997.

Halsall, Guy. *Early Medieval Cemeteries: An Introduction to Burial Archaeology in the Post-Roman West.* Skelmorlie: Cruithne Press, 1995.

———. "Ethnicity and Early Medieval Cemeteries." *Arqueología y Territorio Medieval* 18 (2011): 15–28.

Heather, Peter. "Goths and Huns." In *Cambridge Ancient History. Volume XIII. The Late Empire, AD 337–425,* edited by Averil Cameron and Peter Garnsey, 487–515. Cambridge: Cambridge University Press, 1998. DOI: 10.1017/CHOL9780521302005.017.

Henning, Joachim, Michael McCormick, Lauro Olmo Enciso, Knut Rassman, and Eyub Fikrit. "Reccopolis Revealed: First Geomagnetic Mapping of the Early Medieval Visigothic Royal Town," *Antiquity* 93, no. 369 (2019), 735–51. DOI: 10.15184/aqy.2019.66.

Houten, Pieter. *Civitates Hispaniae: Urbanisation on the Iberian Peninsula during the High Empire.* Ph.D. diss., Leiden University, 2018. https://openaccess.leidenuniv.nl/handle/1887/68032.

Jiménez Sánchez, Juan Anotnio. "Los últimos ludi circenses realizados en Hispania en época visigoda." *Faventia* 28, no. 1 (2006): 99–113.

Kaiser, Alan. *Roman Urban Street Networks.* London: Routledge, 2011. DOI: 10.4324/9780203821817.

Koch, Manuel. "Arianism and Ethnic Identity in Sixth-century Visigothic Spain." In *Arianism: Roman Heresy and Barbar-*

ian Creed, edited by Guido Berndt and Roland Steinacher, 257–70. London: Ashgate, 2014.

Kulikowski, Michael. "The Late Roman City in Spain." In *Die Stadt in der Spätantike — Niedergang oder Wandel?,* edited by Jens-Uwe Krause and Christian Witschel, 129–49. Stuttgart: Franz Steiner Verlag, 2006.

Liebeschuetz, Wolfgang. "The End of the Ancient City." In *The City in Late Antiquity,* edited by John Rich, 1–50. Ashgate: London, 1992.

Martínez Jiménez, Javier. "A Preliminary Study of the Aqueduct of Reccopolis." *Oxford Journal of Archaeology* 34, no. 4 (2015): 301–20. DOI: 10.1111/ojoa.12060.

———. *Aqueducts and Urbanism in post-Roman Hispania.* Gorgias Studies in Classical and Late Antiquity 26. Piscataway: Gorgias Press, 2019.

———. "Urban Identity and Citizenship in the West between the Fifth and Seventh Centuries." *al-Masaq* 32, no. 1 (2020): 81–108. DOI: 10.1080/09503110.2019.1675026.

———. "Water Supply in the Visigothic Urban Foundations of Eio (El Tolmo de Minateda) and Reccopolis." In *New Cities in Late Antiquity: Documents and Archaeology,* edited by Efthymios Rizos, 233–45. Bibliothèque de l'Antiquité Tardive 35. Turnhout: Brepols, 2017.

Martínez Jiménez, Javier, and Carlos Tejerizo García. "Central Places in the Post-Roman Mediterranean: Regional Models for the Iberian Peninsula." *Journal of Mediterranean Archaeology* 28, no. 1 (2015): 81–104. DOI: 10.1558/jmea.v28i1.27502.

Martínez Jiménez, Javier, and José María Moreno Narganes. "Nunc autem a Gothis subversa: The Province of Alicante and the Spanish Mediterranean Towns Between the Byzantine and Visigothic Periods." *Early Medieval Europe* 23, no. 3 (2015): 263–89. DOI: 10.1111/emed.12104

Mateos Cruz, Pedro. "La identificación del xenodochium fundado por Masona en Mérida." In *IV Reunió d'Arqueologia Cristiana Hispànica,* edited by Josep Maria Gurt Esparraguera, and Núria Tena, 309–16. Barcelona: Institut d'Estudis Catalans, 1995.

Mateos Cruz, Pedro, and Isaac Sastre de Diego. "Elementos arquitectónicos tardoantiguos y altomedievales en el Templo
de Diana (Mérida, España)." *Mérida. Excavaciones arqueológicas 7* (2004): 397–415.

Moreno Martín, Francisco. "Circulación de modelos y circularidad de argumentación para el conocimiento de la topografía
cristiana entre la Antigüedad Tardía y la Alta Edad Media," In
*Entre civitas y madina. El mundo de las ciudades en la Penín-
sula Ibérica y en el norte de África (siglos IV–IX),* edited by
Sabine Panzram and Laurent Callegarin, 153–72. Collection
de la Casa de Velázquez 16. Madrid: Casa de Velázquez, 2018.

Navarro Palazón, Julio, and Pedro Jiménez Castillo. "Algunas reflexiones sobre el urbanismo islámico." *Artigrama* 22 (2007):
259–98

Olmo Enciso, Lauro. "La Vega Baja en época visigoda: una investigación arqueológica en construcción." In *La Vega Baja
de Toledo,* edited by Alfonso García and Diego Perís, 69–94.
Toledo: Toletum Visigodo, 2009.

———. "Recópolis: una ciudad en época de transformaciones."
In *Recópolis y la ciudad en la época visigoda,* edited by Lauro
Olmo Enciso, 40–63. Zona Arqueológica 9. Alcalá de Hena-
res: Museo Arqueológico Regional, 2008.

———. "The Royal Foundation of Recópolis and the Urban Renewal in Iberia during the Second Half of the Sixth Century."
In *Post-Roman Towns and Trade in Europe and Byzantium,*
edited by Joachim Henning, 181–99. Berlin: DeGruyter, 2007.

Olmo Enciso, Lauro, Manuel Castro Priego, Amaya Gómez de
la Torre-Verdejo, and Álvaro Sanz Paratcha. "Recópolis y su
justificación científica: la secuencia estratigráfica." In *Recópolis y la ciudad en la época visigoda,* edited by Lauro Olmo Enciso, 64–75. Zona Arqueológica 9. Alcalá de Henares: Museo
Arqueológico Regional, 2008.

Ozcariz Gil, Pablo. *Los conventus de la Hispania Citerior.* Madrid: Dykinson, 2006.

Panzram, Sabine. "Mérida contra Toledo, Eulalia contra Leocadia. Listados 'falsificados' de obispos como medio de autorepresentación municipal." In *Espacios urbanos en el occi-*

dente mediterráneo (S. VI–VIII), edited by Alfonso García, 123–30. Toledo: Toletum Visigodo, 2010.

Pliego Vázquez, Ruth. *La moneda visigoda I. Historia monetaria del Reino visigodo de Toledo (c. 569–711).* Seville: Universidad de Sevilla, 2009.

Pohl, Walter. "Introduction: Strategies of Distinction." In *Strategies of Distinction: The Construction of Ethnic Communities, 300–800,* edited by Walter Pohl and Helmut Reimitz, 1–15. Leiden: Brill, 1998.

Ramírez Sádaba, José Luis. "La primera epigrafía cristiana de Mérida." In *Los orígenes del cristianismo en Lusitania,* edited by Antonio González and Agustín Velázquez, 101–22. Cuadernos Emeritenses 34. Mérida: MNAR, 2008.

Rascón Marqués, Sebastián, and Ana Lucía Sánchez Montes. "Complutum tardoantiguo." In *La investigación arqueológica de la época visigoda en la Comunidad de Madrid,* edited by Jorge Morín de Pablos, 267–91. Zona Arqueológica 8. Alcalá de Henares: Museo Arqueológico Regional, 2006.

Rizos, Efthymios, ed. *New Cities in Late Antiquity. Documents and Archaeology.* Bibliothèque de l'Antiquité Tardive 35. Turnhout: Brepols, 2017.

Sánchez López, Elena, and Javier Martínez Jiménez. *Los Acueductos de Hispania. Construcción y Abandono.* Madrid: Fundación Juanelo Turriano, 2016.

Tejerizo García, Carlos. "Ethnicity in Early Middle Age Cemeteries. The Case of the 'Visigothic' Burials." *Arqueología y Territorio Medieval* 18 (2011): 29–43.

Vidal Castro, Francisco. "Agua y urbanismo: evacuación de aguas en fatwà-s de al-Andalus y el Norte de África." In *L'urbanisme dans l'occident musulmana du Moyen Âge. Aspects juridiques,* edited by Patrice Cressier, Maribel Fierro, and Jean-Pierre van Staëuel, 101–23. Madrid: Casa Velázquez, 2000.

Vigil-Escalera, Alfonso, and Juan Antonio Quirós Castillo, eds. *La cerámica de la Alta Edad Media en el cuadrante noroeste de la Península Ibérica (siglos V–X).* Bilbao: Universidad del País Vasco, 2016.

Ward-Perkins, Bryan. *From Classical Antiquity to the Middle Ages: Urban Public Building in Northern and Central Italy AD 300–850.* Oxford: Oxford University Press, 1984.

6

Augusta Emerita in Late Antiquity: The Transformation of Its Urban Layout During the Fourth and Fifth Centuries CE

Pedro Mateos Cruz

Roman cities were not created as a perennial urban project; quite to the contrary, they constantly evolved, with some researchers stating that they give the sensation of having had building work underway at all times. In archaeological excavations, we often find signs of different types of significant reforms made to the urban fabric that were carried out in just a few years; projects that completed others that had been started some years earlier. These were processes of social, economic, political, and cultural change, which can be seen very clearly in the urban development of these cities.

A clear example of this process was the construction of the provincial center for Imperial worship, which led to the transformation of four blocks of houses and a section of the *cardo maximus,* fifty years after the founding of the Roman colony of

Fig. 1. Ground plan of Augusta Emerita from the Flavian period onwards. By the author.

Augusta Emerita.[1] We have also documented reformation work carried out on the forum, with the construction of the eastern platform over two blocks of houses,[2] or later, in the third century CE, the reformation of several *domus* for the construction of a public building, next to the provincial center for Imperial worship, whose function we are still unable to ascertain.[3] These modifications, to mention just a few examples, gradually transformed the urban landscape, and are a further example of the

---

1   Pedro Mateos Cruz, *El llamado foro provincial de Augusta Emerita. Un conjunto monumental de culto imperial,* Anejos de Archivo Español de Arqueología 42 (Madrid: CSIC, 2006), 321.

2   Rocío Ayerbe Vélez, Teresa Barrientos, and Felix Palma, "Los complejos forenses de 'Augusta Emerita," in *El Foro de Augusta Emerita. Génesis y evolución de sus recintos monumentales,* ed. Rocío Ayerbe Vélez, Teresa Barrientos, and Felix Palma, Anejos de Archivo Español de Arqueología 53 (Madrid: CSIC, 2009), 667–832, at 747–53.

3   Rocío Ayerbe Vélez "La llamada basílica de Laborde: identificación, ubicación y cronología. Intervención arqueológica en la C/ Calvario 8," *Memoria, Excavaciones Arqueológicas en Mérida 2002* (2005): 27–54.

vitality of a city that adapted its urban layout to new circumstances (fig. 1).

Throughout the second and third centuries, new signs of this construction activity in the city are documented, as well as the maintenance of its public vitality. In 261, the governor Clodius Laetus Macrinus dedicated a statue in the forum to the emperor Gallienus, proof of a continuity in administrative life that was uninterrupted until at least this moment in time.[4] At the end of the third century, these dedications to emperors made by governors multiplied in number, indicating that there were indeed signs of a breakdown in the governance of the city during this period.[5] These details probably, in fact, indicate that there were multiple interruptions to the public functioning of the city,[6] if we take into account the previously existing situation, although the same argument may suggest a continuity. The sculpture workshops were likely not as active as they had been in former times. The relief of Maximilian Herculeus[7] is an indication of the decline of the workshops, but also the continuity of the classical official iconographic models.[8] The paintings from the basil-

4 Javier Arce, "Introducción histórica," in *Las capitales provinciales de Hispania: Augusta Emerita,* vol. 2, ed. Xavier Dupré (Rome: "L'Erma" di Bretschneider, 2004), 7–14, at 12.

5 José Luis Ramirez, Agustín Velázquez, and Eulalia Gijón, "Un nuevo pedestal de Galieno encontrado en Mérida," *Anas* 6 (1993): 75–84; José Carlos Saquete, José Luis Mosquera, and Juana Márquez, "Aemilius Aemilianus, un nuevo gobernador de la Lusitania," *Anas* 4–5 (1992): 31–43.

6 Javier Arce, "Augusta Emerita: Continuidad y transformación (ss. IV-VII)," in *Actas del Congreso Internacional 1910–2010, el yacimiento emeritense,* ed. José María Álvarez and Pedro Mateos Cruz (Mérida: Ayuntamiento de Mérida, 2011), 491–504, 491.

7 Javier Arce, "Augusta Emerita en el s. V d. C.," in *Mérida Tardorromana (300–580 d. C.),* Cuadernos emeritenses 22 (Mérida: Museo Nacional de Arte Romano, 2002), 179–194, at 114.

8 Javier Arce, "Augusta Emerita," 492.

ica house[9] and the mosaics from the house "of the Mithraeum"[10] reveal a certain degree of continuity and Roman tradition in the local workshops.[11]

As we have seen, although we cannot compare the dynamism of the city's buildings or art with that of previous periods, it does seem clear that activity persisted at this time, coinciding with the administrative reforms of Diocletian (r. 284–304). The possible choice of the colony of Emerita as the capital of the *Diocesis Hispaniarum* seems to be attested, from a historical perspective, by the interpretation of the *Laterculus Polemii Silvii* and the inclusion of Emerita as the only city in the list of new provinces in Hispania,[12] in the same way as Carthage in Africa, or Sirmium in Illyricum.[13] This argument is the only historical document we have to support this statement, although it should be noted that there are archaeological data that point in this direction. The discovery of the inscription of the *vicarius Octavius Clarus* who declared himself as *famulus Gratiani* serves as further proof of this fact.[14]

In order to underline the fact that the city was a capital, we have to consider a vitally important piece of evidence provided by the appearance of the *missorium* of Theodosius, found in the town of Almandraleja, close to Mérida, which amongst other figures shows the *Vicarius Hispaniarum* in the process of receiving the *codicilli* of his new post from the emperor Theodosius I. This means it would have been a gift from the emperor to

---

9   Antonio Mostalac, "El programa pictórico de la estancia absidada F de la Casa Basílica de Mérida," in *Congreso Internacional: La Hispania de Teodosio,* ed. Ramón Teja (Segovia: Junta de Castilla y León, Consejería y Cultura, 1997): 581–603.

10 Arce, "Augusta Emerita en el s. V d. C.," 115.

11 Arce, "Augusta Emerita," 492.

12 Robert Etienne, "Mérida capitale du vicariat des Espagnes," in *Homenaje a Saenz de Buruaga* (Badajoz: Diputación Provincial de Badajoz, 1982), 201–8.

13 Arce, "Augusta Emerita en el s. V d. C.," 115.

14 Rafael Hidalgo y Guadalupe Méndez, "Octavius Clarus, un nuevo vicarius Hispaniarum en Augusta Emerita," *Memoria, Excavaciones Arqueológicas en Mérida 2002* (2008): 547–64.

the *vicarius*. The reinterpretation made by Jutta Meischner, associating the disk with Theodosius II[15] has been clearly refuted by Javier Arce.[16]

It is difficult to identify the reasons why Augusta Emerita was chosen as the site of the *Vicarius Hispaniarum* due to the lack of historical and archaeological data that could shed light on this matter. The continuity of its economic, cultural, and political activity would have been a basic factor, although we still do not know the historical and political reasons for this choice. Arce suggests that this would have been due to its peripheral geopolitical location in relation to the rest of the cities in the diocese. Well connected to the dioceses of Baetica, Tarraconense, and Cartaginense, it displaced the political axis towards a less conflictive region, with less possibilities of falling into the hands of usurpers and rebels, as was the case with Tarraco and Carthago Nova.[17]

The legal and administrative consequences of this designation, and the arrival of the *vicarius* and all the governing posts of the diocese have been studied in detail by Arce.[18] In terms of its urban development, this period saw a series of transformations made to the city, which must be seen in the light of this new designation, and the impetus that came about as a result of these administrative changes in the old colony. This is the case of the renovation work carried out in the buildings used for leisure purposes and performances.

Epigraphic and archaeological evidence has been found of the renovation of the main buildings used for performances at that time, between the year 335 — in the theater and amphitheater — and 337 — the circus — indicating that they were in continuous use. Apart from the inscriptions referring to this event,

15 Jutta Meischner, "Das Missorium des Theodosius in Madrid," *Jahrbuch des Deutschen Archäologischen Instituts* 3 (1996): 389–432.
16 Javier Arce, "Teodosio I sigue siendo Teodosio I," *Archivo Español de Arqueología* 71 (1998): 169–79.
17 Arce, "Introducción histórica," 12.
18 Arce, "Augusta Emerita en el s. V d. C.," 115.

Fig. 2. General view of the circus of Emerita. By the author.

the decorative sculptures preserved from these buildings clearly serve to date these projects, which can also be seen in the archaeological data provided by excavation work carried out in the theater[19] and the circus.[20]

The restoration of the circus *vetustate con lapsum,* during the period of the sons of Constantine (337–350) (fig. 2) indicates that there was a certain degree of economic recovery, and that it was a result of a deliberate policy for rebuilding public buildings, and the idea that it was unthinkable to have a capital of a diocese without the presence of a circus in all its activity, as

---

19 Pedro Mateos Cruz and Antonio Pizzo, "Los Edificios de ocio y representación en Augusta Emerita: El teatro y el Anfiteatro," in *Actas del Congreso Internacional 1910–2010,* ed. Álvarez and Mateos, 173–94.

20 Ana Montalvo, Eulalia Gijón, and Javier Sánchez, "Circo romano de Mérida. Campaña de 1995," *Memoria 1. Excavaciones Arqueológicas realizadas en Mérida durante 1994 y 95* (1997): 245–58.

demonstrated by mosaics showing circus scenes dating from the middle of the fourth century.[21]

Similarly, the theater was renovated, as referred to in another inscription which describes the poor condition of the building and its restoration between 333 and 335, under the supervision of the *praeses provinciae Lusitaniae,* Severus.[22] We do not know if the alterations made around the building were related to this restoration work, or if they were new projects carried out at this time; these alterations included the abandonment of the outer doorways leading into the theater from the north side of the city, which were made at the same time as the *porticus post scaenam.*[23] These doorways were transformed into shops with direct access to the *cardus* that separated the theater and the amphitheater in a north-south direction.

This new status as a capital led to numerous refurbishments and modifications being made to the urban structure. The incorporation of new governors and institutions, and the logical interest in improving the image of the city, must have provided sufficient impetus to justify the restoration of the main buildings in the colony, and the construction of others of which we are still unaware. This dynamism, and the new needs of the city, brought about substantial changes to the urban fabric, of which we have archaeological evidence in some cases.[24]

21 Antonio Blanco, *Los mosaicos romanos de Mérida,* Corpus de Mosaicos romanos de España (Madrid: CSIC, 1978), 45.

22 Trinidad Nogales, *Espectáculos en Augusta Emerita,* Monografías Emeritenses 5 (Mérida: Museo Nacional de Arte Romano, 2000), 31.

23 Pedro Mateos Cruz and Juana Marquez, "Nuevas estructuras urbanas relacionadas con el teatro romano de Mérida: El pórtico de acceso," *Memoria III. Excavaciones Arqueológicas realizadas en Mérida durante 1997* (1999): 301–20.

24 Pedro Mateos Cruz and Miguel Alba, "De Emerita Augusta a Marida," in *Actas del Simposio Internacional Visigodos y Omeyas: Un debate entre la tardoantiguedad y la Alta Edad Media,* ed. Luís Caballero and Pedro Mateos Cruz, Anejos de Archivo Español de Arqueología 23 (Madrid: CSIC, 2000), 143–68, at 145.

For example, in the case of the urban layout, according to the archaeological data we have documented, the road network remained unchanged; however, a series of modifications were made, such as the privatization of the gateways for the roads, which occurred diachronically from the second to the fourth century, by the houses that occupied these spaces, and which increased their domestic space or used them as *tabernae* for commercial purposes. During the excavation work carried out in Morería, it was found that the street had been fully or partly invaded in order to build baths in two of its houses.[25] This invasion of the streets by houses on occasions is interpreted as something negative, when in fact the only thing it demonstrates is the vitality of the city at this time, and an increase in private enterprise in relation to the public interest.[26] However, this is an interesting aspect when it comes to evaluating the start of the urban transformations that heralded major changes in the concept of the city.

Another situation that has been documented in the streets of Emerita during this period is the laying of new paving over the streets, with diorite stones. Apart from raising the level of the streets, in the case of the *decumanus,* it would have lowered their east–west slope, used to empty their sewers into the River Anas. This new road surface would have covered over the manholes leading into the sewer network, putting the sanitation network at risk, and which may have fallen into disuse by the end of the century, something that is more evident in the fifth century. What we see in the streets of the city, their continuity in the lay-

25 Miguel Alba, "Ocupación diacrónica del Area Arqueológica de Morería (Mérida)," in *Memoria, Excavaciones Arqueológicas en Mérida 1994–1995,* ed. Miguel Alba Calzado, Pedro Mateos Cruz, and Juana Márquez Pérez (Madrid: Consorcio de la Ciudad monumental de Mérida, 1997), 285–315, at 292.

26 Miguel Alba "Diacronía de la vivienda señorial de Emerita (Lusitania, Hispania): Desde las domus altoimperiales y tardoantiguas a las residencias palaciales omeyas (Siglos I–IX)," in *Archeologia e società tra tardoantico e alto medioevo,* ed. Jean Pietro Brogiolo (Padua: Universitá di Padova, 2008), 163–92, at 172.

Fig. 3. Remains of the dwelling known as the "House of Marbles" in the Archaeological Zone of Morería. By the author.

out with changes in their shape and external image, also applies to the majority of the urban structures in Emerita at this time.

As regards the dwellings located in the area within the city walls, apart from the previously mentioned "invasion" of the street found in some cases, excavation work carried out in the archaeological zone of Morería has identified refurbishment work, where the size of some buildings was increased, adding large, vaulted salons in some cases, with private baths (fig. 3).[27]

During this same century, probably during the second half, based on the analysis of the paintings found in the interior,[28] the so called "basilica house" of the theater was built — a domestic structure built by making use of part of the entrance doorways leading into the theater,[29] which meant abandoning public spac-

---

27 Alba, "Ocupación diacrónica del Area Arqueológica de Morería (Mérida)," 290.

28 Mostalac, "El programa pictórico de la estancia absidada F de la Casa Basílica de Mérida."

29 Mateos Cruz and Marquez, "Nuevas estructuras urbanas relacionadas con el teatro romano de Mérida."

es in favor of private occupation. Arce interprets this as a *schola* or *collegium*.[30]

As previously mentioned, during this century, the workshops that contributed to monumentalizing some of the prosperous homes — which altered their floors and walls by installing luxurious mosaics and painted tapestries, and which decorated their rooms — were still operational. This has been deduced from a study of the mosaic in *opus sectile* and the paintings from the house in the citadel, for example, from the paintings in Calle Suarez Somonte with circus scenes and *venationes*[31] or from some of the mosaics and paintings that decorated the so-called "House of the Mithraeum," as well as the cosmogonic mosaic dated by Arce to the mid-fourth century.[32]

Another element that defines the continuity of the urban layout throughout the fourth century is the continued presence of the forum areas, and the main public buildings whose architectural and functional structure was not altered until the fifth century. It is likely that the new status as a capital of the diocese would have led to some type of changes being made to the official architecture of Augusta Emerita, such as that found in a public building belonging to the western platform of the forum, which may have been the *schola iuvenum,*[33] inside which a thermal structure was built, dated from the late imperial period, without the possibility of offering a more detailed chronology.

Apart from this refurbishment carried out on the western platform, we do not have any archaeological or epigraphic data whatsoever that confirms the new transformation work carried

---

30 Javier Arce, Alexandra Chavarria, and Gisela Ripoll, "Theurbandomus in Late Antique Hispania. Examples from Emerita, Barcino and Complutum," in *Housing in Late Antiquity,* ed. Luke Lavan, Lale Özgenel, and Alexander Sarantis, Late Antique Archaeology 3.2 (Leiden: Brill, 2007) 305–36, at 309–11.

31 José Álvarez Sáenz de Buruaga, "Una casa romana con valiosas pinturas, en Mérida," *Habis* 5 (1974): 169–87.

32 Arce, "Augusta Emerita en el s. V d. C.," 117–36.

33 Ayerbe Vélez, Barrientos, and Palma, "Los complejos forenses de 'Augusta Emerita," 747–53, 800.

Fig. 4. Water conduit known as "Los Milagros." By the author.

out in the forum during the fourth century. These were probably not structural reforms, but instead ornamental work, although if they did take place, they have not been documented to date.

As regards the public infrastructures, it is important to note the lack of documentation referring to the re-use of the aqueducts, where the only piece of archaeological data has been provided by excavation work carried out on a section of the conduit of "Los Milagros," (fig. 4) where five coins were found amongst the filling material, all of which dated from the time of Constantine II (337–340) and Constantius II (346–354), although the fact that these coins were in use for a lengthy period means it is impossible to precisely date when they were obliterated.[34] However, due to the lack of a monographic study of these structures, we still do not know the precise date of their construction, their renovations over the centuries, and their re-use.

34 Rocío Ayerbe Vélez, "Intervención arqueológica en la urbanización Jardines de Mérida de la Avda. de la plata. Excavación de un tramo de conducción hidráulica Proserpina-Los Milagros," *Memoria, Excavaciones Arqueológicas en Mérida 1998* (2000): 39–58.

We have also observed the continued development of the walled area of Augusta Emerita during this period. As we will see later on, although the city walls were reinforced with a lining of large blocks of stone for defensive purposes at an unknown moment during the fifth century, not one single renovation has been documented, either in its layout or architectural details, during the fourth century. It is possible that sporadic reformations were made to its structure, affecting the gates, ramparts, and towers that stood on top. For example, raising the height of the *decumanus,* as a result of laying new paving materials, also resulted in changes in the arches of the gates in the wall, whose heights had to be altered.

However, the main urban changes during this period took place outside the city walls. While the pagan funerary areas had maintained their size in the areas around the main roads leading into the city, during this century they seem to have collapsed, and grown in size. In addition to this growth of the necropoli, there was an urban change that is difficult to explain, resulting from the progressive abandonment of the suburban houses, whose owners moved to either refurbished and enlarged houses within the walls, or to new, sumptuous *villae* in the countryside, which extended throughout the ager of Emerita during this century. This was the case in the north-east part of the city, where the abandonment of the suburban *domus* in the area has been documented during this time, such as the "house of the amphitheater," built entirely throughout the first century CE, although with refurbishments made to its walls and floors over the years.[35] This could be connected to the pressure caused by the constant growth of the funerary area known as the "eastern necropolis," confirmed by the discovery of a mausoleum dating from the

---

35 José María Álvarez, "Excavaciones en Augusta Emerita," in *Arqueología de las ciudades modernas superpuestas a las antiguas,* ed. Alberto Balil (Zaragoza: Ministerio de Cultura, 1985), 35–54, at 46.

mid-third century, in an area halfway between the previously documented necropolis and the "house of the amphitheater."[36]

Finally, we have the discovery of new funerary areas from the late Roman period, especially in the south and north-east part of the city, which occupied the abandoned space of the suburban *domus* documented in the area.

Based on the data provided by the urban archaeology, everything would seem to point towards the fact that after becoming capital of the *Diocesis Hispaniarum,* the fourth century in Mérida was characterized by the functional continuity of the main structures that made up its urban layout, although these underwent numerous transformations typical of the passage of time and renovation work, especially in the public sphere, due to the new situation that affected the city during these years. Despite being documented to a lesser extent, these changes announced a new urban concept that would characterize the city over the following centuries. In parallel, during the fourth century, new structures gradually appeared that formed a part of a new cultural context: Christianity, which despite only having a minor impact during this century, would gradually have a profound impact on the society of Emerita over time.

The first signs of Christianity from this century coexisted with a profoundly pagan society, which gradually became permeable to new cultural forms that arose, especially in the main cities of the west following the persecutions of Diocletian and Maximian Herculius. This would lead to the creation of new martyrs, leading to the first signs of Christian architecture in the cities. In Mérida, despite some signs of a Christian community having been documented from the second and third centuries,[37] it was not until the fourth century when the first traces of this

---

36 Alicia Canto, Ana Bejarano, and Félix Palma, "El mausoleo del dintel de los ríos de Mérida, Revue Anabaraecus y el culto de la confluencia," *Madrider Mitteilungen* 38 (1997): 247–94.

37 Isaac Sastre, *Los primeros edificios cristianos de Extremadura. Sus espacios y elementos litúrgicos.* Caelum in terra, Serie Ataecina 5 (Mérida: Asamblea de Extremadura, 2010).

Fig. 5. General view of the excavations carried out inside the church of St. Eulalia. By the author.

new culture appeared in the topography of the city, coinciding with the death of the young Eulalia (d. 304), and the birth of her cult as a martyr, sung by Prudentius in the *Peristephanon*.

These initial expressions of Christianity in Mérida consisted of a series of objects found without a context, associated with funerary rites. On the one hand, we have sarcophagi decorated with Christian motifs,[38] and epitaphs dated from the early part of the fourth century,[39] which are some of the first artistic works that indicate the spread of Christianity in Mérida. On the other hand, from the middle of the century a Christian funerary area

---

38 Pedro Mateos Cruz, "Sarcófagos decorados de época tardorromana en Mérida," *Memoria. Excavaciones Arqueológicas en Mérida: 2000* (2002): 437–48.

39 José Luís Ramírez and Pedro Mateos Cruz, *Inscripciones Cristianas de Mérida,* Cuadernos emeritenses 14 (Mérida: Museo Nacional de Arte Romano, 2000), 17, 20, 51, 63.

grew around what we currently believe to be the building where
Eulalia was worshipped as a martyr. The main buildings that occupied this funerary area are known from excavations carried
out inside the Church of St. Eulalia (fig. 5).[40]

All of these details point towards the fact that throughout
the fourth century there was a Christian community in the
city, whose presence was reflected in the urban development of
Emerita, based on their funerary and religious rites around the
figure of the martyr. Although it has not been documented, it is
possible that other types of Christian funerary areas existed in
Mérida during this same century, associated with the burial of a
local martyr or saint.

As regards the possible presence of a cathedral in the city in
the fourth century, as has been documented in other western
cities[41] we do not have any evidence of any written, architectural
or sculptural remains being found that would be associated with
such a building. This said, other types of evidence have been
found inside the city, such as a Chi Rho painted inside an underground cistern from the Roman period, which belonged to a
house, and which has been tentatively associated with a *domus
ecclesiae*,[42] although so far we have not been able to archaeologically or epigraphically document any other type of Christian
structure in the city from this century.

Therefore, the fourth century in Emerita could be described
as a period of urban and cultural continuity, in which the main
buildings that formed the city during the Early Imperial period
remained in use. In comparison to the introduction of the first
Christian structures, the pagan temples and structures were still
used, with others being built such as the possible *taurobolium,*
defined by its discoverer as a center for Mythraic and taurobolic

40 Pedro Mateos Cruz, *Sta. Eulalia de Mérida. Arqueología y urbanismo,* Anejos de Archivo Español de Arqueología 19 (Madrid: CSIC, 1999).
41 Richard Krautheimer, *Tre capitali cristiane. Topografía e politica* (Turin:
Einaudi, 1987).
42 Javier Heras, "Los cristianos de Mérida y la domus de la Puerta de la Villa,"
Boletín Foro, Consorcio de la Ciudad Monumental de Mérida 59 (2010): 6.

worship, found recently during excavation work carried out on the "Los Blanes" site,[43] which also confirms the existence of a pagan-Christian duality that marked this century in the main cities of Hispania.[44]

In order to recreate the essential features of Emerita during the fifth century, we have to examine the archaeological data provided by the excavations carried out on the site, together with the few historical sources from the period, which are mainly based on the *Chronica* of Hydatius and the presence of Goths and Suevi in the city, recently analyzed by Arce.[45]

As already mentioned, the *vicarii* had lived in Emerita since the reforms of Diocletian. The last known *vicarius* in Emerita was Macrobius, between 399 and 400. It seems that the Roman administration disappeared after it was taken over by the Suevi, Vandals, and Alans, and shared out between them, although in 420 there is a document referring to Maurocellus as *vicarius,* who visited Bracara with his troops in the same year. It would therefore appear that at this time there was still a *vicarius* in Emerita, and as a result, a Roman administration.[46]

Hydatius first refers to the arrival of the Vandal king Geiseric in the city in 429, while news arrived that the Suevian Heremigarius had started to pillage Lusitania, and the Vandal king clashed with the Suevi to prevent the taking of Emerita.[47] The result was the death of Heremigarius in the River Anas at the hands of Geiseric, saving the city, which according to Arce was not sacked or demolished. The other episode narrated in the *Chronica* is the conflict between the Gothic king Theodoric

---

43 Javier Heras, *Un edificio singular de la Mérida tardorromana: un posible centro de culto metróaco y rituales taurobólicos.* Ataecina, Serie de estudios históricos de la Lusitania 8 (Mérida: Asamblea de Extremadura, 2011).

44 Pedro Mateos Cruz and Luís Caballero, "El paisaje urbano de Augusta Emerita en época tardoantigua (ss. IV–VII)," in *Actas del Congreso Internacional 1910–2010,* ed. Álvarez and Mateos, 505–20, at 509.

45 Arce, "Augusta Emerita: Continuidad y transformación (ss. IV–VII)."

46 Arce, "Augusta Emerita en el s. V d. C.," 183.

47 Arce, "Augusta Emerita: Continuidad y transformación (ss. IV–VII)," 497.

and the Suevi in 456, which resulted in the defeat of the Suevi, and the imprisonment and death of Rechiarius.[48] Theodoric remained in Mérida for three months with his troops, before setting off for Gaul in 457.

Between these two military operations, it is important to note the presence of the Suevi in Emerita, as a result of the attempt by Rechila to expand towards the south, having entered the city in 439 with the aim of setting up his operational base in Mérida and controlling Betica, converting the city into the temporary capital of the Suevi kingdom. We know that in 448, Rechila and his court were still in Emerita, as according to Hydatius, the king died in this same year, and was replaced by Rechiarius. For at least ten years, the seat of Suevi power was not Bracara but Emerita, from where they made their first incursions into Baetica, including the conquest of Hispalis in 441, which apparently remained under the control of the Suevi until 458. The following years were marked by Bracara and Emerita sharing the royal privilege for some time, until their invasion of Tarraconense in 456 led the Goths of Theodoric II to enter Hispania and put an end to the reign of the Suevi. The Goths traveled from Gallaecia to Lusitania with their sights set on Emerita, although according to Hydatius, forewarned by what had happened in Bracara, did not provide Rechiarius's troops with an opportunity.[49]

An "objective" interpretation of the *Chronica* reveals, on the one hand, a certain prominence by Emerita during the middle years of this century, in the power struggles that took place in Hispania, and on the other, a series of turbulent periods that must have influenced daily life in the city. Faced with this data, it is logical to ask what the city was like, having hosted the Suevian court while the monarchy used it as a temporarily stable base, and what influence this process had on the urban development

48 Ibid., 498.
49 Pablo Díaz, "El reino suevo de Hispania y su sede en Bracara," in *Sedes Regiae (400–800),* ed. Gisela Ripoll (Barcelona: Real Academia de buenas Letras de Barcelona, 2000), 405–10.

of the city during the fifth century. Following the disappearance of Roman power in Hispania, the city went from being the capital of the Hispaniarum diocese, to becoming the temporary seat of the Suevian monarchy, as an alternative to Bracara.

Archaeologists have traditionally considered the city in late antiquity as having experienced a process of urban decay, with large numbers of abandoned spaces used for sporadic burials, reoccupation, and the re-use of old buildings, together with the construction of poor-quality buildings, in which families lived with allotments and farmyards. Meanwhile, the urban landscape became dotted with new religious buildings, replacing the former centers of public life from the Roman city.

This new image of the city in late antiquity was different, as indicated by Peter Brown, from the classical city, although, "they are not ruinous, decaying cities."[50] Perhaps the concept of the city and its urban features changed, if we consider that this was an urban landscape derived from the Roman design, but now inhabited by the new peoples who were arriving in Hispania with a new culture. This suggests a new attitude towards public life, in which many of the structures from the old city still survived, while other new buildings were erected that would mark the development of these cities over the following centuries.[51]

In the case of Emerita, the fifth century was a period of urban transformation of the fourth century city, the legacy and continuation of the urban landscape from the late imperial period, which shifted towards another, different situation, basically marked by the abandonment of the public buildings that had defined the classical city, and the definitive incorporation of a new culture — Christianity — with new public buildings.

---

50 Peter Brown, *The Making of Late Antiquity* (Cambridge: Harvard University Press, 1978), 29.
51 Rocío Ayerbe Vélez and Pedro Mateos Cruz, "Un nuevo ejemplo de arquitectura pública emeritense en época tardoantigua," in *Navigare necesse est. Homenaje al profesor Luzón,* ed. Jorge García, Irene Mañas, and Fabiola Salcedo (Madrid: Universidad Complutense, 2015), 179–91, at 188.

Fig. 6. Archaeological excavations carried out in the hyposcaenium of the theater of Emerita. By the author.

Throughout the fifth century, Mérida bore witness to the definitive abandonment of the main public buildings from the Roman city, which were gradually occupied by new public, domestic, or productive buildings. This was the case of the theater, which had already been abandoned by this stage, judging by the archaeological evidence found in recent excavation work carried out in the *hyposcaenium* and in the *porticus post scaenam,* as part of the research projects by the Archaeological Institute of Mérida on the two buildings used for public spectacles in the city.[52] The work carried out in the *porticus* revealed the remains of dwellings that once occupied its northern side, including the so-called "sacred hall,"[53] while the *hyposcaenium* seems to have been definitively sealed at the end of this century, judging by the ceramic materials found in the levels covering the stage pit (fig. 6).[54]

The amphitheater had already been abandoned during the fifth century, first losing its decorative elements made of marble, such as the panels that covered the granite podium separating the stands from the arena. The granite blocks used as seating were also removed, although the blocks from the podium remained in place, but we do know that different structures were re-used that had once formed a part of the pictorial and epigraphic decoration of the building.[55] This is the case of the scenes of *venationes* shown on a mural painting found on four ashlar stones from the amphitheater, which were re-used as part of a burial in late antiquity, and a monumental inscription in marble from a building used for performances, which was re-used inside a mausoleum close to the amphitheater itself.[56] During late antiquity, the amphitheater was re-used for domestic purposes,

52 Mateos Cruz and Pizzo, "Los Edificios de ocio y representación en Augusta Emerita."
53 Pedro Mateos Cruz and Begoña Soler, "El aula sacra del teatro de Mérida. Nuevas consideraciones sobre su concepción arquitectónica y la cronología de su pavimento marmóreo," in *Actas del II Congrés Internacional d'Àrqueologia i Mon Antic, August i les Provinces Occidentals 2000 aniversari de la mort d'Àugust* (Tarragona: Fundació Privada Mútua Catalana, 2015), 111–18.
54 I would like to thank Rocío Ayerbe Vélez, archaeologist for the Consortium of the Monumental City of Mérida, and responsible for both excavations, for this unpublished data.
55 Miguel Alba, "Evolución y final de los espacios romanos emeritenses a la luz de los datos arqueológicos (pautas de transformación de la ciudad tardoantigua y altomedieval)," in *Augusta Emerita: Territorios, espacios, imágenes y gentes en Lusitania romana*, ed. Trinidad Nogales, Monografías Emeritenses 8 (Mérida: Museo Nacional de Arte Romano, 2004), 207–56, at 220.
56 Canto, Bejarano, and Palma, "El mausoleo del dintel de los ríos de Mérida," 289.

revealed by the discovery of different personal items in the *vomitorium* of the amphitheater, together with slag from forges built on the same site, documented during excavation work carried out as a part of the same research project.

Finally, we have very little archaeological data regarding the abandonment of the circus in Emerita.[57] The last piece of information we have about it being in use is contained, indirectly, in the epigraph of Sabinianus, a Christian charioteer whose funerary slab, re-used as the covering for a tomb from the adjacent paleochristian basilica of Casa Herrera,[58] has been dated from the fourth century.[59] It seems likely that by the mid-fifth century, the circus had already been abandoned in the same way as the theater and amphitheater, and that its most valuable materials were gradually being plundered.

In the same way as these buildings used for leisure and performance purposes were re-used during this century, we also have data that reveal the gradual abandonment of the main buildings in the forum of the colony, which by the mid-fifth century had undergone a process of transformation in which they lost their original functions. In general, and as indicated by the researchers who have analyzed the urban design of the forum, this transformation "was generally expressed by the plundering of the decorative and structural elements of the buildings, the destruction of their component parts, the recovery of specific areas for commercial purposes, and the appearance of rubbish dumps."[60] Logically, this is a general overview of the situation, requiring more specific details of the exact processes that occurred in each of the areas of public life. During the Roman pe-

57 Eulalia Gijón and Ana Montalvo, "El circo romano de Mérida," in *Actas del Congreso Internacional 1910–2010*, ed. Álvarez and Cruz, 195–208.

58 Luís Caballero and Thilo Ulbert, *La basílica paleocristiana de Casa Herrera en las cercanías de Mérida (Badajoz)*, Excavaciones Arqueológicas en España 89 (Madrid: Ministerio de Cultura, 1976), 178–80.

59 Ramírez and Mateos Cruz, *Inscripciones Cristianas de Mérida*, 99.

60 Ayerbe Vélez, Barrientos, and Palma, "Los complejos forenses de 'Augusta Emerita,'" 828.

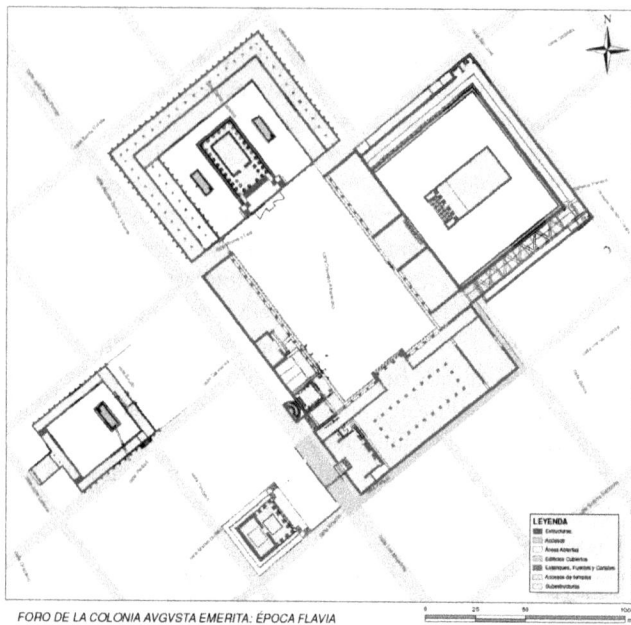

FORO DE LA COLONIA AVGVSTA EMERITA: ÉPOCA FLAVIA

Fig. 7. Reconstruction of the forum from the colony of Augusta Emerita during the Flavian period. Used by permission from Rocío Ayerbe, Teresa Barrientos, and Felix Palma, "Los complejos forenses de 'Augusta Emerita," in *El Foro de Augusta Emerita. Génesis y Evolución de sus Recintos Monumentales,* ed. Rocío Ayerbe, Teresa Barrientos, and Felix Palma, Anejos de Archivo Español de Arqueología 53 (Madrid: CSIC, 2009), 667–832, at 828.

riod, the area of the forum (fig. 7) was arranged around three platforms containing the main public buildings.[61] The central platform contained the temple "of Diana," at its northernmost end, in what we have identified as a *cryptoporticus*. At the other end was the basilica, in front of which was a central square, sur-

---

61 Ibid.

Fig. 8. General view of the "Temple of Diana" dated from the Augustan period. By the author.

rounded by arcades containing the main buildings that comprised the forum, such as the *curia, aerarium,* or *carcer.*

Remains have been documented on the eastern platform — traditionally known as the "portico of the forum" — of an area dedicated to the Imperial cult, which included a temple. Another public space existed to the south of this complex, whose function is unclear. Finally, remains have been found on the western platform of the temple that stood in Calle Viñeros, and a public structure that has been identified as a *schola iuvenum.* Each of these areas suffered from independent processes of abandonment of their buildings, and the plundering and reuse of their spaces. In some cases, we have been able to interpret certain stages of this process.

The temple "of Diana," after being abandoned as a building for Imperial worship, must have been re-used for some other purpose, as it is still in a good state of preservation today (fig. 8). It is possible that after the fifth century it was used for some other type of public purpose, possibly religious, judging by the discovery inside the building of large numbers of architectural decorations, which are now located in the portico of the Renaissance palace of "Los Corbos,"[62] built in its interior, as well as the discovery of several gravestones in the surrounding area.[63] To the east of the so-called temple "of Diana" a building was erected using granite ashlars with external buttresses. Only one of its walls remains in place, which ran perpendicularly to the temple, and whose construction levels indicate that it was built in the mid-fifth century. The characteristics of these remains suggest that it may have been used for public purposes,[64] although we are unable to ascertain its function.

Inside the porticoed spaces, the remains of crucibles were found embedded in the paving, suggesting the presence of forges or metal foundries, and that these workshops were set up inside the buildings that were gradually being dismantled and plundered. In some parts of the porticoed buildings to the south west of the square, levels of abandonment have been found from this century that were prior to the process of dismantling and plundering these buildings. Also, the *cryptoporticus* in this area was filled in, and its space divided up for use as dwellings at a subsequent moment. The archaeological excavations have also revealed that the thermal baths were abandoned at this time, which had been built in the fourth century over the remains of a building identified as a possible *schola iuvenum.*[65]

On the eastern platform, to the south of the monumental area, in a space that is difficult to interpret, but which may have contained the public baths of the forum during the Early Imperial period, a public building once stood that was built in the first half of the fifth century, but which continued to be in use until the end of the sixth century, at which stage it was trans-

62 Pedro Mateos Cruz and Isaac Sastre, "Mobiliario arquitectónico de época tardoantigua en el entorno del templo de Diana. Una propuesta sobre su ocupación entre los siglos VI al IX," *Memoria, Excavaciones Arqueológicas en Mérida 2001* (2004): 397–416.

63 Ramírez and Mateos Cruz, *Inscripciones Cristianas de Mérida,* 279.

64 Ayerbe Vélez, Barrientos, and Palma, "Los complejos forenses de 'Augusta Emerita'," 830.

65 Ibid., 831.

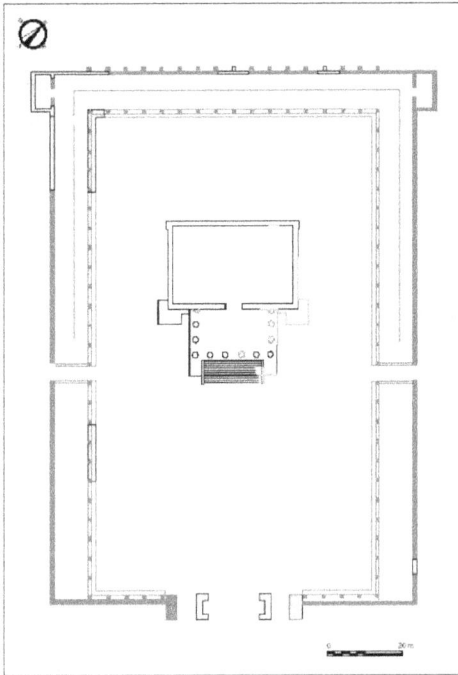

Fig. 9. Reconstruction of the ground plan of the provincial center dedicated to imperial worship in Augusta Emerita. By the author.

formed for domestic use. It is a structure made of *opera mixta* with granite ashlars and large blocks of stone and brick, with buttresses also made of granite ashlars. Only two of the building's rooms have been preserved. Their architectural features and construction technique indicate that this was a public building. The thickness of its walls, the use of external granite buttresses, and the architectural quality of the preserved remains, all point towards it being an example of public architecture from late an-

247

tiquity, as seen in other public buildings in Mérida and the rest of the Iberian Peninsula.[66]

One could also suggest a parallel, contemporary process for the public buildings found in what is known as the provincial complex for Imperial worship (fig. 9). This complex, accessed through what is known as the "Arch of Trajan," the entrance into this monumental space, is defined by a triple portico delimiting a square presided over by a tetrastyle temple with an oblong *cella*.[67] It was built during the Tiberian period, while throughout the fifth century the main buildings were plundered for building materials, losing most of their valuable elements, and dismantled for subsequent use as dwellings in the area of the square and the porticos.[68] Here, the remains of up to five buildings have been found, which were adjacent to the podium of the temple, the walls of the porticos, and the "Arch of Trajan." During this century, layers of rubble accumulated over the marble pavement of the square and the doorway leading into this area, saving it from being plundered.[69]

In general, as can be seen from the data provided by the archaeological excavations carried out in the area, the fifth century was a time of major transformations in the area occupied during Roman times and known as the "forum of the Colony" and the provincial area for Imperial worship. During this process, the main buildings in the public area lost their original function, and some of them were plundered for their decorative and structural elements, as occurred with the granite ashlars that surrounded the concrete nucleus of the temple in Calle Vi-

---

66 Ayerbe Vélez and Mateos Cruz, "Un nuevo ejemplo."

67 Mateos Cruz, *El llamado foro provincial de Augusta Emerita,* 251–76.

68 Miguel Alba and Pedro Mateos Cruz, "Transformación y ocupación tardoantigua y altomedieval del llamado foro provincial," in *El llamado foro provincial de Augusta Emerita,* ed. Mateos Cruz, 355–80, at 360.

69 Xavier Aquilué and Rafael Dehesa, "Los materiales arqueológicos de época romana y tardorromana procedentes de las excavaciones del denominado 'Foro Provincial' de Mérida," in *El llamado foro provincial de Augusta Emerita,* ed. Mateos Cruz, 157–70, at 170.

Fig. 10. Remnants of the defensive structure of the Roman wall inside the archaeological area of Morería. By the author.

ñeros.[70] However, the area was not completely abandoned, and instead the space was used for domestic and commercial purposes. At the same time, other public buildings were erected as part of the official representation of a new political situation that came about following the departure of the Roman authorities. This process of re-using the space must have occurred, based on the archaeological data, during the first half of the fifth century, following the abandonment of these buildings at the end of the fourth century or in the early fifth century. This coincided with the end of the Roman administrative and political power represented in Augusta Emerita by the figure of the *vicarius,* whose presence in the city has been attested until the year 400.

Another important structure in the Roman city, the wall, suffered the transformation of its architectural design, but not its layout. The wall that had defined the internal space of the colony of Augusta Emerita until that time has remained unchanged since the Roman period. Throughout the fourth century, it underwent a series of minor alterations that did not affect its shape

---

70 Ayerbe Vélez, Barrientos, and Palma, "Los complejos forenses de 'Augusta Emerita,'" 831.

or course; now, the Roman wall was reinforced by the construction of an external layer using granite blocks that were re-used
from other buildings, which are visible in many of the known
sections of the Roman wall (fig. 10).

In terms of its structure, the reinforcement of ashlar blocks
that covered the wall at this time had a width of between two
and three meters, consisting of rows of granite material re-used
from previous buildings. Apart from ashlars, a large number of
columns have been identified, together with material from different funerary settings, such as *cupae* and *pulvini*,[71] evidence
of the prior destruction of these pagan funerary spaces before
re-using them as reinforcement materials. The absence of sections with architectural decoration from the public buildings
in the forum made of granite, such as the temple "of Diana,"
the only building that was not plundered, probably due to its
continued re-use, or the temple documented in Calle Viñeros,[72]
mean it is not possible to confirm whether these buildings had
been dismantled at the time the protective "covering" was built.
However, we do have evidence of the re-use of decorative materials from both buildings in structures considered as belonging
to the Emirate period.[73]

One of the substantial reforms that influenced the life of the
city at this time was the re-use of the conduits used to supply,
control, and channel the city's water. The water supply was cut
off during the fifth century, probably because the aqueducts (except for the aqueduct of San Lázaro, which may have been in
use for a longer period) had already been abandoned by this
time, judging by the data from the excavations carried out in the
aqueduct of Los Milagros,[74] although this is still impossible to

---

71 José Beltran and Luís Baena, "Pulvinos monumentales de Mérida," *Anas* 9
    (1996): 105–31, at 110.
72 Felix Palma, "Solar de la calle Viñeros, 17," in *El Foro de Augusta Emerita,* ed.
    Ayerbe Vélez, Barrientos, and Palma, 331–66.
73 Antonio Peña, "La decoración arquitectónica," in *El Foro de Augusta Emer-
    ita,* ed. Ayerbe Vélez, Barrientos, and Palma, 525–82, at 563.
74 Ayerbe Vélez "Intervención arqueológica," 47.

confirm with regard to the rest of the conduits. At this time, the city probably had cisterns and wells, which had been in regular use since the Roman period, in the collective dwellings. Also, the drainage system had become inoperative due to the lack of running water and maintenance work on the sewers, whose manholes located at the city's crossroads had been covered over following the refurbishment of the road system.

One of the most widely documented elements associated with the transformation of the city during the fifth century, and the new situation that came about as a result, is found within the domestic sphere. We have extensive data on the new domestic spaces that appeared, for example, as a result of the abandonment of the public spaces from the fifth century onwards. This is the case of the dwellings documented inside the provincial forum,[75] in the forum of the Colony,[76] in the *peristylium* of the theater, or in the amphitheater,[77] to name just a few examples. In general, these were dwellings that were adapted to the previously existing urban structure, on one floor, and made of material from previously abandoned buildings.

During this same period, the Roman stately homes began to be fragmented, with their courtyards converted into patios, and their rooms used as dwellings for whole families. The way the spaces were used and occupied changed, breaking them up, and leading to the dysfunction of the parts of the former Roman house.[78] Both of these situations — the creation of new private homes in the former public areas, and the subdivision of the old Roman mansions — have been used as arguments to support the increase of population within the city walls during this century, which became crowded in relation to other previous historical

---

75 Alba and Mateos Cruz, "Transformación y ocupación tardoantigua."
76 Palma, "Solar de la calle Viñeros, 17"; Peña, "La decoración arquitectónica," 528–31.
77 Mateos Cruz and Pizzo "Los Edificios de ocio y representación en Augusta Emerita: El teatro y el Anfiteatro."
78 Alba, "Evolución y final de los espacios romanos emeritenses a la luz de los datos arqueológicos," 236.

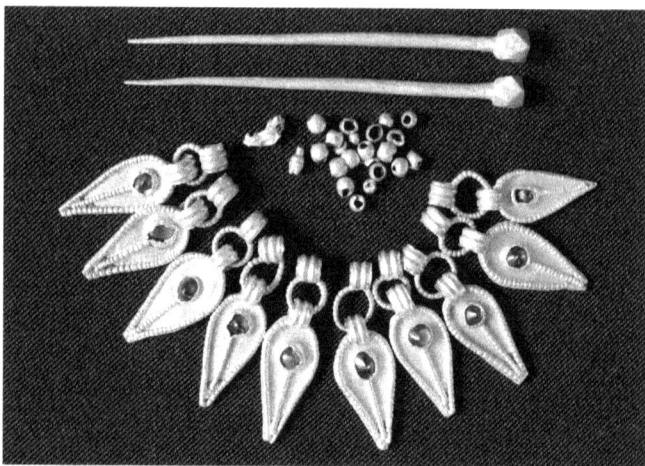

Fig. 11. Grave goods found in one of the tombs from the funerary area of "Los Blanes." Photograph by Consorcio de la Ciudad monumental de Mérida. Used by permission.

periods in the city. However, it is likely that this was only a reflection of a process of urban de-structuring that characterized the city at this time, with abandoned areas, unoccupied buildings and spaces that were sporadically used for burials inside the city and which were not associated with funerary structures, combined with densely occupied housing.

This said, we find the clearest indication of the urban changes that occurred during this century in the area outside of the city walls. The pagan funerary areas were abandoned, destroying the buildings and the tombs inside them. As we have seen, many of the remnants of these structures were re-used in the reinforcement of the city walls, which are full of countless granite ashlar blocks, together with fragments from burials in these funerary areas, such as *pulvini* or *cupae*. In turn, the excavation work carried out on the site of "Los Blanes" revealed a large funerary area, whose final stage contained eleven burials with grave goods and jewelry that were clearly of Suevian origin (fig. 11). The tombs were dated, stratigraphically and from the materials they contained, from between the start and middle of the fifth

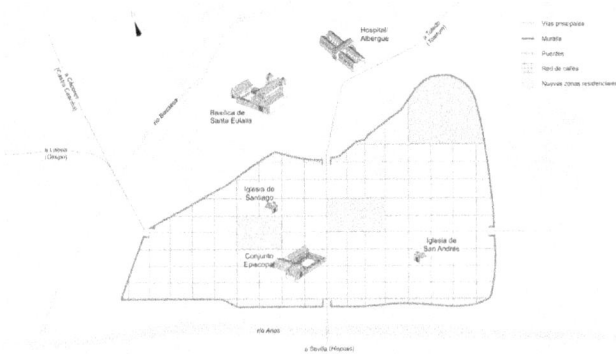

Fig. 12. Ground plan of Augusta Emerita with the main Christian buildings that stood in the city in late antiquity. By the author.

century,[79] confirming the presence of a Suevian military elite in the city at this time.

From the fourth century onwards, Christian funerary areas were created in the city around the burial site of a martyr, such as the large funerary area of St. Eulalia which, as previously mentioned, was destroyed prior to the construction of the basilica in the second half of the fifth century. Due to the extension of these basilicas for funerary purposes, and their dedication to martyrs, in the suburbs of the city, new areas were created around these churches, located within and outside of the city walls.

Here we are seeing a process of urban transformation that reflects the economic, cultural, social, and political changes that occurred in this society during the fifth century and led to a new concept of the city. This new concept was a legacy of the late Roman city, except all of the main landmarks connected with leisure, government, or religion had been eliminated, in parallel with the end of the Roman administration. These public build-

79 Javier Heras and Ana Olmedo, "Ficha de catálogo. Collar," in *Catálogo de la Exposición Hispania Gothorum. S. Ildefonso y el reino visigodo de Toledo,* ed. Rafael García (Toledo: Museo de la Santa Cruz, 2007), 390.

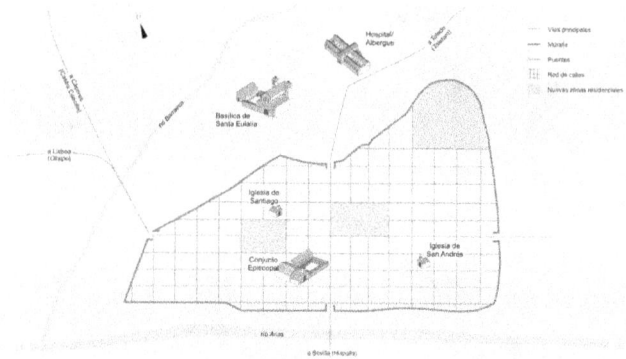

Fig. 13. Reconstruction of the architectural ground plan of the basilica of St. Eulalia. By the author.

ings that were characteristic of a certain architecture of power were replaced by new civil and religious structures beneath the sign of the cross, this time under the power of the bishop, which began to mark the urban development of the cities. And so, throughout the fifth century, the first Christian places of worship appeared, which would gradually spread throughout the entire city over the following centuries (fig. 12).

Outside of the city walls, combining all the religious significance of the funerary areas that had been formerly presided over by a building dedicated to a martyr, new basilicas for funerary and martyrial purposes were built, which during the sixth and seventh centuries would become architectural ensembles with a complex structure. Sources from the period say that they included schools, monasteries, and hospitals, such as the funerary, monastic, and martyrial complex of St. Eulalia.

The suburban basilica of St. Eulalia was built in the second half of the fifth century inside the earlier funerary area. Its architectural features have already been analyzed in previous publications,[80] although it is worth noting that the sanctuary

---

80 Mateos Cruz, *Sta. Eulalia de Mérida.*

was adapted to the architectural layout of the martyrial building which, like the rest of the structures in the necropolis, had been destroyed at a previous time (fig. 13). It seems likely that following the construction of the basilica, the space was once again used as a funerary area, with evidence of burials of privileged individuals in its interior, in crypts that were built to contain the bodies of the bishops of Emerita, as well as certain public figures who lived in the city.

At this time, there must have been other funerary basilicas in the suburbs of Emerita. The *Vitas Patrum Emeritensium*[81] refers to the presence at the end of the sixth century of churches dedicated to different saints and martyrs. These were located inside a Christian funerary area, and so it is likely that they were already in use during the fifth century. Similarly, we know that other churches existed within the city walls during the Visigothic period, in different parts of the city, which were built according to the availability of land and religious needs. However, we have hardly any archaeological data referring to these structures.

It is likely that there was a church close to the so-called temple "of Diana" in the mid-fifth century. We do not believe that it was built by using the remnants of the pagan building itself, as this re-use would have been unusual at such an early date. As previously mentioned, the presence of different funerary epigraphs in the surrounding area,[82] together with fragments of architectural decorations from the Visigothic period (cymatium moldings, capitals and bases), re-used in a building erected in the sixteenth century inside the temple,[83] allow for the hypothesis that this church was present in the area.

Also within the city walls, the *Vitas* indicates that there was a church dedicated to St. Andrew, which probably stood on the site of the now abandoned convent of Santo Domingo, which

---

81 *Vitas Sanctorum Patrum Emeretensium,* ed. Antonio Maya Sánchez, Corpus Christianorum Series Latina 116 (Turnhout: Brepols, 1992).

82 Ramírez and Mateos Cruz, *Inscripciones Cristianas de Mérida,* 279.

83 Mateos Cruz and Sastre, "Mobiliario arquitectónico de época tardoantigua en el entorno del templo de Diana."

was still known as the convent of St. Andrew in the seventeenth century.[84] A series of remnants from the Visigothic period were found during excavation work inside the convent, which could be connected with this structure, although the only sustainable argument is provided by the historical memory of the site, which kept the same name over the centuries.

During this century, it is also likely that the cathedral or *ecclesia senior* already existed, which according to the *Vitas* was known as St. Ierusalem.[85] The only archaeological data associated with the location and architectural features of the cathedral have been provided by a series of decorative materials which appeared in the area around the current co-cathedral church of St. Mary, which include an object that has been identified as a *cathedra,* the seat of the bishop,[86] and an epigraph which was reused as an impost in the gateway leading into the Arab citadel, and which may be connected to the change of the cathedral's dedication from St. Ierusalem to St. Mary, Princess of all the Virgins.[87] These elements have made it possible to suggest a hypothetical location of the Visigothic cathedral in the same position now occupied by the present-day cathedral, taking into account the appearance of these elements in the surrounding area, and historical records that refer to the construction of the "main church of St. Mary" following the re-conquest of the city in 1228, on the site formerly occupied by the Visigothic cathedral.

In summary, we have a series of archaeological data that explain the process of urban transformation that took place in Augusta Emerita during its development from the capital of the Hispaniarum diocese at the start of the fourth century, until it became the temporary base of the Suevian monarchy in Hispania throughout the fifth century. This was a time of transition,

84 Bernabé Moreno de Vargas, *Historia de la ciudad de Mérida* (1633; rpt. Mérida: Diputación Provincial de Badajoz, 1987), 476.
85 *Vitas Sanctorum Patrum Emeretensium,* 4.9.7.
86 María Cruz, *Mérida Visigoda: La escultura arquitectónica y litúrgica* (Badajoz: Diputación Provincial de Badajoz, 1985), 205, n. 182.
87 Ramírez and Mateos Cruz, *Inscripciones Cristianas de Mérida,* 31–35.

in which the structures that had defined the Roman city were gradually removed and replaced by a new concept of the city, associated with its new and different political, cultural, economic, and social condition, where the power of Rome was replaced by the power of other peoples who settled in Emerita during the fifth century. The city did not lose its function as the structuring element of the territory, although it would evolve towards other ways of understanding public space, as a private sphere in relation to the classical city. The buildings used for leisure purposes and performances, the architecture of power, and the rest of the public urban structures from the Roman period gradually lost their function, and were abandoned and replaced by a new type of architecture, which manifested the authority of the church from this moment on.

Bibliography

Primary

Vitas Sanctorum Patrum Emeretensium. Edited by Antonio Maya Sánchez. Corpus Christianorum Series Latina 116. Turnhout: Brepols, 1992.

Secondary

Alba, Miguel. "Consideraciones arqueológicas en torno al s. V en Mérida." In *Memoria, Excavaciones Arqueológicas en Mérida 1996,* edited by Miguel Alba Calzado, Pedro Mateos Cruz, and Juana Márquez Pérez, 361–86. Madrid: Consorcio de la Ciudad monumental de Mérida, 1998.

———. "Diacronía de la vivienda señorial de Emerita (Lusitania, Hispania): Desde las domus altoimperiales y tardoantiguas a las residencias palaciales omeyas (Siglos I–IX)." In *Archeologia e società tra tardoantico e alto medioevo,* edited by Jean Pietro Brogiolo, 163–92. Padua: Università di Padova, 2008.

———. "Evolución y final de los espacios romanos emeritenses a la luz de los datos arqueológicos (pautas de transformación de la ciudad tardoantigua y altomedieval)." In *Augusta Emerita: Territorios, espacios, imágenes y gentes en Lusitania romana,* edited by Trinidad Nogales, 207–56. Monografías Emeritenses 8. Mérida: Museo Nacional de Arte Romano, 2004.

———. "La participación de la iglesia en la transformación del escenario urbano: la cristianización y despaganización de Emerita (ss. V-VII)." In *Modelos edilicios y prototipos en la monumentalización de las ciudades de Hispania,* edited by Manuel Martín Bueno and J. Carlos Sáenz, 83–98. Monografías Arqueológicas 49. Zaragoza: Universidad de Zaragoza, 2015.

———. "Ocupación diacrónica del Area Arqueológica de Morería (Mérida)." In *Memoria, Excavaciones Arqueológicas en Mérida 1994–1995,* edited by Miguel Alba Calzado, Pedro Mateos Cruz, and Juana Márquez Pérez, 285–315. Madrid: Consorcio de la Ciudad monumental de Mérida, 1997.

Alba, Miguel, and Mateos Cruz, Pedro. "Transformación y ocupación tardoantigua y altomedieval del llamado foro provincial." In *El foro provincial de Augusta Emerita: Un conjunto monumental de culto imperial,* edited by Pedro Mateos Cruz, 355–80. Anejos a Archivo Español de Arqueología 42. Madrid: CSIC, 2006.

Álvarez Martínez, José María. "Excavaciones en Augusta Emerita." In *Arqueología de las ciudades modernas superpuestas a las antiguas,* edited by Alberto Balil, 35–54. Zaragoza: Ministerio de Cultura, 1985.

Aquilué, Xavier, and Dehesa, Rafael. "Los materiales arqueológicos de época romana y tardorromana procedentes de las excavaciones del denominado "Foro Provincial" de Mérida." In *El llamado foro provincial de Augusta Emerita. Un conjunto monumental de culto imperial,* edited by Pedro Mateos Cruz, 157–70. Anejos a Archivo Español de Arqueología 42. Madrid: CSIC, 2006.

Arce, Javier. "Augusta Emerita: Continuidad y transformación (ss. IV–VII)." In *Actas del Congreso Internacional 1910–2010, el yacimiento emeritense,* edited by José María Álvarez and Pedro Mateos Cruz, 491–504. Mérida: Ayuntamiento de Mérida, 2011.

———. "Augusta Emerita en el s. V d. C." In *Mérida Tardorromana (300–580 d. C.),* 179–194. Cuadernos emeritenses 22. Mérida: Museo Nacional de Arte Romano, 2002.

———. "Introducción histórica." In *Las capitales provinciales de Hispania: Augusta Emerita,* Volume 2, edited by Xavier Dupré, 7–14. Rome: "L'Erma" di Bretschneider, 2004.

———. "Teodosio I sigue siendo Teodosio I." *Archivo Español de Arqueología* 71 (1998): 169–79. http://aespa.revistas.csic.es/index.php/aespa/article/view/281.

Arce, Javier, Alexandra Chavarria, and Gisela Ripoll. "The urban domus in Late Antique Hispania. Examples from Emerita, Barcino and Complutum." In *Housing in Late Antiquity,* edited by Luke Lavan, Lale Özgenel, and Alexander Sarantis, 305–36. Late Antique Archaeology 3.2. Boston and Leiden: Brill, 2007. https://doi.org/10.1163/ej.9789004162280.i-539.100.

Ayerbe Vélez, Rocío. "Evolución y transformación de un cardo minor y su margo desde época romana hasta nuestros días." *Memoria, Excavaciones Arqueológicas en Mérida 2004* 10, (2007): 185–208.

———. "Intervención arqueológica en la urbanización Jardines de Mérida de la Avda. de la plata. Excavación de un tramo de conducción hidráulica Proserpina-Los Milagros." *Memoria, Excavaciones Arqueológicas en Mérida 1998* (2000): 39–58.

———. "La llamada basílica de Laborde: identificación, ubicación y cronología. Intervención arqueológica en la C/ Calvario, 8." *Memoria, Excavaciones Arqueológicas en Mérida 2002* (2005): 27–54.

Ayerbe Vélez, Rocío, Teresa Barrientos, and Felix Palma, eds. *El Foro de Augusta Emerita. Génesis y Evolución de sus Recintos Monumentales.* Anejos de Archivo Español de Arqueología 53. Madrid: CSIC, 2009.

———. "Los complejos forenses de 'Augusta Emerita.'" In *El Foro de Augusta Emerita. Génesis y Evolución de sus Recintos Monumentales,* edited by Rocío Ayerbe Vélez, Teresa Barrientos, and Felix Palma, 667–832. Anejos de Archivo Español de Arqueología 53. Madrid: CSIC, 2009.

Ayerbe Vélez, Rocío, and Pedro Mateos Cruz. "Un nuevo ejemplo de arquitectura pública emeritense en época tardoantigua." In *Navigare necesse est. Homenaje al profesor Luzón,* edited by Jorge García, Irene Mañas, and Fabiola Salcedo, 179–91. Madrid: Universidad Complutense, 2015.

Barrientos, Teresa. "Arquitectura termal en Mérida. Un siglo de hallazgos." In *Actas del Congreso Internacional 1910–2010, el Yacimiento Emeritense, 10–13 de Noviembre,* edited by José María Álvarez and Pedro Mateos Cruz, 327–42. Mérida: Ayuntamiento de Mérida, 2011.

Beltran, José, and Luís Baena. "Pulvinos monumentales de Mérida." *Anas* 9 (1996): 105–31.

Blanco Antonio. *Los mosaicos romanos de Mérida. Corpus de Mosaicos romanos de España.* Madrid: Ministerio de Cultura, 1978.

Brown, Peter. *The Making of Late Antiquity.* Cambridge: Harvard University Press, 1978.

Caballero, Luís, and Thilo Ulbert. *La basílica paleocristiana de Casa Herrera en las cercanías de Mérida (Badajoz).* Excavaciones Arqueológicas en España 89. Madrid: Ministerio de Cultura, 1976.

Canto, Alicia, Ana Bejarano, and Félix Palma. "El mausoleo del dintel de los ríos de Mérida, Revue Anabaraecus y el culto de la confluencia." *Madrider Mitteilungen* 38 (1997): 247–94.

Cruz, María. *Mérida Visigoda: La escultura arquitectónica y litúrgica.* Badajoz: Diputación Provincial de Badajoz, 1985.

Díaz, Pablo. "El reino suevo de Hispania y su sede en Bracara." In *Sedes Regiae (400–800),* edited by Gisela Ripoll, 403–23. Barcelona: Real Academia de Buenas Letras de Barcelona, 2000.

Etienne, Robert. "Mérida capitale du vicariat des Espagnes." In *Homenaje a Saenz de Buruaga,* 201–8. Badajoz: Diputación Provincial de Badajoz, 1982.

García Sandoval, Eugenio. *Informe sobre las casas romanas de Mérida y excavaciones en la Casa del Anfiteatro.* Excavaciones Arqueológicas en España 49. Madrid: Ministerio de Cultura, 1966.

Gijón, Eulalia, and Ana Montalvo. "El circo romano de Mérida." In *Actas del Congreso Internacional 1910–2010, el Yacimiento Emeritense, 10–13 de Noviembre,* edited by José Maria Álvarez and Pedro Mateos Cruz, 195–208. Mérida: Ayuntamiento de Mérida, 2011.

Heras, Javier. "Los cristianos de Mérida y la domus de la Puerta de la Villa." *Boletín Foro, Consorcio de la Ciudad monumental de Mérida* 59 (2010): 6.

———. *Un edificio singular de la Mérida tardorromana: un posible centro de culto metróaco y rituales taurobólicos.* Ataecina, Serie de Estudios Históricos de la Lusitania. Mérida: Instituto de Arqueología de Mérida, 2011.

Heras, Javier, and Ana Olmedo. "Ficha de catálogo. Collar." In *Hispania Gothorum. S. Ildefonso y el reino visigodo de Toledo,* edited by Rafael García, 390. Toledo: Museo de la Santa Cruz, 2007.

Hidalgo, Luís, and Guadalupe Méndez. "Octavius Clarus, un nuevo vicarius Hispaniarum en Augusta Emerita." *Memoria, Excavaciones Arqueológicas en Mérida 2002* (2008): 547–64.

Jiménez, Alfonso. "Los acueductos de Mérida." In *Augusta Emerita: Actas del Simposio Internacional Conmemorativo del Bimilenario de Mérida,* edited by Antonio Blanco Freijeiro, 111–26. Madrid: Diputación Provincial de Badajoz, 1976.

Krautheimer, Richard. *Tre capitali cristiane.* Topografia e politica. Turin: Einaudi, 1987.

Mateos Cruz, Pedro. "Augusta Emerita: de Capital de la Diócesis Hispaniarum a sede temporal de época visigoda." In *Sedes Regiae (400–800),* edited by Gisela Ripoll, 491–520. Barcelona: Real Academia de las buenas Letras de Barcelona, 2000.

———. "La identificación del xenodochium fundado por Masona en Mérida." In *IV Reunió d'Arqueologia Cristiana Hispànica,* edited by Josep Maria Gurt Esparraguera and Núria Tena, 309–16. Barcelona: Institut d'Estudis Catalans, 1995.

———, ed. *El llamado foro provincial de Augusta Emerita. Un conjunto monumental de culto imperial.* Anejos de Archivo Español de Arqueología 42. Madrid: CSIC, 2006.

———. "Sarcófagos decorados de época tardorromana en Mérida." *Memoria. Excavaciones Arqueológicas en Mérida: 2000* (2002): 437–48.

———. *Sta. Eulalia de Mérida. Arqueología y urbanismo.* Anejos de Archivo Español de Arqueología 19. Madrid: CSIC, 1999.

Mateos Cruz, Pedro, and Miguel Alba. "De Emerita Augusta a Marida." In *Actas del Simposio Internacional Visigodos y Omeyas: Un debate entre la tardoantiguedad y la Alta Edad Media,* edited by Luís Caballero and Pedro Mateos Cruz, 143–68. Anejos de Archivo Español de Arqueología 23. Madrid: CSIC, 2000.

Mateos Cruz, Pedro, and Luís Caballero. "El paisaje urbano de Augusta Emerita en época tardoantigua (ss. IV–VII)." In *Actas del Congreso Internacional 1910–2010, el yacimiento emer-*

itense, edited by José María Álvarez and Pedro Mateos Cruz, 505–20. Mérida: Ayuntamiento de Mérida, 2011.

Mateos Cruz, Pedro, and Juana Márquez. "Nuevas estructuras urbanas relacionadas con el teatro romano de Mérida: El pórtico de acceso." *Memoria III. Excavaciones Arqueológicas realizadas en Mérida durante 1997* (1999): 301–20.

Mateos Cruz, Pedro, and Antonio Pizzo. "Los Edificios de ocio y representación en Augusta Emerita: El teatro y el Anfiteatro." In *Actas del Congreso Internacional 1910–2010, el yacimiento emeritense,* edited by José María Álvarez and Pedro Mateos Cruz, 173–94. Mérida: Ayuntamiento de Mérida, 2011.

Mateos Cruz, Pedro, and Isaac Sastre. "Mobiliario arquitectónico de época tardoantigua en el entorno del templo de Diana. Una propuesta sobre su ocupación entre los siglos VI al IX." *Memoria, Excavaciones Arqueológicas en Mérida 2001* (2004): 397–416.

Mateos Cruz, Pedro, and Begoña Soler. "El aula sacra del teatro de Mérida. Nuevas consideraciones sobre su concepción arquitectónica y la cronología de su pavimento marmóreo." In *Actas del II Congrés Internacional d'Àrqueologia i Mon Antic, August i les Provinces Occidentals 2000 aniversari de la mort d'Àugust,* edited by Jordi Lopez, 111–18. Tarragona: Fundació Privada Mútua Catalana, 2015.

Meischner, Jutta. "Das Missorium des Theodosius in Madrid." *Jahrbuch des Deutschen Archäologischen Instituts* 3 (1996): 389–432.

Mélida, José Ramón. *Catálogo monumental de España: Provincia de Badajoz.* Madrid: Ministerio de Instrucción Pública y Bellas Artes, 1925.

Montalvo, Ana. "Intervención arqueológica en el solar de la Barriada Sta. Catalina: Una aproximación al conocimiento del área Norte de Augusta Emerita." *Memoria, Excavaciones Arqueológicas en Mérida 1997* (1999): 125–52.

Montalvo, Ana, Eulalia Gijón, and Javier Sánchez. "Circo romano de Mérida. Campaña de 1995." *Memoria 1. Excavaciones Arqueológicas realizadas en Mérida durante 1994 y 95* (1997): 245–58.

Moreno de Vargas, Bernabé. *Historia de la ciudad de Mérida.* 1633; rpt. Mérida: Diputación Provincial de Badajoz, 1987.

Mostalac, Antonio. "El programa pictórico de la estancia absidada F de la Casa Basílica de Mérida." In *Congreso Internacional: La Hispania de Teodosio,* edited by Ramón Teja, 581–603. Segovia: Junta de Castilla y León, Consejería y Cultura, 1997.

Nogales, Trinidad. *Espectáculos en Augusta Emerita.* Monografías Emeritenses 5. Mérida: Museo Nacional de Arte Romano, 2000.

Peña, Antonio. "La decoración arquitectónica." In *El Foro de Augusta Emerita. Génesis y Evolución de sus Recintos Monumentales,* edited by Rocío Ayerbe Vélez, Teresa Barrientos, and Felix Palma, 525–82. Anejos de Archivo Español de Arqueología 53. Mérida: CSIC, 2009.

Ramirez, José Luís, Agustín Velázquez, and Eulalia Gijón. "Un nuevo pedestal de Galieno encontrado en Mérida." *Anas* 6 (1993): 75–84.

Ramírez, José Luís, and Pedro Mateos Cruz. *Inscripciones Cristianas de Mérida.* Cuadernos emeritenses 14. Mérida: Museo Nacional de Arte Romano, 2000.

Saquete, José Carlos, José Luís Mosquera, and Juana Márquez. "Aemilius Aemilianus, un nuevo gobernador de la Lusitania." *Anas* 4–5 (1992): 31–43.

Sastre, Isaac. *Los primeros edificios cristianos de Extremadura. Sus espacios y elementos litúrgicos. Caelum in terra.* Serie Ataecina 5. Mérida: Instituto de Arqueología de Mérida, 2010.

Tranoy, Alain. *Hydace, Chronique.* Volume 2. Paris: Les Editions du Cerf, 1974.

Vives, José. "La inscripción del puente de Mérida de época visigoda." *Revista del Centro de Estudios Extremeños* 13 (1939): 1–7.

7

The So-Called "Oriental Quarter" of Ostia: Regions III.XVI–VII, a Neighborhood in Late Antiquity

Michael Mulryan[1]

Introduction

Recent work on Ostia has begun to move away from the focus on the second century CE to the more nuanced and much more difficult task of reconstructing the city in its final few centuries.[2]

1   I would like to thank Philipp Markus for kindly taking the photographs used in this article. They were taken between June and November 2017.
2   Axel Gering, "Plätze und Straßensperren an Promenaden. Zum Funktionswandel Ostias in der Spätantike," *Römische Abteilung* 111 (2004): 299–382; Axel Gering, "Krise, Kontinuität, Auflassung und Aufschwung in Ostia seit der Mitte des 3. Jahrhunderts," in *L'Empire romain en mutation. Répercussions sur les villes romaines dans la deuxième moitié du 3ᵉ siècle*, ed. Regula Schatzmann and Stefanie Martin-Kilchner (Montagnac: Editions Mergoil, 2011), 301–16; Axel Gering "Marmordepots. Zum 'Recycling' des Forums von Ostia im 5. und 6. Jh. n. Chr.," in *Werkspuren. Materialverarbeitung und handwerkliches Wissen im antiken Bauwesen*, ed. Dietmar Kurapkat and Ulrike Wulf-Rheidt (Regensburg: Schnell and Steiner, 2016), 149–66; Luke Lavan, "Public Space in Late Antique Ostia: Excavation and Survey in 2008–2011," *American Journal of Archaeology* 116, no. 4 (2012): 649–91; Luke Lavan, *Public Space in the Late Antique City: AD 284–650*, 2 vols. (Leiden: Brill, 2020); Michael Mulryan, "Christian and Jewish Spaces in Late An-

The difficulties resulting from the rapid clearance excavations of the town from 1938–1941 are well known and do not need to be repeated here,[3] but they leave us with only a small lens of late antique material with which to work. Where recent excavations have been able to touch virgin soil, or closely examine standing remains, alongside shallow sondaging, the continued activity and vibrancy of the town in this late period is clear.[4] As

tique Ostia," in *A Forgotten City: New Archaeological Research on Late Antique Ostia*, ed. Michael Mulryan (forthcoming); and Michael Mulryan, "Cultic Spaces in Late Antique Ostia," in *A Forgotten City*, ed. Mulryan. The difficulties of this period are highlighted by Carlo Pavolini, "A Survey of Excavations and Studies on Ostia (2004–2014)," *Journal of Roman Studies* 106 (2016): 222–28; and Carlo Pavolini, "Per un riesame del problema di Ostia nella tarda antichità: indice degli argomenti," in *Le regole del gioco. Studi in onore di Clementina Panella*, ed. Antonio F. Ferrandes and Giacomo Pardini (Rome: Edizione Quasar, 2016), 385–405.

3   In the written archives at Ostia, the excavation diary from this period contains less details, and part of it is reduced to a list of main finds, although some useful photos exist. The published material over this period consists largely of discussions of new epigraphic and sculptural finds; whole regions we know were unearthed are barely mentioned.

4   On the Porta Marina: Massimiliano David and his Bologna team are still excavating an area around the Porta Marina, part of which includes unexcavated land. Many publications have followed, the most relevant ones include: Massimiliano David, "Una caupona tardoantica e un nuovo mitreo nel suburbio di Porta Marina a Ostia antica," *Temporis signa* 9 (2014): 31–44; Massimiliano David, Dante Abate, Stefano De Togni, Maria Stella Graziano, Dino Lombardo, Alessandro Melega, and Angelo Pellegrino, "Il pavimento del nuovo Mitreo dei marmi colorati a Ostia antica," in *Atti del XXI colloquio dell'Associazione italiana per lo studio e la conservazione del mosaico*, ed. Claudia Angelelli, Daniela Massara, and Francesca Sposito (Tivoli: Arbor Sapientiae, 2016), 369–76; Massimiliano David, Mauro Carinci, Marialetizia Carra, Stefano De Togni, Maria Stella Graziano, and Angelo Pellegrino, "Fenomeni esondativi del Tevere nell'area della città di Ostia tra il I e il V sec. d.C," in *Roma, Tevere, Litorale. Ricerche tra passato e presente*, ed. Giulia Caneva, Carlo M. Travaglini, and Catherine Virlouvet (Rome: Università Roma Tre, Centro per lo studio di Roma (CROMA), 2017), 61–68; Massimiliano David, Mauro Carinci, Maria Stella Graziano, Stefano De Togni, Angelo Pellegrino, and Marcello Turci, "Nuovi dati e argomenti per Ostia tardoantica dal Progetto Ostia Marina," *Mélanges de l'École Française de Rome* 126 (2016): 173–86; Marcelo Turci, "Un complesso termale tardoantico. Il balneum di Musiciolus (IV, XV, 2) nel quartiere fuori Porta Mari-

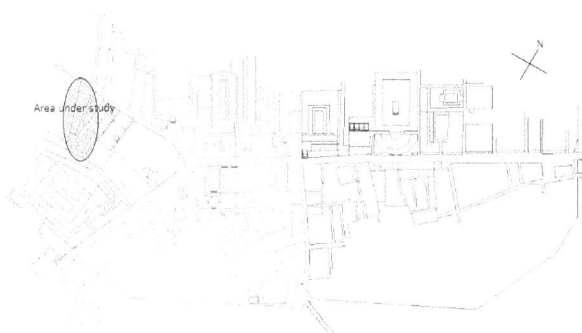

Fig. 1. Plan of Ostia Antica with area under study shown. Adapted by the author with permission from *Ostia Antica Atlas,* http://www.ia-ostiaantica.org/news/atlante-di-ostia-antica.

part of expanding this picture of late Ostia, and a wider under-standing of late antique urban development in general, I would like to move away from the tendency towards *Baugeschichten* (building histories), and focus more on movement and the hu-man actor, by approaching the question in a micro-spatial way. I will do this with a close examination of a small area of the city off the so-called Via della Foce. The area comprises insulas 16–17 on the southern side of this major road that leads up to the Tiber, a region that has been described in the past as an "oriental quarter" (fig. 1).[5] This particular characterization and its impli-cations will be discussed briefly later, but my primary focus is the spatial organization of the area and how it functioned for the actors within it in the final phases of Ostia's existence as a work-

na," *Mélanges de l'École Française de Rome* 126 (2016): 161–71. On the Forum of the Heroic Statue and elsewhere: Lavan, "Public Space in Late Antique Ostia"; and Lavan, *Public Space in the Late Antique City,* vol. 2; Gering, "Krise, Kontinuität, Auflassung und Aufschwung in Ostia seit der Mitte des 3. Jahrhunderts." On the Synagogue: http://www.fastionline.org/record_view.php?fst_cd=AIAC_2521.

5   Ricardo Mar, "El Serapeum Ostiense y la urbanística de la ciudad. Una aproximación a su estudio," *Bolletino di Archeologia* 13–15 (1992): 37–46; cf. Stephen T.A.M. Mols, "The Urban Context of the Serapeum at Ostia," *BA-Besch — Bulletin Antieke Beschaving* 82 (2007): 227–32.

ing town. This can help fill out our picture of how late antique Ostia actually functioned, rather than simply providing a series of building histories.

Methodology

The habit in recent years of utilizing spatial analytical techniques and "urban theory" from the field of architecture and applying it to ancient urban landscapes is a useful and worthwhile pursuit, especially to pick out features that can be missed through structural analysis.[6] However, in many cases, it can tend to result in "common sense" conclusions that could be reached by simpler techniques. So, while a judicious use of these ideas will form part of an analysis of mine elsewhere,[7] here I wish to focus on ideas of movement, accessibility, "openness," and so on through

---

6   This growing field of scholarship has stemmed from the pioneering work of R.A. Raper and Ray Laurence, focusing on Pompeii: R.A. Raper, "The Analysis of the Urban Structure of Pompeii: A Sociological Examination of Land Use (Semi-Micro)," in *Spatial Archaeology*, ed. David L. Clarke (London: Academic Press, 1977), 189–221; R.A. Raper, "Pompeii: Planning and Social Implications," in *Space, Hierarchy and Society: Interdisciplinary Studies in Social Area Analysis*, ed. Barry C. Burnham and John Kingsbury, BAR International Series 59 (Oxford: Oxford University Press, 1979), 137–48; Ray Laurence, *Roman Pompeii: Space and Society* (London: Routledge, 1994). This has also been applied to other well-preserved Roman sites, such as Empúries and of course Ostia: Alan Kaiser, *The Urban Dialogue: An Analysis of the Use of Space in the Roman City of Empúries, Spain,* BAR International Series 901 (Oxford: Oxford University Press, 2000); Hanna Stoeger, *Rethinking Ostia: A Spatial Enquiry into the Urban Society of Rome's Imperial Port-Town* (Boston and Leiden: Brill, 2011). All this work stems from the ideas of the post-war urban theorists, such as Kevin Lynch, *The Image of the City* (Cambridge: Harvard University Press, 1960); Henri Lefebvre, *La production de l'espace* (Paris: Éditions Anthropos, 1974); Edward W. Soja, *Thirdspace: Journeys to Los Angeles and Other Real and Imagined Places* (Oxford: Blackwell, 1996); and Christopher Y. Tilley, *A Phenomenology of Landscape: Places, Paths, and Monuments* (Oxford: Berg, 1994), bringing in ideas of "experience," something now developed within the burgeoning field of "sensory archaeology."

7   Michael Mulryan, "A Space Syntax Analysis of an Ostian Region in Late Antiquity: Regions 3.16–17," forthcoming.

the structural remains, which can also be judged without the need for complex graphs and equations.

One question needs to be addressed here: that of "behavior," and the actions of the "actor," in a particular space being defined by, or defining, the space around it. I think it would be fair to say that modern scholarship has been inevitably influenced by the motivations of twentieth-century town planners in Britain and Europe, who sought to influence behavior and society through their designs.[8] The fact that many of these twentieth-century structures ultimately failed as functional spaces, and within a generation were torn down or almost universally hated, shows that people seem to act in particular ways in a space which appears to be culturally defined, and if that space is actively trying to stop that, or works against that, then problems follow. Equally, modifications, both structural and decorative, to internal and external urban spaces show that such "influence" is a two-way street, as it were, with spaces and human agents within them influencing each other. Spaces are not static; they either work with human experience and movement, or they disappear. The truth behind this question is therefore complex, but it is apparent that the actor ultimately influences the space. There is no clear evidence for the ancient period of builders trying to

8   Established by the rationalist/functionalist ideas of the Congrès internationaux d'architecture moderne (CIAM): Eric Paul Mumford, *The CIAM Discourse on Urbanism, 1928–1960* (Cambridge: MIT Press, 2000). Although this was superseded by more structuralist ideas from the 1960s to 1980s, the concept of architecture having an impact on society continued: see for example Herman Hertzberger, *Architecture and Structuralism: The Ordering of Space* (Rotterdam: Nai010 publishers, 2015). There is still the assumption amongst some current urban theorists that human agency is largely determined by built environments, such as in the work of Alan Penn at UCL, which recently included computer simulations of human behavior in an environment (the "Ikea model"), which assumes an intrinsic lack of movement "freedom," although recent work also acknowledges human influence on the urban environment as well: Kinda Al-Sayed and Alan Penn, "On the Nature of Urban Dependencies: How Manhattan and Barcelona Reinforced a Natural Organization Despite Planning Intentionality," *Environment and Planning B: Planning and Design* 43, no. 6 (2016): 975–96.

influence behavior, yet it is clear that they understood the basic concepts of visibility and accessibility within the urban context.[9]

The changes to this region of Ostia over time also suggests a divergence between the original urban design and functional changes made for practical reasons, which upset any neat design plans that may have been there in the area's original form. This is the task at hand: distinguishing between, on the one hand, plans and design, and, on the other hand, function, movement, and behavior. These are the essential parts of any equation when trying to establish the "character" of the neighborhood. The sums making up the equation include the relationship between the main road through the region, the Via del Serapide, the buildings and spaces on and adjacent to the street, and the human actors operating within all these spaces. I will also not be focusing on a pervading question in some scholarship, that of "public" and "private" space, as this is culturally informed and rarely perceivable from archaeological remains. As such, "public" and "private" are unhelpful definitions, often based on modern perception. Therefore, "accessibility" will be the nearest I will get to such a concept, and this will be based on likely room and building function and location of entrances.

9   Temples on hills and within fora, for example, and see Vitruvius, *On Architecture, Volume I: Books 1–5,* trans. Frank Granger, Loeb Classical Library 251 (Cambridge: Harvard University Press, 1931), 1.7.1–2, 4.5.2. For these ideas in a late antique context, see Claudian, *Panegyricus de sexto consulato Honorii August,* in *On Stilicho's Consulship 2–3. Panegyric on the Sixth Consulship of Honorius. The Gothic Wars. Shorter Poems. Rape of Proserpina,* vol. 2, trans. Maurice Platnauer, Loeb Classical Library 136 (Cambridge: Harvard University Press, 1922), 39–52. For a modern opinion, see Michael Mulryan, *The Religious Topography of Late Antique Rome (A.D. 313–440): A Case for a Strategy* (Ph.D. diss., University College London, 2008); Michael Mulryan, "The Establishment of Urban Movement Networks: Devotional Pathways in Late Antique and Early Medieval Rome," *Theoretical Roman Archaeology* 2011 (2012): 123–34; and, Michael Mulryan, *Spatial "Christianisation" in Context: Strategic Intramural Building in Rome from the 4th–7th c. AD* (Oxford: Archaeopress, 2014).

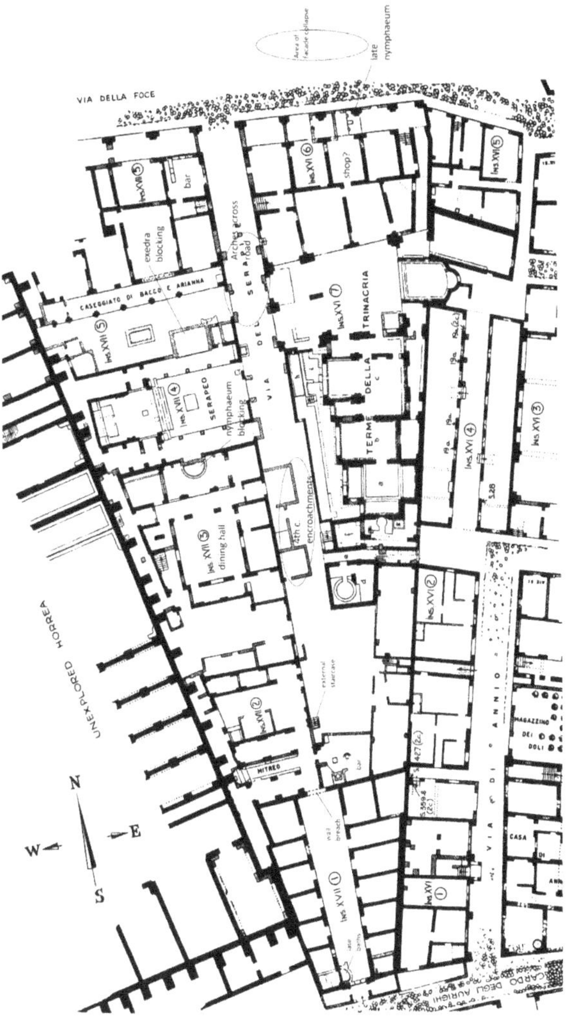

Fig. 2. Adapted from Bloch, "The Serapeum of Ostia and the Brick-Stamps of 123 A.D.: A New Landmark in the History of Roman Architecture," *American Journal of Archaeology* 63 (1959): 225–40, fig. 1 (labels are author's; insula numbers are Bloch's); courtesy of the *American Journal of Archaeology* and Archaeological Institute of America.

The Buildings and Their Chronology (fig. 2)

In order to provide a context for the late antique modifications to and use of this area of Ostia, I will briefly lay out the earlier building phases of the region, and their implications for the actors who used these spaces.[10] Many of these earlier features remained in place into late antiquity, and therefore much of what is discussed here is applicable to how the area "worked" in that period as well.

Trajanic–Hadrianic Phase (98–138 CE)

A few investigations have found some remains of what existed in this area before the Trajanic–Hadrianic period, and which show evidence for earlier walls in a few places at a lower level to the current road surface.[11] However, as far as we can tell, the major building phases for this part of Ostia began in the second century, which created the outline form the neighborhood would take for the next four centuries. This early chronology of this part of Ostia was made more secure with the work of Herbert Bloch in the 1950s, after the area's initial excavation in the late 1930s. He located all the in situ brick stamps in the vicinity and summarized his findings in an important article published in 1959.[12] This said that insula 17 and the Terme della Trinacria (hereafter Baths of Trinacria) on the other side of the road were confirmed to have been built within a wedge-shaped area formed by the pre-existing *horreum* structure to the west (with a *terminus post quem* [TPQ] of 110 CE) and the structures 1–4 in insula 16 to the east. The brick stamps in the Serapeum dated

---

10 A detailed analysis of the dating of the area can be found in *El santuario de Serapis en Ostia*, ed. Ricardo Mar (Tarragona: Universitat Rovira i Virgili, 2001), so this will be an overview with some references to that work and others.

11 Ibid., 36–38.

12 Herbert Bloch, "The Serapeum of Ostia and the Brick-Stamps of 123 A.D.: A New Landmark in the History of Roman Architecture," *American Journal of Archaeology* 63 (1959): 225–40.

overwhelmingly to 123 CE, with the *cella* wall containing one of 124, with others of 125 by the entrance, and a few of 126 found behind the *cella*. The Baths of Trinacria contained stamps mainly from 126, and is likely to have been finished soon thereafter, with modifications to one of its cisterns a few years later and modifications elsewhere c. 200. The portico with shops to the north of the baths (III.XVI.6) likely pre-existed the baths but were modified at the same time, or soon after the baths were constructed, with a blocking wall and a square feature in the portico itself.[13]

This firming up of the dating for the creation of the Serapeum and other nearby structures using brick stamps thus gave a good guide for the other buildings that lay in its immediate surroundings, whose construction techniques and relationship to the firmly dated examples allowed for relative dating from this. Bloch's work was aided by the earlier discovery of a fragment of the Ostian *fasti,* which mentions the dedication of a temple to Serapis on January 24, 127, giving us a firm *terminus ante quem* (TAQ) for its structural completion.[14] At almost the same time as the discovery of this inscription came the uncovering of what was believed to be the temple itself. This identity for this structure was confirmed in 1953 when a pedimental inscription that read IOVI SERAPI was discovered broken in two and reused in a repair to the late paving of a portico "to the right of the Serapeum," although this inscription dates from a later phase (see below).[15] This, coupled with the numerous cult items and dedications related to Serapis and Egypt found in the

---

13 Ibid., 227–28.

14 *Inscriptiones Italiae, Fasti consulares et triumphales,* vol. 13, ed. Attilio Degrassi (Rome: Libreria dello Stato, 1937), 1, 205, 234. This allowed him to discuss the nature of brick production and their use/storage: Bloch, "The Serapeum of Ostia," esp. 234. That is, brick stamps give us a close TPQ, not a precise building sequence, as is assumed from many publications.

15 *Giornale degli Scavi* 30, July 2, 1953; *L'Année épigraphique* (1956): 76; Fausto Zevi, "Iscrizioni e personaggi nel Serapeo," in *El santuario de Serapis en Ostia,* ed. Mar, 188.

temple area and within the baths across the road, present a convincing case for this being a temple to this deity.[16] The fact that both the temple area and the Baths of Trinacria across the road both contain dedications to Jupiter-Serapis or Sol-Serapis may point to some sort of religious/symbiotic relationship between the two spaces at some point in time. However, the contextual details have been lost of their discovery, so why and when they were in these spaces is still debatable (see below).

The in-situ brick stamps discovered by Bloch confirm that most of the buildings east, north, and south of the Serapeum date to soon after 125. The House of Bacchus and Ariadne lies just to the north of the Serapeum temple and its *area sacra*. From brick stamps, we know it was also constructed in the Hadrianic period,[17] and a wide entrance connected it to the Serapeum. This all suggests they were meant to operate as a functional whole, but the precise nature of that function is ambiguous, although one room was for dining. The building also contains a courtyard with a basin, flanked by a portico, with several spaces having high-quality black and white mosaics, one of which depicts Bacchus and Ariadne. The part of this structure located closer to the main Via della Foce road to the north consists of two shops; the one at the corner of the "foce" and "serapide" roads shows a bar counter, something which has now disappeared, and entrances from both roads. As such, we cannot know the date of this bar, nor detect whether it was an original element of the area, or a later addition. Nonetheless, it was clearly installed to benefit from the large amount of foot traffic coming from the main road that ultimately led to the river, and presumably the port, and from customers going into and out of the main entrance to the baths here.

---

16 Michel Malaise, *Inventaire préliminaire des documents égyptiens découverts en Italie* (Boston and Leiden: Brill, 1972), 72–74, n. 19–23, 27, 29–30 (dedications); 79–81, n. 67–77 (objects). See Maria Floriani Squarciapino, *I culti orientali ad Ostia* (Boston and Leiden: Brill, 1962), 19–22 for more detail.
17 Bloch, "The Serapeum of Ostia," with his fig. 1.

Fig. 3. Entrance to the Baths of Trinicaria. Looking southeast.

The entrance to the House of Bacchus and Ariadne from the road was not from the main Via della Foce, but was rather in the southeast part of the building, and was marked by a series of arches that went over the Via del Serapide; the bases for these arches are extant and, through brick stamps found by Bloch, date to 126, so are contemporary with the "house."[18] An entrance down a side road rather than the main Via della Foce implies that the structure was less easily accessible, but was still marked out on the street. This entrance was directly opposite the main (widest) entrance to the Baths of Trinacria, which we have seen dates to c. 126 as well (fig. 3). These set of arches across the road may have marked out a main entrance to the baths for customers and provided shelter from the rain in the process. Perhaps a structure lay above the arches that led from the baths to the "house" over the road? But, certainly, a spatial link was created between the two spaces from this initial phase for actors walking here. The two areas may have had a functional relationship from the start; the finds of Serapic material from the baths and the spatial link between the House of Bacchus and Ariadne and the Serapeum does appear to link all three areas at this earlier

18   See *El santuario de Serapis en Ostia,* ed. Mar, 69, fig. 29.

Fig. 4. Brick pillars south of Baths of Trinacria. Wall of structure 3.XVII.2 behind. Looking southeast.

time. But such a spatial link was broken between the latter two in the next phase (see below) and the finds are not reliable indicators as discussed above.

The buildings south of the Serapeum and baths in this period are also Hadrianic. The so-called "House of the Serapeum," as dated from the brick stamps, was built around 123–125,[19] and, like the House of Bacchus and Ariadne, it could also be entered directly from the *area sacra* of the Serapeum. This also suggests a functional and spatial relationship. This building had a square dining hall (judging by the layout of the colored and black and white floor mosaics for the placement of tables and U-shaped benches) which led directly from the *area sacra* via a corridor and antechamber.

All this suggests that, during this Hadrianic period, the upper, or northern, part of the Via del Serapide was a busy area and one that was influenced and characterized by Serapic worship, with a complex of buildings around the Serapeum spatially related to it. From the late second century at least (when the pedi-

19 Bloch, "The Serapeum of Ostia," with his fig. 1.

mental inscription of IOVI SERAPI is thought to date from — see below) this was apparent from the street to some extent.

To the south of the House of the Serapeum is a building built around 123–126 according to the brickstamps,[20] but again its original purpose is unknown and cannot be accurately assessed with the data we have. The rows of brick and tufa piers and lack of decorative elements from this period may point to a utilitarian role as this is seen in storage buildings elsewhere.[21]

A series of walls to the west of this structure are more mysterious (fig. 4). Brick stamps from the three brick pillars south of the Baths of Trinacria come from 123,[22] but the walls that join them up may not date to this period (*opus reticulatum* judging from what remains on site). The pillars though are at least contemporary with the surrounding buildings and part of the original spatial formulation of the area. The walls that join the pillars, from the Gismondi plan (barely visible today as the area is now overgrown), are much thinner than the surrounding building walls, so we must assume they were for a single-story structure. Interestingly, the series of rooms running north–south, and thus parallel with the west wall of building III.XVI.2, are related to each other, albeit divided by an external staircase (which must lead to the upper floor of III.XVI.2, behind), and are accessible from the Via del Serapide. Their use and purpose are unknown, however. Another cellular room, formed by an east–west running wall, appears to be a later phase and will be dealt with below.

The trapezoid warehouse that is at the end of the street contained no surviving brick stamps, but its relationship with the dated buildings around it means it must date to after the large, mainly unexcavated, *horreum* to the west (dated to c. 110 — see below), but earlier than the utilitarian building to its north

---

20 Ibid.
21 Mar believes it is a service or storage building, possibly connected to the Serapeum sanctuary: *El santuario de Serapis en Ostia,* ed. Mar, 55–57.
22 Bloch, "The Serapeum of Ostia," with his fig. 1.

Fig. 5. Remains of the "bar" and east wall of structure 3.XVII.2. Looking southwest.

Fig. 6. Looking northwest from "bar." Mithraeum is marked by white sign.

(completed c. 126). It was originally designed to be entered only from the south, via the Cardo degli Aurighi, so, in this phase, it would have only been the end wall for the Via del Serapide. Later modifications, however, changed this.

Post-Hadrianic–Mid-Third Century

There is some evidence through brick stamps for modifications in the Baths of Trinacria in the late second century,[23] however, for structural changes after this period we seem to be reliant on wall typologies and relative dating through wall relationships, rather than excavation or later stamps.[24] Several walls can thus be firmly dated to after 125–126, but the wide use of spolia in some and their location within structures and over the street point to a late antique date, but more on this below.

An area with even more ambiguous dating is a cellular room, lying directly east of the entrance to the utilitarian building at the end of the street, that was formed by an east–west running wall, which, from Gismondi again, seems to be a bit thicker and of a later phase than the thin north–south running walls off the Baths of Trinacria, mentioned above.[25] There are no brick stamps and only the very corner of this wall, by the Mithraeum entrance (paralleled with another wall section of the same typology on the other side of the entrance), is visible now; a raised bump in the ground is the only indication of the remainder of the rest of the wall today (figs. 5 and 6). Despite its current poor condition, its relationship with a wall known to be from around 123 (with brickstamp, see above) tells us that it belongs in a later phase — it abuts it and is not intrinsic with it. This later wall is in danger of collapse now, but the first part of it seems to be well-sorted *opus latericium*. A generic mid-second — fourth-century

23 Ibid., 238–39.
24 This seems to be the case judging from ibid. But see *Corpus Inscriptionum Latinarum,* vol. 15.1, ed. Berlin-Brandenburg Academy of Sciences and Humanities (Berlin: Berlin-Brandenburg Academy of Sciences and Humanities, 1891), and Herbert Bloch, "The Roman Brick Stamps not published in Vol. XV of the CIL," *Harvard Studies in Classical Philology* 56–57 (1947): 1–128.
25 The area was unfortunately not well-maintained in the past, and is now generally overgrown with collapsing walls. So, much of what I am discussing here can only be partly verified on the ground, but, where possible, I will mention what we can see today.

date can thus only be given, with a TPQ of 123.[26] Another wall off it is *opus vittatum,* and is of a similar character to the firmly dated fourth century encroachments on the road from the House of the Serapeum (see below). This may be the square feature in this corner shown on the Gismondi plan (which Bloch uses — see fig. 2), rather the remainder of the wall though. This part of the street was a bar or food area, due to the presence of a sunken dolium, a basin, and a well, the latter two barely visible now due to overgrown weeds and plants (fig. 5). This area only seems to have been accessible from the Hadrianic utilitarian building, which, from the early third century, housed a Mithraeum. The implications of this will be explored below, but the blockings that can be seen within and on the east external wall of the Hadrianic utilitarian building (III.XVII.2) may all date from the time of the creation of the Mithraeum within it, c. 204–11, or its repair/modification c. 253–259 (see below), suggestive of the creation of a Mithraic "club" with a bar/food area solely for the club. We can only be speculative here as any useful data is lost and new data is lacking for the area, but, at some point in time, it is likely that a bar only accessible to Mithraists existed here from the third century.

The other changes to the area that have been more firmly, or traditionally, dated from the mid-second century to the mid-third century, i.e. the first alterations to the Hadrianic redevelopment of the area, include:

- A *scholae* or square exedra with aedicula was constructed off a portico north of the *area sacra* of the Serapeum.[27] This (completely?) blocked the wide entrance that existed earlier between the House of Bacchus and Ariadne and the Sera-

---

26 Mar dates it to the post-Hadrianic period it seems: *El santuario de Serapis en Ostia,* ed. Mar, fig. 56a–b.

27 *El santuario de Serapis en Ostia,* ed. Mar, 105–7. An inscription of T. Statilius Optatius may derive from it: Fausto Zevi, "Iscrizioni e personaggi nel Serapeo," 181.

peum complex. Whether a small entrance between the two areas now remained just to its west is difficult to say.

– A large inscription in marble (found reused in a pavement — for which see more below), is thought to have been part of the pediment of the temple or the porch that led to the *area sacra* from the road. According to B. Bollmann, it comes from the late second century.[28] It reads IOVI SERAPI[DI] and marks a redecoration of the temple of Serapis area.[29]

– Modifications in and around the temple of Jupiter-Serapis, and to the north in the House of Bacchus and Ariadne, as well as those in the Baths of Trinacria, have been dated to the Severan period. This includes a new porch for access to the *area sacra* of the temple, and dedications of this date were found within the Serapeum.[30]

– The creation of the Mithraeum of the foot sole within the utilitarian Hadrianic building at the southern edge of the road is believed to date from c. 204–211.[31] It was installed between two sets of piers in the southern part of the building.

Although outside the region we are focusing on, it is worth mentioning the buildings just to the west so as to give us some wider context for the activity that took place in and off the Via del Serapide. To the west lies an *horreum* that contains the typi-

---

28 Cited in Zevi, "Iscrizioni e personaggi nel Serapeo," 188.

29 The early third-century Octavius by Minucius Felix shows that Serapis remained prominent in the town in the early third century, if we take the account literally. He describes a statue to the goddess on, or visible from, the river shore: Minucius Felix, *Octavius,* in *Tertullian, Minucius Felix, Apology. De Spectaculis. Minucius Felix: Octavius,* trans. T.R. Glover and G.H. Rendell, Loeb Classical Library 250 (Cambridge: Harvard University Press, 1931), 2.3–4.

30 *El santuario de Serapis en Ostia,* ed. Mar, 102, 118–30. For the dedications, see Malaise, *Inventaire préliminaire des documents égyptiens découverts en Italie,* 72–74.

31 Michael White, "The Changing Face of Mithraism in Ostia," in *Contested Spaces: Houses and Temples in Roman Antiquity and the New Testament,* ed. David Balch and Annette Weissenrieder (Tübingen: Mohr Siebeck, 2012), 435–92.

cal red *opus latericium* wall type of the Severan period; brick stamps of 110 in other parts of the building show that these are later modifications of a Trajanic structure.[32] Only the edge of the east and a small part of the south wall have been excavated of this warehouse, but we know that it was a very large one, that lay next to two smaller ones from the second century further to the west (with another large one to the north), thanks to the geophysical survey and a small sondage of Michael Heinzelmann in 2000.[33] This confirms that our region lay at the edge of a large working and storage area for the goods from the port. The use of this street needs to be seen in this wider utilitarian context.

The Late Antique Modifications (Mid-Third Century–Mid-Sixth Century)

The form of the area today is broadly that from its final phase of its occupation, of course. Although we cannot rule out the removal of some late "untidy" features by twentieth-century excavators, as occurred elsewhere, this is likely to have been confined to some unrecorded blocking walls.[34] The late antique modifications to this region cannot generally be dated with any precision (we have to rely on relative dating), but there are a few exceptions, which are noted below. Thus, any precise chronology for these late changes cannot really be given. These late modifications can be summarized in this way:

- In the late third or early fourth century the sides of the pronaos of the temple of Serapis were closed (thus extending the *cella*) and a small room with hypocausts, and another with

---

32 Bloch, "The Serapeum of Ostia," 227.
33 Michael Heinzelmann, "Ostia, Regio III. Untersuchungen in den unausgegrabenen Bereichen des Stadtgebietes. Vorbericht zur dritten Grabungskampagne 2000," *Römische Abteilung* 108 (2000): 313–28.
34 More significant occupation features from beyond the sixth century may also have existed here, but again we have no record of them, and they were likely created in a period of "squatter occupation" that we see elsewhere in the city from this time.

buttresses, was created in the House of Bacchus and Ariadne. The dating for these changes seems to be purely from wall typologies.[35]

– The remaining narrow passage by the *schola* between the House of Bacchus and Ariadne and the Serapeum, if there was one, was blocked, the *schola* redecorated and a new portico created. The paving areas of the Serapeum were re-paved partly reusing dedicatory inscriptions, including the large IOVI SERAPI example. All this has been given a generic fourth-century date, with no reasoning given, with the re-paving thought to be early fifth century, again with no rea-soning given.[36] Perhaps this is because the Serapeum is likely to have been abandoned by the time such reuse occurred.

– A possible nymphaeum and wall blocking appear in the por-tico north of the Baths of Trinacria; a façade collapse onto the Via della Foce also occurs. The late antique nymphaeum, apparently dated due to its use of reused material and poorly leveled *opus vittatum,* faces west, rather than towards the Via della Foce. A square room was also created in the portico in the Hadrianic period (well sorted and leveled *opus lat-ericium* — see above), just west of the nymphaeum, so, from that time, the portico had changed function. The west-facing nymphaeum suggests a disconnect with the Via della Foce space, perhaps linked to the closing off of this road to wheeled traffic (see below). Perhaps some blocking walls that shut off the portico from the road existed that were unrecorded at excavation. From what Axel Gering has said about this area in late antiquity, this activity could have taken place within a landscape of ruins and pragmatic reuse following façade col-lapses, notably the façade of this portico (see below).[37]

---

35 *El santuario de Serapis en Ostia,* ed. Mar, 135–42.

36 Ibid., 143; Mar, "El Serapeum Ostiense y la urbanística de la ciudad," 41.

37 Axel Gering, "Ruins, Rubbish Dumps and Encroachment: Resurveying Late Antique Ostia," in *Field Methods and Post-Excavation Techniques in Late Antique Archaeology,* ed. Luke Lavan and Michael Mulryan (Boston and Leiden: Brill, 2013), 249–88.

Fig. 7. Looking north from *horreum* 3.XVII.1 showing neat wall breach.

Fig. 8. Late road encroachment. Looking south.

– A small bath suite in the former *horreum* at the south end of area is created. The small size of it, its widespread use of reused material, its wall typology (*opus vittatum mixtum*), and the source of its water supply (a well from within the

Fig. 9. Late road encroachments. Looking north.

warehouse) all point to a late date.[38] It was entered from the Cardo degli Aurighi via swing doors to the south, but the warehouse building in which it was installed had its north wall knocked through by the entrance to the Mithraeum, presumably at a later date (see fig. 7).

– Modifications to the Mithraeum of the foot sole took place. Among some other repairs and modifications, an altar was added (a coin of Valerian of 253–259 was found in its masonry).[39] The narrowing of the entrance with poorly sorted *opus vittatum* walls can only have a generic late antique date.

– Wall blocking took place between the House of the Serapeum and the Serapeum to the north of it. A series of encroachments over the road were also created here (figs. 8 and 9), which confirms that this was definitively a domus by late antiquity. The former blocking entailed the creation of a

---

38 Grégoire Poccardi "Les bains de la ville d'Ostie a l'époque tardo-antique (fin IIIe–debut VIe siècle)," in *Les cités de l'Italie tardo-antique (IVe–VIe siècle)*, ed. Massimiliano Ghilardi, Christophe J. Goddard, and Pierfrancesco Porena (Rome: Ecole française de Rome, 2006), 167–86, in contrast to Mar (*El santuario de Serapis en Ostia,* 130–32), who thinks it is Severan.

39 White, "The Changing face of Mithraism in Ostia," 489–91.

nymphaeum with a semi-circular basin, while the latter en-croachments were rooms of varying function that have been firmly dated to the fourth century, thanks to a recent excava-tion.[40] The nymphaeum seems to have been dated only from wall typology, but has been given the same phase by Marcel Danner et al.

– The Via della Foce was narrowed and blocked at both ends. The first such activity was just east of the entrance to the Via del Serapide due to a façade collapse during the Severan pe-riod, which was then integrated into a later rebuilding of the area, with the collapse "tidied" and built around and over in situ from the mid-fourth century.[41] The Via della Foce was also blocked by "privately constructed" late spolia walls at its other end, just south of the bivium nymphaeum and by the decumanus crossroads; these walls were removed by the first excavators.[42]

– East–west walls were built sometime in the fourth century at the end of the road enclosing a food area (a partly buried dolia still survives there [see figs. 5 and 6]). Again, generic wall typologies seem to be the basis for the dating.[43]

The function and nature of the temple to Jupiter-Serapis or Sol-Serapis in this later period need to be assessed. As Stephen Mols rightly points out, the Serapic finds from the area almost cer-tainly do not date from the same period,[44] and their archaeolog-ical context has been lost due to the poor nature of the area's ex-cavation, which had no scientific rigor. Thus, any hope of their dating, beyond unreliable stylistic criteria — as well as being

---

40 Marcel Danner et al., "Untersuchungen zur Chronologie der spätantiken Wohnhäuser in Ostia — Vorbericht zu einem Kurzprojekt im Oktober 2012," *Kölner und Bonner Archaeologica* 3 (2013): 217–39.

41 Gering, "Ruins, Rubbish Dumps and Encroachment."

42 Gering, "Plätze und Straßensperren an Promenaden," 354–55, n. 125–26.

43 *El santuario de Serapis en Ostia,* ed. Mar, 143. See below for an examination of the walls in more detail.

44 Mols, "The Urban Context of the Serapeum at Ostia," 229.

able to distinguish between whether we have a recycling dump/ antiquarian collection or a series of in situ finds here — has been lost. Even if these finds were originally from this approximate area, it is not possible to say what date range they cover and whether they can all be attributed to the Serapeum itself.[45] As we cannot reliably date the finds relating to Serapis found in the vicinity (or their deposition date from any stratigraphic data), we have nothing firm to deduce a time when the temple ceased to be active as a place of worship for this or any other deity.[46] The creation of a *domus* separated from the temple on its south side, sometime in the fourth century, may point to a change in the function of the temple, but not necessarily its demise. The access between the temple and the building to the north was blocked in the second century (if we believe Ricardo Mar and Fausto Zevi) after all, and the temple continued to function. Other finds from the temple area are simply listed in the excavation diary, with nothing here, nor in published form, as to their archaeological context. The density of Serapic material from in and around the Serapeum could thus be as much to do with a post abandonment antiquarian collection, or brought together by a devotee eager to protect works from throughout Ostia from eager lime burners, or even Christian iconoclasts in the final period of ancient occupation at the site.[47] Thus, the status of the temple is ambiguous into the fifth century and beyond.

---

45 Contra Dirk Steuernagel, *Kult und Alltag in römischen Hafenstädten. Soziale Prozesse in archäologischer Perspektive* (Stuttgart: Franz Steiner Verlag, 2004), 214.

46 Neither Floriani Squarciapino, *I culti orientali ad Ostia,* nor Malaise, *Inventaire préliminaire des documents égyptiens découverts en Italie,* describe any stratigraphic data nor any dating for the objects beyond approximate stylistic judgements. The excavation diary (*Giornale degli scavi*) is not particularly helpful either.

47 Akin to the finds from the Walbrook Mithraeum in London, some of which may have been ritually buried: see John D. Shepherd, *The Temple of Mithras, London: Excavations by W.F. Grimes and A. Williams at the Walbrook* (London: English Heritage, 1998).

What we can say is that the importance of the Serapeum had diminished by this later period, with the buildings linked to it, both north and south of its *area sacra,* now separated domestic structures. Any relationship with the Baths of Trinacria, aside from the road arches linking the two, cannot be firmly established either. In this way, the Serapic, or "eastern" character of the neighborhood had also diminished, or had been largely lost by this time, especially with the removal of the large pedimental inscription to Jupiter-Serapis that had been visible from the street.

The Impact of the Late Antique Changes on the Movement Economy

The most important aspect of this road as far as its movement economy is concerned was that it was a cul-de-sac, rather than a through road, with a wall of a commercial building marking its south end. By late antiquity, it also had encroachments onto the road outside the House of the Serapeum, which narrowed it and must have further decreased the traffic flow along it. As such, those entering it in late antiquity (and before) were not casual passers-by, but those who specifically wanted and needed to use the baths, visit the temple or Mithraeum, or return to their home in one of the new large houses, or to apartments above the building with the Mithraeum — the only structure around this street in late antiquity where it was possible to have such a use in its lost upper floor: the bottom part of an external staircase survives on the road outside this structure. In other words, this street was rarely for frequent general use as there was no through route, and the road became increasingly narrow and hard to navigate. It had always likely been dark as well, with the arches over the road at the east end providing a gloomy face to the pedestrian from the Via della Foce up to the river. The road was not used to access other parts of Ostia, which gave it its distinctive character. Thus, the street may have been known as the one for the baths or the temple to the general public. It may also have had a seedy reputation, if the "statio cunnilogorum" mosaic in the Baths of Trinacria refers to male prostitutes, and that they still operated in late antiquity.[48]

During this period, the street was still dominated by a large set of widely accessible baths. At its northern end were the large Baths of Trinacria, which seem still to have been operational at the end of the third century at least, due to several interventions within it being dated to this period.[49] This is perhaps a response to the Severan period façade collapse of the portico by the Via della Foce, mentioned above, which must have affected the working of the baths just behind it. According to Mar, the rear waterwheel stopped being used and a pool was converted into an oven in the late fourth century which shows a change of use and a decrease in activity.[50] Much of the baths could still have been utilized, and such activity may have been a response to issues with the aqueduct (required for a waterwheel) rather than a decline in consumer demand in the area.

Thus, the northern end of the street continued to have considerable movement of people for the baths at least. Also at this north end was a portico with shops and a bar facing the main Via della Foce road, west of the entrance to the Via del Serapide. The bar (on the 1950s Gismondi plan, although the counter has now disappeared: see fig. 2) was visible from the road through a portico, so as to benefit from the frequent foot-fall of people going to the river for business or travel. On the east side of the Via del Serapide entrance was another portico, with a buried dolium jar in its westmost cellular room, implying a link with the bar directly opposite on the other side of the Via del Serapide. This portico also, by this period, had a nymphaeum placed within it, but that faced away from the main road, as described above. The

---

48 Cf. Marc Kleijwegt, "Schola Iuvenum seu caplatorum," *Epigraphica* 56 (1994): 29–40, or possibly a crude pun on the "stations" by the theater: http://www.ostia-antica.org/regio3/16/16-7.htm.

49 Theodora Leonora Heres, *Paries: A Proposal for a Dating System of Late-Antique Masonry Structures in Rome and Ostia (A.D. 235–600)* (Amsterdam: Rodopi, 1982).

50 *El santuario de Serapis en Ostia,* ed. Mar, 143.

nymphaeum was hidden from the road, so would only be seen, and indeed was designed to be seen, only once one had entered the portico. This entrance was flanked then by the nymphaeum to the left, as you entered from the main road, and the wall of a pre-existing square room on the right, as noted above. It led through to a cellular room behind, described as a shop. The nymphaeum thus seems to be an embellishment of this through way from the "shop" to the main road and vice versa, suggestive of high frequency use. This nymphaeum has also been seen as a possible bar area.[51]

In this way, in this area by the entrance to the Via del Serapide from the Via della Foce, a bar lay here, across both sides of our side road, for those passing along the main road, drawing them into the beginning of our street. But a portico next to it, that also was originally for the same passers-by, was now altered in use and movement patterning, and perhaps contained another bar. The Severan façade collapse here may have been a factor in these changes. It narrowed and raised the main road, with another set of small baths built opposite this portico on the other side of the road and over the top of the collapse layer. So, this immediate area by late antiquity was one dominated by bath buildings, a bar(s), and the pragmatic use of ruins and the remaining usable spaces. This collapse, just east of the road entrance, seems to have marked the beginning of the encroached, narrower and walled off section of the Via della Foce,[52] so this could explain the continuing presence of bars, and a new nymphaeum here, to go along with the Baths of Trinacria. This was where wheeled traffic could go up to and no further, and so was a traffic and movement hub.

The other end of the Via del Serapide street had a very different "feel"; the pedestrian was invited into the northern end, with its bar(s), nymphaeum, and widely accessible baths; the south-

---

51 Gering, "Plätze und Straßensperren an Promenaden," 354–55 with his fig. 32.
52 Ibid., his fig. 49 implies this.

ern end, in contrast, with its Mithraeum, an associated bar, and a *domus,* may have had a somewhat "clubby" reputation, and may not have been as welcoming to the general Ostian.[53] This is inevitably speculative of course, but it suggests a street that had two contrasting characters; an open, inviting, and busy northern end, that then led to a narrow (due to road encroachments) less frequently used dead end, attended mainly by Mithraists when that shrine was still active. Gering interprets the bar and Mithraeum area at the end of the street (discussed above) to be a single entity club building for Mithraists in the third and fourth centuries.[54] If both areas were active at the same time, perhaps the bar materials were now being used for ritual activity associated with the cult, but it may also have simply been a recreational area for Mithraists. Mar has given us a generic late antique date for the walls around this area which contain the basin, well, and sunken dolium, but we do not know when the Mithraeum went out of use, so we must be cautious when assuming any relationship between the two.

An examination of the walls on site (see above) showed that the walls around the bar, despite now being largely overgrown and in a state of partial collapse, can give us some relative dates, with the square feature at one corner, that formed part of the east-west running wall, likely to be fourth century. So, we can tentatively say that the bar here was created, or closed off from the rest of the road, at that time.

---

53 We need to be careful, of course, with our use of "private" and "public," as I have said. An important corrective was provided by Marlis Arnhold, "Sanctuaries and Urban Spatial Settings in Roman Imperial Ostia," in *A Companion to the Archaeology of Religion in the Ancient World,* ed. Rubina Raja and Jörg Rüpke (London: Wiley-Blackwell, 2015), 293–304. This shows that numerous apparently private religious shrines could actually have been open to many. As mentioned also, "public" and "private" are culturally determined ideas, so our concept of it is probably different from the Romans, and theirs may have also varied over time. For example, a "private house" was also often opened up to the owner's clients, and so on.

54 Gering, "Plätze und Straßensperren an Promenaden," 377, n. 170 with fig. 49 (K5b).

The Mithraeum was certainly still in use in the mid-third century as we have seen, and we have no evidence to suggest it stopped functioning into the fourth, indeed the entrance between the two areas was narrowed by two *opus vittatum* walls, showing that the cult area was likely still in use around this time. The closing off of the area, with access now only possible from the Mithraeum space (an opening in this wall on the Gismondi/ Bloch plan looks like a window feature not an entrance) is the most convincing evidence for a limited use by Mithraists for the bar from that time. Interestingly, the thickness of this closing wall, and the other wall running parallel to the buildings to the east, is about half of that of the other building walls in the vicinity, and suggests they were low boundary walls, or certainly did not support an upper floor. We can imagine a wooden lean-to roof at most that covered the immediate area. All this shows that some people did indeed use this end of the street (especially if the bar was open to the road in its earlier life), or that the Mithraists provided a frequent enough customer base in sufficient numbers to justify its existence here.

The House of the Serapeum has been argued to be a former guild or cult association house, judging by the central dining area arrangement set within a surrounding corridor, and was linked in some way to the temple of Serapis due to the access it had to the temple immediately to the north. This access was blocked some time in late antiquity by a wall with a semi-circular basin that came off it; a set of floor-level niches lie either side of it. It suggests a decorative scheme, probably water related, and has been dated to the same phase as the securely dated road encroachments to the east (more below). In any case, by this time the "house" was now clearly meant to no longer be linked to Serapis, or whatever cult or activity was associated with the temple by this time. Perhaps the creation of the "Mithraic club" area was done so as to replace the loss of this cult association building? Gering suggests remains of a late-fifth-century Christian structure, inter alia, exist in this "house," but it is not clear what he is specifically referring to and how he comes to this interpretation.[55]

The suggestion that the House of the Serapeum was now a *domus* is likely as this was the easiest adaptation to make, and the shape of the ground floor rooms was not greatly altered. Most of the renovations involved blocking former wall openings; there was also the creation of several new smaller rooms, internally, and, most notably, the creation of several new ones projecting east out over the road. This encroachment is similar to the pattern we see elsewhere in the Roman world and Ostia in late antiquity, with "private" space (if we can use that word) asserting itself over what we might call communal or intercommunal space.[56] These encroaching walls are of a well sorted and leveled *opus vittatum* A type, and associative diagnostic finds from one (a new columned stepped entrance porch accessed from the street) gives us a fourth-century date for its construction (fig. 8). The other rooms were constructed at slightly later times it seems, and had varying functions.[57]

Most importantly for us, these walls significantly narrowed the road at this point, from approximately eight meters (twenty-six feet) wide to approximately two meters (six-and-a-half feet) (measured according to the Gismondi plan), restricting both access and movement at the end of the street. This suggests one of two things. Either the street was little-used and so such an encroachment was of minor consequence for the civil authorities; or this became a serious impediment to movement, which effectively "closed off" or severely restricted the accessibility of the end of the road. The end of the road, beyond the encroaching structures off the House of the Serapeum south of the temple, became pedestrian only effectively, with no wheeled vehicle able to get past it easily, thus the area south of and be-

---

55 Gering, "Plätze und Straßensperren an Promenaden," 311, n. 36.

56 See Lavan, *Public Space in the Late Antique City,* vol. 2 (appendix "Street Architecture").

57 Danner et al., "Untersuchungen zur Chronologie der spätantiken Wohnhäuser in Ostia."

Fig. 10. Looking south from wall breach in *horreum* 3.XVII.1. Late baths are at the end.

yond the encroachments may have felt like a separate area from the street to the north. The street did open up once again after the house encroachments however, although the series of thin late antique walls that sectioned off the "Mithraic bar" and the east edge of the road, the latter running off and aligned to the building Caseggiato III.XVI.2 to the east (discussed above), had diminished this area somewhat.

The narrow part of road by these encroachments seems to have been the only way to access this end of the street. On the Gismondi/Bloch plan (fig. 2) it looks like there is a narrow entrance from the inside of one of the House of the Serapeum encroachments onto this southern end of the road, but this does not appear on site today. Also, the only other potential form of access to this part of the road, and the road in general, was from a narrow corridor that went through the south part of the Baths of Trinacria. One came out from it onto the street to face one of the encroaching House of the Serapeum walls which narrowed the exit considerably, yet the Gismondi/Bloch plan shows walls blocking this corridor. Brick stamps found by Bloch here date to

123,[58] and this was also a service area: here lay the main furnace and heating installations for the baths, as well as a waterwheel. As such the only real way to access both ends of the Via del Serapide was from the entrance from the Via della Foce.

Beyond the Mithraic area at the end of the road there was originally no access from this direction to the apparently disused *horreum* to the south. However, at some unknown point, an entranceway was created by the entrance to the Mithraeum, which involved knocking through the north wall of the storage building. This entrance was only accessible via the building housing the Mithraeum, but we do not know whether the breach occurred when the Mithraeum was still in use. At the southern end of this warehouse (III.XVII.1), a small bath suite was created in the late antique period; we cannot be more specific than that (see above) (fig. 10). There is, at least, the enticing possibility of a separate entrance for Mithras devotees to the baths, possibly for a ritual purpose. Why an entrance was made through an apparently disused building seems odd though; perhaps it was made when this part of the *horreum* was actually still in use, but it seems it was not blocked up again. It provided a less than glamorous entrance to the bath suite now installed at its southern end, but it did at least mean there was now access to it for Mithraists and potentially limited access for others from the north. For those with this access, mainly Mithraists one would assume, this changed the character of the street entirely; it meant they could now reach the Cardo degli Aurighi from the Via del Serapide, and a set of baths, perhaps for their out of hours use. For these people, the road was no longer a cul-de-sac, but for most people it still was. The uncertain dating of this wall breach means we need to be cautious in assuming it was not a post antique/abandonment development, but the cut of the walls reaches down to the Roman level, and it is neat, so it does seem to be an ancient breach (see fig. 7).

58 Bloch, "The Serapeum of Ostia," his fig. 1.

Yet, an embellishment at the southern end of this warehouse, with secondary walls, on the Cardo degli Aurighi, and a raising of the level—an embellishment that also included the south façade of the building next door (a commercial structure of some sort: III.XVI.1)—indicates that this was intended to be the main entrance to a new set of baths for the general public. We cannot be certain of the date of these modifications, but they may be contemporary with the new baths. The new entrance has a bolt hole and two pivot holes on either side, meaning it had two swing doors, perhaps one for people going in, the other for those coming out, a door arrangement designed for busy, free flowing movement. In this way, the wall breach in the north wall of the warehouse by the Mithraeum was a secondary entrance, perhaps for the Mithraic use of the baths, or to access the well that lay in the warehouse. The creation of the baths at this end of the warehouse and the existence of these swing doors suggests the southern edge of our neighborhood, on the Cardo degli Aurighi, had a high movement economy in late antiquity.

Conclusion

We can say that, by late antiquity, the Via del Serapide was not a typical street, but neither was it particularly "oriental" in character. The dual nature of the street is interesting; the northern half, nearest the Via della Foce, was busy and sought to draw in people from that main thoroughfare. The Foce was a main road to the port area, so this is unsurprising. The southern part of the road in late antiquity had a very different character. A physical and perceptual change occurred in the road with the encroachments from the House of the Serapeum from the fourth century that narrowed the road considerably, and led to an area for Mithraists, and possibly residents of potential flats in the upper floors of the Hadrianic building. This was a dead end; but this changed at some point for those with access to the Mithraeum area, where they could enter the warehouse as a back way into the baths installed at its far end. It was this "dead end" character for most residents of the town that meant the Via del Serapide was not widely used beyond the Baths of Trinacria. The number of Serapists in the town cannot have been the majority either, so the baths and the surrounding bars were the main draw for most. Unlike most of the streets in Ostia, it led nowhere.

The eastern character of the street is doubtful. The frequent Serapic finds and dedicatory inscriptions are from within and near the temple, but the vague nature of the description of find spots, and lost stratigraphic data, means we cannot distinguish between antiquarian collection, the remnants of post antique robbing activity, or near in situ use.[59] It should also be noted that the Serapic complex, initially comprising the temple and *area sacra* itself with the two buildings north and south if it, already began to diminish sometime in the second century, with the square exedra blocking the connection between the Serapeum and the House of Bacchus and Ariadne to its north. The building to its south was then separated from it in late antiquity. Elsewhere, the street is typically late antique Ostian in the buildings that lay off it: two houses, a building with a Mithraeum, porticoes and shops, a nymphaeum, active baths, all exist alongside the pragmatic use of ruined areas.

What does this street and its movement economy tell us about Ostia in late antiquity? It says that the town was still vibrant and active, but its streets were narrower and areas changed in use for practical reasons. The pedestrian and goods traffic became less important, with larger houses appearing, but with bars and movement nodes continuing. This active northern end of our road suggests a longevity for the use of the river, with people clearly continuing to utilize the road that led to it. The street also shows the importance Mithraism held within the city

---

59 The in situ shrine to Serapis in a building to the south of our area is a far more convincing example of wider Serapic activity in this part of Ostia, from the Severan period (Angelo Pellegrino, "Note sul culto di Serapide ad Ostia," *Miscellanea greca e romana* 13 (1988): 225–41). The underlying assumption made that Serapists were necessarily Greek or Graeco-Egyptian is highly questionable, especially in Ostia where the majority of the dedicatory inscriptions to the god are in Latin.

at this time; the Mithraeum here seems to have had its own bar and entrance to a set of baths. The Via del Serapide is thus highly representative of late antique Ostia; a vibrant, "messy" street and area; one that would have seemed different to an Ostian of the early imperial period, but not entirely unfamiliar.

Bibliography

Primary

Claudian. *Panegyricus de sexto consulatu Honorii August. In On Stilicho's Consulship 2–3. Panegyric on the Sixth Consulship of Honorius. The Gothic War. Shorter Poems. Rape of Proserpina.* Volume 2. Translated by Maurice Platnauer. Loeb Classical Library 136. Cambridge: Harvard University Press, 1922. DOI: 10.4159/DLCL.claudian_claudianus-panegyric_sixth_consulship_emperor_honorius.1922.

Corpus Inscriptionum Latinarum. 17 Volumes. Edited by Berlin-Brandenburg Academy of Sciences and Humanities. Berlin: Berlin-Brandenburg Academy of Sciences and Humanities, 1863–1986.

Inscriptiones Italiae, Fasti consulares et triumphales. Volume 13. Edited by Attilio Degrassi. Rome: Libreria dello Stato, 1937.

Minucius Felix. *Octavius.* In Tertullian, Minucius Felix. *Apology. De Spectaculis. Minucius Felix: Octavius.* Translated by T.R. Glover and Gerald H. Rendell. Loeb Classical Library 250. Cambridge: Harvard University Press, 1931. DOI: 10.4159/DLCL.minucius_felix-octavius.1931.

Vitruvius. *On Architecture, Volume I: Books 1–5.* Translated by Frank Granger. Loeb Classical Library 251. Cambridge: Harvard University Press, 1931. DOI: 10.4159/DLCL.vitruvius-architecture.1931.

Secondary

Al-Sayed, Kinda, and Alan Penn. "On the Nature of Urban Dependencies: How Manhattan and Barcelona Reinforced a Natural Organisation Despite Planning Intentionality." *Environment and Planning B: Planning and Design* 43, no. 6 (2016): 975–96. DOI: 10.1177/0265813516650200.

Arnhold, Marlis. "Sanctuaries and Urban Spatial Settings in Roman Imperial Ostia." In *A Companion to the Archaeology of Religion in the Ancient World,* edited by Rubina Raja and Jörg Rüpke, 293–304. London: Wiley-Blackwell, 2015. DOI: 10.1002/9781118886809.ch22.

Bloch, Herbert. "The Roman Brick Stamps not Published in Vol. XV of the CIL." *Harvard Studies in Classical Philology* 56–57 (1947): 1–128. DOI: 10.2307/310746.

———. "The Serapeum of Ostia and the Brick-Stamps of 123 A.D. A New Landmark in the History of Roman Architecture." *American Journal of Archaeology* 63 (1959): 225–40. DOI: 10.2307/501844.

Danner, Marcel, et al. "Untersuchungen zur Chronologie der spätantiken Wohnhäuser in Ostia—Vorbericht zu einem Kurzprojekt im Oktober 2012." *Kölner und Bonner Archaeologica* 3 (2013): 217–39.

David, Massimiliano. "Una caupona tardoantica e un nuovo mitreo nel suburbio di Porta Marina a Ostia antica." *Temporis signa* 9 (2014): 31–44.

David, Massimiliano, Dante Abate, Stefano De Togni, Maria Stella Graziano, Dino Lombardo, Alessandro Melega, and Angelo Pellegrino. "Il pavimento del nuovo Mitreo dei marmi colorati a Ostia antica." In *Atti del XXI colloquio dell'Associazione italiana per lo studio e la conservazione del mosaico,* edited by Claudia Angelelli, Daniela Massara, and Francesca Sposito, 369–76. Tivoli: Arbor Sapientiae, 2016.

David, Massimiliano, Mauro Carinci, Marialetizia Carra, Stefano De Togni, Maria Stella Graziano, and Angelo Pellegrino. "Fenomeni esondativi del Tevere nell'area della città di Ostia tra il I e il V sec. d.C." In *Roma, Tevere, Litorale. Ricerche tra passato e presente,* edited by Giulia Caneva, Carlo M. Travaglini, and Catherine Virlouvet, 61–68. Rome: Università Roma Tre, Centro per lo studio di Roma (CROMA), 2017.

David, Massimiliano, Mauro Carinci, Maria Stella Graziano, Stefano De Togni, Angelo Pellegrino, and Marcello Turci. "Nuovi dati e argomenti per Ostia tardoantica dal Progetto Ostia Marina." *Mélanges de l'École Française de Rome* 126 (2016): 173–86.

Floriani Squarciapino, Maria. *I culti orientali ad Ostia.* Boston and Leiden: Brill, 1962. DOI: 10.1163/9789004296107.

Gering, Axel. "Krise, Kontinuität, Auflassung und Aufschwung in Ostia seit der Mitte des 3. Jahrhunderts." In *L'Empire ro-*

main en mutation. Répercussions sur les villes romaines dans la deuxième moitié du 3ᵉ siècle, edited by Regula Schatzmann and Stefanie Martin-Kilchner, 301–16. Montagnac: Editions Mergoil, 2011.

———. "Marmordepots. Zum 'Recycling' des Forums von Ostia im 5. und 6. Jh. n. Chr." In *Werkspuren. Materialverarbeitung und handwerkliches Wissen im antiken Bauwesen,* edited by Dietmar Kurapkat and Ulrike Wulf-Rheidt, 149–66. Regensburg: Schnell and Steiner, 2016.

———. "Plätze und Straßensperren an Promenaden. Zum Funktionswandel Ostias in der Spätantike." *Römische Abteilung* 111 (2004): 299–382.

———. "Ruins, Rubbish Dumps and Encroachment: Resurveying Late Antique Ostia." In *Field Methods and Post-Excavation Techniques in Late Antique Archaeology,* edited by Luke Lavan and Michael Mulryan, 249–88. Boston and Leiden: Brill, 2013.

Heinzelmann, Michael. "Ostia, Regio III. Untersuchungen in den unausgegrabenen Bereichen des Stadtgebietes. Vorbericht zur dritten Grabungskampagne 2000." *Römische Abteilung* 108 (2000): 313–28.

Heres, Theodora Leonora. *Paries: A Proposal for a Dating System of Late-Antique Masonry Structures in Rome and Ostia (A.D. 235–600).* Amsterdam: Rodopi, 1982.

Hertzberger, Herman. *Architecture and Structuralism: The Ordering of Space.* Rotterdam: Naio10 publishers, 2015.

Kaiser, Alan. *The Urban Dialogue: An Analysis of the Use of Space in the Roman City of Empúries, Spain.* BAR International Series 901. Oxford: Oxford University Press, 2000.

Kleijwegt, Marc. "Schola Iuvenum seu caplatorum." *Epigraphica* 56 (1994): 29–40.

Laurence, Ray. *Roman Pompeii: Space and Society.* London: Routledge, 1994. DOI: 10.4324/9780203283158.

Lavan, Luke. "Public Space in Late Antique Ostia: Excavation and Survey in 2008–2011." *American Journal of Archaeology* 116, no. 4 (2012): 649–91. DOI: 10.3764/aja.116.4.0649.

———. *Public Space in the Late Antique City.* AD 284–650, 2 Volumes. Leiden: Brill, 2020.

Lefebvre, Henri. *La production de l'espace.* Paris: Éditions Anthropos, 1974. DOI: 10.3406/homso.1974.1855.

Lynch, Kevin. *The Image of the City.* Cambridge: Harvard University Press, 1960.

Malaise, Michel. *Inventaire préliminaire des documents égyptiens découverts en Italie.* Boston and Leiden: Brill, 1972.

Mar, Ricardo, ed. *El santuario de Serapis en Ostia.* Tarragona: Universitat Rovira i Virgili, 2001.

———. "El Serapeum Ostiense y la urbanística de la ciudad. Una aproximación a su estudio." *Bolletino di Archeologia* 13–15 (1992): 31–51.

Mols, Stephen T.A.M. "The Urban Context of the Serapeum at Ostia." *BABesch — Bulletin Antieke Beschaving* 82 (2007): 227–32. DOI: 10.2143/BAB.82.1.2020772.

Mulryan, Michael. "A Space Syntax Analysis of an Ostian Region in Late Antiquity: Regions 3.16–17." Forthcoming.

———. "Christian and Jewish Spaces in Late Antique Ostia." In *A Forgotten City: New Archaeological Research on Late Antique Ostia,* edited by Michael Mulryan. Forthcoming.

———. "Cultic Spaces in Late Antique Ostia." In *A Forgotten City: New Archaeological Research on Late Antique Ostia,* edited by Michael Mulryan. Forthcoming.

———. *Spatial "Christianisation" in Context: Strategic Intramural Building in Rome from the 4th–7th c.* AD. Oxford: Archaeopress, 2014.

———. "The Establishment of Urban Movement Networks: Devotional Pathways in Late Antique and Early Medieval Rome." *Theoretical Roman Archaeology 2011* (2012): 123–34. DOI: 10.2307/j.ctvh1dgs4.15.

———. *The Religious Topography of Late Antique Rome (A.D. 313–440): A Case for a Strategy.* Ph.D. diss, University College London, 2008.

Mumford, Eric Paul. *The CIAM Discourse on Urbanism, 1928–1960.* Cambridge: MIT Press, 2000.

Pavolini, Carlo. "A Survey of Excavations and Studies on Ostia (2004–2014)." *Journal of Roman Studies* 106 (2016): 199–236. DOI: 10.1017/S0075435816001015.

———. "Per un riesame del problema di Ostia nella tarda antichità: indice degli argomenti." In *Le regole del gioco. Studi in onore di Clementina Panella,* edited by Antonio F. Ferrandes, and Giacomo Pardini, 385–405. Rome: Edizione Quasar, 2016.

Pellegrino, Angelo. "Note sul culto di Serapide ad Ostia." *Miscellanea greca e romana* 13 (1988): 225–41.

Poccardi, Grégoire. "Les bains de la ville d'Ostie a l'époque tardo-antique (fin IIIe–debut VIe siècle)." In *Les cités de l'Italie tardo-antique (IVe–VIe siècle),* edited by Massimiliano Ghilardi, Christophe J. Goddard, and Pierfrancesco Porena, 167–86. Rome: Ecole française de Rome, 2006.

Raper, R.A. "Pompeii: Planning and Social Implications." In *Space, Hierarchy and Society: Interdisciplinary Studies in Social Area Analysis,* edited by Barry C. Burnham and John Kingsbury, 137–48. BAR International Series 59. Oxford: Oxford University Press, 1979.

———. "The Analysis of the Urban Structure of Pompeii: A Sociological Examination of Land Use (Semi-Micro)." In *Spatial Archaeology,* edited by David L. Clarke, 189–221. London: Academic Press, 1977.

Shepherd, John D. *The Temple of Mithras, London: Excavations by W.F. Grimes and A. Williams at the Walbrook.* London: English Heritage, 1998.

Soja, Edward W. *Thirdspace: Journeys to Los Angeles and Other Real and Imagined Places.* Oxford: Blackwell, 1996.

Steuernagel, Dirk. *Kult und Alltag in roemischen Hafenstaedten. Soziale Prozesse in archaeologischer Perspektive.* Stuttgart: Franz Steiner Verlag, 2004.

Stoeger, Hanna. *Rethinking Ostia: A Spatial Enquiry into the Urban Society of Rome's Imperial Port-Town.* Boston and Leiden: Brill, 2011.

Tilley, Christopher Y. *A Phenomenology of Landscape: Places, Paths, and Monuments.* Oxford: Berg, 1994.

Turci, Marcelo. "Un complesso termale tardo-antico. Il balneum di Musiciolus (IV, XV, 2) nel quartiere fuori Porta Marina." *Mélanges de l'École Française de Rome* 126 (2016): 161–71.

White, Michael. "The Changing Face of Mithraism in Ostia." In *Contested Spaces: Houses and Temples in Roman Antiquity and the New Testament,* edited by David Balch and Annette Weissenrieder, 435–92. Tübingen: Mohr Siebeck, 2012.

Zevi, Fausto. "Iscrizioni e personaggi nel Serapeo." In *El santuario de Serapis en Ostia,* edited by Ricardo Mar, 171–200. Tarragona: Universitat Rovira i Virgili, 2001.

8

Looking through Landscapes: Ideology and Power in the Visigothic Kingdom of Toledo

Isabel Sánchez Ramos[1]

The collapse of Roman order at the end of the fifth century pro-vided the impetus for local political change.[2] Cities continued to have great importance as axes of the articulation of political power from the end of the sixth century, and the urban world of the center of the Iberian Peninsula underwent a phase of unique development.[3] New cities were founded (Reccopolis), and the

1 This work was produced as part of the research project Urban Landscapes of Power in the Iberian Peninsula from Late Antiquity to the Early Middle Ages (ULP.PILAEMA), supported by funding from the Marie Skłodowska-Curie Actions "Horizon 2020-MSCA-IF-EF-ST-2016," under grant agreement No. 740123. Parts of this chapter have been translated from the original Spanish by Patricia Di Gialleonardo, University of Buenos Aires, Humanities College.
2 Santiago Castellanos and Iñaki Martín, "The Local Articulation of Central Power in the North of the Iberian Peninsula (500–1000)," *Early Medieval Europe* 13, no. 1 (2005): 1–41, at 10. See also José Carlos Sánchez and Michael G. Shapland, eds., *Churches and Social Power in Early Medieval Europe: Integrating Archaeological and Historical Approaches* (Turnhout: Brepols, 2015).
3 Mayke de Jong, Frans Theuws, and Carine van Rhijn, eds., *Topographies of Power in the Early Middle Ages* (Boston and Leiden: Brill, 2001).

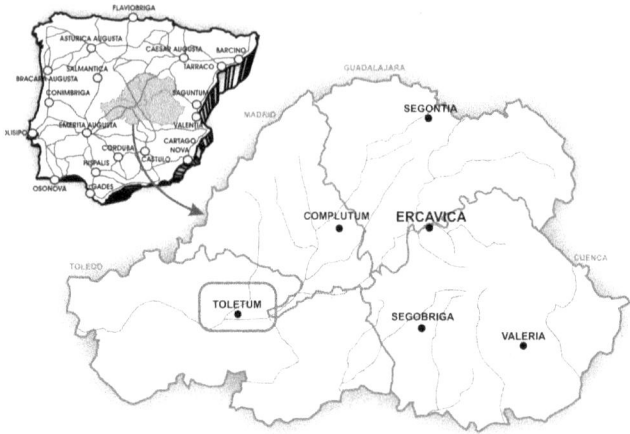

Fig. 1. Location of Toledo in the Iberian Peninsula and the main settlements cited in the text. Adapted by the author from Rafael Barroso, Jesús Carrobles, and Jorge Morín, "La articulación del territorio toledano entre la Antigüedad tardía y la Alta Edad Media (ss. IV al VIII d.C.)," in *Visigodos y Omeyas: el territorio,* ed. Luis Caballero, Pedro Mateos and Tomás Cordero (Madrid: CSIC, Anejos de AEspA LXI, 2012), 263–304. Printed with permission.

urban character of ancient urban settlements was strengthened, converted into important episcopal sites (Barcelona and Valencia), and endowed with illustrious architecture (Toledo). There are even examples of aristocratic residences in the territory nearest to the most relevant cities (e.g., Los Hitos and Pla de Nadal).

The *Regnum Gothorum* in the Iberian Peninsula began its process of political and territorial consolidation in the middle of the second half of the sixth century, when an ambitious cultural and legislative program, perfectly elaborated, was set into action in order to achieve the unification of ancient Roman Hispania. Archaeological and documental records demonstrate a continued monumentalization process of the kingdom's capital, Toledo, and its territory, throughout the seventh century. Toledo was an economic center of power inside a system in which bishops had extensive fiscal responsibilities and exercised increasingly significant political authority resulting in a marked increase in long-distance communication among church elites coming from different geographical areas. Spanish bishops, Toledo's included,[4] managed economic resources and interacted with each other and with a diverse array of individuals and areas for social and religious power.[5]

Toledo, in contrast, for example, to Mérida — as discussed in this volume by Pedro Mateos Cruz — was not burdened by an "historical weight," by well-established elite communities and networks that could significantly rival royal authority in the city. It was a relatively new city, on top of an easily defensible site and in a central geographic location, in the middle of the peninsula (fig. 1). The definitions of local, regional, and central boundaries of authority in Visigothic Spain stem from longstanding historiographical controversies and remain hotly debated within Visigothic Studies today.[6] The prevailing argument is still that the kingdom, from its Toledo location, sought to — and to a considerable measure did — create political and even religious unity within this highly diverse society, with its relatively independent local elites and cultural traditions.[7] This diversity has tended to be read in contrast to or as a problem for the argu-

4 Roger Collins, "Julian of Toledo and the Royal Succession in Late Seventh-Century Spain," in *Early Medieval Kingship*, ed. Peter H. Sawyer and Ian Wood (Leeds: University of Leeds, 1977), 30–49.

5 Castellanos and Martín, "The Local," 12.

6 Pablo Díaz, "Extremis mundi partibus. Gallaecia tardoantigua: periferia geográfica e integración política," in *Comunidades locales y dinámicas de poder en el norte de la peninsula ibérica durante la Antigüedad Tardía,* ed. Urbano Espinosa Ruiz and Santiago Castellanos (Logroño: Universidad de la Rioja, 2006), 201–15, at 213; Santiago Castellanos, "La construcción del poder político visigodo y los horizontes locales: canals de participación y de hostilidad," in *De Roma a los bárbaros. Poder central y horizontes locales en la cuenca del Duero,* ed. Santiago Castellanos and Iñaki Martín Viso (León: Universidad de León, 2008), 145–70, at 152.

7 Pablo Díaz, "City and Territory in Hispania in Late Antiquity," in *Towns and Their Territories Between Late Antiquity and the Early Middles Ages,*

ment of a unified kingdom. However, I would postulate that the extensive urban interactions resulting from the diversity of local and regional institutions, practices, and social organizations, such as competing episcopal administrations, may have been, in fact, powerful instruments precisely *for* building central power, rather than undermining it.

The effectiveness of the centralization of the power of the Visigothic monarchy over the rest of the territory is evaluated through the network of established and consolidated bishoprics in the seventh century and evidenced by the Visigothic councils. The kingdom's attempts at territorial unification can be traced back, as well, to the coinage of the *tremeses* of the year 576 with the solo legend of Liuvigild represented as king with diadem and mantle.[8] The royal monopoly on the minting of coins must be related to the collection of taxes, a formula more than contributing to the process of consolidation and unification of the Visigothic state together with the intervention in the new urban planning of Toledo from the second half of the sixth century. An excellent example of the monumental expression of the elites and the impact of their ideological project on the urban landscape is the exceptional foundation of Reccopolis by Liuvigild.[9] This royal foundation, discussed in the chronicles by John of Biclar and Isidore of Seville, was a new city inspired by the Byzantine peninsular foundations, as well as the urban infrastructures and functions that characterized them, that is, the presence of walls and the existence of large *horrea* for cereal storage.[10] Other elements that suggest a relationship of depen-

ed. Gian Pietro Brogiolo, Nancy Gauthier and Neil Christie (Boston and Leiden: Brill, 2000), 3–35, at 33.

8   Ruth Pliego, *La moneda visigoda* (Seville: Universidad de Sevilla 2009).

9   Lauro Olmo, "The Materiality of Complex Landscapes: Central Iberia During 6th–8th Centuries A.D.," in *New Directions in Early Medieval European Archaeology: Spain and Italy Compared. Essays for Riccardo Francovic*, ed. Sauro Gelichi and Richard Hodges (Turnhout: Brepols, 2015), 15–42.

10 Efthymios Rizos, "Centres of the Late Roman Military Supply Network in the Balkans: a Survey of *horrea*," *Jahrbuch des Römisch-Germanischen Zentralmuseums* 60 (2013): 659–96, at 665.

dency of peripheral territories with Toledo are the slates found in the southwest of the Meseta, in the case of those of Diego Álvaro (Ávila), which refer to the existence of a tax imposed by the central, royal authorities.[11] However, the slates of El Cortinal de San Juan (Salvatierra de Tormes, Salamanca), reflect the economic benefits and social control that the local elites gained from the management of the collection of taxes.[12] The imports of African ceramics found in cities (Toledo and Reccopolis) and settlements in the interior of the Iberian Peninsula (Los Hitos and Gózquez de Arriba) also show both the continuity of a long-distance overseas trade and operation of land routes in the seventh century, as well as the capacity of the local elites and the monarchy to acquire these products.[13]

In terms of architectonic evidence, the main problem is the absence of excavated or preserved buildings and of archaeological contexts for the hundreds of sculptures that are scattered throughout the royal capital.[14] Toledo presents a real problem for archaeologists because of centuries of destruction to and continued occupation of the city, not because of an inability of late antique elites to construct new buildings of prestige in order to seek and recover their role in the territory.[15] Archae-

---

11 Iñaki Martín, "Colapso político y sociedades locales:el Noroeste de la península ibérica (siglos VIII–IX)," *Reti Medievali Rivista* 17, no. 2 (2016): 1–35, at 6.

12 Ibid., 7.

13 Michel Bonifay and Dario Bernal, "Recópolis. Paradigma de las importaciones africanas en el *Visigothorum Regnum,* Un primer balance," in *Recópolis y la ciudad en la época visigoda,* ed. Lauro Olmo, Zona Arqueologica 9 (Madrid: Museo Arqueológico Regional, 2008), 98–115, at 102.

14 Most of them have been preserved and reused in subsequent buildings because of their lasting capacity to serve as imaginary capital: whether as legitimization for a military occupation during the tenth century, or an early modern (sixteenth- and seventeenth-century) symbolic defense of Toledo against other cities, such as Burgos or Madrid.

15 Javier Arce, "Campos, tierras y uillae en Hispania (siglos IV–VI)," in *Visigodos y Omeyas: el territorio,* ed. Luis Caballero, Pedro Mateos Cruz, and Tomás Cordero, Anejos de Archivo Español de Arqueología 61 (Madrid: CSIC, 2012), 21–30.

ologists have also been able to document the collapse of the ancient territorial model of the Roman Empire and its substitution by a genuine Visigothic one. This model is characterized by the appearance of new monumental complexes after the large Roman *villae* were abandoned, in which monastic and sacred complexes (e.g., Los Hitos, Melque, and Guarrazar) linked to the elites of Toledo acquired a marked preference.[16] The city's architecture was especially influenced by this and was consequently transformed into the clearest image of the court and the religious elites. However, archaeologists are faced with buildings that present serious problems of visibility when the architectonic landscape is studied, and there are relatively few well-known case-studies of Toledo.

Toledo during the Roman and Late Roman Empire

Toledo belonged to the interior Carthaginian Roman province also known as Carpetania, which differed from the maritime and most eastern area, where the provincial capital Carthago Nova (Cartagena) was located. One of the reasons for the success of Toledo from its foundation in Roman times was its strategic location at a ford of the Tagus River and its status as a natural border between the fertile territories of Roman Baetica and the northern plateau. These features undoubtedly determined its later historical development, reaching its apex when the city was chosen as the permanent *sede regia* of the Visigothic court in Hispania.

The Roman city was established over a mass of rock, on the old Carpetanian *oppidum*. This forced inhabitants to level the land by building large terraced areas and laying out new road axes aimed at achieving a certain orthogonality of the urban

16 Rafael Barroso Cabrera, Jesús Carrobles, and Jorge Morín de Pablos, "La articulación del territorio toledano entre la Antigüedad tardía y la Alta Edad Media (ss. IV al VIII d.C.)," in *Visigodos y Omeyas,* ed. Caballero, Mateos Cruz, and Cordero, 263–304.

structure. The result was the construction of an authentic urban façade, in which the spectacular complexes built along the main roads going northwards (Vega Baja) stood out. Another main route of the urban nucleus, Huerta del Rey, allowed access to Toledo through the bridge over the Tagus River (the Bridge of Alcántara), considered to be one of the most outstanding landmarks of Roman engineering in Hispania along with the Bridge of Alcántara, also over the Tagus, in Lusitania (the province of Cáceres). Toledo's perimeter was determined by a walled enclosure with an extension of about sixty hectares (148 acres), comparable to the walls raised in the main provincial capitals: Tarraco, Córdoba, Carthago Nova, and Augusta Emerita. These cities were upgraded by a large public building program similar to that supposed to have taken place in Toledo, with the Roman forum as the center of urban life and designed to be used as a multifunctional public space.

The location of Toledo's Roman forum in the area now between the end of Plata Street and the Plaza de San Vicente can be inferred out of the great grounding works and the emergence of reliefs and sculptures as part of the architectonic decoration of an important public space. However, the several buildings of the forensic set (curia, basilica, temple, square, *tabernae,* etc.) remain unsurveyed, which makes it difficult to define the religious, economic, and commercial activity in Roman and late antique Toledo. However, in the city of Reccopolis (Zorita de los Canes), the documented commercial district, along with several productive spaces, is one of the best examples available in Spain to assess the degree of activity and competitiveness in the city and its surroundings during the Visigothic period. Returning to Roman Toledo, the entertainment buildings (circus, theater, and amphitheater) were installed outside the city's walls in the northwestern extramural suburb, presumably when the city acquired the status of a *municipium*. Particularly, the circus kept on working until quite late, according to findings of *terra sigillata hispanica tardia* (TSHT), as well as the discovery of Hippolytus's ivory (390–400), a piece that was part of a *sella* or chair of a member of the highest administration, for instance, the provincial governor or the diocese's vicar.

Toledo barely reached the administrative status of Roman municipium. But, on the grounds of the urban characteristics already described (walls, public and entertainment architecture, functions and services), it should be compared, as said before, to the major Roman *coloniae*. The spatial extent of Toledo's urban pattern can be considered, in a broad sense, as a basic indicator to assess the competition and rivalry with the nearby urban centers. The result of the poll is easy: the inner Carthaginiense had a pyramidal territorial organization in keeping with urban and productive factors, services and communication, with Toledo in the front of this hierarchy of settlements. Toledo's urban pattern far exceeded that of other cities of its immediate environment as Consabura (Consuegra) and Complutum (Alcalá de Henares), which is smaller in size, along with its growing importance during late antiquity, to the detriment of the rest of the cities in the central plateau that began a process of transformation and decay of no return (e.g., Segobriga, Ercavica, Titulcia, etc.). For these reasons, Toledo's interaction from the fifth century on is only comparable with other Hispanic centers of power of remote location, such as Barcelona, Cartagena, Mérida, Seville, or Valencia. It is comparable also to the Mediterranean coast, evident now thanks to a recovered set of imported marble Christian sarcophagi from Rome's sculpture workshops, equivalent in number to the recovered ones in Zaragoza, and other luxury objects found in such a careless condition as those in the circus, namely, the aforementioned Hippolytus's ivory piece, and a chandelier from Byzantine Egypt (sixth–seventh century), all of which reflect the high purchasing power of Toledo's urban elites in these times.

In late antiquity, Toledo was prominent, from the start, on account of its ecclesiastical supremacy — from its episcopal religious authority in the fifth century, to its becoming a metropolitan see in the year 610. Where the archaeological testimonies from late antiquity, including its period as the Visigothic capital, are not numerous, in contrast, the written testimonies of ecclesiastical and legal character stand out. The superiority that Toledo would hold in urban, administrative, and religious terms in respect to the nearby cities or settlements inside the Iberian Peninsula seems *a priori* unquestionable, given its status as royal capital and episcopal metropolitan venue. This suggests the presence of a monumental architecture, the existence of buildings for power, the economic capacity of the local aristocracy, as well as an active exchange and communication with other cities of similar category. But the current archaeological evidence is not enough for scholars to develop more accurate results. In fact, despite prevailing suggestions on the settlement of the main urban structural components in Toletum, it is still unclear which buildings and public spaces related to trade, and which to the civic and religious functions in the Roman city or the equivalent elements in the Visigothic city.

Places of Power in Toledo: The Townscape in Late Antiquity

The definitive establishment of the Visigothic court in Toledo happened during the reign of Theudis (531–548),[17] specifically following the promulgation of his procedural costs law, dated to November 24, 546.[18] The historical circumstances, and, above all, the desire to extend Visigothic rule over the wealthy province of Baetica, encouraged the Visigothic monarchs to leave Toledo for Seville until, with the accession to Athanagild (554–567), the court finally settled in the city along the Tagus, Toledo.[19] Other cities of the Central Plateau near Toledo, such as

---

17 Jesús Carrobles, "Toledo 284–546. Los orígenes de la capitalidad visigoda," in *Regia sedes Toletana I: La topografía de la ciudad de Toledo en la Antigüedad tardía y alta Edad Media,* ed. Jesús Carrobles, Rafael Barroso Cabrera, Jorge Morín de Pablos, and Fernando Valdés (Toledo: Toledo Diputación de Toledo, Real Fundación de Toledo, 2007), 45–92.

18 Fidel Fita, "Noticia de una ley de Teudis desconocida, recientemente descubierta en un palimpsesto de la catedral de León," *Boletín de la Real Academia de la Historia* 14, no. 6 (1889): 473–95.

19 Céline Martin, *La Géographie du pouvoir dans l'Espagne visigothique* (Lille: Presses Universitaires du Septentrion, 2003).

Fig. 2. Topography of Toledo in Late Antiquity: 1. Possible location of the St. Mary Episcopal church; 2. Sculpture and liturgical furniture associated to the Visigothic Episcopal group (St. Ginés and Convent of St Pedro Mártir); 3. Possible location of the praetorian ecclesia (St. Mary of the Alficén church?); 4. Proposed localization of the Visigothic palace (Alcázar-Santa Cruz Hospital-Convento Santa Fe); 5. Residential area outside the walls construction (Vega Baja); 6. Possible location of the martyrial Basilica of St Eulalia (Hermitage of Cristo de la Vega); 6. Late antique cemeteries (Hermitage of Cristo de la Vega). Image by the author.

Segóbriga, Ercávica, Valeria, and Alcalá de Henares, were also episcopal seats, but they presented an unstructured topographical arrangement, a small population, and an urban landscape marked by one or few ecclesiastical buildings. For this reason, Toledo should be compared to other peninsular cities further afield that were important economic and fiscal centers driven by local elites, such as Valencia, Zaragoza, Seville, Mérida, and Barcelona, with which Toledo would undoubtedly maintain "diplomatic" exchanges. In these urban centers, what stood out were the walls — a privileged space occupied by the civil and episcopal power — and commercial and production areas engaged in overseas trade (Barcelona and Valencia) and the reselling of

merchandise through the main roads of terrestrial communication (Seville and Mérida). However, the *urbs toletana* had a
specific form of an aulic complex that met the dependencies of
a true imperial court: the royal palace, the chancellery, the treasure chamber, the palatine church, etc. All this formed the administrative picture of the kingdom that, in the seventh century,
would crystallize into a political unit, the Officium Palatinum,
in charge of the government of the kingdom and constituted
by *viri inlustres* or *proceres* and even *duces*.[20] From the conciliar
documentation of the seventh century, it is evident also that Toledo had three churches which served as the settings for the celebration of councils and which marked the essential milestones
of the Visigothic urban topography: the episcopal see of Santa
Maria, the *ecclesia praetorensis* of the Holy Apostles, and the
martyrial basilica of Santa Leocadia in the *suburbium,* of which,
unfortunately, we do not have any precise archaeological knowledge (fig. 2).[21]

The Palatine Complex

Although some studies insist on placing the Visigothic palace
outside of the walls, in the area called the Vega Baja, and next
to the late antique St. Leocadia Church,[22] I propose, with other

---

20 Claudio Sánchez-Albornoz, "El Aula Regia y las asambleas políticas de los
godos," *Cuadernos de Historia de España* 5 (1946): 5–110.

21 Pere de Palol, "Resultados de las excavaciones junto al Cristo de la Vega,
supuesta basílica conciliar de Sta. Leocadia, de Toledo. Algunas notas de
topografía religiosa de la ciudad," in *Actas del Congreso Internacional del
XIV Centenario del III Concilio de Toledo (589–1989)* (Toledo: Arzobispado
de Toledo, 1991), 787–832; Isabel Velázquez and Gisela Ripoll, "Toletum, la
construcción de una urbs regia," in *Sedes Regiae (ann. 400–800),* ed. Gisela
Ripoll and José Maria Gurt, Memorias de la Real Academia de Buenas Letras 25 (Barcelona: Reial Acadèmia de Bones Lletres, 2000), 521–78, at 550;
Luis J. Balmaseda, "En busca de las iglesias toledanas de época visigoda," in
Hispania Gothorum: San Ildefonso y el reino visigodo de Toledo, ed. Rafael
García Serrano (Toledo: Don Quijote, 2007), 197–214.

22 Eugen Ewig, "Résidence et capitale pendant le Haut Moyen Age," *Revue Historique* 230 (1963): 25–72; Velázquez and Ripoll, "Toletum," 558–63; Lauro

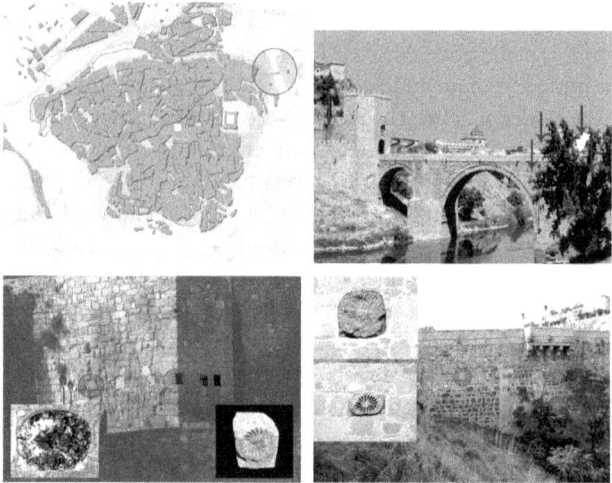

Fig. 3. The Visigothic palatine complex, demonstrating reliefs and sculptural material reused during medieval construction (e.g., the Gate and Bridge of Alcántara). In Rafael Barroso Cabrera and Jorge Morín de Pablos, *Regia sedes Toletana II. El Toledo visigodo a través de su escultura monumental* (Toledo: Diputación de Toledo, Real Fundación de Toledo, 2007b), 124, 127, and 134. Printed with permission.

scholars, that the Visigothic palace and the *praetorium* (palatine) church of the Apostles Peter and Paul related with it were both located in the upper area of the city, near the later alcázar (Islamic citadel), in conjunction with the control of the Roman bridge over the Tagus river (fig. 3).[23] An important argument for locating the royal palace in this urban area is the urban plan-

Olmo, "Nuevos paisajes urbanos y consolidación del estado en época visigoda," in *Hispania Gothorum,* ed. García Serrano, 161–80; Ramón Teja and Silvia Acerbi, "El palacio visigodo y el circo de Toledo: hipótesis de localización," *Reti Medievali Rivista* 11, no. 2 (2010): 81–86.

23 Rafael Barroso Cabrera, Jesús Carrobles, Jorge Morín de Pablos, and Isabel Sánchez, "El paisaje urbano de Toledo en la Antiguedad tardía," *Revue Antiquité Tardive* 23 (2015): 329–52, at 345.

ning, itself inherited from the late Roman period when the city was set up as a military settlement managing the transport of *annona,* but also that the Tagus was the key to controlling the road network, leading from Mérida and Córdoba to Zaragoza and Gaul.[24] The *praetorium* probably was separated from the rest of the city by another wall, forming a real *suburbium* within it, such as it appears solely in the royal foundation of Reccopolis (Zorita de los Canes, Guadalajara). Thus, this Visigothic *praetorium* or citadel would probably correspond to the previous Roman *castellum* and its medieval evolution, like the *alficén* or *alcazaba* (fortress). The discovery of many important elements of decorative sculpture used as *spolia* at the Alcantara's Gate, renovated by Abd al-Rahman III in the tenth century, seems to confirm this identification.[25]

Emphasizing this are the reliefs decorated with medallions that enclose a *gallonado* motif and which are equally represented in the Toledan site of Los Hitos — related to the ostentation of power — and can be compared with the rounds of the palace of Santa María del Naranco and of the Palatine churches of San Miguel del Lillo and Santa Cristina de Lena (ninth century).[26] The Visigothic aristocracy and especially those of its members who were part of the *Palatial Officium* — whose offices included an urban *comes* — had to have their own prestigious buildings

24 Jesús Carrobles and Santiago Palomero, "Toledo: un vado y una ciudad estratégica," *Revista del Instituto Egipcio de Estudios Islámicos en Madrid* 30 (1994): 245–61; Fernando Valdés Fernandez, "Un puente sobre el Tajo. El proceso de islamización de la ciudad de Toledo," in *Regia sedes Toletana I,* ed. Carrobles et al., 165–206.

25 Rafael Barroso Cabrera, Jesús Carrobles, and Jorge Morín de Pablos, "Toledo visigodo y su memoria a través de los restos escultóricos," in *Spolien im Umkreis der Macht: Akten der Tagung in Toledo vom 21.bis 22. September 2006 = Spolia en el entorno del poder,* ed. Thomas G. Schattner and Fernando Valdés Fernández (Mainz am Rhein: P. von Zabern, 2009), 171–97.

26 Rafael Barroso Cabrera and Jorge Morín de Pablos, "Toledo en el contexto de la escultura hispanovisigoda peninsular," in *Regia sedes Toletana I,* ed. Carrobles et al., 21–64.

within the city,[27] which undoubtedly would copy palatial iconographic and architectural models.[28]

The Episcopal Complex of St. Mary

The major architectural changes detected in the Iberian episco-
pacies took place between the second half of the sixth century
and the beginning of the seventh century, that is, when the state
structure of the Visigothic monarchy was consolidated and with
it the network of bishoprics following the meeting of the Third
Council of Toledo in 589.[29] During this Visigothic period, the
bishop of Toledo achieved primacy over the rest of the bishops
of the kingdom—the result of a long process that was parallel
to the consolidation of the city as royal court and had its main
milestones in the Third Council, the promulgation of the De-
cree of Gundemar (610) and in the Twelfth Council of Toledo
(681) with the promulgation of the so-called privilege of election
(canon 6).[30]

Toledo had been a bishopric from the beginning of the fourth
century, when a certain Melancio subscribed to the minutes of

27 Isabel Escrivá, Jorge Morín de Pablos, Albert Ribera i Lacomba, Miquel
    Rosselló, and Isabel Sánchez, "Estudio y propuesta de reconstrucción," in
    Pla de Nadal (Riba-roja del Túria). El Palacio de Tevdinir, ed. Albert Ribera
    i Lacomba (Valencia: Ajuntament, 2015), 36–41.
28 The documentation of this type of civil complexes in Toledo defends the
    Visigothic origin of a series of buildings that have begun to be studied in
    Barcelona and Mérida. See *El siglo VII frente al siglo VII: Arquitectura,* ed.
    Luis Caballero, Pedro Mateos Cruz, and Maria Angeles Utrero, Anejos de
    Archivo Español de Arqueología 51 (Madrid: CSIC, 2009), 91–132.
29 Abilio Barbero, "Las divisiones eclesiásticas y las relaciones entre la Iglesia y
    el Estado en la España de los siglos VI y VII," in *La Historia en el contexto de
    las Ciencias humanas y sociales: Homenaje a Marcelo Vigil Pascual,* ed. Ma-
    ria José Hidalgo de la Vega (Salamanca: Universidad de Salamanca, 1989),
    185–88; and Jesús Peidró, "La región de la Oróspeda tras Leovigildo. Orga-
    nización y administración del territorio," *Verdolay-MAM* 11 (2008): 263–76.
30 12 Toledo 31, 29; José Vives, *Concilios visigóticos e hispano-romanos* (Madrid
    and Barcelona: CSIC, 1963), 407; Fernándo González, "Consolatio (Concilio
    Toledano VII)," *Voces* 5 (1994): 61–64.

the council of Eliberri, while the first references that seem to allude to the episcopal space is the council of Toledo held in the year 400 and assembled in the *ecclesia Toleto*.[31] This apparently neutral denomination refers to the *ecclesia principalis,* as opposed to the other two conciliar basilicas, the Praetorian and that of St. Leocadia, located both in their respective suburbs of the palatine neighborhood and the Vega Baja.

The conciliar records also reveal a dedication of the cathedral church to the Virgin Mary, a title that was frequent for other episcopal sees. Interesting in this regard is that the appearance in the sixteenth century of an epigraph dated to the year 587, during the reign of Reccared, which commemorates the Catholic re-consecration of the Basilica of Santa Maria ("ecclesia sanctae Mariae virginis"). The inscription is considered further testimony to Reccared's policy of returning assets seized by Liuvigild to Catholics during the civil war with Hermenegild.[32]

The epigraph further suggests that Reccared was commemorating a re-consecration of a church near the ancient Roman forum that, until then, would have been Arian. Theudis, it seems, used the *ecclesia intramuros* for the celebration of Arianism. This would mean that, at least temporarily, the congregation of the faithful and the development of the Catholic episcopal liturgy would take place in a different urban space, as has been

---

31 Conc. Elib. 1, 1; Vives, *Concilios,* 1.

32 "+In nomine D[omi]ni consecra/ta eclesia S[an]cte Marie/ in catolico die primo/idus aprilis anno feli/citer primo regni d[omi]ni/ nostri gloriosissimi Fl[auii] Reccaredi regis era/DCXXV." In José Vives, *Inscripciones cristianas de la España romana y visigoda* (Barcelona: CSIC, 1942): ICERV suppl. 302; See also Juan Francisco Rivera, "La catedral de Toledo. Museo de Historia, II. Época visigoda," *Boletín de la Real Academia de Toledo* 64–65 (1950–1951): 32–35; Javier Santiago, "El hábito epigráfico en la Hispania visigoda," in *VIII Jornadas Científicas sobre documentación de la Hispania altomedieval (siglos VI–X),* ed. Juan Carlos Galende Díaz, Javier Santiago Fernández, Nicolás Ávila Seoane, Manuel Salamanca López, and Leonor Zozaya Montes (Madrid: Universidad Complutense de Madrid, 2009), 291–344, at 318; Rafael Barroso Cabrera and Jorge Morín de Pablos, "La ciuitas regia Toletana en el contexto de la Hispania de la séptima centuria," in *Regia sedes Toletana I,* ed. Carrobles et al., 97–161, at 99; Velázquez, "La inscripción," 261–80.

Fig. 4. The episcopal group of St. Mary, including reliefs and sculptural evidence associated with the episcopal complex and reused in modern constructions. Adapted by the author from Rafael Barroso Cabrera and Jorge Morín de Pablos, *Regia sedes Toletana II. El Toledo visigodo a través de su escultura monumental* (Toledo: Diputación de Toledo, Real Fundación de Toledo, 2007b), 114, 134, passim. Printed with permission.

shown to be the case in Barcelona, when the city served as the royal see.[33] As for its location, it has been assumed that the episcopal complex of Toledo is under the foundations of the current Gothic cathedral, where the former mosque was built (fig. 4).[34] This seems to be inferred not only from the traditional overlapping of sacred spaces, but also from a piece of news transmitted by the *Muqtabis* of Ibn Hayyan, which states that in 871 there was a church attached to the mosque.[35] But the recent excavations carried out in the cloister of the cathedral have not provided new archaeological data on this controversial issue, so that, for sure, the only element that could support this hypothesis is the sculptural group reused in the walls of the nearby alley of San Ginés.[36]

The Martyrdom of St. Leocadia

Written sources allude to episcopal burials in the martyrial Basilica of St. Leocadia, which was consecrated by king Sisebut in 618.[37] The royal bishops Eugenius II, in 657, and Ildefonsus, in 667, were buried in this place according to the *Apologeticus martyrum* by Eulogius of Córdoba.[38] The Catholic Councils also

---

33 Julia Beltrán de Heredia, "Nuevos datos sobre el cristianismo en Barcino. Los orígenes de la Basílica de los Santos Mártires Justo y Pastor," in *Costantino i costantinidi: l'innovazione costantinianna, le sue radici e i suoi sviluppi. Atti del XVI Congresso Internazionale di Archeologia Cristiana*, ed. Olof Brandt, Vicenzo Fiocchi Nicolai, and Gabriele Castiglia (Vatican City: PIAC, 2016), 1550.

34 Eduardo Carrero, "Presbiterio y coro en la catedral de Toledo. En busca de unas circunstancias," *Hortus Artium Medievalium* 15, no. 2 (2009): 315–28, at 325.

35 Barroso Cabrera and Morín de Pablos, "La ciuitas," 104.

36 Barroso Cabrera and Morín de Pablos, "Toledo en el contexto de la escultura hispanovisigoda peninsular."

37 Eulog. Cord. Apol. 16: "[…] currente Aera DCLVI […] Toleto quoque beatae Leocadiae aula miro iubente preadicto principe [s.c. Sisebutus] culmine alto extenditur […]," in *Corpus Scriptorum Muzarabicorum,* vol. 2, ed. Juan Gil, Anejos de Emerita 28 (Madrid: CSIC, 1973), 475–93, at 483.

38 Barroso Cabrera et al., "El paisaje," 37.

emphasize the prestigious funerary character of St. Leocadia for hosting the tombs for the Visigothic kings. Yet, it is difficult to imagine that there was not already a monument dedicated to St. Leocadia before 618, given the funerary nature of this space and the fame that the saint would later achieve. It is probable that Sisebut only undertook the monumentalization of an old *cella memoriae* or martyrium to elevate the importance of Leocadia's cult in and role as patron of Toledo. The prestige of St. Leocadia of Toledo is remembered (or invented?) in various post-Visigothic sources, such as the *Chronicle of 754,* the *Albeldense Chronicle,* the so-called *Chronicle of Moro Rasis,* and the Pseudo-Isidoriana.[39]

Nevertheless, this church of St. Leocadia has not been confirmed archaeologically, nor has any other kind of funerary structure or epitaph that could be associated with the local Toledan elites. However, in the northwestern extramural region (today, Hermitage Cristo de la Vega), there once stood a sturdy construction, perhaps belonging to a building similar to a classroom.[40] The building reuses plundered Roman stonework in the construction, but it stands out for its significant use of buttresses that suggest a rectangular floor plan for a central nave with flying buttresses, possibly to anchor a vaulted ceiling or the presence of a crypt, much like those documented at San Antolín (Palencia) and La Alberca (Murcia), and that appear in St. Leocadia's crypt in Oviedo. Thus, as argued in a previous

---

39 *Chronica muzarabica* 14 (*Corpus Scriptorum Muzarabicorum,* vol. 1, ed. Juan Gil, Anejos de Emerita 28 [Madrid: CSIC, 1973], 20); *Chronica Albeldensis* XIII. 64; XIV. 24 (Juan Gil, José Moralejo, and Juan I. Ruiz de la Peña, eds., *Crónicas Asturianas* [Oviedo: University of Oviedo, 1985], 96, 165, 169); *Crónica Rasis* XCV (*Crónica del Moro Rasis: versión del Ahbār Mulūk al-Andalus,* ed. Diego Catalán and Maria Soledad de Andrés, Fuentes Cronísticas de la Historia de España 3 [Madrid: Gredos, 1975], 191); *Historia Pseudoisidoriana* 7, ed. Theodor Mommsen, Monumenta Germaniae Historica Auctores Antiquissimi 11 (Berlin: Weidmann, 1894), 377–88, at 382.

40 Palol, "Resultados," 790.

publication,[41] this structure should be identified as a mausoleum that shares the same dynamic with other Iberian sacred spaces.

Prestigious Residential Buildings outside the Walls

The suburban sector that stretched east of the old Roman circus experienced a significant transformation of its residential, commercial, and craft spaces in the second half of the sixth century.[42] Some of the verified constructions that correspond to extensive properties delimited in surface by enclosures, have been interpreted as the palatium of the Visigothic kings.[43] On this point, I refer to the hypothesis above, that, in contrast, defends the location of the royal palace and the new spaces of power in the upper part of the city walls — practically unknown by archeology, but where the late imperial public complexes would have been — perhaps following the same spatial scheme that has been recognized in other cities such as Barcelona; that is, in proximity to other representative urban groups linked to the ecclesiastical elites.[44]

The excavations carried out in recent years in the Vega Baja have allowed the definition of several spaces of representation that have clear parallels with the constructions located in different peninsular areas, which in Toledo should be understood as the continuity of a privileged or aristocratic residential occupation now related to the presence of the elites (senior officials) of

41 Barroso Cabrera, Carrobles, and Morín de Pablos, "El paisaje," 60.

42 María del Mar Gallego García, ed., *La Vega Baja de Toledo* (Toledo: Toletum Visigodo, 2009); Lauro Olmo, "Ciudad y estado en época visigoda: Toledo, la construcción de un nuevo paisaje urbano," in *Espacios urbanos en el Occidente mediterráneo (s. VI–VIII)*, ed. Alfonso García, Ricardo Izquierdo Benito, Lauro Olmo, and Diego Peris (Toledo: Toletum Visigodo, 2010), 89.

43 Juan M. Rojas and Antonio J. Gómez, "Intervención arqueológica en la Vega Baja de Toledo. Características del centro político y religioso del Reino Visigodo," in *El siglo VII frente al siglo VII: Arquitectura*, ed. Luis Caballero, Pedro Mateos Cruz, and Maria Angeles Utrero, Anejos de Archivo Español de Arqueología 51 (Madrid: CSIC, 2009), 45–89.

44 Barroso Cabrera, Carrobles, and Morín de Pablos, "Arquitectura," 24.

the royal headquarters. A good example of this is the presence of thermal baths and spaces documented in this sector.[45] The system of axiality, the existence of two floors, and the rectangular classrooms that characterize these sets, as well as the presence of porticos and pillars attached to the exterior facades, is common to other prestigious buildings, such as the possible palace of the *dux* Teodomir identified in Pla de Nadal (Riba-Roja de Túria) or the central rooms documented in military complexes such as Sant Julià de Ramis (Girona), as well as in the residences of the Morerías and the citadel of Mérida.[46]

Aristocratic Proprieties in the Territory of the Visigothic *sedes regia*

Corresponding to the conciliar records, close to Toledo there were several monasteries under the patronage of Sts. Cosmas and Damian (this one otherwise known as Agali or Agaliense, from its situation *ad Galiense iter* [on the way to Gallia]), St. Michael, the Holy Cross, St. Vincent, and St. Eulalia of Mérida. Written sources also provide further useful information about the religious complexes around the countryside of Toledo. The monastery Deibiensis, founded by Ildefonsus for virgins in a family-owned property and probably located in Los Yébenes (Toledo),[47] and the *coenobium* Cabensis (of unknown location),

---

45 Rojas and Gómez, "Intervención," 63.

46 Escrivá et al., "Estudio," 40; José M. Nolla, "Ciudades, torres y castella. La defensa de la Vía Augusta," in *Las fortificaciones en la Tardoantigüedad. Élites y articulación del territorio (siglos V–VIII d.C.),* ed. Raúl Catalán, Patricia Fuentes, and José Carlos Sastre (Madrid: Ediciones La Ergástula, 2014), 43–56; Miguel Alba, "Diacronía de la vivienda señorial de Emerita (Lusitania, Hispania): Desde las domus altoimperiales y tardoantiguas a las residencias palaciales omeyas (Siglos I–IX)," in *Archeologia e società tra tardo antico e alto medioevo,* ed. Gian Pietro Brogiolo and Alexandria Chavrría Arnau (Padua: BPR Publishers, 2008), 163–92.

47 Luis A. García Moreno, "El hábitat rural disperso en la península ibérica durante la Antigüedad tardía," *Antigüedad y Cristianismo* 8 (1991): 265–74, at 269.

were the most famous monasteries founded in this territory.[48] Another one is only known by a few verses composed by Eugenius ("St. Felix quae est in Tatanesio") and could be located equally near Toledo in the village of Totanés, somewhere between Melque and Los Yébenes. From Eugenius's poem, it appears that it was a foundation linked to some important figure of the Visigothic court.

Thanks to recent archaeological research, our knowledge of the architectural complexes in the Toledan countryside during the Visigothic period is more accurate; this has enabled a better understanding of the evolution of the city's architecture and urbanism. Of particular interest here are the so-called private churches of more modest size that were built by rural owners and had restricted burial uses, hence the following two paradigmatic funerary and monastic monuments located in the central plateau of the Iberian Peninsula.[49]

Los Hitos (Arisgotas, Orgaz)

There is a large mausoleum, with some spaces surrounding it — a church included — which could have been an aristocratic residence. The main building of Los Hitos, used as a mausoleum, maintained similar features to other prestigious constructions documented in the Iberian Peninsula, characterized by a tripartite plan and appearance of buttresses. Indeed, the importance of Los Hitos is that it offers new types and building associations dated reasonably to the seventh century.[50] The use of annexing supports for the outside walls to raise the parietal height of the building — with views of a vaulted ceiling or the construction of a higher floor — is a characteristic that links this building to other examples among its contemporaries in the Iberian Peninsula,

48 Balmaseda, "En busca," 208.
49 Jorge Morín de Pablos and Isabel Sánchez, *Los Hitos. Arisgotas-Orgaz, Toledo: De palacio a panteón visigodo* (Madrid: Audema editorial, 2015), 47.
50 Isabel Sánchez, Jorge Morín de Pablos, and José Ramón de la Cal, "The Archaeological Site of 'Los Hitos' (Spain) and the Visigoth Landscape of Toledo's Region During Late Antiquity (7th c.)," forthcoming.

Fig. 5. Los Hitos: Residential and later funeral building. Picture by the author.

including those buildings pertaining to residential architecture[51] and others with funerary or sacred functions.[52] This type of solution was also used even to the extent of palace architecture in the Asturian kingdom of Oviedo from the eighth to ninth centuries. It is possible that Los Hitos was the burial place or pantheon for a figure and his family from the high nobility in Toledo on a *latifundium* that likewise could have held an important religious center (fig. 5). This would explain the existence of the lengthy inscription and the pagan altar held in the current parish church with a *loculus* to store relics.[53]

51 Escrivá et al., "Estudio," 41.
52 Luis Real, "Portugal: cultura visigoda e cultura moçarabe," in *Visigodos y Omeyas. Un debate entre la Antigüedad tardía y la Alta Edad Media,* ed. Luis Caballero and Pedro Mateos Cruz, Anejos de Archivo Español de Arqueología 23 (Mérida: CSIC, 2000): 21–75.
53 After ending the archaeological excavation in November 2016, we are working on the study and interpretation of the architectonical complex and the

Santa María de Melque (San Martín de Montalbán)

Santa María de Melque represents one of the early medieval ecclesiastic complexes in Spain with a long history of excavations
and studies since the 1980s.[54] This site has recently been the object of new studies[55] that propose that the monumental complex
was later transformed into a monastery, with its origins dating
to a funerary building for elite tombs.[56] The building was erected
in the center of an enclosure delimited by an altitude that allowed visual surveillance of the area, turning it into a point of
reference. Its architectural model bears a cross-shaped plan with
a straight headwall outside and the shape of a horseshoe arch inside, and a portico at the bottom. An *arcosolium,* which was used
for privileged burials, is located precisely at the southern arm of
the cross. This is a clear indicator that the church was raised to
serve as a monumental pantheon. The decorative elements and
different archaeological findings documented at Melque point
to a chronological window between the mid-seventh-century
and the beginning of the eighth century.[57] Its promoter could
have been someone from the same royal family, or at least one of
the *primates* or *fideles regis* frequently alluded to in the literature
from the time. The identity of this person is unknown without
explicit textual or epigraphic evidence, but it would be unavoid-
able for this individual not to have been documented in sources
from the time, given the magnitude and unique characteristics

material evidence recorded in order to reach new results from this site (see
Sánchez et al., "The Archaeological Site of 'Los Hitos'").

54 Luis Caballero, "El monasterio de Balatalmelc, Melque (San Martín de
Montalbán, Toledo). En el centenario de su descubrimiento," in *Monasteria
et territoria. Elites, edilicia y territorio en el Mediterráneo medieval (siglos
V–XI),* ed. Jorge López, Artemio Martínez, and Jorge Morín de Pablos BAR
International Series 1720 (Oxford: Archaeopress, 2007), 91–119.

55 Luis J. Balmaseda, "Algunos problemas de la escultura visigoda toledana", in
Escultura decorativa tardorromana y altomedieval en la Península Ibérica,
ed. Luis Caballero and Pedro Mateos Cruz, Anejos de Archivo Español de
Arqueología 41 (Mérida: CISC, 2007), 275–99, at 290.

56 Barroso Cabrera, Carrobles, and Morín de Pablos, "Arquitectura," 57–63.

57 Arbeiter, "Alegato," 255.

Fig. 6. St. Maria de Melque church: south façade. Picture by the author.

of this endeavor, and also considering the complex's proximity to the Visigothic capital (fig. 6).[58] This space for elite burials and private tombs would be destined immediately thereafter to be replaced with the monastery dedicated to working the land for economic gain. Its location was strategic in order to control the

---

58 Following Barroso Cabrera and Morín de Pablos's hypothesis from the ancient references transmitted by Eugenius of Toledo (Eug., *Carm.* 27–29) about a noble named Evantius, it is quite possibly he was the same *uir inluster Scanciarum* who signed the minutes of the Eighth Council of Toledo (653 CE). These authors propose the identification of the pantheon of Melque with the large construction cited in this text about the tumulus of Nicolaus, that is, Evantius's father (Sánchez et al., "The Archaeological Site of 'Los Hitos,'" 50). Significant is the fact that Eugenius allocated three poetic compositions to gloss the figure of this Nicolaus, who also said he had a noble origin (*nobilis et magno*), a claim clarified by the weapons (*dextrae beliger*). More relevant is that one of these epitaphs explicitly indicated the existence of a real building (*aula, sacra fabrica*) where laid his remains (Barroso Cabrera, Carrobles, and Morín de Pablos, "Arquitectura," 61–62).

passage of livestock through the transhumance networks — the glens — traveling from the north of the Central System toward the valleys of the former Roman province of Baetica. The geographic placement of the monastery complex at Melque is not only a simple funerary monument erected to commemorate the memory of nobles in the kingdom, but also stands as a magnificent example of the enormous social and economic power of the Visigothic elites in the territory of the capital city.

Conclusions

The interactions, networks, and rivalries between Toledo and the nearby cities of Carthaginensis represent a phenomenon that is difficult to trace from the archaeological perspective. Archeology attempts to unravel the social history of the Visigothic *sedes regia,* but it is tough to build arguments based on the material evidence, which bears witness to those symptoms of conflict and social identity to which this volume is dedicated. Nevertheless, it is possible to indirectly approach this discussion through other factors, for example, the study of landscape management (i.e., communication channels) and the role of the episcopal elites and their use of ecclesiastical assemblies.

In terms of the landscapes of power at the center of the Visigothic kingdom, and the center of the peninsula, the disappearance and/or decay of old urban centers (e.g., Segóbriga and Valeria) meant a shift of authority towards cities supported by the new political power of Toledo (e.g., Reccopolis). Some ancient Roman cities were reduced to empty reflections of past splendor thanks to the continuity of their ecclesiastical structures (e.g., Alcalá de Henares), and the ostentation of the rank — more symbolic than practical — of episcopal sees (e.g., Ercávica).

Two great events also had a special impact on the history of the Visigothic kingdom, on the relationship that the royal city maintained with its environment, as well as on territorial organization. On the one hand, we have the conquest of Cartagena and a part of the Spanish coast by Byzantium, which would prompt a new ecclesiastical organization of the Hispanian Church, with the subsequent founding of new bishoprics. The Byzantine conquest of Cartagena forced the bishoprics of the interior territory of Carthaginensis to be linked more closely to the seat of Toledo, the *de facto* metropolitan see.

On the other hand, we have the foundation of the city of Reccopolis, one of the most symbolic acts of Liuvigild's reign. It is a large city whose dimensions perfectly match those of other major urban centers of the time (Mérida, Zaragoza, and Seville). The urban structure appears clearly inspired by Byzantine models of new creation, such as Iustiniana Prima (Caričin Grad, Serbia), an influence that can also be seen in Toledo itself. Therefore, we can see here the reflection of the urban structure of Visigothic Toledo, with its praetorian space separated from the city proper by a wall. From the strategic point of view, Reccopolis was well situated, within the road network that connects Toledo with Zaragoza and Septimania.

Also, in the case of Ercávica, its monastery and bishopric allow scholars to track the interactions between the main cities of the territory of the Visigothic royal seat. Written sources from the reign of Luivigild's son and successor Reccared demonstrate numerous personal relationships between changing social and religious circles and the transforming functions of the economic and political interests of the Visigothic monarchy. For example, references to the transfer of a part of the funds of the monastery of Ercávica to the monastery of Toledo, and especially the appointment of the abbot Eutropius of Ercávica as bishop of Valencia, which led to the final decline of the monastery of Servitano, and the city. It is in this context that one should interpret the epistolary relationship of Eutropius and Licinianus of Cartagena to be "cordial" and free of conflicts and competitiveness.

Eutropius played a fundamental role in the kingdom's conversion to Catholicism under Reccared, who would reward him with the bishopric of Valencia, an influential and strategic episcopal center in the western Mediterranean. The relationship with the court in Toledo also influenced the evolution of the bishopric of Ercávica and its possible material transfer to the nearby city of Reccopolis.

Reccopolis's foundation allows us to suspect that it was the continuation of the decayed municipality of Ercávica as an urban entity. Although the basilica of Reccopolis does not reach the extremes of ornamental luxury that can be sensed in the ruins of Iustiniana Prima, it seems evident that it would have been conceived by Liuvigild as an authentic Arian cathedral. The capricious circumstances that led to the conversion of the Visigoths to Catholicism had to turn Reccopolis into a magnificent seat for the decaying bishopric of Ercávica. As a hypothesis, then, it should not be ruled out that, with the occasion of Reccared's accession to power, the basilica of Reccopolis was reconsecrated as Catholic, in the style of what also happened at the same time with the church of Santa María de Toledo, and in the episcopal see of Barcelona.

Thus, the study of the archaeological records and documentary sources presented in this chapter highlights the existence of a building program developed in Toledo and its territory in the second half of the seventh century. These changes were the result of the earlier reorganization of the Visigothic kingdom after the celebration of the Third Council (589) and the Fourth Council (633) of Toledo. The consolidation of the *regnum Visigothorum* was also the result of the action of monarchs as prominent as Athanagild or Liuvigild. Since this period, the promotion of Toledo as *urbs regia* was a continuous process, due to the increasing evolution of the *aula regia* and the Toledan episcopate, the metropolitan range of Carthaginensis provincia awarded to Toledo in 610 by Gundemar, and the Iberian ecclesiastical primacy in 681 on occasion of the provisions adopted by the bishops of the Twelfth Council of Toledo. Also, the Christianization of the territory was a phenomenon that one must not understand as a simple alteration of beliefs, but as the articulation of each productive space within a network of civil and ecclesiastical power drawn from the royal city that connected the elites with the more developed rural settlements.[59] Therefore, late antique architecture that was sacred or funerary in nature could be considered another economic exponent in the administration of the territory.[60] These constructions-turned-churches, or perhaps privileged churches used as burial spaces, are an argument in favor of the transformation of former estates of the secular aristocracy into the foundations for monasteries during the seventh century.[61] This was a common, well-known practice in written sources, and confirmed by archaeological evidence at Santa María de Melque, Carranque,[62] and El Saucedo. All of them can be interpreted as a sign of the ability of the ruling classes of the Visigothic kingdom to search for and consolidate new sources of wealth, through the creation of ecclesiastical and civil complexes that would acquire a strong role in the landscape.

---

59 José Carlos Sánchez, "Power and Rural Landscapes in Early Medieval Galicia (400–900 AD): Towards a Re-Incorporation of the Archaeology into the Historical Narrative," *Early Medieval Europe* 21, no. 2 (2013): 140–68, at 161.

60 Sánchez, "Power," 160.

61 Neil Christie, "Landscapes of Change in Late Antiquity and the Early Middle Ages: Themes, Directions and Problems," in *Landscapes of Change: Rural Evolutions in Late Antiquity and the Early Middle Ages. Late Antiquity and Early Medieval Studies,* ed. Neil Christie (Aldershot: Routledge, 2004), 1–37, at 13.

62 Carmen Fernández-Ochoa, Manuel Bendala, and Virginia García, "Últimos trabajos arqueológicos en el yacimiento de Carranque (Toledo). 2004–2005," in *Actas de las I Jornadas de Arqueología de Castilla-La Mancha,* ed. Juan Manuel Millán Martínez and Concepción Rodríguez Ruza (Cuenca: Ediciones de la Universidad de Castilla-La Mancha — Junta de Comunidades de Castilla-La Mancha, 2007), 743–53, at 749.

Bibliography

Primary

Chronica Albeldensis. In *Crónicas Asturianas,* edited by Juan Gil, José L. Moralejo, and Juan I. Ruiz de la Peña. Oviedo: University of Oviedo, 1985.

Chronica muzarabica. In *Corpus Scriptorum Muzarabicorum,* Volume 1, edited by Juan Gil. Anejos de Emerita 28. Madrid: CSIC, 1973.

Historia Pseudoisidoriana. Edited by Theodor Mommsen. Monumenta Germaniae Historica Auctores Antiquissimi 11. Berlin: Weidmann, 1894.

Crónica del Moro Rasis: versión del Ahbār Mulūk al-Andalus. Edited by Diego Catalán and Maria Soledad de Andrés. Fuentes Cronísticas de la Historia de España 3. Madrid: Gredos, 1975.

Eulog. Cord. Apol. = Apologeticus martyrum. In *Corpus Scriptorum Muzarabicorum,* Volume 2, edited by Juan Gil, 475–93. Anejos de Emerita 28. Madrid: CSIC, 1973.

Vives, José. *Concilios visigóticos e hispano-romanos.* Madrid and Barcelona: CSIC, 1963.

———. *Inscripciones cristianas de la España romana y visigoda.* Barcelona: CSIC, 1942.

Secondary

Alba, Miguel. "Diacronía de la vivienda señorial de Emerita (Lusitania, Hispania): Desde las domusaltoimperiales y tardoantiguas a las residencias palaciales omeyas (Siglos I–IX)." In *Archeologia e società tra tardo antico e alto medioevo,* edited by Gian Pietro Brogiolo and Alexandria Chavrría Arnau, 163–92. Padua: BPR Publishers, 2008.

Arbeiter, Achim. "Alegato por la riqueza del inventario monumental hispanovisigodo." In *Visigodos y Omeyas. Un debate entre la Antigüedad tardía y la alta Edad Media,* edited by Luis Caballero and Pedro Mateos Cruz, 251–53. Anejos de Archivo Español de Arqueología 23. Madrid: CSIC, 2000.

Arce, Javier. "Campos, tierras y uillae en Hispania (siglos IV–VI)." In *Visigodos y Omeyas: el territorio,* edited by Luis Caballero, Pedro Mateos Cruz, and Tomás Cordero, 21–30. Anejos de Archivo Español de Arqueología 61. Madrid: CSIC, 2012.

Balmaseda, Luis J. "Algunos problemas de la escultura visigoda toledana." In *Escultura decorativa tardorromana y altomedieval en la Península Ibérica,* edited by Luis Caballero and Pedro Mateos Cruz, 275–99. Anejos de Archivo Español de Arqueología 41. Mérida: CISC, 2007.

Balmaseda, Luis J. "En busca de las iglesias toledanas de época visigoda." In *Hispania Gothorum. San Ildefonso y el reino visigodo de Toledo,* edited by Rafael García Serrano, 197–214. Toledo: Don Quijote, 2007.

Barbero, Abilio. "Las divisiones eclesiásticas y las relaciones entre la Iglesia y el Estado en la España de los siglos VI y VII." In *La Historia en el contexto de las Ciencias humanas y sociales: Homenaje a Marcelo Vigil Pascual,* edited by Maria José Hidalgo de la Vega, 185–88. Salamanca: Universidad de Salamanca, 1989.

Barroso Cabrera, Rafael, and Jorge Morín de Pablos. "La ciuitas regia Toletana en el contexto de la Hispania de la séptima centuria." In *Regia sedes Toletana I: La topografía de la ciudad de Toledo en la Antigüedad tardía y alta Edad Media,* edited by Jesús Carrobles, Rafael Barroso Cabrera, Jorge Morín de Pablos, and Fernando Valdés Fernández, 97–161. Toledo: Diputación de Toledo, Real Fundación de Toledo, 2007.

———. "Toledo en el contexto de la escultura hispanovisigoda peninsular." In *Regia sedes Toletana II. El Toledo visigodo a través de su escultura monumental,* edited by Rafael Barroso Cabrera and Jorge Morín de Pablos, 21–64. Toledo: Diputación de Toledo, Real Fundación de Toledo, 2007.

Barroso Cabrera, Rafael Jesús Carrobles, and Jorge Morín de Pablos. "Toledo visigodo y su memoria a través de los restos escultóricos." In *Spolien im Umkreis der Macht: Akten der Tagung in Toledo vom 21. bis 22. September 2006 = Spolia en el entorno del poder,* edited by Thomas G. Schattner and Fernando Valdés Fernández, 171–97. Mainz am Rhein: P. von Zabern, 2009.

Barroso Cabrera, Rafael, Jesús Carrobles, and Jorge Morín de Pablos. "Arquitectura de poder en el territorio toledano en la Antigüedad tardía y época visigoda. Los palacios de Toledo como referente en la edilicia medieval." In *La ciudad medieval: de la casa principal al palacio urbano,* edited by Jean Passini and Ricardo Izquierdo Benito, 1–69. Toledo: Junta de Comunidades de Castilla-La Mancha, Consejería de Educación, Ciencia y Cultura, 2011.

———. "La articulación del territorio toledano entre la Antigüedad tardía y la Alta Edad Media (ss. IV al VIII d.C.)." In *Visigodos y Omeyas: el territorio,* edited by Luis Caballero, Pedro Mateos Cruz, and Tomás Cordero, 263–304. Anejos de Archivo Español de Arqueología 61. Madrid: CSIC, 2012.

Barroso Cabrera, Rafael, Jesús Carrobles, Jorge Morín de Pablos, and Isabel Sánchez. "El paisaje urbano de Toledo en la Antiguedad tardia." *Revue Antiquité Tardive* 23 (2015): 329–52. DOI: 10.1484/J.AT.5.109387.

Beltrán de Heredia, Julia. "Barcino, de colonia augustea a sede regia en época visigoda. Las transformaciones urbanas a la luz de las nuevas aportaciones de la arqueología." In *Arqueología, Patrimonio y desarrollo urbano problemática y soluciones,* 31–49. Gerona: Institut de Recerca Històrica de la Universitat de Girona, 2010.

———. "Nuevos datos sobre el cristianismo en Barcino. Los orígenes de la Basílica de los Santos Mártires Justo y Pastor." In *Costantino i costantinidi: l'innovazione costantinianna, le sue radici e i suoi sviluppi. Atti del XVI Congresso Internazionale di Archeologia Cristiana,* edited by Olof Brandt, Vicenzo Fiocchi Nicolai, and Gabriele Castiglia, 1549–66. Vatican City: PIAC, 2016.

Bonery, André. "La cathédrale des ariens et la fin de l'arianaisme a Narbonne, Gallo-romaines, wisigoths et francs en Aquitaine, Septimanie et Espagne." In *Gallo-romains, Wisigoths et Francs en Aquitaine, Septimanie et Espagne: Actes des VIIe Journées internationales d'Archéologie merovingienne,* edited by Patrick Périn, 155–60. Rouen: Association française d'archéologie mérovingienne, 1991.

Bonifay, Michel, and Dario Bernal. "Recópolis. Paradigma de las importaciones africanas en el *Visigothorum Regnum*, Un primer balance." In *Recópolis y la ciudad en la época visigoda*, edited by Lauro Olmo, 98–115. Zona Arqueologica 9. Madrid: Museo Arqueológico Regional, 2008.

Caballero, Luis. "El monasterio de Balatalmelc, Melque (San Martín de Montalbán, Toledo). En el centenario de su descubrimiento." In *Monasteria et territoria. Elites, edilicia y territorio en el Mediterráneo medieval (siglos V–XI),* edited by Jorge López, Artemio Martínez, and Jorge Morín de Pablos, 91–119. BAR International Series 1720. Oxford: Archaeopress 2007.

Caballero, Luis, and Margarita Fernández. "Notas sobre el complejo productivo de Melque (Toledo)." *Anejos de Archivo Español de Arqueología* 72 (1999): 199–239. DOI: 10.3989/aespa.1999.v72.302.

Carrero, Eduardo. "Presbiterio y coro en la catedral de Toledo. En busca de unas circunstancias." *Hortus Artium Medievalium* 15, no. 2 (2009): 315–28. DOI: 10.1484/J.HAM.3.65.

Carrobles, Jesús. "Toledo 284–546. Los orígenes de la capitalidad visigoda." In *Regia sedes Toletana I: La topografía de la ciudad de Toledo en la Antigüedad tardía y alta Edad Media,* edited by Jesús Carrobles, Rafael Barroso Cabrera, Jorge Morín de Pablos, and Fernando Valdés Fernández, 45–92. Toledo: Diputación de Toledo, Real Fundación de Toledo, 2007.

Carrobles, Jesús, and Santiago Palomero. "Toledo: un vado y una ciudad estratégica." *Revista del Instituto Egipcio de Estudios Islámicos en Madrid* 30 (1994): 245–61.

Castellanos, Santiago. "La construcción del poder político visigodo y los horizontes locales: canals de participación y de hostilidad." In *De Roma a los bárbaros. Poder central y horizontes locales en la cuenca del Duero,* edited by Santiago Castellanos and Iñaki Martín Viso, 145–70. León: Universidad de León, 2008.

Castellanos, Santiago, and Iñaki Martín. "The Local Articulation of Central Power in the North of the Iberian Peninsula

(500–1000)." *Early Medieval Europe* 13, no. 1 (2005): 1–41. DOI: 10.1111/j.1468-0254.2005.00147.x.

Christie, Neil. "Landscapes of Change in Late Antiquity and the Early Middle Ages: Themes, Directions and Problems." In *Landscapes of Change. Rural Evolutions in Late Antiquity and the Early Middle Ages. Late Antiquity and Early Medieval Studies,* edited by Neil Christie, 1–37. Aldershot: Routledge, 2004.

Collins, Roger. "Julian of Toledo and the Royal Succession in Late Seventh-Century Spain." In *Early Medieval Kingship,* edited by Peter H. Sawyer and Ian Wood, 30–49. Leeds: University of Leeds, 1977.

Del Mar Gallego García, María, ed. *La Vega Baja de Toledo.* Toledo: Toletum Visigodo, 2009.

Díaz, Pablo. "City and Territory in Hispania in Late Antiquity." In *Towns and Their Territories Between Late Antiquity and the Early Middles Ages,* edited by Gian Pietro Brogiolo, Nancy Gauthier, and Neil Christie, 3–35. Boston and Leiden: Brill, 2000.

———. "Extremis mundi partibus. Gallaecia tardoantigua: periferia geográfica e integración política." In *Comunidades locales y dinámicas de poder en el norte de la peninsula ibérica durante la Antigüedad Tardía,* edited by Urbano Espinosa Ruiz and Santiago Castellanos, 201–15. Logroño: Universidad de la Rioja, 2006.

Eger, Christoph. "Guarrazar." In *El tiempo de los bárbaros. Pervivencia y transformación en Galia e Hispania (ss. V–VI d.C.),* edited by Jorge Morín de Pablos, Jorge Lópe, and Artemio Martínez, 563–65. Zona Arqueológica 11. Alcalá de Henares: Museo Arqueológico Regional, 2010.

Escrivá, Isabel, Jorge Morín de Pablos, Albert Ribera, Miquel Rosselló, and Isabel Sánchez. "Estudio y propuesta de reconstrucción." In *Pla de Nadal (Riba-roja del Túria). El Palacio de Tevdinir,* edited by Albert Ribera i Lacomba, 36–41. Valencia: Ajuntament, 2015.

Ewig, Eugen. "Résidence et capitale pendant le Haut Moyen Age." *Revue Historique* 230 (1963): 25–72.

Fernández-Ochoa, Carmen, Manuel Bendala, and Virginia García. "Últimos trabajos arqueológicos en el yacimiento de Carranque (Toledo). 2004–2005." In *Actas de las I Jornadas de Arqueología de Castilla-La Mancha,* edited by Juan Manuel Millán Martínez and Concepción Rodríguez Ruza, 743–53. Cuenca: Ediciones de la Universidad de Castilla-La Mancha — Junta de Comunidades de Castilla-La Mancha, 2007.

Fita, Fidel. "Noticia de una ley de Teudis desconocida, recientemente descubierta en un palimpsesto de la catedral de León." *Boletín de la Real Academía de la Historia* 14, no. 6 (1889): 473–95.

García Moreno, Luis A. "El hábitat rural disperso en la península ibérica durante la Antigüedad tardía." *Antigüedad y Cristianismo* 8 (1991): 265–74.

———. "Guarrazar y la conquista islámica." In *Actas de las VII Jornadas visigodas tesoro de Guarrazar. 16, 17 y 18 de mayo de 2014,* edited by Luis A. García Moreno and Juan Manuel Rojas, 6–9. Guadamur: Ayuntamiento de Guadamur, 2014.

González, Fernándo. "Consolatio (Concilio Toledano VII)." *Voces* 5 (1994): 61–64.

Le Jan, Regin. "Convents, Violence and Competition for Power in Seventh-Century Francia." In *Topographies of Power in the Early Middle Ages,* edited by Mayke De Jong, Carine Van Rhijn, and Frans Theuws, 243–69. Boston and Leiden: Brill, 2001.

Martin, Céline. *La Géographie du pouvoir dans l'Espagne visigothique.* Lille: Presses Universitaires du Septentrion, 2003. DOI: 10.4000/books.septentrion.53176

Martín, Iñaki. "Colapso político y sociedades locales: el Noroeste de la península ibérica (siglos VIII–IX)." *Reti Medievali Rivista* 17, no. 2 (2016): 1–35. http://www.rmojs.unina.it/index.php/rm/article/view/5009.

Morín de Pablos, Jorge. "Guarrazar (trèsor de)." In *Les barbares,* edited by Bruno Dumézil, 676–79. Paris: PUF, 2016.

Morín de Pablos, Jorge, and Isabel Sánchez. Los Hitos. *Arisgotas-Orgaz, Toledo: De palacio a panteón visigodo.* Madrid: Audema, 2015.

Nolla, José M. "Ciudades, torres y castella. La defensa de la Vía Augusta." In *Las fortificaciones en la Tardoantigüedad. Élites y articulación del territorio (siglos V–VIII d.C.),* edited by Raúl Catalán, Patricia Fuentes, and José Carlos Sastre, 43–56. Madrid: Ediciones La Ergástula, 2014.

Olmo, Lauro. "Ciudad y estado en época visigoda: Toledo, la construcción de un nuevo paisaje urbano." In *Espacios urbanos en el Occidente mediterráneo (s. VI–VIII),* edited by Alfonso García, Ricardo Izquierdo, Lauro Olmo, and Diego Peris, 87–111. Toledo: Toletum Visigodo, 2010.

———. "Nuevos paisajes urbanos y consolidación del estado en época visigoda." In *Hispania Gothorum: San Ildefonso y el reino visigodo de Toledo,* edited by Rafael García Serrano, 161–80. Toledo: Don Quijote, 2007.

———."The Materiality of Complex Landscapes: Central Iberia During 6th–8th Centuries A.D." In *New Directions in Early Medieval European Archaeology: Spain and Italy Compared. Essays for Riccardo Francovic,* edited by Sauro Gelichi and Richard Hodges), 15–42. Turnhout: Brepols, 2015.

Palol, Pere de. "Resultados de las excavaciones junto al Cristo de la Vega, supuesta basílica conciliar de Sta. Leocadia, de Toledo. Algunas notas de topografía religiosa de la ciudad." In *Actas del Congreso Internacional del XIV Centenario del III Concilio de Toledo (589–1989), 787–832.* Toledo: Arzobispado de Toledo, 1991.

Peidró, Jesús. "La región de la Oróspeda tras Leovigildo. Organización y administración del territorio." *Verdolay-MAM* 11 (2008): 263–76.

Pliego, Ruth. *La moneda visigoda.* Seville: Universidad de Sevilla, 2009.

Real, Luis. "Portugal: cultura visigoda e cultura moçarabe." In *Visigodos y Omeyas. Un debate entre la Antigüedad tardía y la Alta Edad Media,* edited by Luis Caballero and Pedro Mateos Cruz, 21–75. Anejos de Archivo Español de Arqueología 23. Mérida: CSIC, 2000.

Rivera, Juan Francisco. "La catedral de Toledo. Museo de Historia, II. Época visigoda." *Boletín de la Real Academía de Toledo* 64–65 (1950–1951): 32–35.

Rizos, Efthymios. "Centres of the Late Roman Military Supply Network in the Balkans: A Survey of *horrea*." *Jahrbuch des Römisch-Germanischen Zentralmuseums* 60 (2013): 659–96.

Rojas, Juan M. "El primer año de trabajos en Guarrazar. La confirmación de un yacimiento arqueológico." In *Actas de las VII Jornadas visigodas tesoro de Guarrazar. 16, 17 y 18 de mayo de 2014,* edited by Luis A. García Moreno and Juan Manuel Rojas, 9–57. Guadamur: Ayuntamiento de Guadamur, 2014.

Rojas, Juan M., and Antonio J. Gómez. "Intervención arqueológica en la Vega Baja de Toledo. Características del centro político y religioso del Reino Visigodo." In *El siglo VII frente al siglo VII: Arquitectura,* edited by Luis Caballero, Pedro Mateos Cruz, and Maria Angeles Utrero, 45–89. Anejos de Archivo Español de Arqueología 51. Madrid: CSIC, 2009.

Sánchez, José Carlos. "Power and Rural Landscapes in Early Medieval Galicia (400–900 AD): Towards a Re-Incorporation of the Archaeology into the Historical Narrative." *Early Medieval Europe* 21, no. 2 (2013): 140–68. DOI: 10.1111/emed.12013.

Sánchez-Albornoz, Claudio. "El Aula Regia y las asambleas políticas de los godos." *Cuadernos de Historia de España* 5 (1946): 5–110.

Sánchez, Isabel, Jorge Morín de Pablos, and José Ramón de la Cal. "The Archaeological Site of 'Los Hitos' (Spain) and the Visigoth Landscape of Toledo's Region During Late Antiquity (7th c.)." Forthcoming.

Santiago, Javier. "El hábito epigráfico en la Hispania visigoda." In *VIII Jornadas Científicas sobre documentación de la Hispania altomedieval (siglos VI–X),* edited by Juan Carlos Galende Díaz, Javier Santiago Fernández, Nicolás Ávila Seoane, Manuel Salamanca López, and Leonor Zozaya Montes, 291–344. Madrid: Universidad Complutense de Madrid, 2009.

Teja, Ramón, and Silvia Acerbi. "El palacio visigodo y el circo de Toledo: hipótesis de localización." *Reti Medievali Rivista* 11, no. 2 (2010): 81–86.

Valdés Fernández, Fernando. "Un puente sobre el Tajo. El proceso de islamización de la ciudad de Toledo." In *Regia sedes Toletana I: La topografía de la ciudad de Toledo en la Antigüedad tardía y alta Edad Media,* edited by Jesús Carrobles, Rafael Barroso Cabrera, Jorge Morín de Pablos, and Fernando Valdés Fernández, 165–206. Toledo: Diputación de Toledo, Real Fundación de Toledo, 2007.

Velázquez, Isabel. "La inscripción de consagración de la catedral de Toledo." In *Excavaciones en el claustro de la catedral de Toledo,* edited by Martín Almagro, José María Barranco, and Markel Gorbea, 261–80. Bibliotheca Archaeologica Hispana 33. Madrid: Real Academia de la Historia, 2011.

———. "Las inscripciones del tesoro de Guarrazar." In *El tesoro visigodo de Guarrazar, Libro V. De las coronas y las cruces,* edited by Alicia Perea, 340–46. Madrid: CSIC, 2001.

Velázquez, Isabel, and Gisela Ripoll. "Toletum, la construcción de una urbs regia." In *Sedes Regiae (ann. 400–800),* edited by Gisela Ripoll and José Maria Gurt, 521–78. Memorias de la Real Academia de Buenas Letras 25. Barcelona: Reial Acadèmia de Bones Lletres, 2000.

341

9

Locating Carthage in the Vandal Era

Mark Lewis Tizzoni

Carthage long held a dominant position in the Roman provinces of North Africa and in the western Mediterranean as a
whole. It was the seat of the proconsuls and then of the Diocese
of Africa, possessing all the wealth, prestige, and civic/urban
infrastructure which accompanied this position. All of this gov-
ernmental apparatus was nestled within a large population and
situated on a major maritime nexus. And Carthage was indeed
extremely wealthy.[1] Vandal-era Carthage represents a complex
late antique city; one looking both inward and outward. It functioned both as the heart of the Vandal kingdom and as the central hub of a massive international maritime network spanning
much of the late Roman and post-Roman world. The Vandal
capital accrued more political authority as the center of this
new polity than it had as the center of Roman Africa. Without
doubt, the Vandal invasion and occupation of Carthage in 439
CE brought substantial changes and, in many ways, fundamen-

---

1   See, for example, Gareth Sears, *Late Roman African Urbanism: Continuity
    and Transformation in the City,* BAR International Series 1693 (Oxford: Ar-
    chaeopress, 2007), 41–45.

tally altered the socio-political and religious framework of both the city and the wider region. Yet, Carthage remained Carthage. The city continued as a major religious, cultural, and intellectual center with influence far beyond itself. It also continued as an administrative center through which, by the later fifth and early sixth centuries, the Hasding monarchs and the Vandal nobility controlled large swathes of post-Roman North Africa alongside Sardinia, Corsica, the Balearics, and portions of Sicily. [2]

One of the significant ways in which Carthage changed, however, was how it interacted with other urban centers.[3] The aim of this study is to examine these interactions, to locate Carthage's changing position within the Mediterranean world. Carthage, in effect, possessed two hinterlands: its immediate hinterland under Vandal suzerainty; and its wider hinterland, often geographically distant, which it acquired and held by virtue of its maritime nature and prominence. This chapter will establish the position of Carthage during the Vandal era both within and without the Vandal polity. This will involve an investigation particularly of economic and ecclesiastical evidence. This study will also examine the cultural and intellectual interactions between Carthage and the wider Mediterranean world, particularly focusing on the ways in which the Vandal rulers sought to depict and promote the city. The evidence of the Vandal-era Carthag-

2   For the conception of the Hasding rulers and the Vandal nobility as separate groups, largely based on the continuation of the initial settlement patterns established by Gaiseric, see the argument in Andrew Merrills and Richard Miles, *The Vandals* (Oxford and Malden: Wiley Blackwell, 2010), 68–71. The late Roman population figure for the provinces of Africa is likely to have been around three million, on which see Christian Courtois, *Les Vandales et l'Afrique* (Paris: Arts et Métiers Graphiques, 1955), 105–7. For the geographic extent, see below.
3   The city itself also underwent changes in its urban fabric, etc. The scholarship here is substantial. A good summary of late antique Carthage, with references, can be found in Gareth Sears, *The Cities of Roman Africa* (Stroud: The History Press, 2011), 116–21.

inian poets, especially those of the *Anthologia Latina,* plays a central role in this discussion.[4]

Carthage's position in the wider world and its relationship with other urban centers was complex and at times contradictory. The conquered African provinces which made up the Vandal kingdom provided Carthage with its largest, most immediate and most firmly held hinterland. This region consisted of several larger and more prominent cities alongside a large number of small urban centers and plentiful farmland, ranging from massive *latifundia* through to collective *"agroville"*-type settlements, down to marginal peasant-owned farmsteads, the majority of which continued to function throughout the Vandal period.[5] Upon the capture of Carthage in 439 CE, Gaiseric set about implementing an innovative system of settlement that would establish himself and his Vandal army in the new kingdom: the so-called *sortes Vandalorum,* the nature of which has proven controversial.[6] Despite this controversy, a sufficiently accurate sketch can be presented.[7] Within his likely somewhat-exaggerated accounts of savage despoliation and exile, Victor of Vita provides the basic facts of the occupation: the Vandals appropriated large swathes of the prime agricultural lands for their own use and for that of the Hasding royal family.[8] These

---

4   On the *Anthologia Latina,* see note 69 below.

5   Merrills and Miles, *The Vandals,* 152–62.

6   For the dispute and the line of reasoning followed here see Yves Modéran, "L'établissement territorial des Vandales en Afrique," *Antiquité Tardive* 10 (2002): 87–122; Merrills and Miles, *The Vandals,* 66–68; and, Andreas Schwarcz, "The Settlement of the Vandals in North Africa," in *Vandals, Romans and Berbers: New Perspectives on Late Antique North Africa,* ed. Andrew H. Merrills (Aldershot: Ashgate, 2004), 49–57. For a conveniently organized summation of the dispute, see Yves Modéran, *Les Vandales et l'Empire romain,* ed. Michel-Yves Perrin (Arles: Éditions Errance, 2014), 155–67.

7   A complete understanding of the precise physical structure of the Vandal settlement in Africa likely represents an impossibility, nor would it be of vital importance to the present study.

8   Victor of Vita, *Historia persecutionis africanae provinciae sub Geiserico et Hunirico regibus Wandalorum,* ed. Karl Halm (Berlin: Weidmann, 1879),

settlements, the *sortes Vandalorum,* were contained within the province of Zeugitana, and appear to have developed into a solid territorial bloc, which Andrew Merrills and Richard Miles describe as a "Vandal Pale."[9]

This arrangement solidified Carthage's position in several ways. The Vandal population was centered on Carthage, where the Hasding court was typically to be found, with an agricultural monetary base radiating out from it within its immediate province.[10] Carthage was very much the Vandal *polis,* as it were, upon which the Vandals were centered and where they drew, and spent, their revenue. This arrangement also provided Carthage with an immediate and firmly held hinterland, replete with both small and larger urban centers and agricultural estates. This afforded Carthage a reliable supply of the mercantile goods necessary for its wealth: agricultural produce — such as wheat, olive oil, and wine — and manufactured wares — such as African Red Slipware (ARS), and fish-based produce.[11] This, in turn, allowed Carthage to maintain its vast mercantile efforts uninterrupted by the Vandal occupation. This hinterland relied upon Carthage, with its harbor and fleet, for its continued economic success, and Carthage relied on them for their production. This relationship also gave Vandal Carthage a solid powerbase to leverage its wider power and influence. This was especially true in terms of the physical support this territory

---

1.13. For a discussion of the settlement and Victor of Vita's testimony thereof, see Merrills and Miles, *The Vandals,* 60–70. For a discussion of Victor of Vita and how to treat his text, see ibid., 184–93.

9   Ibid., 68.

10 The Hasding court traveled to some extent, although this travel was largely confined to the suburbs of Carthage, and so not, in reality, outside of the city's immediate powerbase. For this travel, see ibid., 78.

11 The economic prosperity was not solely rooted on olive oil supplemented by the production of fine ceramics, but was rooted in the production also of wine, wheat, and fish products. See Matthew S. Hobson, *The North African Boom: Evaluating Economic Growth in the Roman Province of Africa Proconsularis (146 B.C.–A.D. 439), Journal of Roman Archaeology* Supplementary Series 100 (Portsmouth: Journal of Roman Archaeology, 2015), 155.

gave to the Vandal army, which drew its income directly from the land, and not from taxes, thus freeing the Vandal kingdom from one of the largest state expenses in the ancient world.[12] Certainly, Carthage had controlled the proconsular province prior to the Vandal occupation, but with the Vandal takeover the footing of this control shifted. No longer was the prime farmland held by absentee Italian senators, the emperor, nor even native-born Romano-Africans; it was now held by the Vandals.[13] To this end, Vandal Carthage and Zeugitana resemble something of a large, late-antique *synoikismos* (civic union): while the legal status of Zeugitana's cities remained, in practical terms they were fundamentally oriented towards Carthage and served the city in its external relations. The apparent establishment of Arianism as the official church within Zeugitana further testifies to this special relationship between Zeugitana and Carthage within the wider Vandal state.[14]

Carthaginian rule extended well beyond Zeugitana (or as it was also known, Africa Proconsularis). Following the Vandal conquest of the city, Carthage ruled over much of the heartlands of the territory that comprised the Diocese of Africa. This region, covering Zeugitana, Byzacena, eastern Numidia, and part of Tripolitania was itself replete with urban centers.[15] These ur-

---

12 Merrills and Miles, *The Vandals,* 167–68.

13 Full knowledge of the redistribution of land is wanting, but the substantial imperial holdings certainly did not remain in the hands of the emperor, and, even taken with some reservations, Victor of Vita's account indicates that many landholders did indeed lose their estates. For the size of the imperial estates see Brian Herbert Warmington, *The North African Provinces from Diocletian to the Vandal Conquest* (Westport: Greenwood, 1971), 62–63.

14 The Vandals established Arianism as the legal state religion in the *sortes Vandalorum,* and the evidence points to the interpretation of this law as applicable to the entirety of Zeugitana. For this argument, followed here, Merrills and Miles, *The Vandals,* 68, and Modéran, "L'établissement," 107–10.

15 The extent of Vandal control in North Africa fluctuated and ultimately tapered down as the Vandal century wore on. This final reduction in territory stems, perhaps mostly, from the assertion of indigenous Berber power in, on, and beyond the old Roman limes. At the height of Vandal power, Car-

ban centers ranged from large cities like Hadrumetum and Hippo Regius down to small villages which processed and shipped olive oil, down all the way to farmsteads. Landowners across the region were intent upon maximizing their agricultural production for Mediterranean-wide shipment.[16] The Vandals maintained the Roman tax system — if in a form that the Byzantines later found overly complex and indecipherable — and these cities directed their taxes to Carthage, instead of the imperial capital.[17] Carthage thus became the final destination of a large amount of tax income that had formerly flowed north across the Mediterranean. With the advent of the Vandal Kingdom, Carthage truly became a capital city once more.

As Carthaginian rule extended beyond Zeugitana, so too did it extend beyond the shores of Africa. The full extent of the Vandal "empire" is a matter for debate, but, from the latter decades of the fifth century to the end of the Vandal kingdom in 533/534, Carthage controlled Sardinia, Corsica, the Balearics, and parts of Sicily.[18] Perhaps inadvertently, this reconstructed a state resembling somewhat that of ancient Punic Carthage. These possessions provided a key market for the Carthaginian trade fleet as well as an expanded tax base for the city and its rulers. The Vandal overseas possessions, however, were far from the sole trading partners of Carthage. The distribution of ARS, in certain of its definable types, shows the distribution of particular goods likely moved through Carthage in the Vandal period.[19] While

thage controlled most of Numidia and parts of the Mauretanias, although for how long is unknown. For the extent of Vandal authority see Modéran, *Les Vandales,* 143–52 and Merrills and Miles, *The Vandals,* 63–66.

16 Hobson, *The North African Boom,* 160.

17 For a summary of the taxation system of the Vandals see Merrills and Miles, *The Vandals,* 163–67.

18 Ibid., 129–40, and Modéran, *Les Vandales,* 152–53.

19 The study of ARS is vast and detailed. A summation in regards to the Vandal era, with bibliography, can be found at Jonathan Conant, *Staying Roman: Conquest and Identity in Africa and the Mediterranean, 439–700* (Cambridge: Cambridge University Press, 2012), 90–95. The most complete coverage of the topic is Michel Bonifay, *Études sur la céramique romaine tardive*

the evidence can be interpreted in various ways, production of ARS remained strong throughout the Vandal period, if nonetheless altered from the decades preceding the Vandal conquest.[20] Workshops in the northern region continued to ship through Carthage reaching markets across the Mediterranean.[21] Despite certain shifts and fluctuations, Carthage retained its trade connections with the Eastern Mediterranean in the Vandal period.[22] One eastern area which particularly retained strong trade links to Carthage during the Vandal period was the Nile Delta.[23] The link between Carthage and Egypt is further driven home by the notable presence of Egyptians (often associated with the circus) in the poems of Luxorius and others found in the *Anthologia Latina*.[24] In the West, Carthaginian wares continued to circulate in the older markets like Italy, but also entered into newer markets in southern and eastern Spain and, near the end of the

d'Afrique, BAR International Series 1301 (Oxford: Archaeopress, 2004). For the North African economy, and the role of ARS within it, see Hobson, *The North African Boom,* albeit focused on the pre-Vandal period. The foundational studies for ARS are the various works of John W. Hayes, beginning with his *Late Roman Pottery* (London: British School at Rome, 1972).

20 While certain types undoubtedly decreased in production, this need not be read as an overall decrease or decline. It should be noted also that ARS only shows one aspect of the North African economy. Wheat, one of the key exports, does not show up in the archaeological record, for example. See Conant, *Staying Roman,* 51.

21 Ibid., 96 and Christopher Wickham, *Framing the Early Middle Ages: Europe and the Mediterranean, 400–800* (Oxford: Oxford University Press, 2005), 721ff.

22 Conant, *Staying Roman,* 92–93. Byzantine gold continued to flow into North Africa throughout the Vandal period. Cécile Morrisson, "L'Atelier de Carthage et la diffusion de la monnaie frappe dans l'Afrique vandal et byzantine (439–695)," *Antiquité Tardive* 11 (2003): 65–84, at 77. These eastern trade routes had their origin in late antiquity (Hobson, *The North African Boom,* 107).

23 Bonifay, *Études sur la céramique,* 454–56 and Conant, *Staying Roman,* 93.

24 Four examples from Luxorius are AL 288/R 293, AL 319/R 324, both of which discuss Egyptian charioteers, and AL 348/R 353, regarding an Egyptian hunter, whose epitaph is given in AL 349/R 354. On editions and numbering used for the *Anthologia Latina,* see note 69 below.

Vandal century, Marseille.[25] In effect, Carthaginian goods continued to ply the Mediterranean, and Carthaginian sailors and ships continued to be a common sight in the ports of the Roman and post-Roman worlds.

The numismatic evidence adds another dimension to Carthage's position in its wider economic and political context. The Hasdings famously minted their own coinage in Carthage, initially in the form of pseudo-imperial issues and then in the form of signed openly Vandalic issues, all in bronze and silver.[26] Being small issues, these coins were more the domain of everyday transaction than of long-distance trade, and so their distribution shows us the immediate monetary zone of Carthage itself. Substantial hordes of Vandal coins were found in locations in Numidia and Mauretania Sitifensis dating to the later Vandal era, but the preponderance of finds within Africa are from Zeugitana.[27] This fits with the picture created by our other sources and effectively outlines the areas under most direct Vandal control. The Vandal coinage also appears substantially in the Mediterranean isles which formed part of the Vandal "empire" as well as southern Spain, confirming the strong trade links between Carthage and Spain seen in the distribution of the ARS.[28] There are also substantial finds from Southern Italy and Rome.[29] While it is possible that these finds could date from the Byzantine period, the Southern Italian link makes sense within the Vandal context: Naples is close to Carthage, and was the site of the first great exile of African Catholic churchmen led by Quodvultdeus, the bishop of Carthage, after Gaiseric's conquest of the city in

---

25 Conant, *Staying Roman,* 93–94.
26 Morrisson, "L'Atelier de Carthage," 66. The Hasdings produced coinage throughout the Vandal century, although the dated issues come from the later period. The iconography of the latter issues is important for a full understanding of the Vandal kingdom in Africa, and will be discussed below.
27 Ibid., 80, with map. The large hordes in Numidia and Mauretania Sitifensis are likely the result of military affairs, rather than regular circulation.
28 Ibid., 81, with map, 83.
29 Ibid., 82–83.

439.[30] Dating these finds to the Vandal era is also supported by the noticeably different distribution of coinage minted in Carthage by the Byzantines.[31] There are also a number of hordes of Vandal-era coins in the Peloponnesus, and while they may have arrived after the fall of the Vandals in 533, there is circumstantial evidence to place them earlier.[32] It should be noted also that our literary evidence serves to confirm some of these links: Fulgentius of Ruspe wrote confidently of the ability to travel not only to Alexandria but to various points east, and we know also of substantial contact between Africa and Constantinople.[33]

The numismatic evidence, then, shows a close Carthaginian economic sphere including areas under direct Vandal control (Zeugitana, near Numidia, and the western Mediterranean islands) as well as areas outside direct Vandal control, namely southern Spain and Southern Italy. The fact that these coins represent small day-to-day exchange currency most likely indicates the presence of substantial amounts of Carthaginians operating in these regions. These cities and towns were either firmly within the economic hold of Carthage or participants with the city in a strong mutual economic partnership.

Trade and taxes, however, were not the sole expression of Carthage's "external relations": the city was also the center of a, at various times, large-scale piracy operation. In the first half of the Vandal century, when Carthage was ruled by Gaiseric, at certain times the city's relations with other urban centers could be described as "predatory." Setting out from Carthage, Vandal naval raids hit targets from Gallaecia to Alexandria, instilling

30 Victor of Vita, *Historia persecutionis* 1.15.
31 Morrisson, "L'Atelier de Carthage," 83–84. The coins of Byzantine Carthage have, for example, a much stronger distribution in inland Gaul, Sicily, and inland Italy.
32 Morrisson notes their lack of distribution in military areas, which one would expect. Ibid., 82. The distribution also matches the area of Vandal pirate raids, for the significance of this, see below.
33 For Fulgentius, Conant, *Staying Roman,* 95, for African travelers to Constantinople and the east in general, ibid., 76–83.

fear along the way.[34] Sicily and Sardinia were hit in the opening
foray in 440 and likely Southern Italy, but peace was made in
442 with the second Romano-Vandal treaty.[35] While there were
isolated raids in the intervening years, the next major phase of
Vandal piracy erupted in 455. This second wave of piracy most
famously resulted in the sack of Rome in that year, a pillaging
which resulted in the transportation of a massive amount of
wealth to the city of Carthage. Prominent amongst the spoils
of the raid was the menorah taken by Titus from the Temple
in Jerusalem in 70 CE.[36] More importantly, the Carthaginian
raiders took three women from the imperial family, Eudoxia,
the wife of Valentian III, and their daughters Eudocia and Pla-
cidia — the eldest daughter Eudocia being the fiancée of Gaiseric's son Huneric. The Sack of Rome was followed by years of
raids spanning the Mediterranean islands, Italy, and Greece but
consciously focused on Southern Italy and the Adriatic coasts.[37]
This state of affairs continued until the final peace between Gaiseric and the imperial authorities in 476. All in all, these raids
were part of a wider strategy employed by Gaiseric to secure
the Vandal kingdom's, and thus Carthage's, political position in
the wider Mediterranean world.[38] With Gaiseric's death in 477,
Carthage ended its career as a pirate base.

In the context of urban interactions, this period of piracy
represents part of Carthage's complex and conflicting history.
Long the center of peaceful trade, Carthage became, for a time,
a major disruptor of said peaceful trade. For the purposes of
the present investigation, this period of piracy served to ce-
ment the city's legacy as a dominant military power. While the
later Vandal kings conducted no raids, they retained the power

---

34 Merrills and Miles, *The Vandals,* 109.
35 Ibid., 111, with a synthesis of the primary sources.
36 Procopius, *History of the Wars, Volume II: Books 3–4 (Vandalic War),* ed.
    and trans. Henry B. Dewing, Loeb Classical Library 81 (Cambridge: Har-
    vard University Press, 1916), 2.9.5.
37 Merrills and Miles, *The Vandals,* 118.
38 This is the theory put forth by ibid., 109–24, and it has strong merit.

to do so. It would be difficult to imagine that this continuing latent threat did not aid Carthaginian merchants in their continued endeavors. The main areas of piracy correspond to the areas where Vandal-era Carthaginian coinage appears outside of Africa. These raids, either intentionally or not, had a direct economic effect in helping to establish a stronger Carthaginian economic and mercantile position in the areas hit by the raids. While some of the regions were subsequently conquered by the Vandals, this is not the case for all, and this continued intimidation likely helped to secure the strong position of Carthaginian merchants within these cities. In addition to strengthening the position of Carthaginian merchants through the threat/memory of force, these raids served to fill the coffers of the Hasding monarchs and the Vandal elites who resided in and around the city. This, in turn, helped to fund Hasding euergetism long after the raids stopped.

The much wider shift in Vandal Carthage's network of urban interactions, however, was a dramatic shift in its economic orientation. This is perhaps the most important aspect of the effects of the Vandal occupation on the urban history of Carthage. This "reorientation" began when the Vandals ended the *annona,* the annual state-funded grain shipments from Africa to Rome, and thereby severed the Rome–Carthage axis, upon which the stability of the western Mediterranean economy may well have rested.[39] Meanwhile, the economy of Vandal Africa remained robust: agricultural production continued at the levels it had held prior to the invasion and cities likewise maintained their levels of manufacturing, continuing to produce the various trade goods which accompanied the agricultural produce across the Mediterranean.[40] The termination of the *annona* system affected Carthage in several ways. One aspect of this massive shift

39 Ibid., 147–51 and Hobson, *The North African Boom,* 150ff. Also, see Wickham, *Framing,* 88, 711–12.

40 Merrills and Miles, *The Vandals,* 148–49 (for continued agricultural production) and 153 (for urban manufacturing).

was to open up the trade possibilities available to the Carthaginian fleet. Carthaginian merchants were now free to favor Naples over Rome, as the numismatic evidence suggests they may well have, and likewise to ply both sides of the Mediterranean at will. Part of this shift was directed towards the Vandal overseas territories of Sardinia, Sicily, and Corsica.[41] This also accounts for the increase in Spanish trade discussed above. With the focus no longer on Rome, it also freed increasing numbers of eastern merchants to make for the port of Carthage to sell their wares in exchange for African agricultural produce.[42] All of this encouraged Carthage to orient itself with different cities on new networks, providing new markets for Carthaginian goods, and bringing new and different goods into the port of Carthage.

Also important for the position of Carthage in the wider Mediterranean, the end of the Rome–Carthage axis ended the effective trade monopoly the Carthaginian fleet held in the western Mediterranean. Under the Roman *annona* system, African shippers were subsidized by the imperial government: alongside the foodstuffs that made up the *annona,* these shippers, the *navicularii,* were "free" to load various other agricultural and manufactured goods for sale in the Roman markets.[43] While the *navicularii* were drawn, and drew their goods, from across the African provinces, by the fifth century they were all centrally organized and run collectively by the *vicarius* of Africa, based in Carthage.[44] This centralized the massive trade of the *annona* upon the city. It also served to direct other African trade interests to Carthage, as its fleet's shipping rates were far

41 Ibid., 150.
42 Ibid., 150–51.
43 The *navicularii* also received substantial benefits and tax breaks, Warmington, *Provinces,* 60–62. For Carthage's role in the *annona* see also Wickham, *Framing,* 709–12. The produce was collected and sent in large fleets, Carthage possessed the authorities responsible for this, and the apparatus necessary to do it. Shippers were at times restricted from loading private cargoes onto public shipments, but ARS seems always to have traveled, alongside, most likely, other things. Ibid., 711.
44 Warmington, *Provinces,* 60–61.

lower than its competitors operating outside the *annona* system. After the Vandal conquest, and several decades of piracy and war, the Carthaginian *annona* system no longer functioned, and so its fleet no longer had its imperially-funded competitive advantage. As a result, the North African economy was no longer directed to the port of Carthage and entered into a phase of decentralization. This is confirmed in the distribution of imperial gold issues in finds from the Vandal period, which have a strong distribution in Mauretania and western Numidia.[45] Likewise, Vandal-era trade between North Africa and Marseilles was monopolized by Byzacena, not Carthage, until the second quarter of the sixth century.[46] Indeed, Byzacena appears to have particularly flourished in this new atmosphere.[47] While Vandal-era Carthage nevertheless retained a central position in the North African mercantile trade, its central economic controls were no longer present, and it operated in a much more populated world of competing mercantile interests.[48]

Evidence stemming from the religious sector also sheds light on Carthage's position during the Vandal era. As already noted, the expulsion of the bishop of Carthage and a large number of Romano-African Catholic clergy at the inception of the Vandal century created a link between Carthage and Naples. These expulsions form an important aspect in Vandal Carthage's interactions with other urban centers. Every city, town, and region where the Vandal monarchs exiled their Catholic clergy was brought closer into the ecclesiastical, cultural, and intellectual orbit of the Vandal kingdom, itself centered upon Carthage. The most important of these centers during the last half of the Van-

---

45 Morrisson, "L'Atelier de Carthage," 78–79. During the Byzantine era, the distribution of imperial gold is strongly centered upon Zeugitana and Byzacena, with smaller numbers in Numidia and only very limited finds in Maurentania.

46 Conant, *Staying Roman,* 92–93.

47 Merrills and Miles, *The Vandals,* 149.

48 It continued to control Zeugitana, for example, one of the richest provinces in the Mediterranean at the time.

dal century were the cities of Sardinia, Cagliari in particular.[49] Indeed, from the beginning of Thrasamund's reign in 496, Cagliari "became the focal point of the African Church in exile."[50] During the reign of Thrasamund (496–523) there was royal interest in interfaith dialogue between Arians and Catholics, even if it was indeed driven by the king's desire to strengthen the position of the Arian Church.[51] Sardinia was perfectly suited to this role: it moved the African Catholic clergy to a place that was both peripheral and central. It was more challenging for them to stir up trouble there, as they were physically removed from their congregations, but yet they remained accessible. Sardinia was, as we have seen, closely linked to Carthage and part of its direct economic hinterland. Yet, for this, its seaborne separation allowed the clergy to be kept precisely at arm's length. Sardinia also presented the African churchmen with work to distract them from their African duties: evangelization. The Vandal-era exiles left an indelible African mark on the religious and intellectual culture not only of Sardinia, but also of Corsica and the Balearics. In the latter islands, especially in more rural areas, and in the interior of Sardinia, these African clerics undertook perhaps the first wave of sustained efforts at spreading Christianity, and the Church in these islands took on a strong African flavor.[52] The active intellectual efforts of these exiled bishops also served to connect the western Mediterranean islands not only

49 Merrills and Miles, *The Vandals*, 137–39. Waves of African clerics were exiled to Sardinia under kings Huneric and Thrasamund, from the early 480s until the early 520s.
50 Ibid., 138.
51 This interest manifested itself in the famous debates between Thrasamund and Fulgentius of Ruspe between 516/517 and 518/519, discussed, for example, in ibid., 197.
52 North African saints are prominent in these areas, and the ecclesiastical architecture of especially Corsica bears an African stamp. Ibid., 138–40. North African saints also appear in the south of Italy, particularly Naples (such as Saint Gaudiosus of Naples, one of the exiles who accompanied Quodvultdeus and the cult of Saint Restituta, a North African martyr venerated in the city).

much more firmly to Carthage, but also brought them back into closer touch with wider Mediterranean currents. They additionally cultivated stronger connections with Rome during their exile, and when recalled to Africa under Hilderic, this served to strengthen the ecclesiastical connection between Carthage and Rome.[53] As such, the religious expulsions undertaken by the Vandal monarchs served to strengthen and deepen Carthage's connections with its wider western Mediterranean economic and political hinterland.

The legacy of the exiling of the African Catholic Church hierarchy is more complex than this, however. While Carthage's connections outside of Africa may have been strengthened by this exile, as the city became the main hub of communication and cultural and intellectual discourse, it had nearly the opposite effect within Africa itself. In the early phase, the bishop of Carthage, Quodvultdeus, served as a leader of the exiles, but as the decades wore on Hasding policies progressively weakened the Catholic Church in Zeugitana.[54] It is important to note also that while the Vandal efforts to weaken the Catholic Church in Africa targeted other areas, they were far more sustained in Carthage and Zeugitana, where the Vandal population was centered.[55] As the upper echelons of the African Catholic Church became a government-in-exile, its leadership shifted focus from place to person. In due course, the most prominent intellectual amongst the African Catholics became the effective leader of the Church: this person was Fulgentius of Ruspe. It was with him that Thrasamund debated and when Hilderic restored the

53 Ibid., 138–39.

54 On the opposite side of this, of course, Carthage served as the center of the Arian Church in Africa throughout the Vandal century, but how this influenced interactions with other centers in Africa beyond those already established through connections with the Vandals themselves is difficult to establish.

55 Merrills and Miles, *The Vandals,* 188 and Yves Modéran, "L'Afrique et la persécution vandale," in N*ouvelle Histoire du Christianisme, des origines à nos jours. III Les Églises d'Orient et d'Occident,* ed. Luce Pietri (Paris: Desclée-Fayard, 1998), 247–78.

African Catholics, it was Fulgentius that led the restored church back to Africa.[56] This shift in power served to decentralize Carthage's religious authority within the African Church.[57]

Once restored, Bonifatius, the bishop of Carthage, asserted his religious primacy across North Africa, in his letter to the Council of Iunci in 523, for example, but assertion and reality are not the same.[58] This shift can be witnessed in the Council of Carthage in 525, held two years after Hilderic restored the Church. The goal of the council appears to have been to (re-)assert Carthaginian primacy within the African Catholic Church.[59] The council was poorly attended, with only fifty-two bishops or their representatives in attendance, of which thirty-seven were from Zeugitana, nine from eastern Numidia, three from coastal Byzacena, two from Tripolitania, and one from Mauretania.[60] For context, the Council of Carthage in 439 had 164 bishops in attendance solely from Zeugitana. As Merrills and Miles, alongside Courtois, point out, this disparity demonstrates the damage done to the African Catholic Church during the Vandal century,

---

56 For the debates, Ferrandus, *Vita Fulgentii,* ed. and trans. Gabriel-Guillaume Lapeyre (Paris: Lethielleux, 1929), 20–23; and for his leading the exiled bishops back to Carthage, 26–27 (which also outlines his influence and popularity in the city). See also Merrills and Miles, *The Vandals,* 196–98.

57 Miles argues that the successive exiles weakened the Catholic African episcopate not only in an ecclesiastical sense, but also in terms of their overall authority within Romano-African society. Richard Miles, "The *Anthologia Latina* and the Creation of Secular Space in Vandal Carthage," *Antiquité Tardive* 13 (2005): 305–20, at 313.

58 Merrills and Miles, *The Vandals,* 201–2.

59 Courtois, *Les Vandales,* 305. This seems to be a reasonable summation of the council's central goals, certainly the actions of the council support this interpretation. One of the main decisions of the council was to overturn a ruling of the regional council of Byzacena at Iunci in 523. For this ruling, see Merrills and Miles, *The Vandals,* 201 and, for lengthier discussion, Courtois, *Les Vandales,* 304–9.

60 Three of the Numidian representatives appear to have been of Zeugitanan origin, Courtois, *Les Vandales,* 308. Unfortunately, we do not possess numbers for the Council of Iunci in 523, as this would provide the best comparison. There were nine additional delegates whose sees are unknown, who are not typically counted in the number. Ibid., 305, 307.

in terms of the persecutions, even when taking into account ca-
veats such as practical difficulties, etc.[61] The numbers tell several things, but the geographic distribution of the attendees at
the 525 Council provides the real demonstration of Carthage's
new position in the North African religious landscape. Bonifatius had called upon the Church of Africa, but the only bishops
who came were those whose cities were closely and unavoid-
ably tied to Carthage. Thus, Zeugitana, the stronghold of the
Vandals, attended, alongside eastern Numidia, and a handful of
other coastal cities in the other provinces. The most important
absences were the leaders of the Church in Byzacena; Liberatus,
the metropolitan of Hadrumetum, who sent only a legate, and
Fulgentius of Ruspe. Carthage's religious authority within Africa
had, in effect, been regionalized to the areas directly subordinate to Carthage and its Vandal rulers.[62] In effect, after nearly a
century of Vandal rule, Carthage's religious primacy extended
only as far the political authority of its Vandal rulers and the
economic pull of its infrastructure and enterprise.[63] This is not,

61 The exile of some 500 African bishops in the aftermath of the Council of
    Carthage in 484 certainly has some influence on the numbers here, at the
    very least in terms of bishoprics whose bishops may well not have returned
    from exile. Merrills and Miles, *The Vandals,* 202; Courtois, *Les Vandales,*
    307.

62 For a map and a convenient list of attendees, Courtois, *Les Vandales,* 305–7,
    with discussion 304–9. Courtois likewise argues to this effect on page 308.
    To the reasons given in the present essay, namely the physical disconnection
    of Carthage from the African Catholic Church and subsequent loss of in-
    tellectual/theological authority during the exile, Courtois adds three more:
    the loss of Zeugitanan bishops during the persecution with a subsequent
    loss in numbers to the Carthaginian party, then the increase in provincial
    independence spurred by this weakness, and, lastly, the growth of the mo-
    nasticism and its independence of spirit. Ibid., 308.

63 Likely enough, Carthage's prime position in the African Catholic Church
    was weakened by the city's service as the focal point of the African Ari-
    an Church. As the long history of Donatism shows, Late Antique African
    Christians could be rather less than forgiving in such matters.

however, to say that Carthage accepted this diminished position.[64]

Indeed, the city, and her rulers, were far from conceding defeat. While the Vandals solidified the political power of the city, it slipped in terms of economic and religious authority. Yet, neither the city nor its rulers were willing to see Carthage diminished, and, as such, undertook a concerted program to restore and increase its prominence and prestige. At the center of the Vandal state there had always been a religious conflict between the Arian Vandals and the Catholic Romano-Africans they ruled.[65] This conflict was always an aspect of Vandal Carthage's relations with other urban and rural centers. In the latter half of the Vandal century there was also a concerted effort to bridge this divide amongst the kingdom's elites through an emphasis on shared secular culture. This shared secular culture became the foundation of Vandal-Romano-African relations.[66] It is also in this secular cultural world that Carthage increasingly reasserted itself in the final decades of the fifth and the first decades of the sixth century and where the Hasding cultural program was focused.

This program was a concerted cultural effort to (re-)assert the dominance of the city of Carthage. It channeled itself through various different forms of cultural expression. One of these channels was the Hadings's sponsorship of poetry. As Miles outlines, the Vandal court refocused the cultural, artistic, and especially poetic efforts of North Africa upon their capital city; instead of the best and brightest of Africa taking ship to Italy or

---

64 Metropolitan Bonifatius, however, may well have: there were no more attempts at a general Council of Carthage during his tenure. Courtois, *Les Vandales*, 308. The bishop, however, did not entirely reflect his city in this defeat.

65 Being late antique North Africa, the conflict was not a simple dichotomy. When the Vandals took Carthage, there were still populations of Donatists and Manichaeans, but the main power struggle/power share was between the Arians and the Catholics.

66 This hypothesis is convincingly laid out and argued by Richard Miles, "The *Anthologia Latina*," 305–20, particularly at page 309.

Constantinople, they flocked to Carthage.[67] During the Vandal century, Carthage became one of the most important and most vital centers of Latin poetry in the Roman/post-Roman world; during its heyday, it certainly dominated the field. Its most prolific poet was Blossius Aemilius Dracontius, and his works, both Christian and secular, demonstrate the extent of learning that existed in Vandal-era Carthage.[68] Yet, while the works of Dracontius serve as an ornament to the city, the most "Carthaginian" pieces are not these grand works, but the shorter, feistier poems of the *Anthologia Latina*.[69] These poems are curious, fiercely secular, oftentimes odd, but mostly entertaining glimpses into

67 Ibid., 309.
68 For Dracontius and the extent of his learning see Claude Moussy, "Introduction," in *Dracontius: Oeuvres I*, ed. Claude Moussy and Collette Camus (Paris: Les Belles Lettres, 2002), 7–31 (biography) and 55–77 (education/use of sources), and also Mark Lewis Tizzoni, *The Poems of Dracontius in their Vandalic and Visigothic Contexts* (Ph.D. diss., University of Leeds, 2012), 32–146. For a short summation, Merrills and Miles, *The Vandals*, 205 and 215–17.
69 The *Anthologia Latina* (AL) is a curious collection of short poems (many of which are *epigrammata*) compiled at some point in time near the Byzantine conquest of North Africa. The collection contains some Classical Latin pieces alongside 108 poems that are of clear Vandal-era, North African origin. These African works are by various authors, the majority of which are named. The most prolific of these authors is Luxorius, whose poems account for 88 of the 108 North African pieces. The number of Vandal-era North African texts in the collection may well be higher than the numbers quoted here, which are derived from Miles, "The *Anthologia Latina*." For this, see, Nigel M. Kay, *Epigrams from the Anthologia Latina: Text, Translation and Commentary* (London: Duckworth, 2006), 1–13. For a discussion of the *Anthologia Latina*, see Yitzhak Hen, *Roman Barbarians: The Royal Court and Culture in the Early Medieval West* (Basingstoke: Palgrave Macmillan, 2007), 78–83 and, among others, Morris Rosenblum, *Luxorius: A Latin Poet among the Vandals* (New York: Columbia University Press, 1961), 25–35. For the texts themselves, there are two main edited collections, *Anthologia Latina I*, ed. David R. Shackleton Bailey (Stuttgart: Teubner, 1982) and *Anthologia Latina sive poesis latinae supplementum. Pars Prior: Carmina in codicibus scripta. Fasciculus I: Libri Salmasiani aliorumque carmina*, ed. Alexander Riese (Leipzig: Teubner, 1894). Numbering differs, and this essay gives Shackleton Bailey's numbering first, followed by Riese's.

the lives of Romano-African and Vandal elites in and around Carthage and the world which they created. The poems of the *Anthologia Latina* chronicle the efforts of the Romano-African literary elite to promote the prestige of their city. Together, they paint a vivid picture of the city and its cultural life. The urban life of Carthage witnessed in these poems is vibrant, multi-faceted, and, in keeping with the late antique reputation of the city, rather raucous. These poems paint images with their verse of the art that adorned the homes of Vandal and Romano-African aristocrats, and of their beautiful gardens, of baths and a palace built by monarchs, and of the glories of the circus.[70] They celebrate the great learning of Carthage alongside its bawdy underbelly.[71] Collected together, as indeed they were, they portray a Carthage that was a rival for Classical Rome, conveyed in the language and style of late antiquity. Importantly, they portrayed this Carthage to the students who flocked to study in the city's schools from across Africa. In turn, these students became part of the powerful secular cultural world centered on the city, and so further increased the cultural dominance of Carthage in its wider African context.

The focused efforts of the Hasdings in their glorification of Carthage, however, go far beyond the Romano-African collection of *epigrammata* that is the bulk of the *Anthologia Latina*.[72] One aspect of this is the short panegyric of Florentius preserved within the collection. This text represents a conscious effort to glorify king Thrasamund, but that is ultimately not the full focus

---

70 Examples for nearly all of these can be found in Luxorius. Some examples can be found at AL 329/R 334 and AL 330/R 335 (ekphrases), AL 327/R 332 and 299/R 304 (on gardens), AL 289/R 294 (one of many on charioteers), and AL 194/R 203 (on Hilderic's palace at Anclae), and, for the baths, Felix's poems AL 201–205/R 210–214.

71 The most cursory glance at Luxorius's verses drives both points home quite quickly.

72 The foundational text for the Vandal glorification of Carthage is Frank M. Clover, "Felix Karthago," *Dumbarton Oaks Papers* 40 (1986): 1–16. The following paragraph is an analytical summary of Clover's argument.

of the text.[73] The main thrust of the text comes at the end, and takes the form of a rather forceful encomium on the city of Carthage, whose power is then tied to that of Thrasamund.[74] This conscious attachment of the glory of Carthage with Vandal political power represents a key aspect of the Vandal cultural program. In addition to dating time in the Vandal realm by regnal years, which asserted Hasding authority along imperial routes, the Vandal kingdom employed the *anno Carthaginis,* which ran from the Vandal conquest of the city in 439.[75] This placement of the foundation of Vandal power in Africa as the conquest of Carthage firmly asserted the dominance of the city: the previous Vandal settlements in Africa were as nothing, Carthage was Africa. These assertions of Carthaginian authority were furthered by the iconography of the Vandal coinage.[76] Several issues featured the personification of Carthage with the inscription *Felix Karthago,* including an issue of Hilderic (r. 523–530). This image of Lady Carthage stemmed from earlier imperial coinage, but the Vandal-era mint at Carthage also drew inspiration from the city's Punic past.[77] This iconographic return to the independent pre-Roman past of the city is a strong assertion of Carthaginian authority. The memory of Punic Carthage as the great rival of Rome is with us still; its use in the late fifth century was highly charged.

The *encomia,* the iconography, the glorification of Carthage was indeed an expression of municipal pride, as Clover asserts. However, it was also more than that. These depictions of proud Lady Carthage and the strong, independent history of the Punic past were an assertion of the independent power of the city of

---

73 *AL* 371/R 376.

74 A full translation of the poem can be found at Clover, "Felix Karthago," 9.

75 Ibid., 8. For a detailed discussion of the calculation of time in the Vandal kingdom, Frank M. Clover, "Timekeeping and Dyarchy in Vandal Africa," *Antiquité Tardive* 11 (2003): 45–63.

76 Clover, "Felix Karthago," 2–8 discusses the iconography of Carthage, particularly in reference to coinage.

77 Ibid., 4–8. This iconography included palm trees and horse's heads.

Carthage that had been "returned" to her through the Vandal occupation. All of these artistic and numismatic efforts were coupled with building projects that added to the monumental glory of the city. The most popular form of architecture in Roman and post-Roman Africa appears to have been the baths.[78] Thus we find Thrasamund constructing a bath complex in the Carthaginian suburb of Alienae.[79] Yet, Thrasamund does not simply construct these baths: he has them celebrated in poetry. Alienae is briefly mentioned in the panegyric of Florentius, but the real effort is represented by a series of poems attributed to a Felix, all twelve lines long, which culminate in a complex hexameter production that involves acrostic, mesostich, and telestich in praise of Thrasamund and his baths.[80] These five poems were likely featured on the walls of the bath complex itself, adding another dimension to the monumentality of the building.[81] Together, these efforts made a massive statement. The Vandals had made Carthage proud and independent once more; this, certainly, was the image they sought to project. This promotion of Carthage, whether in verse or stone, or in silver and bronze, asserted Carthaginian independence and affirmed Carthage's ancient and modern position as the capital of an empire.

These efforts to amplify the prestige of Carthage amongst the cities of the Mediterranean took on an imperial bent during the reign of Hilderic. Indeed, Hilderic's projects are vital for an understanding of Carthage's cultural interactions in the final decades of Vandal rule. Hilderic was a member of the Theodosian dynasty through his mother, Eudocia. Hilderic appears to have developed his imperial heritage into a central aspect of his rule.[82] A key element in this development was his construction

---

78 Sears, *Cities of Roman Africa*, 125–26. For the importance of baths for propaganda, Leone, *End of the Pagan City*, 117.

79 Merrills and Miles, *The Vandals*, 223–24.

80 AL 371/R 376, line 20.

81 Merrills and Miles, *The Vandals*, 222.

82 This argument is developed in Merrills and Miles, *The Vandals*, 76 and 222 and more fully in Andrew H. Merrills, "The Secret of my Succession: Dy-

of a new palace at Anclae, a suburb of Carthage.[83] This suburban palace is celebrated in a poem of Luxorius (*AL* 194/R 203)
and elaborated upon further in a poem by Felix (*AL* 206/R 215),
which provides an *ekphrasis* upon the images within.[84] These
images celebrate the imperial heritage of Hilderic, depicting
Valentinian III, Theodosius, and Honorius. This multifaceted
cultural production — a royal palace, full of imperial imagery,
celebrated in Latin verse — served to enhance the imperial identity of Hilderic. As Hilderic continued to associate his rule with
the city of Carthage, this imperial identity was in turn asserted
for the city itself.[85] In the final decades of Vandal rule Carthage
was not simply being marketed as an independent royal center,
but as an imperial capital.

Thus, with Vandal Carthage's power somewhat diminished in
the economic and religious spheres, the city's ruling elite sought
actively to promote its culture. As such, it not only retained but
grew its cultural hold on North Africa. It remained the center
of learning in North Africa and fostered a flourishing of poetic
endeavor, indeed becoming one of the chief sources of Latin poetry in the decades surrounding the year 500. By funding the efforts of the poets and by furnishing its schools with students, the
Vandal and Romano-African elites of Carthage allowed the city
to retain its cultural dominance in Africa. Likewise, as the heart
of the secular culture fostered by these elites in an effort to bring
a stable common-ground to the Vandal kingdom, the city's symbolic dominance in African affairs was solidified. Hilderic's imperial program furthered this symbolic dominance. Another dimension to this strengthening of the dominant cultural position

---

nasty and Crisis in Vandal North Africa," *Early Medieval Europe* 18, no. 2
(2010): 135–59.

83 Merrills and Miles, *The Vandals,* 222.

84 Discussed in Merrills and Miles, *The Vandals,* 222, with reference to the
scholarship on the subject.

85 Hilderic, it should be noted, produced silver Felix Karthago issues, bearing
his name and portrait opposite Lady Carthage inscribed with Felix Karthago.

of Carthage in North Africa was the development of the city's suburbs. The two key Hasding construction projects discussed above both took place in the suburbs of Carthage, the baths in Alienae and the palace in Anclae.[86] The possession of suburbs, and of royal, indeed "imperial," estates within them evoked the situation of Rome in the Golden Age.[87] This connection to Rome was amplified by the literary celebration of these suburbs and their estates found in the poetry of the *Anthologia Latina*.[88] This served to drive home Carthage's independent *imperium* under the Vandals, and thus to solidify the city's authority both within Africa and beyond.

The history of Vandal-era Carthage's urban interactions is thus complex, multifaceted, and, at times, contradictory. This history is underpinned by two main historical factors: the severing of the Rome–Carthage trade axis centered upon the *annona* and the city's newfound status as the capital of an independent state. The severing of the Rome–Carthage axis fundamentally reoriented Carthage's economic position within the wider Mediterranean world. It continued to operate from a solid, wealthy base of agricultural and industrial production (Zeugitana) held firm by the settlement of the Vandal aristocracy, but its relationships outside of its immediate province shifted. Rome was no longer the main trade focus of the city, and the Vandal period saw Carthage's trade connections expand massively, including increased trade with the Eastern Mediterranean and Spain. Yet, this expansion of opportunity also led to some decline in Carthage's economic dominance within Africa itself. Without the

---

86 The *Anthologia Latina* testifies to other such estates, most notably in the verse of Luxorius. Luxorius, for example, speaks of the gardens (replete with paintings) and pools of one Fridamal (R 304 and R 305).

87 Penelope J. Goodman, *The Roman City and Its Periphery: From Rome to Gaul* (Oxford: Routledge, 2007), 7–38.

88 Rome's suburbs feature prominently in the literature of Classical Rome, largely because the elites who produced that literature inhabited those same suburbs. Ibid., 7–25. Indeed, the intentional connection between the *Anthologia Latina* and the poetry of Classical Rome is driven home by the inclusion within the collection of Classical Roman pieces.

subsidized runs of the *annona* being organized through Carthage, the open market led to an increase in competition. Indeed, much of Carthage's competition came from Hadrumetum in Byzacena, within the Vandal kingdom. Hadrumetum and Byzacena likewise asserted their independence from Carthage in the religious sphere, with their poor attendance at the council in 525.

The Vandal era did, nevertheless, see an overall expansion of Carthaginian authority, largely stemming from its position as capital of the Vandal state. Part of this shift was increased dominance in Sardinia, Corsica, and the Balearics. Carthage's dominance in these areas was not solely political, but also economic, and, through an odd course of events, religious. While these areas were brought under Carthaginian control through military conquest, they were brought close to the city through a strong trade in everyday goods, witnessed in the small Vandal currency found there. Equally as deep was the connection formed between Carthage and Cagliari through the exile of the African Catholic Church to the latter in the early sixth century. Carthage's status as the Vandal capital also shifted its relationship with other urban centers within the Vandal realm through the redirection of the old Roman tax system to the city. Carthage was no longer a proconsular city, but, in effect, an imperial one. In the early period, Carthage expressed her independent power through piracy and the cities of the Mediterranean feared her fleets. With the death of Gaiseric, however, Carthage shifted away from aggression, yet remained, to an extent, more dominant because of it. In the latter half of the Vandal century, Carthage's rulers sought to assert the city's cultural dominance, rather than its military. Its power and independence were proclaimed by the poets who flocked to the city and worked under the patronage of its Romano-African and Vandal elites. Carthage not only retained its cultural and intellectual dominance within Africa, but developed this dominance into a great flourishing of the arts. Late antique Carthage was one of the great cities of the Roman world, dominant and powerful. The Vandal occupation did not end this, but it did reorient the city within its wider network of urban interactions.

Bibliography

Primary

Anthologia Latina I. Edited by David R. Shackleton Bailey. Stuttgart: Teubner, 1982.

Anthologia Latina sive poesis latinae supplementum. Pars Prior: Carmina in codicibus scripta. Fasciculus I: Libri Salmasiani aliorumque carmina. Edited by Alexander Riese. Leipzig: Teubner, 1894.

Ferrandus. *Vita Fulgentii. Vie de Saint Fulgence de Ruspe de Ferrand, Diacre de Carthage.* Edited and translated by Gabriel-Guillaume Lapeyre. Paris: Lethielleux, 1929.

Procopius. *History of the Wars, Volume II: Books 3–4 (Vandalic War).* Edited and translated by Henry B. Dewing. Loeb Classical Library 81. Cambridge: Harvard University Press, 1916.

Victor of Vita. *Historia persecutionis africanae provinciae sub Geiserico et Hunirico regibus Wandalorum.* Edited by Karl Halm. Berlin: Weidmann, 1879.

Secondary

Bonifay, Michel. *Études sur la céramique romaine tardive d'Afrique.* BAR International Series 1301. Oxford: Archaeopress, 2004.

Clover, Frank M. "Felix Karthago." *Dumbarton Oaks Papers* 40 (1986): 1–16. DOI: 10.2307/1291526.

———. "A Game of Bluff: The Fate of Sicily after A.D. 476." *Historia: Zeitschrift für alte Geschichte* 48, no. 2 (1999): 235–44.

———. "Timekeeping and Dyarchy in Vandal Africa." *Antiquité Tardive* 11 (2003): 45–63. DOI: 10.1484/J.AT.2.300249.

Conant, Jonathan P. "Europe and the African Cult of Saints, Circa 350–900: An Essay in Mediterranean Communications." *Speculum* 85, no. 1 (2010): 1–46. DOI: 10.1017/S0038713409990935.

———. *Staying Roman: Conquest and Identity in Africa and the Mediterranean, 439–700.* Cambridge: Cambridge University Press, 2012.

Courtois, Christian. *Les Vandales et l'Afrique.* Paris: Arts et Métiers Graphiques, 1955.

Goodman, Penelope J. *The Roman City and Its Periphery: From Rome to Gaul.* Oxford: Routledge, 2007. DOI: 10.4324/9780203446256.

Hayes, John W. *Late Roman Pottery.* London: British School at Rome, 1972.

Hen, Yitzhak. Roman Barbarians: *The Royal Court and Culture in the Early Medieval West.* Basingstoke: Palgrave Macmillan, 2007. DOI: 10.1057/9780230593640.

Hobson, Matthew S. *The North African Boom: Evaluating Economic Growth in the Roman Province of Africa Proconsularis (146 B.C.–A.D. 439).* Journal of Roman Archaeology Supplementary Series 100. Portsmouth: Journal of Roman Archaeology, 2015.

Holum, Kenneth G. "The Classical City in the Sixth Century: Survival and Transformation." In *The Cambridge Companion to the Age of Justinian,* edited by Michael Maas, 87–112. Cambridge: Cambridge University Press, 2005. DOI: 10.1017/CCOL0521817463.004.

Humphrey, John H. "Vandal and Byzantine Carthage: Some New Archaeological Evidence." In *New Light on Ancient Carthage,* edited by John Griffiths Pedley, 85–120. Ann Arbor: University of Michigan Press, 1980.

Kay, Nigel M. *Epigrams from the Anthologia Latina: Text, Translation and Commentary.* London: Duckworth, 2006.

Leone, Anna. *The End of the Ancient City: Religion, Economy, and Urbanism in Late Antique North Africa.* Oxford: Oxford University Press, 2013. DOI: 10.1093/acprof:oso/9780199570928.001.0001.

Lepelley, Claude. "The Survival and Fall of the Classical City in Late Roman Africa." In *The City in Late Antiquity,* edited by John Rich, 50–76. London: Routledge, 1992.

Liebeschuetz, Wolfgang. "The End of the Ancient City." In *The City in Late Antiquity,* edited by John Rich, 1–49. London: Routledge, 1992.

Merrills, Andrew H. "The Secret of My Succession: Dynasty and Crisis in Vandal North Africa." *Early Medieval Europe* 18, no. 2 (2010): 135–59. DOI: 10.1111/j.1468-0254.2010.00293.x.

Merrills, Andrew H., and Richard Miles. *The Vandals.* Oxford and Malden: Wiley Blackwell, 2010. DOI: 10.1002/9781444318074.

Miles, Richard. "The *Anthologia Latina* and the Creation of Secular Space in Vandal Carthage." *Antiquité Tardive* 13 (2005): 305–20. DOI: 10.1484/J.AT.2.301785.

Modéran, Yves. "L'Afrique et la persécution vandale." In *Nouvelle Histoire du Christianisme, des origines à nos jours. III Les Églises d'Orient et d'Occident,* edited by Luce Pietri, 247–78. Paris: Desclée-Fayard, 1998.

———. *Les Vandales et l'Empire romain.* Edited by Michel-Yves Perrin. Arles: Éditions Errance, 2014.

———. "L'établissement territorial des Vandales en Afrique." *Antiquité Tardive* 10 (2002): 87–122. DOI: 10.1484/J.AT.2.300429.

Morrisson, Cécile. "L'Atelier de Carthage et la diffusion de la monnaie frappe dans l'Afrique vandal et byzantine (439–695)." *Antiquité Tardive* 11 (2003): 65–84. DOI: 10.1484/J.AT.2.300250.

Moussy, Claude. "Introduction." In *Dracontius: Oeuvres I,* edited by Claude Moussy and Collette Camus, 7–136. Paris: Les Belles Lettres, 2002.

Rosenblum, Morris. *Luxorius: A Latin Poet Among the Vandals.* New York: Columbia University Press, 1961.

Schwarcz, Andreas. "The Settlement of the Vandals in North Africa." In *Vandals, Romans and Berbers: New Perspectives on Late Antique North Africa,* edited by Andrew H. Merills, 49–57. Aldershot: Ashgate, 2004.

Sears, Gareth. *Late Roman African Urbanism: Continuity and Transformation in the City.* BAR International Series 1693. Oxford: Archaeopress, 2007.

———. *The Cities of Roman Africa.* Stroud: The History Press, 2011.

Tizzoni, Mark Lewis. *The Poems of Dracontius in their Vandalic and Visigothic Contexts.* Ph.D. diss, University of Leeds, 2012.

Warmington, Brian Herbert. *The North African Provinces from Diocletian to the Vandal Conquest.* rpt. Westport: Greenwood, 1971.

Wickham, Christopher. *Framing the Early Middle Ages: Europe and the Mediterranean, 400–800.* Oxford: Oxford University Press, 2005. DOI: 10.1093/acprof:oso/9780199264490.001.0001.

10

Good Neighbors and Good Walls: Urban Development and Trade Networks in Late Antique South Gaul

Douglas Underwood

Introduction

The Roman Empire, as a political entity, can be (and often is) conceptualized as a nested bundle of center–periphery relationships. Rome served as the center for the provinces, the provincial capitals served as the center for the second-rank towns, and so on. In many regards, this model is helpful — it helps track socio-economic flows from peripheral spaces to central nodes and gives some structure to the network of cities that composed the empire of the first three centuries CE. Yet, this kind of hierarchical viewpoint, which sees only vertical relationships, can obscure the horizontal relationships and interactions between cities of similar size and importance. Looking at the various links — personal, cultural, and economic — between a single region or across neighboring regions can begin to supplement the (generally) unidirectional periphery-to-center model with a more nuanced picture of relationships between neighbors.

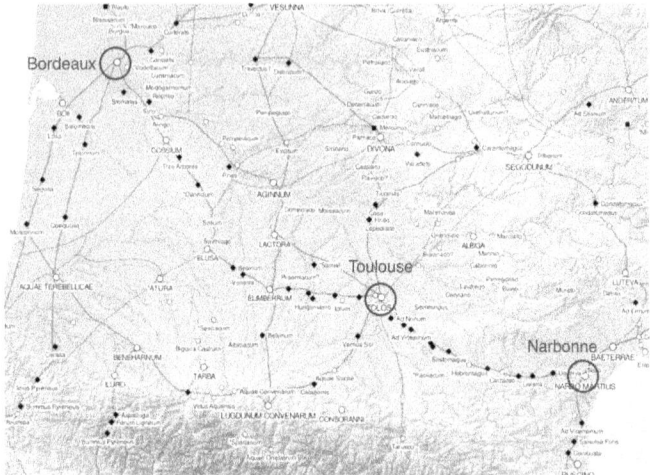

Fig. 1. South Gaul. From the Digital Map of the Roman Empire. Pelia-
gos Project, http://pelagios.org/maps/greco-roman/.

The corridor across the south of France linking the Mediterranean and the Atlantic (fig. 1) provides a case study in which to
look at these kinds of horizontal connections, as there is strong
literary and archaeological evidence for the links between its cities. This network had three major nodes, with Toulouse (Roman
Tolosa) in the center connected to port cities on both coasts,
Bordeaux (Burdigala) near the Atlantic and Narbonne (Narbo)
the Mediterranean, with a number of smaller cities between.
This paper will then survey the relationships along this network
of cities, focusing on the period of the third to fifth centuries.
This is a particularly interesting time for this region — the dominion of the Roman state in Gaul was beginning to falter, finally culminating with the settlement of the Visigoths in Aquitania
in the early fifth century, with their capital at Toulouse, and the
expansion of their kingdom into Narbonensis. While this study
does not aim to set out any new methodologies for understanding the links between urban centers in the Roman period, it
will explore what can be gathered from the current evidence for

links as they are known and to build a composite picture of a more horizontal relationship between a group of cities.

There are difficulties, as always, in such an undertaking, most directly in finding specific evidence for links between cities. We must look across a range of evidence to catch glimpses of interactions. Often connections can be seen in literary accounts which note individuals moving around the empire. For the cities of southern Gaul, the accounts of the two most prolific authors of the period, Ausonius (c. 310–395) and Sidonius Apollinaris (c. 430–489) will provide the most insight into how and why the aristocratic and educated classes moved along this corridor. For example, Ausonius's *Commemoratio professorum Burdigalensium* recounts the lives of thirty-five teachers from the author's hometown of Bordeaux. While not biographies as such, these elegies do give some indications of the abodes of the individual teachers and how and why they move between places. Beyond textual accounts, links can be explored between cities by examining their built heritage and how architectural and urbanistic models were shared and adapted. This has historically been seen as a center-to-periphery phenomenon, where provincial artists and architects looked to Rome or Italy for their models.[1] More recently, however, scholars have begun to take tentative steps to understand how art and architecture may have worked in a more localized context.[2] The cities of south Gaul changed significantly in late antiquity in terms of urban defense, public monuments and spaces, and Christianization; this paper will sketch

---

1   Perhaps best summarized by John Bryan Ward-Perkins in his *Roman Imperial Architecture* (New Haven: Yale University Press, 1981) in a comment about the western provinces: "a civilization which in almost all its manifestations stemmed more or less directly from Italy" (214).

2   See Lynne C. Lancaster, *Innovative Vaulting in the Architecture of the Roman Empire: 1st to 4th Centuries CE* (New York: Cambridge University Press, 2015) on the spread of vaulting innovations, or for a more general picture, see Natalie Kampen, "Roman Art and Architecture in the Provinces and beyond the Roman World" in *The Oxford Handbook of Greek and Roman Art and Architecture,* ed. Clemente Marconi (New York: Oxford University Press, 2014), 395–416.

Fig. 2. Mosaic of the Narbonne traders in the piazzale delle corporazioni, Ostia. Photo: Sailko, Wikimedia commons.

out the growing body of archaeological evidence and recent work on the evolution of each city between the third and fifth centuries, looking at the ways in which their urban trajectories interacted with and reflected local and regional developments. Finally, connections between neighbors can also be seen in trading partners, as for example, in the Piazzale delle Corporazioni at Ostia, where mosaics represented the corporations of guilds and traders who brought in goods from around the empire, like the group of shippers from Narbonne (fig. 2). For the cities of south Gaul, an exploration of the creation and distribution of a locally made imitation fineware pottery called *dérivées de sigillées paléochrétiennes* (known more concisely as DSP), will provide evidence of these kinds of trade between the cities and the economic networks across this linked corridor.

Geography

Starting in the west, Bordeaux sits along a bend in the Garonne (Garumna) river, just south of its outlet into the Garonne Estuary, on to the Bay of Biscay and the Atlantic Ocean. In antiquity, the city was confined to the west bank of the river, and not connected to the east, except by ferry.[3] Upriver (that is, south-east) from Bordeaux, almost halfway between the Atlantic and Mediterranean and close to the upper-most navigable point of the Garonne River is Toulouse. Roman Toulouse was primarily confined to the east bank of the river, but there were impor-tant urban features in the west, like the amphitheater in modern Purpan, northeast of the city. Continuing east, Toulouse is about 40 kilometers (25 miles) west of the Seuil de Naurouze gap, the watershed between the Atlantic and Mediterranean, which sits at 217 meters (711 feet) above sea level. A few small rivers flow from this point and join the Aude (Atax) river, which flows from the Pyrenees, near Carcassonne. Following the river down toward the Mediterranean, Narbonne sits about a dozen miles from the coast, on a small projection of land which dominates the surrounding low plains. In this way, Narbonne was stra-tegically placed with easy overland access to both the Roman province of Hispania as well as river access to the interior of Gaul and the Gulf of Lion. The total distance between Bordeaux and Narbonne is 429 kilometers (267 miles). Between the major nodes in this network were smaller centers as well, such as Car-cassonne (Carcasso), Bram (Ebriomagus), Lectoure (Lactora), and Agen (Aginnum).

A trip between the sea and the ocean was possible by river, following the Aude from the Mediterranean coast inland for a distance, then up through the gap overland, and then by the Garonne from Toulouse down to the Atlantic. This route is re-ported by Strabo, who says, "from Narbo traffic goes inland for a short distance by the Atax River, and then a greater distance by land to the Garumna River; and this latter distance is about eight hundred or seven hundred stadia [c. 125–110 kilometers/79–68 miles]. And the Garumna, too, flows to the ocean."[4] After the

3   Robert Étienne, *Histoire de Bordeaux 1, Bordeaux antique* (Bordeaux: Fé-dération historique du Sud-Ouest, 1962), 18.

4   Strabo, *Geography, Volume II: Books 3–5,* trans. Horace Leonard Jones, Loeb Classical Library 50 (Cambridge: Harvard University Press, 1923), 4.1.14: "ἐκ δὲ Νάρβωνος ἀναπλεῖται μὲν ἐπὶ μικρὸν τῷ Ἄτακι, πεζεύεται δὲ πλέον ἐπὶ

conquest of the region by Rome in the second century BCE, a major road — the Via Aquitania — was built, which paralleled, to some extent, the course of the rivers.[5]

Historical Background

The area north of the Pyrenees came under Roman dominion over several decades, beginning not long after the Second Punic War, as Rome began to exert more influence along the coastal route between Italy and the Iberian Peninsula. A colony was established at Narbonne around 118 BCE, and a Roman garrison housed at Toulouse at the end of the second century BCE, both near earlier *oppida* settlements.[6] Roman control over the area, and specifically over the movement of goods, is clear from the early first century BCE: Fonteius was accused by the Gauls of unfairly taxing wine moving from Narbonne to Bordeaux during his governorship there in the late 70s BCE.[7] While remaining marginally under Roman control, there were a number of serious tribal uprisings and rebellions in Gaul in the early first century BCE. Starting in 58 BCE, Caesar's campaigns brought a stronger Roman military and administrative presence to the region, especially the north and west. He largely conquered the region of Aquitaine in 56 BCE, although there were revolts until the early 30s BCE. Southern Gaul, already somewhat Romanized, benefited from greater stability of the increasing presence of Roman administration and the development of more trade

τὸν Γαρούναν ποταμόν, καὶ τοῦθ᾽ ὅσον ὀκτακοσίων ἢ ἑπτακοσίων σταδίων· ῥεῖ δὲ καὶ ὁ Γαρούνας εἰς τὸν ὠκεανόν."

5   For more information on the Roman road network radiating from Toulouse, see Michel Labrousse, *Tolouse antique, des origins à l'établissement des wisigoths* (Paris: Boccard, 1968), 334–60.

6   Narbonne: Albert Lionel Frederick Rivet, *Gallia Narbonensis: Southern France in Roman Times* (London: B.T. Batsford, 1988), 47–48; Toulouse: Charles Ebel, *Transalpine Gaul: The Emergence of a Roman Province,* Studies of the Dutch Archaeological and Historical Society 4 (Boston and Leiden: Brill, 1976), 93.

7   Étienne, *Bordeaux antique,* 94–98.

routes. Augustus reorganized Gaul soon after 27 BCE, creating the province of Narbonensis with its capital at Narbonne, and the province of Aquitania, with its capital at Saintes (Mediolanum Santonum), in addition to the other Gallic provinces of Lugdenensis and Belgica. Likely in conjunction with this reorganization, Toulouse was re-founded, some seven kilometers (four miles) away from the *oppidum,* as a Roman colony.[8] Slightly later in the early first century CE, Bordeaux was rebuilt along a Roman-style plan, adopting an orthogonal street grid.[9] In short, by the mid-first century CE at the latest, the cities of south Gaul were politically Roman and had largely adopted Roman urban forms, like walls, *capitolia,* baths, fora, and spectacle buildings.

During the following two and a half centuries southern Gaul benefited from the *pax Romana,* and witnessed an increase in economic activity, driven in part by the trade networks established across the region. Strabo, for example, notes that Narbonne is wonderfully situated for trade, communication and providing the necessities of life."[10] Additionally, Bordeaux, situated near the confluence of the Dordogne and Garonne rivers, was an important trading post for goods moving, via the Atlantic, to and from northern France and eventually England.[11] Toulouse thus served as a central hub of this trans-Gallic trade network. While the cost of transporting cargo across south Gaul would have been somewhat higher than sailing around the Iberian Peninsula (due to the costs associated with some overland transport), it was still a major axis for trade, and the fastest and most direct route from anywhere in the Mediterranean to the Bay of Biscay. The continuing centrality of this route is seen in the *Itinerarium Burdigalense* of 333, which outlines the pilgrim-

---

8 Labrousse, *Tolouse antique,* 144.
9 Étienne, *Bordeaux antique,* 87. Bordeaux probably did not obtain Latin rights until the later first century and seems only to have become the provincial capital in the second or third century (possibly not until the Diocletianic reforms).
10 Strabo, *Geography,* 4.1.14.
11 Étienne, *Bordeaux antique,* 136.

age route to Jerusalem from Bordeaux.[12] It lists the *mutationes,* the changing stations, the *mansiones,* guest houses, as well as the *civitates* along the route. Between Bordeaux and Narbonne, the cities of Bazas (Vasatas), Eauze (Elusa), Auch (Auscius), and Toulouse (Tolosa) are listed. The route of the *Itinerarium* (being a road journey) did not utilize the riverine shortcuts, even on the descent down the Aude valley to Narbonne.

The first troubles for this region came during the mid-third century CE, when Gaul — particularly the northern regions of Belgica, Germania Superior, and Germania Inferior — suffered "barbarian" invasions in several waves from the 250s to the 270s.[13] While southern Gaul was mostly (although not completely) untroubled by these early incursions, notable changes to the urban fabric began to occur around this time, perhaps as a consequence of increasing uncertainty, which would, within a century or so, lead to a quite distinct "late Roman" city. These include the construction of urban fortifications, the tailing off of major urban monumental construction, the first signs of the Christianization of the landscape, the encroachment on public spaces, amongst others (discussed further below).[14] Beyond the breakdown of the *limes,* a weak central government in Rome

---

12 Of course, this route was for transportation, not specifically for commerce. For more information on the whole document see Jas Elsner, "The *Itinerarium Burdigalense*: Politics and Salvation in the Geography of Constantine's Empire," *The Journal of Roman Studies* 90 (2000): 181–95.

13 Simon Esmonde Cleary, *The Roman West, AD 200–500: An Archaeological Study* (Cambridge: Cambridge University Press, 2013), 23–40.

14 There are a number of good studies on the evolution of the late antique urban landscape. Besides the aforementioned Esmonde Cleary (*The Roman West*), which covers Gaul and Spain there are also very good single-region surveys covering the rest of the west: Bryan Ward-Perkins, *From Classical Antiquity to the Middle Ages: Urban Building in Northern and Central Italy, AD 300–850* (Oxford: Oxford University Press, 1984); Neil Christie, *From Constantine to Charlemagne: An Archaeology of Italy, AD 300–800* (Ashgate: Aldershot, 2006), ch. 3; Michael Kulikowski, *Late Roman Spain and Its Cities* (Baltimore: John Hopkins University Press, 2004); and Anna Leone, *Changing Townscapes in North Africa from Late Antiquity to the Arab Conquest* (Bari: Edipuglia, 2007).

during this period, with over twenty-five claimants to the throne between 235 and 284, and the breakaway "Gallic Empire" under Postumus from 260 to 269 (which lasted under several others until 274, although portions of Narbonensis were brought under Roman control by Claudius Gothicus at the end of Postumus's reign) resulted in a turbulent half-century for southern Gaul.[15]

The fourth century, however, saw a return of relative peace and prosperity after the troubles of the third. Under Diocletian's reorganization of the provinces, Narbonensis and Aquitania were divided into five provinces: Narbonensis I and II, Aquitania I and II and Novempopulana, each with their own capital; Narbonne maintained its administrative importance and Bordeaux was made the provincial capital, if it was not, by this point, already the provincial capital. Yet, by the later fourth century, the bonds connecting southern Gaul to the imperial center of Rome began to fray. While the narrative is broad and complex (and mostly beyond the scope of this study), the important points for this region focus on one of the Germanic tribes that had entered the empire in the later fourth century, the Visigoths, led by Alaric, who infamously besieged and sacked Rome in 410. In the aftermath, they moved into Gaul, and the tribe was eventually given a large portion of the province of Aquitania along the Garonne river in 418.[16] The Visigoths were not content with this grant and soon began to expand their to territory, effectively extinguishing Roman dominion in southwest Gaul.[17] Over the next generation, they continued to expand into Spain, displacing or conquering two further Germanic tribes, the Vandals and

---

15 John F. Drinkwater, *The Gallic Empire: Separatism and Continuity in the North-Western Provinces of the Roman Empire, A.D. 260–274* (Stuttgart: Franz Steiner Verlag Wiesbaden, 1987), ch. 1.

16 The "Visigothic Settlement," as this transaction is known, is a particularly unclear and contested historical event. For two recent interpretations (including the argument for 418 over 419), see the chapters (1 and 2, respectively) by Schwarcz and Kulikowski in *Society and Culture in Late Antique Gaul*, ed. Ralph Mathisen and Danuta Shanzer (Aldershot: Ashgate, 2001).

17 Guy Halsall, *Barbarian Migrations and the Roman West, 376–568* (Cambridge: Cambridge University Press, 2007), 228–33.

Alans, who had settled there. Thus, by the middle of the fifth century, the Visigoths under their king Euric (r. 466–484) controlled most of the former regions of Gaul and Spain from their capital at Toulouse.[18]

The Visigoths maintained this kingdom until the Franks, another Germanic tribe unified by the skilled general Clovis, began to push downwards from the lower Rhine region. The Visigoths ceded the south-west and their Toulouse fell to the Franks in 507 after the battle of Vouillé.[19] The coastal region around Narbonne was brought into the Visigothic kingdom when the city was handed over by the Roman *comes* Agrippinus to the Visigothic king Theuderic II (r. 453–466).[20] The Franks ruled most of Gaul for several centuries, but never conquered the coastal region of Septimania, the old Roman province of Gallia Narbonensis. This territory, outside of briefly falling into Ostrogothic hands, remained part of the Visigothic kingdom until it was conquered by the Muslim armies of Al-Samh ibn Malik in 719.[21]

Literary Connections

Turning to the specific links between Bordeaux, Toulouse, Narbonne, and points between, we can look across several kinds of evidence — both historical and archaeological. To begin the survey, the lives of individuals and the orbit of connections they created and reinforced can show the personal links between cities, indicating how people and ideas moved. In this regard, two late antique Gallic authors, Ausonius and Sidonius Apollinaris, provide the richest insights into the people and places of south Gaul across the fourth and fifth centuries.

---

18 Peter J. Heather, *The Fall of the Roman Empire: A New History of Rome and the Barbarians* (Oxford: Oxford University Press, 2006), 415–25.

19 Roger Collins, *Visigothic Spain, 409–711* (Malden: Blackwell, 2004), 33.

20 Frank Riess, *Narbonne and Its Territory in Late Antiquity: From the Visigoths to the Arabs* (Farnham: Ashgate, 2016), 57.

21 Riess, *Narbonne and Its Territory,* 227.

Ausonius was born in Bordeaux to a well-to-do family.[22] He was educated there as well as in Toulouse and moved to Constantinople for a time, before turning to a teaching career in his hometown. Some thirty years later, he was brought into the imperial household by Valentinian I (r. 364–375) as a tutor for the future emperor Gratian (r. 375–383).[23] His prose, poetry and letters are important for understanding the aristocratic literati of fourth-century Gaul. In one of his poems, the *Ordo urbium nobilium,* in which he writes about twenty major cities around the empire, Bordeaux, Toulouse, and Narbonne all feature — in fact, they are three out of the five Gallic cities commemorated, alongside Trier and Arles.[24] This highlights the continued significance, even if from the perspective of a native son, of the cities of south Gaul.

But we get a better glimpse of the lives and movements of individuals in the aforementioned *Commemoratio professorum Burdigalensium.*[25] While there are many relocations recorded in the poems, both within Gaul as well as around the empire, there are a few key cases of movement across the Garonne-Aude corridor. Sedatus, who hails from Bordeaux (poem 19) moved around a good deal, or so it seems, but settled in Toulouse. Exuperius similarly moved a good deal in his career, eventually gaining an imperial post. Ausonius reports his early career moves: born in Bordeaux, then "the councillors of Toulouse, that home of Pallas, received you with adoration, but soon drove you as lightly away. Then Narbo harbored you."[26] Similarly, Marcellus was driven away from his homeland of Bordeaux,

22 Hugh G. Evelyn White, "Introduction," in Ausonius, *Volume I: Books 1–17,* Loeb Classical Library 96 (Cambridge: Harvard University Press, 1919), vi–xlv, at viii.

23 Ibid., x.

24 Riess, *Narbonne and Its Territory,* 38.

25 Ausonius, *Poems Commemorating the Professors of Bordeaux,* in *Volume I: Books 1–17,* trans. Hugh G. Evelyn-White, Loeb Classical Library 96 (Cambridge: Harvard University Press, 1919).

26 Ausonius, *Commemoratio,* 17: "Palladiae primum toga te venerata Tolosae mox pepulit levitate pari. Narbo inde recepit."

but "in Narbo, you found the country you had lost."[27] Ausonius himself can be considered here, as he started his education at Bordeaux, but probably finished it in Toulouse. After spending some time in Constantinople, Ausonius returned to Bordeaux to begin his own teaching career. Similarly, his maternal uncle, Aemilius Arborius, was born at Dax, began teaching at Toulouse and then eventually moved to Narbonne before venturing further abroad.[28] From these handful of cases, we can see that movement between Bordeaux, Toulouse, and Narbonne was not uncommon, and largely driven by career motivations, but also some personal affinities for certain people and places.

Sidonius Apollinaris, one of the most celebrated fifth-century writers, was born in Lyon (Lugdunum) to a political family — his father was the Prefect of Gaul and his grandfather the Praetorian Prefect of Gaul.[29] He married the daughter of the Emperor Avitus (r. 455–456), and himself became urban prefect of Rome. Importantly, he became bishop of Clermont-Ferrand (Augustonemetum), where he was captured by the Visigoths in the early 470s as they expanded their control over Gaul.[30] In another instance in this conflict, he was kept in Bordeaux for several months by Euric, the Visigothic king.[31] With his extensive travels as well as being a witness to the Roman loss of Gaul, Sidonius is a prime source for the culture and politics of the fifth century. His letters especially show the movements of people and their connections across regions in this tumultuous period. He writes to a number of friends and colleagues that lived across Gaul, and particularly in the towns and cities between Bordeaux

27 Ausonius, *Commemoratio*, 18: "amissam […] Narbo dedit patriam."
28 Ausonius, *Parentalia*, in *Volume I: Books 1–17*, trans. Hugh G. Evelyn-White, Loeb Classical Library 96 (Cambridge: Harvard University Press, 1919), 3.11–12.
29 Jill Harries, *Sidonius Apollinaris and the Fall of Rome, AD 407–485* (Oxford: Clarendon Press, 1994), 26.
30 Ibid., 169.
31 Ormonde M. Dalton, *The Letters of Sidonius* (Oxford: Clarendon Press, 1915), xlv.

and Narbonne.[32] In general, the links between these places are not as immediately apparent as they are in Ausonius, as Sidonius and his social circle spend relatively little time discussing the cities they visit. Yet some connections are still apparent. For example, in *Epistle* 8.12, Sidonius questions why his friend Trygetius has tarried in Bazas (Vasatium), a town along the road to Toulouse, only twelve miles from Bordeaux, instead of visiting him in Bordeaux.[33] He attempts to entice a visit with the offer of local oysters, fair weather, and companionship, while trying to imagine what possible hindrances could have kept Trygetius from traveling this short distance.

Thus, we can see that short trips along this network, while still somewhat burdensome, were not outrageous expectations for friends; movement along this corridor was considered regular in the fifth century.

Material Connections

While the literary evidence for connections between cities is useful for understanding why and how frequently individuals traveled from one to another, the picture it presents is, naturally, quite limited. It shows the views of a relatively narrow band of society — here educators and aristocrats — who have the ability to record their experiences. There was a significant portion of Roman society that left no or little trace in the textual record. To further understand the interactions between these localities, as non-literary (or at least those whose writings have survived) citizens understand and experienced them, we can turn to the material record, which is somewhat more egalitarian in terms of the agents that participated in it. There are two distinct strands that can shed light on the relationship between Bordeaux, Toulouse, and Narbonne, as well as the smaller centers between

---

32 Harries, *Sidonius Apollinaris,* 7–10.
33 Sidonius, *Poems. Letters: Books 3–9,* trans. William Blair Anderson, Loeb Classical Library 420 (Cambridge: Harvard University Press, 1965).

them. The first is the urban development of the three cities, where we will be able to trace out some hints of motivation, including competition, in the building of public monuments and the development of the urban landscape. The second is in the ceramic record, especially looking at the movement of DSP, a late antique regional fineware pottery style that was produced in south Gaul, distinguished by its use of stamped decoration.[34]

Urban Development

The cities between the Atlantic and Mediterranean along the Aude–Garonne corridor changed considerably between the Roman conquest and that of the Franks — not surprising for a period of over six centuries. The first phase came in the second and first centuries BCE, as Roman-type cities began to be established, either *ex novo* or replacing earlier *oppida* — the fortified villages that constituted the bulk of the settlement-types in pre-Roman Gaul.[35] The early years of all the cities in this region were marked with the development of Roman urban forms, most visible in an orthogonal street grid, along with public monuments like temples and baths, as an ever-expanding road system led to increased wealth and the elites, including the emperor or the imperial household, took up the practice of monumental euergetism. For example, *capitolia* were constructed at both Toulouse and Narbonne; while both are partially known archaeologically, only Toulouse's is reasonably well dated to the second half of the first century CE.[36] The cities in this region continued to develop

---

34 Of course, relying too heavily on the ceramic record is not without its troubles, as noted by Simon T. Loseby in "The Ceramic Data and the Transformation of the Roman World," in LRCW 2. *Late Roman Course Wares, Cooking Wares and Amphorae in the Mediterranean: Archaeology and Archaeometry,* ed. Michel Bonifay and Jean-Christophe Trégrila (Oxford: Archaeopress, 2007), 2–5.

35 Greg Woolf, *Becoming Roman: The Origins of Provincial Civilization in Gaul* (Cambridge: Cambridge University Press, 1998), 109.

36 Jean-Charles Arramond and Jean-Luc Boudartchouk, "Le Capitolium de Tolosa?" *Gallia* 54 (1997): 203–38, at 217.

along the same lines over the next two centuries, although most major public building was in place by the mid-first century CE.

The cities of south Gaul — and of much of the Roman empire — began to undergo significant changes from the third century onwards.[37] While there is little direct evidence for destruction (e.g., at the hands of invaders) at any point in the third century, the urban forms of these cities (as with many throughout Gaul, and indeed, throughout much of the Western empire) started to change notably in the aftermath of the crises. The drivers behind these changes are both diverse and difficult to fully identify, and, in any case, too expansive to do justice to here.[38] Nevertheless, the ways that late antique cities, or at least Gallic cities, were changing can be fairly superficially summarized: city walls were constructed around a comparably small core, either through the construction of a circuit wall around a previously undefended town or through the re-establishment of existing (largely Augustan-era) fortifications; urban population declined and burials began to infiltrate *pomerium* boundaries; public monuments and spaces (from temples to amphitheaters) were progressively disused, and then either spoliated for building materials or re-used for various purposes like housing and small-scale industry; the orthogonal street-system was encroached upon and distorted; urban spaces, and eventually public spaces, were gradually Christianized, that is, converted to religious usage. Eventually, the stereotypical medieval town, with strong fortifications, winding alleys centered around churches comes into view.

However, such an overview does not tell the full story — it highlights the major trends, but fails to take into account any local variation, both in terms of what happened in each locality and in terms of chronology. Such changes to late antique cit-

---

37 This is best summarized in Marc Heijmans, "La place des monuments publics du Haut-Empire dans les villes de la Gaule méridionale durant l'antiquité tardive (IVᵉ–VIᵉ s.)," *Gallia* 63 (2006): 25–41.

38 See Douglas Underwood, *(Re)using Ruins: Public Building in the Cities of the Late Antique West, A.D. 300–600* (Boston and Leiden: Brill, 2019).

ies did not constitute a single wave of transformation sweeping over the Roman empire. Rather, there was considerable dispar-ity in how and to what degree changes took place as a result of the size and economic vitality of a city, its demographic changes, historical events and the like. For example, in the above-noted list of urban evolutions, a number of Gallic cities, particularly those with functional early walls, like Marseille and Toulouse, did not construct a reduced enceinte.[39] But Autun, which did have a larger Augustan wall, only utilized one small corner of it, combining the old with a new section to create a small enclosed city.[40] And the chronology of the construction of these enceintes ranged over two centuries: at Bordeaux (see below), there is fair evidence for a late-third century construction, while at Saint-Bertrand-de-Comminges in the Pyrenees, the wall was a fifth century project.[41] As a further illustration of this complexity, we can look briefly at baths in late antique Gaul. Again, at St-Bertrand-de-Comminges, both the primary temple and baths adjacent to the forum were destroyed in the late fourth or early fifth century. However, shortly after this demolition, a small (less than 300 m²/3229 sq. feet) bath suite, made of low quality and differing materials, was built in the peribolos, or enclosure, of the temple precinct, adjacent to the old baths.[42] These baths went out of use by the middle of the fifth century. In contrast, Les Thermes de la place Villeneuve-Bargemont in Marseille, otherwise a thriving late antique city, were abandoned in the second half of the fourth century; we know little about the us-age of other baths in that city in this period, so it is unknown whether public bathing disappeared entirely or only this single

---

39 Marseille: Simon T. Loseby, "Marseille: A Late Antique Success Story?" *Journal of Roman Studies* 82 (1992): 165–85; Toulouse: see below.

40 Johnson, *Late Roman*, 84.

41 Jason Wood, "The Wall Top of the Late-Roman Defences at Saint-Bertrand-de-Comminges: Interim Report." *Journal of Roman Archaeology* 15 (2002): 297–309.

42 Heijmans, "La place," 36.

edifice.[43] Still, this shows that even in a vibrant city, some buildings still were disused. Thus, the evolution of cities in late antique Gaul is not a single uniform process, where all the changes happened to all cities at the same time and rate. As a result, we must look more closely at each city to understand its development. The following section will (albeit somewhat superficially, given the scope of this study) look at the particular changes in the cities of the Garonne-Aude corridor, especially to see what is similar or different between these three sites in the third to sixth centuries, in order to establish what their development in late antiquity can say about links between them.

The most substantial change to cities in late antique Gaul was the construction of urban fortifications.[44] These walls were bigger and more extensive than almost any other public monument built by the Romans and were the most common new urban monument built after the third century, and in many places were the only new major construction beyond an early church or cathedral. They also imposed a clear and definite boundary on the urban landscape, which limited interaction and funneled movement towards set perforations in a few impermeable boundaries. The three major nodes on the Garonne–Aude corridor, as well as some smaller cities, were fortified in this period. It is worth noting that a significant number of Gallic cities built walls over the period c. 300–500 CE, and this should not be considered a particularly localized phenomenon; nevertheless, the chronology and characteristics of these fortifications will suggest some links between the cities they enclosed.

---

43 Loseby, "Marseille," 169–70; Heijmans, "La place," 35.

44 For a broad, but somewhat outdated survey, see Stephen Johnson, *Late Roman Fortifications* (London: B.T. Batsford, 1983), ch. 2. More updated studies include Pierre Garmy and Louis Maurin, eds., *Enceintes romaines d'Aquitaine. Bordeaux, Dax, Périgueux, Bazas* (Paris: Éditions de la Maison des sciences de l'homme, 1996); Marc Heijmans, "La mise en défense de la Gaule méridionale aux IVe–VIe s." *Gallia* 63 (2006): 59–74. More recent studies have recognized that the fortification of Gaul was a much longer process than the fifty or so years that Johnson allows.

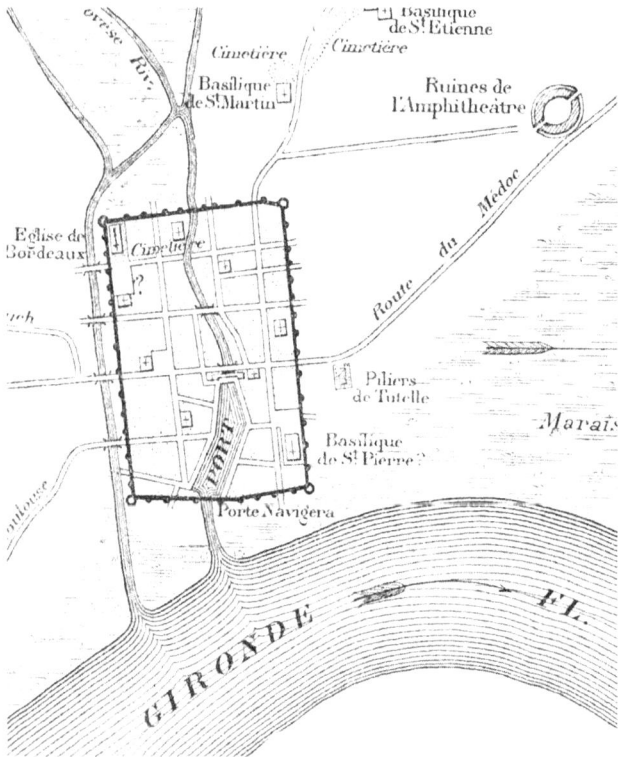

Fig. 3. Plan of Bordeaux. Adapted from Camille Jullian, *Histoire de Bordeaux depuis les origines jusqu'en 1895* (Bordeaux: Feret et fils, 1895), 87.

At Bordeaux, a rectangular-shaped fortification wall, running c. 2.34 kilometers (1.45 miles) and enclosing 32.5 hectares (80 acres), was constructed in the later third century (fig. 3).[45]

---

45 Dany Barraud, Jacques Linères, and Louis Maurin, "Bordeaux," in *Enceintes romaines d'Aquitaine: Bordeaux, Dax, Périgueux, Bazas,* ed. Garmy and Maruin, 15–80, at 49. The dating comes from a few pieces of evidence, none individually convincing, but together providing a reasonable consensus. A bath on the rue des Frères-Bonnes was destroyed to create the no-man's

Fig. 4. Late Antique Wall. Adapted from Camille Jullian, *Histoire de Bordeaux depuis les origines jusqu'en 1895* (Bordeaux: Feret et fils, 1895), 46.

The wall was constructed in the typical Roman fashion, with a concrete and rubble core faced on both sides. The lower courses of the wall (c. 6 meters/20 feet) were faced with *opus quadratum,* which was primarily or almost exclusively made of *spolia,* and the upper courses with small block work (known generally as *petit appareil*) (fig. 4). The exact height of the wall is unknown, but likely reached 9 to 10 meters (29–32 feet), and the width ranges from 4 meters (13 feet) near the base to 2.5 meters (8 feet)

land outside the wall, and coins from 261–266 and 274 were found in the backfill. In the wall itself, the latest datable epigraphic element notes the consulship of Postumus (260) and two coins noting Claudius Gothicus, dated to 270–273 and 275, were found in the fabric of the wall. For more details, see Cécile Doulan, *Bordeaux,* Carte archeologique de la Gaule 33.2 (Paris: Académie des Inscriptions et Belles-Lettres, 2013), 198.

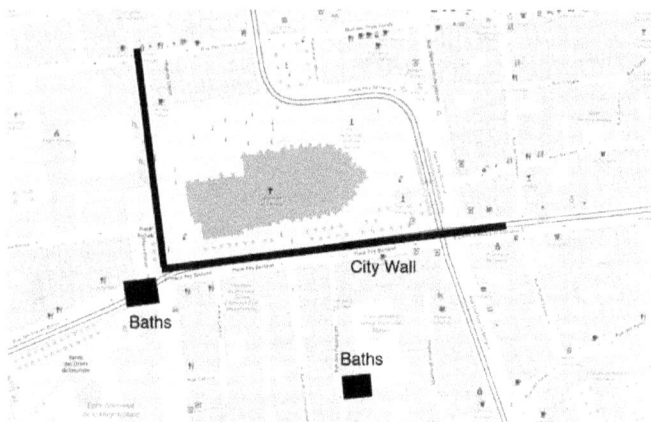

Fig. 5. Southwest corner of Late Antique Wall and Destroyed Baths. Image by the author; map data: Open Street Maps.

near the top. [46] The wall was equipped with semi-circular towers, slightly larger on the four corners, placed at seemingly irregular distances, as the surviving evidence for sixteen such towers indicates.[47] There is less evidence for gates, although there were at least three — the north and south exit of the *cardo maximus* and the western exit of the *decumanus* (the east was occupied by the port and river).

There are several points of evidence for the chronology of construction of the Bordeaux wall.[48] First, there are two coins from the thermal establishment to the south of the Cathedral, likely destroyed for the construction of the wall (fig. 5). One is of Gallienus (dated to 261–266) and the abovementioned Tetricus. From this site also came dateable ceramics, particularly Hayes 50A (dated 240–325), and an intermediary form between Hays 48 A (220–270) and B (260–320). In 1867, a coin of Claudius II,

---

46 Bernard Bachrach, "The Fortification of Gaul and the Economy of the Third and Fourth Centuries," *Journal of Late Antiquity* 3, no. 1 (2010): 38–64, at 44; Barraud, Linères, and Maurin, *Bordeaux,* 66.

47 Barraud, Linères, and Maurin, *Bordeaux,* 61.

48 Ibid., 75–76.

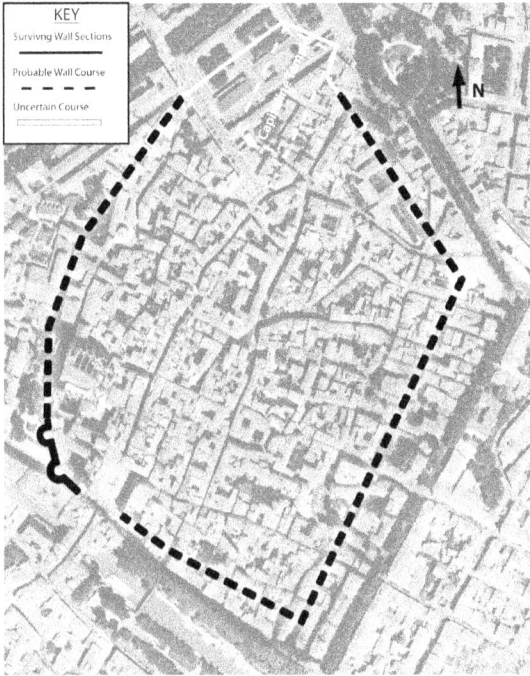

Fig. 6. Plan of Narbonne. Figure by the author; map data: Google.

called Gothicus, was found in between two large stones at the base of the wall. This coin has been dated to between 270 and 273. More recently, excavations in 2001–2003 near the cathedral uncovered another coin of Claudius Gothicus, which has been dated to after 275.[49] Specifically how these precise dates have been concluded by scholars is not clear (especially as Claudius died in 270), but a late-third century chronology is still clear. The latest inscription that has currently been uncovered from within the wall is a spolia epitaph that notes a consulship of Pos-

49 Doulan, *Bordeaux,* 198.

Fig. 7. Narbonne Wall. Photo by the author.

tumus in 260.[50] Further, the discovery of a necropolis not far beyond the north face of the wall, in which the earliest tombs have been dated to the early fourth century, provides a *terminus ante quem* (TAQ) for the wall.[51] In all, the evidence points to a construction date in the late third century.

At Narbonne, a 1.6-kilometer (1 mile), roughly pentagonal wall was built to enclose 17 hectares (42 acres) of the city (fig. 6). This fortification was built fully in *opus quadratum,* which was mostly faced with *spolia* largely turned inward towards the core (fig. 7). The wall was nearly 4 meters (13 feet) thick near its base, and rose to 1 meter (3 feet) near the top, which has been estimated to be well over 4 meters (13 feet).[52] The wall was given towers, but evidence for only five has survived; these suggest semi-circular projections with flat backs approximately 32 me-

---

50 *CIL* XIII.633. *Corpus Inscriptionum Latinarum,* vol. 13 (Berlin: De Gruyter, 1968).
51 Doulan, *Bordeaux,* 198.
52 Michel Gayraud, *Narbonne antique: des origines à la fin du IIIe siècle* (Paris: Ed. du Boccard, 1981), 287.

Fig. 8. Plan of Toulouse. Figure by the author; map data: Google.

ters (105 feet) apart, totaling between forty-five and fifty overall. There is little evidence for gates, but there must have been two, where the Via Domitia left the city, and more likely four at minimum, at the intersections of the wall and the major roads.

The date of the fortifications at Narbonne is not certain, but likely late antique. It was once thought to have been constructed in the years just before the Visigothic settlement in south Gaul in the early fifth century.[53] It is now believed to date to around the last quarter of the third century, based on two coins, a small bronze of Gallienus and a slightly larger bronze of Maximian, ap-

---

53 F.-P. Thiers, "Notes sur l'enceinte préwisigothique de Narbonne," *Bulletin de la commission archeologique du Narbonne* 1 (1891): 158–69, at 168.

parently found within the wall (although their precise find-spot was not recorded), which provide a *terminus post quem* (TPQ) of 260 CE for the Gallienus coin and 288 for that of Maximian.[54] Additionally, a *spolia* block from the wall carried an inscription dedicated to Philip the Arab (244–249 CE) from the residents of Beziers.[55] Altogether, the combined evidence suggests a late third to possibly fourth century date for the walls of Narbonne.

Toulouse presents a slightly different case, as it was already supplied with a fortification wall, likely not long after the time of its foundation as a colony in the early first century CE. This early fortification wall ran a lunate course of about 3.5 kilometers (2 miles) and enclosed 90 hectares (222 acres) (although the inhabited area did not fill this area at this point, if it did ever), starting and ending on the Garonne, 790 meters (2,591 feet) apart, with a mixture of round, U-shaped and polygonal towers (fig. 8).[56] A relatively recent excavation at the Hôpital Larrey site in the northeast has provided a detailed stratigraphy — collaborated by numismatic evidence — including sigillata pottery from Montans and La Graufesenque which provide a date of 30 to 60 CE for construction. Two samples of the bricks from the wall, moreover, were subjected to archaeomagnetic testing; this returned dates of 0–40 CE and 0–30 CE,[57] suggesting that the early wall at Toulouse was constructed around 30–40 CE. It seems that the city never grew to fully fill out the large enclosed

54 Dominique Moulis, "Le rempart de l'antiquité tardive," in *Narbonne et le Narbonnais,* ed. Éric Dellong, Carte archeologique du Gaule 11.1 (Paris: Académie des Inscriptions et Belles-Lettres, 2002), 140–47, at 147.

55 *CIL* XII.4227. *Corpus Inscriptionum Latinarum,* vol. 12 (Berlin: De Gruyter, 1963). Unfortunately, as is the case with the coins, these finds were brought to light before systematic, scientific excavation procedures were commonplace, and, as such, their exact find-spot has not been recorded.

56 Daniel Cazes, "La ville dans ses murs," in *Palladia Tolosa: Toulouse romaine,* ed. Musée Saint-Raymond (Toulouse: Musée Saint-Raymond, 1988), 61–67, at 61.

57 Raphaël de Filippo, "Nouvelle définition de l'enceinte romaine de Toulouse," *Gallia* 50 (1993): 181–204, at 191.

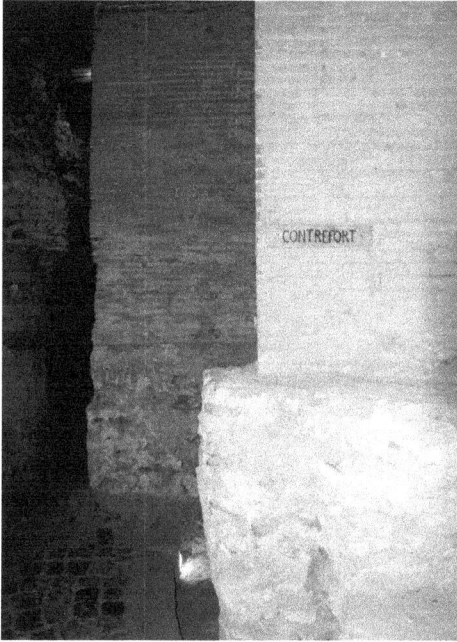

Fig. 9. Late Antique Wall and Contrefort, Toulouse. Photo by the author.

space, as indicated by excavations in the 1990s along the line of wall, which showed vacant spaces until the fourth century CE.[58]

In late antiquity, a new wall was constructed to close off the riverside left open by the early wall. The construction of the late Roman wall at Toulouse, with a superstructure entirely in brick (fig. 9), differs from that of the early wall, which features several meters of *opus vittatum mixtum* (*petit appareil*) in a lower section topped with *opus testaceum*.[59] The wall itself consists of two parallel brick faces, measuring 0.58 and 0.59 meters (1.90 and 1.94 feet) thick, cut through with transversal walls to form

58 Ibid.
59 Ibid., 193.

Fig. 10. Spolia from Late Antique Wall, Toulouse. Photo by the author.

2-meter (6.5 feet) wide compartments for a concrete and rubble fill.[60] It was not provided with towers, but 13 contreforts have been discovered.[61] At Toulouse, the *spolia* in the late wall (fig. 10), none of which has been given anything beyond a vague first or second century date, may indicate a TPQ of the second century.[62] An archaeomagnetic investigation of a large sample of

60 Georges Baccrabère, *Le rempart antique de l'Institut catholique de Toulouse* (Toulouse: Institut catholique de Toulouse, 1974), 11–12.
61 Georges Baccrabère and Alain Badie "L'enceinte du Bas-Empire de Toulouse," in *La civilisation urbaine de l'antiquité tardive dans le Sud-Ouest de la Gaule: actes du IIIᵉ Colloque Aquitania et des XVIᵉ Journées d'Archéologie Mérovingienne, Toulouse, 23–24 juin 1995,* ed. Louis Maurin and Jean-Marie Pailler (Bordeaux: Éditions de la Féderation Aquitania, 1996), 128.
62 Baccrabère, *Le rempart antique,* 19–20.

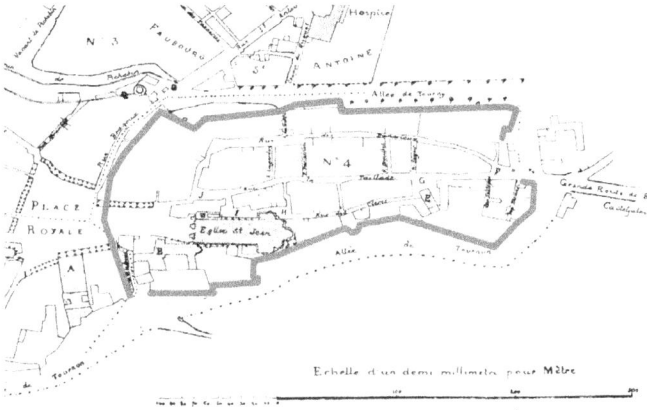

Fig. 11. Plan of Bazas. Adapted from Camille Jullian, "L'Enciente gallo-Romaine de Bazas," *Revue des Études Anciennes* 27, no. 2 (1925): 176.

bricks was carried out, but the results have been inconclusive.[63] As a result, the mid-first century must be taken as only a TPQ, but the wall likely dates from the second century at the earliest, if the *spolia* are any indication.

Yet, beyond the three major urban centers along this route, smaller settlements in the region were also fortified in late antiquity. A wall was built around Bazas (Vasatium) in this period, although the evidence about it is not particularly extensive; accounts of sieges by the Visigoths and the Huns, in Paulinus of

---

63 Ibid., 20. The test returned two dates, 190 and 275 CE. The investigator noted a curious fact that both dates, and even a date between the two, are possibilities for when these bricks were made. More recently Alain Badie ("Note à propos des matériaux utilizes pour la construction du rempart de l'Institut Catholique et nouvelles hypothèses pour sa dataion," in *Tolosa: Nouvelles recherches sur Toulouse et son territoire dans l'Antiquité* [Rome: École française de Rome], 564–68) has suggested, based on the same tests, that the bricks were more likely from the middle of the first century. He also argues that the bricks were cut down, thus implying they were reused from an original context, meaning that the production date of the bricks has little to do with the date of this fortification.

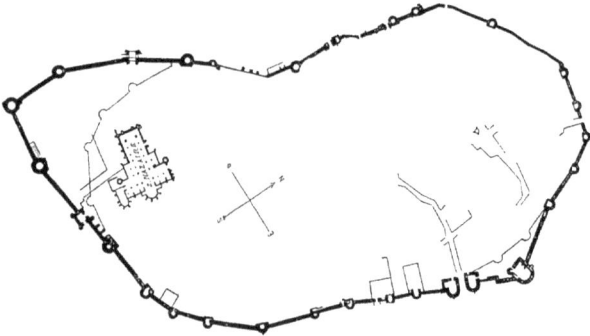

Fig. 12. Plan of Carcassonne. Image: Eugène Viollet-le-Duc, *La cité de Carcassonne (Aude)* (Paris: Ve. A. Morel et cie, 1866), fig. 16.

Pella (377–c. 461) and Gregory of Tours (538–594), respectively, mention a wall, suggesting that it was in place before the beginning of the fifth century.[64] A few limited rescue excavations have revealed some physical details, such as several differing kinds of masonry (although primarily *petit appareil*), a height of over 3 meters (10 feet) and a circumference of about 640 meters (2,100 feet), enclosing close to 2 hectares (5 acres) (fig. 11).[65] No direct chronological evidence was found in these excavations.

Carcassonne is perhaps one of the most famous fortified towns, as the Roman walls (repaired and restored in the middle ages) have largely survived to the present and present the modern visitor with an impressive sight. The original Roman wall

---

64 Paulinus of Pella, *The Eucharisticus of Paulinus Pellaeus,* in Ausonius, Paulinus Pellaeus, *Volume II: Books 18–20. Paulinus Pellaeus: Eucharisticus,* trans. Hugh G. Evelyn White, Loeb Classical Library 115 (Cambridge: Harvard University Press, 1921), vv. 383–89; Gregory of Tours, *Glory of the Martyrs,* trans. Raymond Van Dam, Translated Texts for Historians 4 (Liverpool: Liverpool University Press, 2004), 12.

65 Louis Maurin and Jean-Francois Pichonneau, "Bazas," in *Enceintes romaines d'Aquitaine: Bordeaux, Dax, Périgueux, Bazas,* ed. Garmy and Maruin, 162–64.

Fig. 13. Carcasonne Wall. Photo by the author.

was built around a natural outcropping, running 1 kilometer (.62 miles) and enclosing slightly more than 7 hectares (17 acres) (fig. 12). This wall was built in *petit appareil* masonry (fig. 13), approximately 3 meters (10 feet) thick, and featured little *spolia,* beyond some pieces embedded in the foundations.[66] The wall would have stood more than 7 meters (23 feet) in height. Twenty-one U-shaped towers at Carcasonne are at least partially Roman, or on the original foundation (fig. 14).[67] There would have been, based on generally accepted calculations, between thirty-four and thirty-eight towers on the original circuit, depending on how the major gates were flanked.[68] There is one current gateway that stands on the site of a Roman gate, although there were possibly four originally, and two smaller posterns survive

66 Jean Guilaine and Daniel Fabre, *Histoire de Carcassonne* (Toulouse: Privat, 1984), 37.
67 Guilaine & Fabre (ibid., 36), unhelpfully, say there are "une vingtaine" original towers.
68 Ibid., 37.

Fig. 14. Carcasonne Tower. Photo by the author.

as well.[69] In terms of dating, the Hierosolymitan itinerary of 333 describes the city as a *castellum,* which seems to connote a walled fortress of some kind, which the ring of walls circling the high outcropping of the Roman town would have easily resembled.[70] However, excavations in 1995 revealed ceramics that have been dated to no earlier than 375 in a construction fill of the wall.[71] Around the same time, archaeomagnetic tests were undertaken on two sets of bricks, showing that they were not

---

69 Ibid., 38.
70 Raymond Chevallier, *Roman Roads,* trans. N.H. Field (London: Batsford, 1976), 37.
71 Jean-Pascal Fourdrin, "Vestiges d'un parapet antique près de la tour du Sacraire Saint-Sernin à Carcassonne," *Journal of Roman Archeology* 15 (2002): 311–16, at 311; Jean-Pascal Fourdrin, "L'enceinte antique de Carcassonne (Secteur Nord)," in *Carcassonne, études archéologiques,* ed. Frédérik

Fig. 15. Palais Gallien. Adapted by the author from Arène de Bx by A1AA1A, Wikicommons.

made in the second or fourth century, intimating instead that they were therefore third or fifth century.[72] Theoretically, either date is acceptable, although a third-century date would indicate that the bricks were reused in the wall, as the pottery evidence points to a post-fourth century date.

Altogether, these five fortification walls share a number of similarities. Unfortunately, their chronology is not precise enough to say conclusively that they were definitively built at the same time, even if they are all almost certainly late antique. The walls of Narbonne and Bordeaux have the most evidence for their dating, and both were likely constructed in the final years of the third century and so can be considered together. These two circuits share similarities beyond chronology: they both en-closed a much smaller area than the city likely covered, although

Letterlé (Carcassonne: Société d'études scientifiques de l'Aude), 105–29, at 114.

72 Fourdrin, "L'enceinte antique," 114.

the enclosed space at Bordeaux was almost double that of Narbonne (seventeen vs thirty-two hectares/forty-two vs seventy-nine acres); both walls employed much *spolia* in their facings; finally, there are some further similarities in the width, height and towers of these fortifications, which are also seen at Carcassonne. While there is no direct evidence for central planning and execution of these walls[73] — and in fact the minor variations and differences between them suggests that there was no organized construction — the similarities, basic as they are, show some loose links between these cities. They were dealing with a new, less-secure position in the world of late antique Gaul, and their similar, yet still individual, responses to these challenges perhaps hints at some degree of communication between them. In some sense, these late antique walls (perhaps excepting Toulouse) have enough in common to suggest that there was an exchange of ideas between the four settlements; indeed, the similarities seen in many Gallic walls across the wider region.[74]

There are further late antique urban developments that link the cities along this corridor. At the same time that fortifications were being erected, their spectacle buildings were going out of use — either abandoned or destroyed. The amphitheater at Bordeaux (fig. 15), called the Palais Gallien, was damaged in a fire in the late third or possibly fourth century — which some scholars have connected to the Germanic invasions of 276 — and never repaired, although certain parts of it have survived to the present in good condition.[75] At Agen (Aginnum), a small city

---

73 As has been argued for certain groupings of walls (though not necessarily these) by a range of scholars like Stephen Johnson (*Late Roman Defences* [London: B.T. Batsford, 1983], 114–16) and Carmen Fernández Ochoa and Ángel Morillo ("Walls in the Urban Landscape of Late Roman Spain: Defense and Imperial Strategy," in *Hispania in Late Antiquity: Current Approaches,* ed. Kim Bowes and Michael Kulikowski, The Medieval and Early Modern Iberian World 24 [Leiden: Brill, 2005], 299–340).

74 Although, as noted above, a thorough examination of the chronology and features of each would be necessary to demonstrate a connection.

75 Jean-Claude Golvin (*L'amphithéâtre Romain: essai sur la théorisation de sa forme et de ses fonctions* [Paris: De Boccard, 1988], 214) reports that this date

midway between Bordeaux and Toulouse, the amphitheater was destroyed and supposedly "backfilled" by no later than the second half of the fourth century.[76] The Toulouse amphitheater (which was actually a few kilometers from the city at Purpan) was abandoned by the second half of the fourth century.[77] There is less archaeological evidence about the Narbonne amphitheater; Heijmans has suggested that it must have been in ruins by the fourth century, as it was not mentioned by either Sidonius or Ausonius.[78] This should not be taken as particularly strong evidence, as it is based only on the silence of two sources, neither of which was trying to exhaustively describe the city. Whatever the case here, overall there is a notable trend of the abandonment of spectacle buildings in the cities of the Garonne-Aude passageway in the fourth century. This is partially echoed in the disuse of bath buildings as well, as with the baths in Bordeaux on the modern Rue des Frères-Bonie, just beyond the line of the ancient city wall, which were destroyed and leveled, likely in connection to this construction.[79] At Toulouse, the discovery of stamped ceramics in a drain suggested the abandonment

for the fire is based on excavations by Étienne in the 1950s and 1960s, where a layer of ash was found. Such a precise chronology from excavation should, as always, raise some doubts.

76 Bruno Bizot and Myriam Fincker, "Un amphithéâtre antique à Agen," *Aquitania* 10 (1992): 49–74.

77 Michel Fincker, Claude Domergue, and Jean-Marie Pailler, "L'Amphithéâtre de Toulouse, récemment dégagé," *Dossiers d'Archéologie* 116 (1987): 46–51, at 46.

78 Heijmans, "La place," 38.

79 However, not all baths were going out of use in this period. In general terms, the largest baths in provincial cities were the most likely to be abandoned (see Underwood, *Reusing Ruins,* for a wider discussion of this trend). The Îlot Saint-Christoly baths, for example, which were very small — around 230 m² (2,476 square feet) — continued to be used until the end of the fifth century (see Dany Barraud and Louis Maurin, "Bordeaux au Bas-Empire: de la ville païenne à la ville chrétienne (IIIe–VIe s.)," in *La civilisation urbaine de l'antiquité tardive dans le Sud-Ouest de la Gaule,* ed. Maurin and Pailler, 35–54, at 51.

Fig. 16. Piliers de Tutelle. From Claude Perrault, *Les dix livres d'architecture de Vitruve,* 2nd edn. (Paris: Jean Baptiste Coignard, 1684), 219.

of the bath complex on Rue du Languedoc street in the fourth century.[80]

Beyond these key public monuments, urban space began to be transformed in similar ways across these towns in late antiquity. Fora in these three cities began to suffer material decline in

---

80 Alain Bouet, *Les thermes privés et publics en Gaule Narbonnaise,* vol. 1, Collection de l'École Français de Rome 320 (Rome: École française de Rome, 2003), n. 84.

the fifth century. At Bordeaux, the forum has never been conclusively discovered, and several locations have been proposed.[81] There has been a suggestion, however, that the monument known as the "Piliers de Tutelle" (fig. 16, a drawing made shortly before it was destroyed) was connected to the forum complex, or perhaps a secondary civic center.[82] No matter the precise function, the complex that contained this civic monument was left outside of the newly built city walls in the late third century.[83] More clear cases of the transformation of fora come from Toulouse and Narbonne. In the former, the Capitolium was destroyed around the end of the fourth into the beginning of the fifth century.[84] The history of the site for the following century or so is uncertain, but a chapel to Saturninus, commemorating his place of martyrdom, was built there in the later sixth century, likely reusing stone from the temple.[85] At Narbonne, the Capitolium was destroyed by 455. A TAQ is provided by reused elements of the temple that were discovered in the funerary church of Saint Felix, which was not built over the ruins of the temple, but at a short distance to the west.[86]

---

81 Doulan, *Bordeaux,* 49.

82 Heijmans, "La place," 33.

83 It is uncertain how the erection of the wall impacted extra-mural settlements due to limited excavation, but the Piliers de Tutelle survived mostly intact until the seventeenth century, possibly suggesting that the area, and the putative forum, was fairly depopulated leading to the survival of the monument.

84 Jean-Luc Boudartchouk, Henri Molet, and Catherine Viers, "Le Capitolium de Toulouse, L'église Saint-Pierre-et-Saint-Géraud et le martyre de l'Évêque Saturnin: nouvelles données," *Mémoires de la Société Archéologique du Midi de la France* 65 (2005): 15–50, at 22–23.

85 Ibid., 23. The church of Saint-Pierre-et-Saint-Géraud was built in the middle ages over the few remains of the temple platform and this early chapel.

86 Marc Heijmans, "Les espaces civiques dans les villes de Gaule Narbonnaise, IIe–IVe siècle," in *Les espaces publics d'Hispanie et de l'Occident romain entre les IIe et IVe s. Urbanisme civique en temps de crise,* ed. Laurent Brassous and Alejandro Quevedo, Collection de la Casa de Velázquez 149 (Madrid: Casa de Velázquez, 2015), 53, and Frank Riess, *Narbonne and Its Territory,* 89.

These conversions bring us to the final category of significant urban change, the Christianization of the urban topography. All three cities had major intra- (as well as extra-) mural churches built in the fourth or early fifth century. At Bordeaux, the first cathedral (as the city is attested to have had a bishop from at least the council of Arles in 314) was built in the later fourth or early fifth century, just north of the current Saint-André Cathedral. It was twenty-eight meters (ninety-two feet) long, likely of a three-aisled plan, with a polygonal apse and paved with poly-chromatic mosaics.[87] The whole episcopal complex was situated just inside the line of the late antique walls. Moreover, the funer-ary churches of Saint Seurin and Saint Etienne were established a few hundred meters outside the walls within a major necropo-lis. Sarcophagi from these churches suggest a date of at least the fifth century, and possibly earlier.

At Narbonne, four early Christian churches are known. The earliest documented is the cathedral, which was built in 445, as noted in an inscription thought to have been placed over the lintel.[88] The inscription notes that this edifice replaced an ear-lier church that burnt down; little is known of this earlier build-ing, beyond a hypothesized foundation date of 313, following the Edict of Milan. Beyond the principal church, excavations in the 1970s revealed a basilica at a site called Clos de la Lom-barde, some 300 meters (984 feet) from the north edge of the city wall. A large peristyle villa had been on the site until the late third century, and an aisled basilica was built over it in the early fourth.[89] The precise chronological sequence between these two structures is not fully understood, which precludes the possibil-ity of positively identifying the villa as a church-house that was expanded to accommodate a growing Christian community. There is some evidence in the area for destruction and abandon-ment in the third century, possibly intimating that the conver-

---

87 Doulan, *Bordeaux,* 57.

88 *CIL,* XII.5336.

89 Riess, *Narbonne and Its Territory,* 121.

sion to a church took place after the villa had been abandoned.[90] Whatever the precise relationship between these two phases, the basilica is likely the earliest Christian structure in Narbonne, and one of the earliest in Gaul. There was additionally a church said to contain the remains of St. Paul, the first bishop of Narbonne, on the site of the current Saint-Paul basilica, south of the Roman city. While it is possible that this church was built in the fifth or sixth centuries, no clear evidence has been found to confirm the date.[91]

Finally, there was the previously-mentioned St. Felix, which was built in 455, according to an inscription found in 1927.[92] Excavations in 1994 revealed a portion of the basilica with a protruding apse, almost immediately beyond the late antique city wall. This church was also, like the Clos de la Lombarde church, built above a Roman house; however, the house was only built in the third century, not long before the church conversion.[93] There is literary evidence for this church. In Gregory of Tour's *Glory of the Martrys,* Alaric is recorded as having ordered the lowering of the roof of the building which was obstructing his view of the Liviere plain.[94] It has been suggested that St. Felix may have been the Arian cathedral of Narbonne, a proposition further strengthened by Alaric's authority over the building and his ability to alter its height at will.[95]

The Arian/Nicaean church divide can also be seen at Toulouse, the capital of the Visigothic state in the fifth century, until

---

90 Ibid., 122.
91 Ibid., 116.
92 Ibid., 85.
93 Olivier Ginouvez, "Le site de Saint-Félix à Narbonne: une église d'origine paléochrétienne et son environnement funéraire (V[e]–XVIe siècle)," *Archéologie du Midi médiéval* 17 (1999): 25–46, at 29.
94 Gregory of Tours, *Glory of the Martyrs,* 91.
95 Riess, *Narbonne and Its Territory,* 121. Churches in the fifth century may have had Visigothic patronage. See Ralph Mathisen and Hagith S. Sivan, "Forging a New Identity: The Kingdom of Toulouse and the Frontiers of Visigothic Aquitania (418–507)," in *The Visigoths: Studies in Culture and Society,* ed. Alberto Ferreiro (Boston and Leiden: Brill, 1999), 1–62, at 48.

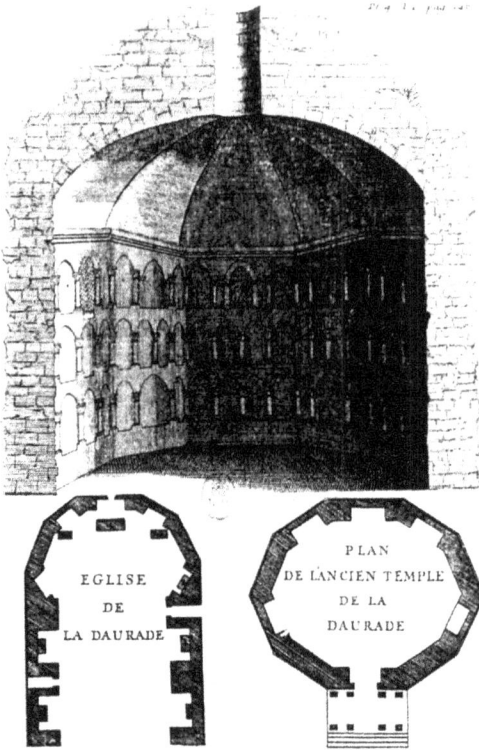

Fig. 17. Notre-Dame de La Daurade, plan, proposed elevation. Image in public domain. From Jacques Martin, *La religion des Gaulois tirée des plus pures sources de l'Antiquité,* vol. 1 (Paris: Chez Saugrain, 1727), 146.

507. Like Narbonne, there is evidence for four Paleochristian churches in Toulouse: a cathedral situated inside the walls, two funerary/martyrial churches over the site of a Roman cemeteries and the Notre Dame de la Daurade, in addition to the later sixth-century church built over the remains of the Capitolium noted above. Unfortunately, for most of these structures, which survive partially and have had limited excavation at points over the last hundred years, dating evidence is limited or non-exis-

tent. The best dated is the funerary church of Saint-Sernin, some 200 meters (656 feet) north of the city wall, noted in the *Passio sancti Saturnini,* which states that the bishop Exuperius (who took office in 405) dedicated the project begun by his predecessor, Silvius.[96] Despite this reasonable dating evidence, however, there is little understanding of the building itself, which was destroyed in the eleventh century when the present Romanesque church was built. Another funerary church, above the church of Saint-Pierre-des-Cuisines and slightly less than 100 meters (328 feet) north of the city wall, was excavated in 1995. This scientific study revealed a substantial fifth- or sixth-century transept church, which replaced an earlier and more primitive edifice with a nave, porch, and two side structures to the north and south.[97]

The episcopal church, likely built in the late fourth or early fifth centuries, was situated below the present Cathedral Saint-Etienne. Nothing remains of this early church except for a column capital found in 1983.[98] It has been suggested that a double-church episcopal complex comprised this primitive Saint Etienne along with the church of Saint Jacques some 50 meters (164 feet) to the south, with the other buildings of the complex (e.g. baptistry, bishops residence, etc.) between them.[99] The evidence for the whole complex is not particularly strong; in fact, even the dating evidence for the bishop's church is derived from archaeological work in the surrounding area, which showed a new late fourth or early fifth century road of substantial (six meters/twenty feet) width and an increase in building in the neigh-

96 Jean Guyon, "Toulouse, la première capital du royaume Wisigoth," in *Sedes Regiae (ann. 400–800),* ed. Gisela Ripoll and Joseph M. Gurt (Barcelona: Reial Academia de Bones Lletres, 2000), 219–14, at 227.

97 Quitterie Cazes, Jean Catalo, and Patrice Cabau, *L'ancienne église Saint-Pierre-des-Cuisines à Toulouse,* Mémoires de la Société archéologique du Midi de la France 48 (Toulouse: Hotel d'Assézat, 1988).

98 Guyon, "Toulouse, la première capital du royaume Wisigoth," 226.

99 Ibid., 224.

boring streets, seemingly indicating an occupation of a previously marshy and little-developed region.[100]

The final church in Toulouse is the most enigmatic. The church of Notre Dame de la Daurade (fig. 17), situated near the Garonne within the city walls, was destroyed in 1761, yet its rich decorative mosaics (which gave the church its name of Santa Maria deaurata) are known from records from the early eighteenth century.[101] In terms of construction, dates from the fourth to sixth centuries for the decoration of the building (to say nothing of its original construction, if different — Guyon, for example, suggests that this may have been a reused mausoleum) have been proposed based on parallels in style and iconography.[102] Moreover, there are doubts as to whether the building was a Catholic church, an Arian church, or even the funerary chapel for the Visigothic kings. Notably, the church is not located outside the walls, but is fairly central, only 350 meters (1,148 feet) from the forum. A connection with the Visigoths, and thus its hypothetical purpose, hinges on the chronology of the structure, which remains uncertain. The rich decoration, showing scenes from the New Testament and figures from the Old around Christ and the Virgin, would seem to suggest a royal connection, as does the proximity to the suspected Visigothic palace at the site of the Hôpital Larrey, and there should be no expectation for any obvious signs of Arianism in the iconography of the building.[103]

In sum, we can see in the physical evolution of the cities along this trade route in south Gaul a notable number of similarities. The most substantial change to the urban topography was the installation of walls, which at Narbonne and Bordeaux, enclosed

---

100 Ibid.
101 Ibid., 236.
102 Ibid., 238.
103 Drawing inferences from Bryan Ward-Perkins's work in Ravenna ("Where Is the Archaeology and Iconography of Germanic Arianism?" in *Religious Diversity in Late Antiquity*, ed. David Gwynn and Susanne Bangert, Late Antique Archaeology 6 [Boston and Leiden: Brill, 2010], 265–89).

a small part of the city. In all three, as best we can tell, the forum area — central to Roman cities — lost its importance around the beginning of the fifth century. Similarly, spectacle buildings were falling out of use at points in the fourth century, and baths probably nearer the beginning of the century. At the same time, new buildings and spaces — largely Christian — were being developed. While dating evidence is not particularly robust for this period, at all three cities, at least one church is known from the early fifth century, and more substantial cathedrals were in situ before the middle of the century.

However, the extant evidence does not permit us to see explicit links between the cities from these developments. That is to say, there is no way to connect a change in one city to a change in another through an individual or group. Broadly speaking, many similar transformations were taking place in cities across the west, and especially in Gaul. Yet the similar timing of these changes across Bordeaux, Toulouse, and Narbonne — three linked cities but with their own individual contexts — shows three cities that all came to similar solutions to the changing demands on urban space in the fourth and fifth centuries. It is not unreasonable, then, to see a connection between their responses to these conditions. The well-established road and riverine links meant that all three cities were certainly in communication with one another, possibly even more than with any other cities. We may easily imagine then these cities looking to their immediate neighbors for understanding how to deal with the new urban situation in late antiquity.

Trade Links

One final aspect of the connection between these three cities is trade. Without a doubt, as a result of the river networks and geography of south Gaul, there was always significant movement of goods between these cities. We know that with the advent of Roman hegemony across south Gaul, this trade increased and remained important throughout the imperial period. Much of this, as with many aspects of Roman economic activity, has left minimal impact on the archaeological record. Ceramics, however, do survive in large quantities; they can generally stand in as a proxy for broader trade patterns, in part because they moved along established trading routes, and in part because some pottery vessels like amphorae carried some of the agricultural commodities that were traded over distances.[104] A diachronic study of the variety of pottery — from the above-noted transport amphorae to domestic fine- and course-wares, imported or locally made — circulating in south Gaul is beyond the scope of this study.[105] While such an approach could speak to the movement of goods (and hence people) between these neighboring cities, a brief look at one particular kind of late antique pottery produced in south Gaul must suffice here to illuminate some of these connections.

In this vein, we can look at the group of fine table wares known as DSP, which was made from about the end of the fourth century through the sixth.[106] It imitated other forms of stamped fineware like the ubiquitous African Red Slip that circulated across the later Roman Empire, yet DSP was generally not exported outside of Gaul.[107] The pottery was slip coated and fired in an oxidizing environment to produce an orangey coat, although certain producers fired in a reducing atmosphere to generate a grey exterior.[108]

104 A good introduction to the topic can be found in Andrew Wilson, "Approaches to Quantifying Roman Trade," in *Quantifying the Roman Economy: Methods and Problems*, ed. Alan Bowman and Andrew Wilson, Oxford Studies on the Roman Economy (Oxford: Oxford University Press, 2009), 213–49.

105 Besides the fact that there is no single volume which covers the range of ceramics across this region.

106 Jacqueline Rigoir, Yves Rigoir, and Lucien Rivet, "Cruches et pots en sigillee paleochretienne," in *Actes du congrès de la Société française d'étude de la céramique antique en Gaule, Caen, 28–31 mai 1987* (Marseille: S.F.É.C.A.G., 1987), 193–206.

107 Claude Raynaud, "Céramique Estampée grise et orangée dite 'dérivée de sigillée paléochrétienne'," *Lattara* 6 (1993): 410–18, at 410.

108 Esmonde Cleary, *The Roman West*, 325.

It has been well-established that DSP was produced in three regions — the Atlantic/Aquitanian, Languedoc, and Provencal groups — and many individual producers in each region have been found.[109] More recently, excavations have revealed the notable production of DSP in the Midi-Pyrénées, but this is not yet a recognized region. The Provencal group, centered around Marseille, is not directly connected to the Aude–Garonne corridor, although it is worth noting the economic connections here that stretched across the Gulf of Lion. Within each region, for the most part, the ateliers producing this pottery were based in, or very nearby to, cities. For the Languedoc group, two major producers have been identified, one near Narbonne and the other near Carcassonne. The products of these workshops were slightly more restricted chronologically, seemingly only circulating from the last third of the fourth century through the middle of the fifth. And for the Atlantic/Aquitanian group, while the exact production site has not been located, the most likely center is in or near Bordeaux. This group was being produced from the fifth to seventh centuries, with a clear peak in the sixth.[110] Further, kilns producing a similar style of pottery to that of Bordeaux have been located in Toulouse, along with a number of other sites in the surrounding territory, including Albi, Lectoure, and Cahors — all along or not far from the Garonne valley.[111] Within Toulouse, one of the two identified kilns is near the Cathedral Saint-Etienne, noted above (and the other is near the Hôpital Larrey site, also noted above in connection to a putative Visigothic palace).[112]

---

109 Ibid.

110 Chaidron Cyrille, "Note sur la découverte de dérivées de sigillées paléochrétiennes dans le Nord de la France," *Revue archéologique de Picardie* 3–4 (2008): 247–51, at 247.

111 Christien Dieulafait, Jean-Luc Boudartchouk, Jacques Lapart, Laurent Llech, Raphaël de Filippo, Patricia Kalinowsky, and Sylvie Soulas, "Céramiques tardives en Midi-Pyrénées Premières approaches," in *La civilisation urbaine de l'antiquité tardive dans le Sud-Ouest de la Gaule,* ed. Maurin and Pailler, 165–77, at 266.

112 Ibid., 269.

Most revealing about DSP is how it moved around south France. While much work remains to be done on the distribution and the exact chronology of each regional type, it seems clear that the fineware imitation was not confined to the region it was produced in. For example, two pieces of clearly Languedocian pottery were discovered in Saint-Bertrand-de-Comminges, which was normally supplied with pots from the Atlantic group, likely produced near Bordeaux.[113] Or, in Toulouse, DSP imports from both the Languedoc and Atlantic regions have been discovered, with the latter coming in when the former seems to no longer have been imported.[114] Moreover, direct connections are seen between Bordeaux, Toulouse, and Narbonne in the influence each regional style had with the others. This is clearly seen with the decoration on certain pots produced in Toulouse which were clearly influenced by those from the Languedoc region, seen in similarities between "des chrismes, des oiseaux, des arcatures ("the chi-rho, the birds, the arches")." [115]

Simon Esmonde Cleary sums up the significance of the movement of DSP quite clearly:

This would seem to be good evidence for the existence of a considerable commercial nexus in south-western Gaul, probably in important part mediated through urban centers such as Bordeaux itself, Toulouse and Saint- Bertrand-de-Comminges, supporting the contention that these places still had important commercial functions. [...] If anything, these industries right across southern Gaul from the Atlantic to the Mediterranean seem to have been displaying even more vigor than the TSHT [terra sigillata hispanica tardia] of the northern part of Iberia. So southern Gaul could colourably

---

113 Jean-Froiçois Meffre, Jacqueline Rigoir, and Yves Rigoir, "Les dérivées des sigillées paléochrétiennes du groupe atlantique," *Gallia* 31, no. 1 (1973): 207–63, at 210.

114 Diuelafait "Céramiques tardives," 275.

115 Ibid., 269.

be argued to have been enjoying a period of economic prosperity through at least the first half of the fifth century.[116]

The flourishing economic activities suggested by the confirmed and ample movement of regional pottery in late antique Gaul show the connections and links between cities that remained active throughout this period.

Conclusions

It is clear that the cities along the Aude–Garonne corridor had strong links, culturally, but also economically, due to the human and physical geography that was exploited throughout the Roman period. In late antiquity, those connections began to be tried, as the breakaway Gallic empire, reorganization under Diocletian, and eventual Gothic settlement and dissolution of the Roman political system fundamentally changed the power dynamics in the region. It is within this context of shifting dominions that the connections between Bordeaux, Toulouse, and Narbonne should be considered, and their continued existence be noted. As we have seen, the literary evidence from Ausonius points to a continued movement of individuals — especially for professors — in the fourth century. There is less clear indication of these kinds of travels in the fifth century in Sidonius, but still some hint of a mobile, aristocratic class engaged in politicking as the Visigoths began to expand their territory beyond Aquitania. The physical evidence from the urban development equally confirms the continued connections in this region — similarities between walls, especially Narbonne and Bordeaux, and in the patterns of disuse of baths and spectacle buildings, while all part of a broader late antique urbanism, do show particular links. The evidence from the early churches in south Gaul also demonstrate a number of chronological and typological parallels, with aisled basilicas first appearing in the mid-to-later fourth cen-

116 Esmonde Cleary, *The Roman West*, 423–24.

tury, and becoming widespread in the fifth. In all these developments, there is no indication of central planning or of specific and direct communication between cities, which would show a precise link. Instead, we should imagine an exchange of ideas between the settlements in this corridor, brought along with the traders, aristocrats, and others who traveled between them. How those new ideas were implemented depended on the local dynamics, coupled with any historical exigencies. Any exchange will never have been fully uniform across the region or indeed across the empire — some places, like Rome, attracted more people and had more resources for executing incoming ideas. Conversely, some places will have been more resistant to outside ideas and new ways of doing. This model, of idea exchange and receptiveness, seems to me to be a way to understand some aspects of cultural change — like the persistently thorny concept of Romanization — in the ancient world.

And so, while this variety of connections is intrinsically useful for understanding the communication, economic and otherwise, between neighboring cities on a well-trodden route, these connections are also remarkable in light of how they change with the establishment of the Visigothic kingdom and its attempts — and somewhat gradual successes — to gain control over southern Gaul, from the Atlantic to the Mediterranean. The conquest of the whole of south Gaul by the Visigoths in the course of the fifth century brought an already weakened Roman rule to a close, although significant elements of the administrative system still continued to more-or-less function. Similarly, in the ceramic evidence, there is continued movement between these network nodes, into the fifth centuries, even so far as facilitating the copying of styles. Indeed, as Esmonde Cleary notes about the Atlantic and Languedoc DSP production areas, "Neither of these centres seems to have been much troubled by the Visigothic settlement in Aquitaine or the subsequent wars in the south-east."[117]

117 Ibid., 476–77.

However, the story began to change later in that century: "but again the second half of the fifth century seems to have been a period during which the volume and distribution of these centres declined. Of course, some, notably DSP, did continue to be produced and to circulate into the sixth century, but in a more restricted range of forms, in smaller quantities and over lesser distances than had been the case in the earlier fifth century."[118] Here then, we see that trade patterns were not immediately disrupted by this political change, but that by a combination of multifarious causes of various origins, including regime change, they were impacted by the end of the fifth century. The other connections linking these cities began to fray under the Visigoths — not necessarily caused by their reign per se, but as a result of broader economic and cultural shifts at the end of the Roman Empire. Cities began to be organized around ecclesiastical leadership, rather than the strictly civil. Trade became more local in its horizon. Depopulation and other pressures led to economic decline and reduced wealth for capital projects, like walls or other public monuments.[119] And thus, the relationships that had been established and maintained between cities under the Roman Empire largely disappeared for south Gaul by the sixth century, as their constituent parts — cultural, economic, and ideological — ebbed.

---

118 Ibid., 475.
119 The Visigoths, for example, built few new fortifications and instead simply repaired the third-century walls.

Bibliography

Primary

Ausonius. *Parentalia.* In *Volume I: Books 1–17,* translated by Hugh G. Evelyn-White. Loeb Classical Library 96. Cambridge: Harvard University Press, 1919. DOI: 10.4159/DLCL. ausonius-parentalia.1919.

———. *Poems Commemorating the Professors of Bordeaux.* In *Volume I: Books 1–17,* translated by Hugh G. Evelyn-White. Loeb Classical Library 96. Cambridge: Harvard University Press, 1919.

Corpus Inscriptionum Latinarum, vol. 12. Berlin: De Gruyter, 1963.

Corpus Inscriptionum Latinarum, vol. 13. Berlin: De Gruyter, 1968.

Gregory of Tours. *Glory of the Martyrs.* Translated by Raymond Van Dam. Translated Texts for Historians 4. Liverpool: Liverpool University Press, 2004.

Paulinus of Pella. *The Eucharisticus of Paulinus Pellaeus.* In *Ausonius, Paulinus Pellaeus. Volume II: Books 18–20. Paulinus Pellaeus: Eucharisticus,* translated by Hugh G. Evelyn White. Loeb Classical Library 115. Cambridge: Harvard University Press, 1921. DOI: 10.4159/DLCL.paulinus_pellaeus-eucharisticus.1921.

Sidonius. *Poems. Letters: Books 3–9.* Translated by William Blair Anderson. Loeb Classical Library 420. Cambridge: Harvard University Press, 1965.

Strabo. *Geography, Volume II: Books 3–5.* Translated by Horace Leonard Jones. Loeb Classical Library 50. Cambridge: Harvard University Press, 1923.

Theodosian Code. In *The Theodosian Code and Novels: and the Sirmondian Constitutions.* Translated by Clyde Pharr. Princeton: Princeton University Press, 1952.

Secondary

Arramond, Jean-Charles, and Jean-Luc Boudartchouk. "Le Capitolium de Tolosa?" *Gallia* 54 (1997): 203–38. DOI: 10.3406/galia.1997.2997.

Bernard Bachrach. "The Fortification of Gaul and the Economy of the Third and Fourth Centuries." *Journal of Late Antiquity* 3, no. 1 (2010): 38–64. DOI: 10.1353/jla.0.0056.

Baccrabère, Georges. *Le rempart antique de l'Institut catholique de Toulouse.* Toulouse: Institut catholique de Toulouse, 1974.

Baccrabère, Georges, and Alain Badie. "L'enceinte du Bas-Empire de Toulouse." In *La civilisation urbaine de l'antiquité tardive dans le Sud-Ouest de la Gaule: actes du IIIᵉ Colloque Aquitania et des XVIᵉ Journées d'Archéologie Mérovingienne, Toulouse, 23–24 juin 1995,* edited by Louis Maurin and Jean-Marie Pailler, 125–29. Bordeaux: Éditions de la Féderation Aquitania, 1996.

Badie, Alain. "Note à propos des matériaux utilizes pour la construction du rempart de l'Institut Catholique et nouvelles hypothèses pour sa dataion." In *Tolosa: Nouvelles recherches sur Toulouse et son territoire dans l'Antiquité,* edited by Jean-Marie Pailler, Collection de l'École française de Rome 281, 564–68. Rome: École Française de Rome.

Barraud, Dany, Jacques Linères, and Louis Maurin. "Bordeaux." In *Enceintes romaines d'Aquitaine: Bordeaux, Dax, Périgueux, Bazas,* edited by Pierre Garmy and Louis Maurin, 15–80. Paris: Maison des sciences de l'homme, 1996.

Barraud, Dany, and Louis Maurin. "Bordeaux au Bas-Empire: de la ville païenne à la ville chrétienne (IIIe–VIe s.)." In *La civilisation urbaine de l'antiquité tardive dans le Sud-Ouest de la Gaule: actes du IIIᵉ Colloque Aquitania et des XVIᵉ Journées d'Archéologie Mérovingienne, Toulouse, 23–24 juin 1995,* edited by Louis Maurin and Jean-Marie Pailler, 35–54. Bordeaux: Éditions de la Féderation Aquitania, 1996.

Bizot, Bruno, and Myriam Fincker. "Un amphithéâtre antique à Agen." *Aquitania* 10 (1992): 49–74.

Boudartchouk, Jean-Luc, Henri Molet, and Catherine Viers. "Le Capitolium de Toulouse, L'église Saint-Pierre-et-

Saint-Géraud et le martyre de l'Évêque Saturnin: nouvelles données." *Mémoires de la Société Archéologique du Midi de la France* 65 (2005): 15–50.

Bouet, Alain. *Les thermes privés et publics en Gaule Narbonnaise.* 2 Volumes. Collection de l'École Français de Rome 320. Rome: École française de Rome, 2003.

Cazes, Daniel. "La ville dans ses murs." In *Palladia Tolosa: Toulouse romaine*, edited by Musée Saint-Raymond, 61–67. Toulouse: Musée Saint-Raymond, 1988.

Cazes, Quitterie, Jean Catalo, and Patrice Cabau. *L'ancienne église Saint-Pierre-des-Cuisines à Toulouse.* Mémoires de la Société archéologique du Midi de la France 48. Toulouse: Hotel d'Assézat, 1988.

Chevallier, Raymond. *Roman Roads.* Translated by N.H. Field. London: B.T. Batsford, 1976.

Christie, Neil. *From Constantine to Charlemagne: An Archaeology of Italy, AD 300–800.* Ashgate: Aldershot, 2006.

Collins, Roger. *Visigothic Spain, 409–711.* Malden: Blackwell, 2004. DOI: 10.1002/9780470754610.

Cyrille, Chaidron. "Note sur la découverte de dérivées de sigillées paléochrétiennes dans le Nord de la France." *Revue archéologique de Picardie* 3–4 (2008): 247–51. DOI: 10.3406/pica.2008.3142.

Dalton, Ormonde Maddock. *The Letters of Sidonius.* Oxford: Clarendon Press, 1915.

Dieulafait, Christien, Jean-Luc Boudartchouk, Jacques Lapart, Laurent Llech, Raphaël de Filippo, Patricia Kalinowsky, and Sylvie Soulas. "Céramiques tardives en Midi-Pyrénées Premières approaches." In *La civilisation urbaine de l'antiquité tardive dans le Sud-Ouest de la Gaule: actes du IIIe Colloque Aquitania et des XVIe Journées d'Archéologie Mérovingienne, Toulouse, 23–24 juin 1995*, edited by Louis Maurin and Jean-Marie Pailler, 265–77. Bordeaux: Éditions de la Féderation Aquitania, 1996.

Doulan, Cécile. *Bordeaux.* Carte archeologique de la Gaule 33.2. Paris: Académie des Inscriptions et Belles-Lettres, 2013.

Drinkwater, John F. *The Gallic Empire: Separatism and Continuity in the North-Western Provinces of the Roman Empire, A.D. 260–274.* Stuttgart: Franz Steiner Verlag Wiesbaden, 1987.

Ebel, Charles. *Transalpine Gaul: The Emergence of a Roman Province.* Studies of the Dutch Archaeological and Historical Society 4. Boston and Leiden: Brill, 1976.

Elsner, Jas. "The Itinerarium Burdigalense: Politics and Salvation in the Geography of Constantine's Empire." *The Journal of Roman Studies* 90 (2000): 181–95. DOI: 10.2307/300206.

Esmonde Cleary, Simon. *The Roman West, AD 200–500: An Archaeological Study.* Cambridge: Cambridge University Press, 2013. DOI: 10.1017/CBO9781139043199.

Étienne, Robert. *Histoire de Bordeaux 1, Bordeaux antique.* Bordeaux: Fédération historique du Sud-Ouest, 1962.

Fernández Ochoa, Carmen, and Ángel Morillo. "Walls in the Urban Landscape of Late Roman Spain: Defense and Imperial Strategy." In *Hispania in Late Antiquity: Current Approaches,* edited by Kim Bowes and Michael Kulikowski, 299–340. The Medieval and Early Modern Iberian World 24. Leiden: Brill, 2005.

De Filippo, Raphaël. "Nouvelle définition de l'enceinte romaine de Toulouse." *Gallia* 50 (1993): 181–204. DOI: 10.3406/galia.1993.2937.

Fincker, Michel, Claude Domergue, and Jean-Marie Pailler. "L'Amphithéâtre de Toulouse, récemment dégagé." *Dossiers d'Archéologie* 116 (1987): 46–51.

Fourdrin, Jean-Pascal. "L'enceinte antique de Carcassonne (Secteur Nord)." In *Carcassonne, études archéologiques,* edited by Frédérik Letterlé, 105–29. Carcassonne: Société d'études scientifiques de l'Aude, 2009.

———. "Vestiges d'un parapet antique près de la tour du Sacraire Saint-Sernin à Carcassonne." *Journal of Roman Archaeology* 15 (2002): 311–16. DOI: 10.1017/S1047759400013994.

Garmy, Pierre, and Louis Maurin, ed. *Enceintes romaines d'Aquitaine: Bordeaux, Dax, Périgueux, Bazas.* Paris: Maison des sciences de l'homme, 1996.

Gayraud, Michel. *Narbonne antique: des origines à la fin du IIIe siècle*. Paris: du Boccard, 1981.

Ginouvez, Olivier. "Le site de Saint-Félix à Narbonne: une église d'origine paléochrétienne et son environnement funéraire (Ve–XVIe siècle)." *Archéologie du Midi médiéval* 17 (1999): 25–46. DOI: 10.3406/amime.1999.924.

Golvin, Jean-Claude. *L'amphithéâtre Romain: essai sur la théorisation de sa forme et de ses fonctions*. Paris: De Boccard, 1988.

Guilaine, Jean, and Daniel Fabre. *Histoire de Carcassonne*. Toulouse: Privat, 1984.

Guyon, Jean. "Toulouse, la première capital du royaume Wisigoth." In *Sedes Regiae (ann. 400–800)*, edited by Gisela Ripoll and Joseph M. Gurt, 219–40. Barcelona: Reial Academia de Bones Lletres, 2000.

Halsall, Guy. *Barbarian Migrations and the Roman West, 376–568*. Cambridge: Cambridge University Press, 2007. DOI: 10.1017/CBO9780511802393.

Harries, Jill. *Sidonius Apollinaris and the Fall of Rome, AD 407–485*. Oxford: Clarendon Press, 1994.

Heather, Peter J. *The Fall of the Roman Empire: A New History of Rome and the Barbarians*. Oxford: Oxford University Press, 2006.

Heijmans Marc. "La mise en défense de la Gaule méridionale aux IVe–VIe s." *Gallia* 63 (2006): 59–74. DOI: 10.3406/galia.2006.3284.

———. "La place des monuments publics du Haut-Empire dans les villes de la Gaule méridionale durant l'Antiquité tardive (IVe–VIe s.)." *Gallia* 63 (2006): 25–41. DOI: 10.3406/galia.2006.3281.

———. "Les espaces civiques dans les villes de Gaule Narbonnaise, IIe–IVe siècle." In *Urbanisme civique en temps de crise. Les espaces publics d'Hispanie et de l'Occident romain entre les IIe et IVe s.* edited by Laurent Brassous and Alejandro Quevedo, 47–61. Collection de la Casa de Velázquez 149. Madrid: Casa de Velázquez, 2015.

Johnson, Stephen. *Late Roman Fortifications*. London: B.T. Batsford, 1983.

Jullian, Camille. *Histoire de Bordeaux depuis les origines jusqu'en 1895.* Bordeaux: Feret et fils, 1895.

———. "L'Enciente gallo-Romaine de Bazas." *Revue des Études Anciennes* 27, no. 2 (1925): 119–21. DOI: 10.3406/rea.1925.2356.

Kampen, Natalie. "Roman Art and Architecture in the Provinces and beyond the Roman World." In *The Oxford Handbook of Greek and Roman Art and Architecture,* edited by Clemente Marconi, 395–416. New York: Oxford University Press, 2014.

Kulikowski, Michael. *Late Roman Spain and Its Cities.* Baltimore: John Hopkins University Press, 2004.

Labrousse, Michel. *Tolouse antique, des origins a l'établissement des wisigoths.* Paris: Boccard, 1968.

Lancaster, Lynne C. *Innovative Vaulting in the Architecture of the Roman Empire: 1st to 4th Centuries CE.* New York: Cambridge University Press, 2015. DOI: 10.1017/CBO9781107444935.

Leone, Anna. *Changing Townscapes in North Africa from Late Antiquity to the Arab Conquest.* Bari: Edipuglia, 2007.

Loseby, Simon T. "Marseille: A Late Antique Success Story?" *Journal of Roman Studies* 82 (1992): 165–85. DOI: 10.2307/301290.

———. "The Ceramic Data and the Transformation of the Roman World." In *LRCW 2. Late Roman Course Wares, Cooking Wares and Amphorae in the Mediterranean: Archaeology and Archaeometry,* edited by Michel Bonifay and Jean-Christophe Trégrila, 1–14. Oxford: Archaeopress, 2007.

Martin, Jacques. *La religion des Gaulois tirée des plus pures sources de l'Antiquité.* Volume 1. Paris: Chez Saugrain, 1727.

Mathisen, Ralph, and Hagith S. Sivan. "Forging a New Identity: The Kingdom of Toulouse and the Frontiers of Visigothic Aquitania (418–507)." In *The Visigoths: Studies in Culture and Society,* edited by Alberto Ferreiro, 1–62. Boston and Leiden: Brill, 1999.

Mathisen, Ralph, and Danuta Shanzer, ed. *Society and Culture in Late Antique Gaul.* Aldershot: Ashgate, 2001.

Maurin, Louis, and Jean-Francois Pichonneau. "Bazas." In *Enceintes romaines d'Aquitaine: Bordeaux, Dax, Périgueux, Bazas,* edited by Pierre Garmy and Louis Maruin, 155–66. Paris: Maison des sciences de l'homme.

Meffre, Jean-Froiçois, Jacqueline Rigoir, and Yves Rigoir. "Les dérivées des sigillées paléochrétiennes du groupe atlantique." *Gallia* 31, no. 1 (1973): 207–63. DOI: 10.3406/galia.1973.2630.

Moulis, Dominique. "Le rempart de l'antiquité tardive." In *Narbonne et le Narbonnais,* edited by Éric Dellong, 140–47. Carte archeologique du Gaule 11.1. Paris: Académie des Inscriptions et Belles-Lettres, 2002.

Perrault, Claude. *Les dix livres d'architecture de Vitruve.* Paris: Jean Baptiste Coignard, 1684.

Raynaud, Claude. "Céramique Estampée grise et orangée dite 'dérivée de sigillée paléochrétienne." *Lattara* 6 (1993): 410–18.

Riess, Frank. *Narbonne and Its Territory in Late Antiquity: From the Visigoths to the Arabs.* Farnham: Ashgate, 2016. DOI: 10.4324/9781315597218.

Rigoir, Jacqueline, Yves Rigoir, and Lucien Rivet. "Cruches et pots en sigillee paleochretienne." In *Actes du congrès de la Société française d'étude de la céramique antique en Gaule, Caen, 28–31 mai 1987,* edited by Lucien Rivet, 193–206. Marseille: S.F.É.C.A.G, 1987.

Rivet, Albert Lionel Frederick. *Gallia Narbonensis: Southern France in Roman Times.* London: B.T. Batsford, 1988.

Thiers, F.-P. "Notes sur l'enceinte préwisigothique de Narbonne." *Bulletin de la commission archeologique du Narbonne* 1 (1891): 158–69.

Underwood, Douglas. *(Re)using Ruins: Public Building in the Cities of the Late Antique West, A.D. 300–600.* Boston and Leiden: Brill, 2019. DOI: 10.1163/9789004390539.

Viollet-le-Duc, Eugène. *La cité de Carcassonne (Aude).* Paris: Ve. A. Morel et Cie, 1866.

Ward-Perkins, Bryan. *From Classical Antiquity to the Middle Ages: Urban Building in Northern and Central Italy, AD 300–850.* Oxford: Oxford University Press, 1984.

———. *Roman Imperial Architecture.* New Haven: Yale University Press, 1981.

———. "Where Is the Archaeology and Iconography of Germanic Arianism?" In *Religious Diversity in Late Antiquity,* edited by David Gwynn and Susanne Bangert, 265–89. Late

Antique Archaeology 6. Boston and Leiden: Brill, 2010. DOI: 10.1163/22134522-90000137.

Wilson, Andrew. "Approaches to Quantifying Roman Trade." In *Quantifying the Roman Economy: Methods and Problems,* edited by Alan Bowman and Andrew Wilson, 213–49. Oxford Studies on the Roman Economy. Oxford: Oxford University Press, 2009. DOI: 10.1093/acprof:o so/9780199562596.003.0009.

Wood, Jason. "The Wall Top of the Late-Roman Defences at Saint-Bertrand-de-Comminges: Interim Report." *Journal of Roman Archaeology* 15 (2002): 297–309. DOI: 10.1017/S1047759400013982.

Woolf, Greg. *Becoming Roman: The Origins of Provincial Civilization in Gaul.* Cambridge: Cambridge University Press, 1998. DOI: 10.1017/CBO9780511518614.

Contributors

Lisa Kaaren Bailey is a Associate Professor in History, and in Classics and Ancient History at the University of Auckland in New Zealand. She is the author of *Christianity's Quiet Success: The Eusebius Gallicanus Sermon Collection and the Power of the Church in Late Antique Gaul* (Notre Dame: University of Notre Dame Press, 2010) and *The Religious Worlds of the Laity in Late Antique Gaul* (New York & London: Bloomsbury, 2016).

Michael Burrows completed his Ph.D. in Medieval History at the University of Leeds. His doctoral thesis is an investigation of violence in the western provinces of the Roman Empire and the successor states in late antiquity. The particular focus of the thesis is on violence as an expression of power in social relationships, and what episodes of violence can reveal about life and agency among the lower classes in late antiquity/the Early Middle Ages. He has worked closely with his peers at the University of Leeds on the Networks and Neighbours project (https://networksandneighbours.org/) and with the Texts and Identities series. He has taught undergraduate modules on late ancient and medieval Europe and the Mediterranean at the University of Leeds, and has delivered papers on a range of topics, from the Roman Principate to Merovingian Gaul.

Ann Christys is an independent scholar of the Arabic and Latin historiography of Spain from the eighth to eleventh centuries. Her most recent book is *Vikings in the South: Voyages to Iberia and the Mediterranean* (London: Bloomsbury, 2015).

Michael J. Kelly is Visiting Assistant Professor in Comparative Literature and Judaic Studies at Binghamton University (SUNY) and Director of the international, open-access project Networks and Neighbours (https://networksandneighbours.org/). His teaching and research focus on the relationship between literature and history, critical theory, and the philosophy of history. His recent publications include the volumes *Theories of History: History Read Across the Humanities* (London: Bloomsbury, 2018),* edited with Arthur Rose, and, with Dominique Bauer, *The Imagery of Interior Spaces* (Earth: punctum books, 2019). He is currently adapting two novels for the stage, with their author, Ariana Harwicz.

Dimitris J. Kyrtatas is Professor of Late Antiquity at the University of Thessaly. He was born in 1952 in Athens and educated in Thessaloniki and London. From 1985 until 2001 he lectured at the University of Crete and in 2002 moved to the University of Thessaly. His main field of research is the social and religious history of the Greek world in the Roman period. He has published many books, including *The Social Structure of the Early Christian Communities* (New York and London: Verso, 1987) and articles on related topics.

Javier Martínez Jiménez is a Postdoctoral Researcher at the Faculty of Classics at the University of Cambridge, member of the "Impact of the Ancient City" ERC-funded project, and a Postdoctoral By-Fellow at Churchill College. He received his doctorate in archaeology from Oxford University, researching on the continuity of aqueducts in Visigothic and early Islamic Spain, supervised by Bryan Ward-Perkins. He has been in charge of the survey and excavation of the aqueduct of Reccopolis in Spain and the excavation of the late antique complex at Casa Herrera

(Mérida). His publications include papers on urbanism in post-Roman Spain, late antique ideas of citizenship and identity, and the continuity and role of aqueducts in the post-Roman period.

Pedro Mateos Cruz is Director of the Institute of Archeology of Mérida. He is currently engaged in research exploring the world of Roman public architecture and is leading projects such as "The Monumental Ensemble of Imperial Worship of Augusta Emerita," "The Roman theater and amphitheater of Augusta Emerita," and "The Roman Theater of Medellín." He also directs research projects on the arch of the Boario forum in Rome and the archaeological excavations at the *Contributa Iulia* site.

Michael Mulryan is an Honorary Research Fellow at the University of Kent, and is Associate Researcher at the École Normale Supérieure, Paris. He is interested in late antique Roman urbanism and has edited and contributed to volumes looking at late pagan and early Christian spaces in Rome and Constantinople, field methodology on late antique sites, and the late antique environment. His book *Spatial "Christianisation" in Context: Strategic Intramural Building in Rome from the 4th–7th Century A.D.* (Oxford: Archaeopress, 2014) focused on the spatial impact and pragmatic location of some early Christian buildings. He was the assistant director and archivist for the Kent section of the Late Antique Ostia field project from 2008 to 2012.

Isabel Sánchez Ramos is an archaeologist currently based at the Institute of Archaeology, University College London under a Marie Skłodowska-Curie Individual Fellowship. She is a specialist in late antiquity archaeology and the early medieval period. Her main line of research is based on understanding landscape transformations of ancient Roman cities in Western Europe from the fourth to the eighth centuries CE (from the collapse of the Roman Empire to the early medieval period). She has received several long-term Ph.D. fellowships and postdoctoral contracts in renowned institutions, such as the Spanish Research Council at Rome, the Centre Camille Jullian at Aix-en-Provence, the University of Barcelona, the Ausonius Institute, and the Institute of Advanced Studies at Paris, among others. Her professional experience spans a range of areas: archaeological heritage management, fieldwork, transferring and organizing R&D activities, public dissemination, and leadership of research projects (e.g., IdaVe Project at Idanha-a-Velha). She has been invited to participate in several congresses, meetings, and various international conferences around Europe. She has published widely in Spanish and across a range of platforms.

Mark Lewis Tizzoni is an Assistant Professor of Classical and Medieval Studies at Bates College. His research centers on issues of identity, cultural change, and transcultural interactions in the Late Antique and Early Medieval Mediterranean, particularly as witnessed in the Latin poetry of North Africa and Iberia. His teaching focuses on the pre-modern history of Africa and the Mediterranean. He has recently published a chapter on Isidore of Seville's early reception in the Brill Companion to Isidore of Seville and an article on Eugenius II of Toledo in *Visigothic Symposia 2* (visigothicsymposia.org).

Douglas Underwood is an independent scholar, having recently completed a Ph.D. at the University of St Andrews. He is the author of *Re(using) Ruins: Public Building in the Cities of the Late Antique West, 300–600* (Boston and Leiden: Brill, 2019). His primary research deals with urbanism and public monuments from the imperial period to late antiquity. He has contributed articles to *Late Antique Archaeology* and others and has an upcoming chapter in *Companion to Cities in the Graeco-Roman World* with Blackwell.

Ian Wood taught at the University of Leeds from 1976 to 2015, retiring as professor emeritus. His monographs include *The Merovingian Kingdoms* (New York: Routledge, 1994), *The Missionary Life* (New York: Routledge, 2001), and *The Modern Origins of the Early Middle Ages* (Oxford: Oxford University Press, 2013). His most recent book is *The Transformation of the Roman*

West (Kalamazoo: Arc Humanities Press, 2018). He was elected to the British Academy in 2019.

Index